Foreign Policies of EU Member States

Foreign Policies of EU Member States provides a clear and current overview of the motivations and outcomes of EU Member States regarding their foreign policy-making within and beyond the EU. It provides an in-depth analysis of intra-EU policy-making and sheds light, in an innovative and understandable way, on the lesser-known aspects of the inter-EU and extra-EU foreign policies of the twenty-eight Member States. The text has an innovative method of thematic organisation in which case study state profiles emerge via dominant foreign policy themes. The text examines the three main policy challenges currently faced by the twenty-eight Member States:

- First, EU Member States must cooperate within the mechanisms of the EU, including the Common Foreign and Security Policy (CFSP).
- Second, EU Member States continue to construct their own inter-EU foreign policies.
- Third, the sovereign prerogative exercised by all EU Member States is to construct their own foreign policies on everything from trade and defence with the rest of the world.

This combination of clarity, thematic structure and empirical case studies make this an ideal textbook for all upper-level students of European foreign policy, comparative European politics and European studies.

Amelia Hadfield is the Director of the Centre for European Studies (CEFEUS) and the Jean Monnet Chair in European Foreign Affairs, at Canterbury Christ Church University, UK.

Ian Manners is a Professor in the Department of Political Science at the University of Copenhagen, Denmark.

Richard G. Whitman is Professor of Politics and International Relations and Head of the School of Politics and International Relations at the University of Kent, UK. He is also Associate Fellow at Chatham House and an Academic Fellow at the European Policy Centre.

'For the many scholars and students who have used the first edition of *The Foreign Policies of EU Member States* as a key reference and resource, this second edition is very welcome. It also represents a significant advance in our understanding of foreign policies in the EU, combining as it does analysis based on the geopolitical orientations and roles of the member states with their engagement in a series of cross-cutting issues, and enables important comparative conclusions to be drawn. The result is a rich and provocative collection of case-studies as well as a stimulating comparative analysis.'

Michael Smith, *University of Warwick, UK*

'This most welcomed edited book provides an indispensable contribution to studying and understanding EU foreign policy by linking the diverse historic and geostrategic foundations of Member States' identity and preferences, to those domestic dimensions' influence on forging a "common" foreign policy across often rather contentious foreign policy fields. It is thus an invaluable read for academics', as much as for actual foreign policy-makers' interested in comprehending the challenge of achieving "unity in diversity" in EU foreign policy-making.'

Ingo Peters, *Freie Universität Berlin, Germany*

Foreign Policies of EU Member States

Continuity and Europeanisation

**Edited by Amelia Hadfield,
Ian Manners and Richard G. Whitman**

Routledge
Taylor & Francis Group

LONDON AND NEW YORK

First published 2017
by Routledge
2 Park Square, Milton Park, Abingdon, Oxon OX14 4RN

and by Routledge
711 Third Avenue, New York, NY 10017

Routledge is an imprint of the Taylor & Francis Group, an informa business

British Library Cataloguing-in-Publication Data
A catalogue record for this book is available from the British Library

Library of Congress Cataloging-in-Publication Data
Names: Hadfield, Amelia, editor. | Manners, Ian, editor. | Whitman, Richard G.,
    editor.
Title: Foreign policies of EU member states : continuity and Europeanisation /
    edited by Amelia Hadfield, Ian Manners and Richard G. Whitman.Other titles:
    Foreign policies of European Union member states
Description: Abingdon, Oxon ; New York, NY : Routledge, 2017. | Includes
    bibliographical references and index.
Identifiers: LCCN 2016046507 | ISBN 9780415670050 (hardback) |
    ISBN 9780415670067 (pbk.) | ISBN 9781315276724 (ebook)
Subjects: LCSH: European Union countries—Foreign relations. | Regionalism—
    Political aspects—European Union countries. | European Neighbourhood
    Policy (Program) | Geopolitics—European Union countries.
Classification: LCC JZ1570.F657 2017 | DDC 327.4—dc23
LC record available at https://lccn.loc.gov/2016046507

ISBN: 978-0-415-67005-0 (hbk)
ISBN: 978-0-415-67006-7 (pbk)
ISBN: 978-1-315-27672-4 (ebk)

Typeset in Times New Roman
by Apex CoVantage, LLC

Printed and bound in Great Britain by
TJ International Ltd, Padstow, Cornwall

Contents

Figures

Tables

Contributors

Chad Damro is Senior Lecturer of Politics and International Relations as well as Jean Monnet Chair and Director of the Jean Monnet Centre of Excellence at the University of Edinburgh.

Madalina Dobrescu is a Junior Research Fellow in the European Neighbourhood Policy Chair at the College of Europe, Natolin Campus (Warsaw, Poland).

Simon Duke is a Professor at the European Institute of Public Administration (EIPA), Maastricht, Netherlands, and a Senior Research Fellow at Maastricht University.

Tobias Etzold is a Research Associate and leader of the project Research Centre Norden at the German Institute for International and Security Affairs in Berlin.

Amelia Hadfield is Jean Monnet Chair in European Foreign Affairs and Director of the Centre for European Studies at Canterbury Christ Church University.

Hiski Haukkala is an Associate Professor of International Relations at the School of Management at the University of Tampere, Finland.

Ana E. Juncos is a Reader in European Politics at the School of Sociology, Politics and International Studies at the University of Bristol.

Robert Kissack is an Associate Professor and Head of Studies at the Institute Barcelona d'Estudis Internacionals (IBEI) in Spain.

Simon Lightfoot is a Senior Lecturer in European Politics at the University of Leeds.

Ian Manners is Professor in the Department of Political Science at the University of Copenhagen.

Jocelyn Mawdsley is a Senior Lecturer in European Politics in the School of Geography, Politics and Sociology at Newcastle University.

Meltem Müftüler-Baç is a Professor of International Relations and Jean Monnet Chair at Sabanci University in Istanbul (Turkey).

Jan Orbie is an Associate Professor at the Department of Political Science and Director of the Centre for EU Studies at Ghent University (Belgium).

Annemarie Peen Rodt is Associate Professor at the Institute for Strategy of the Royal Danish Defence College in Copenhagen.

Karolina Pomorska is an Assistant Professor at the Department of Politics, Faculty of Arts and Social Science at Maastricht University.

Kristi Raik is a Senior Research Fellow at the Finnish Institute of International Affairs (FIIA) and Adjunct Professor at the University of Turku.

Tobias Schumacher is a Professor and a holder of Jean Monnet Chair in European Neighbourhood Policy at the College of Europe, Natolin Campus (Warsaw, Poland).

Luis Simón is a Research Professor at the Institute for European Studies at the Vrije Universiteit Brussel.

Stelios Stavridis is an ARAID Senior Research Fellow in the Research Unit on European and International Studies/ZEIS of the University of Zaragoza in Spain.

Ben Tonra is a Professor of International Relations at the University College Dublin School of Politics and International Relations.

Richard G. Whitman is Professor of Politics and International Relations and Director of the Global Europe Centre at the University of Kent.

Alasdair R. Young is a Professor in the Sam Nunn School of International Affairs at the Georgia Institute of Technology.

Acronyms

ACP	African, Caribbean and Pacific states
AFSJ	Area of Freedom, Security and Justice
BiH	Bosnia and Herzegovina
BNA	Bilateral Non-surrender Agreement
BRICs	Brazil, Russia, India, China
BSEC	Black Sea Economic Cooperation
BSR	Baltic Sea Region
BWI	Bretton Woods Institutions
CAC	Codex Alimentarius Commission
CAP	Common Agricultural Policy
CAR	Central African Republic
CBSS	Council of the Baltic Sea States
CCP	Common Commercial Policy
CEI	Central European Initiative
CEN	European Committee for Standardization (Comité Européen de Normalisation)
CENELEC	European Committee for Electrotechnical Standardization
CFA	Chartered Financial Analyst
CFSP	Common Foreign and Security Policy
CIS	The Commonwealth of Independent States
COEST	Working Party on Eastern Europe and Central Asia
COJUR	EU Council Working Group on Public International Law
COREPER	Committee of Permanent Representatives in the European Union
COREU	Correspondence Européenne
CSDP	Common Security and Defence Policy
DCFTA	Deep and Comprehensive Free Trade Area
DG	Directorate General
DRC	Democratic Republic of Congo
DSACEUR	Deputy Supreme Allied Commander for Europe
EaP	Eastern Partnership
EC	European Commission
ECJ	European Court of Justice
ECN	European Competition Network
ECSC	European Coal and Steel Community
EDA	European Defence Agency
EDC	European Defence Community

EDF	European Development Fund
EEA	European Economic Area
EEAS	European External Action Services
EEC	European Economic Community
EMP	European Mediterranean Partnership
EMU	Economic and Monetary Union
ENP	European Neighbourhood Policy
ENPI	European Neighbourhood Policy Instrument
EP	European Parliament
EPC	European Political Cooperation
ESDI	European Security and Defence Identity
ESDP	European Security and Defence Policy
ESS	European Security Strategy
ETA	European Technical Assessment
ETSI	European Telecommunications Standards Institute
EU	European Union
EUFOR Althea	European Union Force Althea (Bosnia and Herzegovina)
EUMC	European Union Military Committee
EUMS	European Union Military Staff
EUNAVFOR	European Union Naval Force
EURATOM	European Atomic Energy Community
EUREMA	Intra EU Relocation from Malta
EURONEST	EU Neighbourhood East Parliamentary Assembly
EUROSUR	European Border Surveillance System
EUSBSR	European Union Strategy for the Baltic Sea Region
EUTM	European Union Training Mission
FAC	Foreign Affairs Council
FAO	Food and Agriculture Organization of the United Nations
FCO	Foreign and Commonwealth Office
FPA	Foreign Policy Analysis
FYROM	Former Yugoslav Republic of Macedonia
GAC	General Affairs Council
GAERC	General Affairs and External Relations Council
GDP	Gross Domestic Product
HR/VP	High Representative/Vice-President
ICC	International Criminal Court
ICN	International Competition Network
IEA	International Energy Agency
IEC	International Electrotechnical Commission
IMF	International Monetary Fund
IR	International Relations
ISAF	The International Security Assistance Force
ISO	International Standards Organization
ISR	Intelligence, Surveillance and Reconnaissance
JHA	Justice and Home Affairs
MAP	Membership Action Plan
MEDA	Maryland Economic Development Association
MENA	Middle East and North Africa

MEP	Member of the European Parliament
MFA	Ministry of Foreign Affairs
MP	Member of Parliament
MS	Member State
NATO	North Atlantic Treaty Organization
ND	Northern Dimension
NGO	Non-Governmental Organization
NOC	Network and Optical Communications
NPT	Non-Proliferation Treaty
NSS	National Security Strategy
ODA	Official Development Aid
OECD	Organization for Economic Co-operation and Development
OSCE	Organization for Security and Co-operation in Europe
PCA	Partnership and Cooperation Agreement
PfP	Partnership for Peace
PiS	Law and Justice Party in Poland
PS	Parti Socialiste (France)
PSC	Political and Security Committee
PSOE	Spanish Socialist Party
QMV	Qualified Majority Voting
R&D	Research and Development
RES	Renewable Energy Resources
RtoP	Responsibility to Protect
SAA	Stabilization and Association Agreements
SAP	Stabilization and Association Process
SDSR	Strategic Defence and Security Review
SHAPE	Supreme Headquarters of Allied Powers in Europe
TACIS	Technical Assistance to the Commonwealth of Independent States and Georgia
TEU	Treaty on European Union
TFEU	Treaty on the Functioning of the European Union
UfM	Union for the Mediterranean
UN	United Nations
UNCHR	United Nations Commission on Human Rights
UNGA	General Assembly of the United Nations
UNPROFOR	United Nations Protection Force
UNSC	United Nations Security Council
UNSCR	United Nations Security Council Resolution
WEOG	Western Europe and Other Group
WEU	Western European Union
WTO	World Trade Organization

Preface

This volume has been almost a decade and a half in the making. After completing a volume on the foreign policies of EU Member States in 2000, Manners and Whitman began a discussion on the ongoing evolution of European foreign policy-making. The successive enlargements of the EU in the early twenty-first century raised the question as to whether the EU's newest members were demonstrating the same characteristics in foreign policy-making as the more longer-standing EU members.

EU treaty reform, and most especially the Treaty of Lisbon with a drawing together of the EU's external relations under the new umbrella of external action made clear that examining policies beyond the Common Foreign and Security Policy (CFSP) and the Common Security and Defence Policy (CSDP) was essential to gain a full grasp of the wider complex of EU foreign policy-making. The UK referendum vote to exit the EU on the 23rd June adds uncertainty to the future of the EU's foreign policy.

The interests of Hadfield in trying to organise thinking on the contemporary landscape of Member States in EU foreign policy gave rise to the three-way editorial team of this volume.

The University Association for Contemporary European Studies (UACES) facilitated the development of the collective thinking of the contributors to this volume via the support of Collaborative Research Network (CRN) funding that allowed our authors to exchange ideas as the thinking behind their chapters evolved. We are grateful to UACES for their support.

We would also like to acknowledge the assistance of Michal Gloznek for his energy and efforts in organising the manuscript into a publishable format. Finally, we would like to extend our thanks to Routledge for their patience in what has been an extended publishing endeavour.

Amelia Hadfield, Ian Manners,
Richard G. Whitman

Introduction

Conceptualising the foreign policies of EU Member States

Amelia Hadfield, Ian Manners
and Richard G. Whitman

> Geknetet in Gleichmut, essen die Menschen, meine Nachbarn, täglich ihr Brot. Keiner will Asche sein.
>
> (Huchel, 1984)[1]

The European Union's Member States have embarked on a unique project in seeking to create a collective foreign, security and defence policy. Through shared institutions and the gradual forging of common approaches, the EU has sought to develop a greater international profile over recent decades. This collective foreign policy endeavour has been pursued whilst national foreign policies themselves have evolved. EU foreign policy and Member State foreign policy therefore operate in a symbiotic but uneasy relationship. It is this relationship, and the internal and external impacts upon this dual exercise in foreign policy construction, which is the central focus of this volume. For scholars and practitioners alike, the challenge of understanding the foreign policy nuances between the European Union (EU) and its twenty-eight Member States presents an added level of difficulty. As this text illustrates in its two-part structure, there is both a quantitative issue in terms of assessing sensibly the sheer number of EU Member States, and a qualitative aspect to discerning both their individual foreign policy profile and the contribution they make *as members* to the architecture of EU external affairs.

Naturally, many things have changed since Manners and Whitman (2000) first tackled the rationale and construction of the foreign policies of EU Member States. The objective at that stage was simply to get to grips with the substance of each of the foreign policies of the fifteen EU Member States. At that point, focusing empirically upon the change, process and action of national and EU-level policy-making illustrated the principal tension between discrete 'national' foreign policies and a growing body of 'Europeanised' foreign policies. Now, however, the many factors that have come to constitute EU membership for all EU states, both old and new, hold the key to a comprehensive understanding of the single most important dynamic of EU foreign policy: the ongoing tension – both positive and negative – between the aims and objectives of national foreign policy-making and an increasingly wide range of cross-cutting EU foreign policies. Those tensions translate into the innumerable demands, both external and internal, placed upon Member States as a function of EU membership, as well as upon EU policy-makers to construct appreciably 'European' strategies. The resulting combination presents Member States with the difficult task of balancing national attitudes, interests and even sovereignty against demands for ever greater common foreign policy; defending national interests while defining collective interests and managing domestic austerity budgets in the face of Eurozone instability. As will be seen, while EU membership has in the past fifteen years blurred some quintessential differences between national and EU-level policy-making, other areas, including security and defence have remained largely untouched.

Continuity and change in EU foreign policy-making

Current EU foreign policy-making is driven chiefly by an overarching duality: first, areas of policy-making remain largely national in their characteristics, rendering European foreign and security significantly overdetermined by the national interests of its constituent members. Such areas include diplomacy, security and defence, energy security and, more recently, neighbourhood migration and asylum. Second, changes in the institutional and diplomatic structures of the EU have reinforced or created a set of deeply integrated policies held in common across all states. These include trade, climate change, freedom security and justice, and, to a lesser extent, enlargement, which taken together demonstrate the emergence of a common European strategy. This volume seeks to explore two methods by which EU membership is fashioned: geopolitically via the regional value-sets that Member States in the regions of Europe now share (Part I); and institutionally via the exercise of collective policy-making (Part II). We explore how the particularisms that constitute the national interests of Member States and the imperatives of constructing a common European foreign policy have produced both a *range of change* between EU Member States as individual units and *modes of action* across them, as a group of institutionalised, even habituated actors.

Since the turn of the century, the greatest change to both the substantive nature of the EU and its emerging diplomatic system has been the addition of Member States through three successive waves of enlargement. Given the focus upon the central contributions of Member States to the EU foreign policy-making mix, their ability to collaborate as well as their proclivity for conflict, and the enormously widened sphere of influence (generated by the increasing geopolitical extent of a Union across twenty-eight states), we use enlargement policy to help set the stage. As explored later in this chapter, enlargement encapsulates, but also renders oppositional, the key themes of deepening and widening, of *communautaire* and intergovernmental decision-making and, most importantly, the complex inter-relationship of Europeanisation and national political cultures, against the terrain of EU foreign policy.

A new analytical framework

The original Manners and Whitman (2000) text tackled a threefold challenge. The first challenge was to provide a clear empirical overview of the foreign policies of the fifteen EU Member States, both in terms of their ability to make distinct 'national' foreign policy, and Europeanised foreign policy pursuant to their role as Member States. The second task was to examine the ensuing observations of both top-down (Europeanising) and bottom-up (nationalising) forces within a conceptual framework that captured the dynamics of change, process and action. The final challenge was to merge observations from this framework into the increasingly interdisciplinary debate at that time regarding the nature of a distinctive Foreign Policy Analysis (FPA) approach which would ultimately entail 'possibilities for creating an FPA of EU states' and the examination of the EU itself as a foreign policy actor (Manners and Whitman, 2000: 1).

A number of major developments in the past decade have further made the case for a substantially transformed approach to the analysis of the foreign policies of EU Member States. First, the EU has expanded dramatically in terms of its membership. There is a host of new raw empirical material that now needs to be identified, categorised and explained.

While the first edition presented an encyclical appraisal of the individual foreign policies of the (then) fifteen Member States, this volume must contend with twenty-eight new members. How have these states operated within the EU external relations framework while simultaneously formulating their own foreign policies? Has the national content of their foreign policies been transformed or remained unaffected by EU membership? Equally, is the construction of EU foreign policy itself a truly integrative, Europeanising process, or is it a platform for the forces of increased nationalisation?

Second, a new text is needed to account for the institutional impact rendered by the harsh lessons arising from the failure of the Constitutional Treaty and the reforms initiated in 2009 with the Lisbon Treaty. As is well known, Lisbon sought to increase the overall *consistency* of the EU's range of external policies in the areas of economic, monetary, development assistance and energy. Strengthened horizontal integration was intended to generate better vertical integration via a more *coherent* approach to tackling global problems. The European External Action Service (EEAS) was established as the institutional interface for the objectives of consistency and coherence; designed to High Representative Lady Ashton's warnings that 'the EU can be too slow, too cumbersome, too bureaucratic' and could only 'bring together the many levers of influence' with the production of 'a single political strategy' (Ashton, 2010). This in turn would prepare the EU for a series of increasingly international tasks by endowing it 'with stronger institutional capacity and policy instruments to make it a more *effective* international actor in foreign and security terms' (Edwards, 2013: 276, emphasis added).

Chief among these endowments was the establishment of the EEAS as a one-stop shop for progressing the aims of EU diplomacy at the EU level. Because of the strategic importance of the EEAS within the overall EU foreign policy structure, chapters on security and defence by Ana E. Juncos and Annemarie Peen Rodt, and EU diplomacy by Simon Duke, examine the varied effects that the EEAS has had upon the EU's actorness. From a positive perspective, Member States have largely accepted the changes entailed in the Lisbon Treaty as a complex but ultimately necessary method of streamlining foreign policy, while remaining generally ambivalent about the EEAS' ability to be both *procedurally efficient* in the construction of EU policies and *practically effective* in their implementation. More critical perspectives however suggest that the Treaty has produced key vulnerabilities within the EU's foreign policy machinery that the EEAS has not been able to remedy (a good example being the European Neighbourhood Policy).

Third, theory-making itself has altered in the range of questions being asked about the EU and its methods of decision-making, even if some of the traditional modes of enquiry remain largely unchanged. State-centric definitions of foreign policy continue to pit state and governmental activities (Smith, 1988) against broader process of external relations. The field of investigation in FPA thus comprises both narrow definitions describing the activities of a generic executive and Ministry of Foreign Affairs (MFA) in managing official state relations against a backdrop of broader external relations populated by states and non-states engaging in a wider range of state and societal action. Lastly, where necessary, the text addresses the inevitable changes brought about by the UK's June 2016 Referendum, bringing to an end its membership of the EU in 2019. Specific challenges regarding the disassociation of a Member State from the EU via Article 50 of the Treaty on European Union need to be considered alongside the broader challenges to the EU, in terms of the composition of its membership and the overall nature of its foreign policy (as seen in Chapters 2 and 11 and the Conclusion).

The burgeoning field of European foreign policy

The majority of foreign policy analysis falls in the area between state-centric foreign policy and institutionally derived external affairs. Manners and Whitman (2000) made reference for example to studies undertaken in the 1990s, including comparative attempts to explore 'the impact of membership on individual Member States' (Wallace and Paterson, 1978); analyses on the specific types of EU foreign policy, chiefly the Common Foreign and Security Policy (Hill); and the impact of EU foreign policy upon the classic mechanisms of IR theory, including interparadigm and agency-structure considerations (Carlsnaes and Smith, 1994). If EU foreign policy had – in the early 2000s – begun to 'come of age', then it has, with more than a decade of subsequent theorising, certainly attained a maturity reflected in the variety of ontologies, epistemologies and methodologies on offer (Manners and Whitman, 2000: 4). As suggested later in this chapter, while the overall categories have not shifted that much, the nature of their contents has yielded a variety of fruitful additions. The history, membership increase and geopolitical development of the EU, alongside theoretic developments thus provides a host of material for scholars (including our own contributors) to continue on from the original Manners and Whitman, and make useful observances of the EU as a twenty-first-century foreign policy actor.

(i) Actorness and effectiveness

The body of literature analysing EU foreign policy has flourished, even proliferated in the last decade and a half. Within this canon, a number of distinct, yet closely interlinked facets of analysing the EU's interactions with the outside world have emerged. First are the series of works taking as their foundation constructivist concepts, building on the 'presence, opportunities, capabilities' triptych established by Bretherton and Vogler (1999) and constituting the concept of 'actorness'. In recent years, this has been recalibrated to examine the 'effectiveness' of the EU as a measure of its overall impact. Since its inception in the 1950s, the (now) European Union has undergone a series of developments that have been both incremental in nature and ground-breaking in effect. Initially classified as a hybrid intergovernmental organisation, the EEC was subsequently reclassified as a 'mixed actor' (Young, 1972), a label that still fell short of capturing EU's true essence. IR and FPA scholars (both attached to the allure of typologies) began conceptualising the EU as a unique global actor (Bretherton and Vogler, 1999). In the mid-1990s, the trend shifted to assessing the EU's *actorness*. Actorness analyses generally employ a comparative-empirical approach, utilising other international actors as international benchmarks against which the EU as an actor, and the effectiveness of its foreign policies can be evaluated (Niemann and Bretherton, 2013: 263). Initial definitions of EU actorness included the attributes of presence, capability and opportunities (Bretherton and Vogler, 1999), as well as characterisations of recognition, authority, cohesion and autonomy (Jupille and Caporaso, 1998). More recently – and possibly out of frustration at the overwhelming ambiguity of its outputs – studies have turned towards assessing the nature and quality of EU *effectiveness* (see Edwards, 2013; Elsig, 2013; Groen and Niemann, 2013; Niemann and Bretherton, 2013).

Investigating whether the EU as an 'actor' is like, or unlike any other international actor remains a key fascination for scholars, and the jury is decidedly split. Die-hard perspectives of the EU's unrelenting *sui generis* qualities argue that multiperspectival conceptualisations and more rigorous empirical assessments of the EU continue to confirm it as the ultimate hybrid polity of the international system. Other perspectives (see Ruggie, 1998; Rosamond,

2005; Hettne, 2008; Wunderlich, 2008) suggest that as an entity the EU's presence is sporadic, its capability badly hobbled, and a variety of opportunities fatally missed, and that the EU as an 'actor' can no longer be taken for granted. From this perspective, contemporary effectiveness-oriented analyses may be more relevant in highlighting areas where the EU has or has not worked effectively, and arguing that neither the EU, nor its quality of actorness is an especially unique phenomenon in comparison to other multilevel, semi-supranational polities. Indeed, we suggest that the less effective the EU's overall multilevel actorness, both substantively, and as a function of external perceptions (Chaban and Holland, 2014), the greater the role for nationally driven policy content (whether traditional or resurgent), and ultimately the less *sui generis* the overall enterprise.

(ii) *Determining EU power*

Having established, and on occasion taken for granted, the actorness and uniqueness of the EU in foreign policy terms (Niemann and Bretherton, 2013), recent studies have also explored the unique nature of power as represented, and utilised, by the EU (Niemann and Bretherton, 2013). Foreign policy dynamics can usefully be categorised into inputs and outputs (Smith, Hadfield and Dunne, 2016). Explorations of national value-sets (Lucarelli and Manners, 2006; Mayer and Vogt, 2006); geopolitical particularities (Gower and Timmins, 2011); and market preferences of Member States (Elsig, 2002; Dür and Manfred, 2011; Young and Peterson, 2014), as well as the range of national and EU decision-making dynamics (Hill, 1996; Manners and Whitman, 2000; Smith, 2004), help refine categories of EU foreign policy 'inputs', while 'outputs' incorporate the different forms of power that the EU simultaneously represents (hard, soft, integrated, economic, civilian, normative, regional etc.) (see Duchêne, 1972; Bull, 1982; Rosecrance, 1998; Bretherton and Vogler, 1999; Manners, 2002; Meunier and Nicolaïdis, 2006; Telo, 2007; Moravcsik, 2009) and ensuing modes of actorness.

Assessing the type and quality of power wielded by the EU is an area that lacks much in the way of scholarly consensus. The fundamental question raised could not be simpler: 'What sort of power is the EU?'. Yet the responses constitute a veritable riot of perspectives, ranging from an 'integrative power' (Koops, 2011), a 'small power' (Toje, 2011) or conversely a 'quiet superpower' to 'civilian power Europe' (CPE) (Duchêne, 1972), to 'normative power Europe' (NPE) (Manners, 2002), to a transformative power or indeed a motley combination of all of these. Some scholars have opted to describe the EU purely from an economic point of view, arriving at the conclusion that it is a 'conflicted trade power' (Meunier and Nicolaïdis, 2006), or simply a 'trade power', and that, on this basis, the EU has been an effective FP actor since its earliest days (Elsig, 2013). In recent years, definitions of power have themselves shifted within FPA, and the widening spectrum of hard/soft/smart categories has not always provided a workable foundation for EU scholars, any more than the EU's own hybrid/civilian/normative spectrum has provided FPA or security scholars with a convincing European exemplar. For the time being, the EU's increasingly complex structure seems to stymie scholars in this area, as much as it inspires them.

(iii) *EU versus Member State tensions*

A third area of enquiry has focused upon the ongoing tensions between individual Member State consolidation in terms of retaining core competences, uploading national preferences and EU-level acquisitiveness in accruing competences and downloading institutional influence. Here, the 'form' rather than the content is the focus: the nature, distribution and decision-making accompanying the spread of those policies classified as external. The ambiguous nature of EU power complicates the ongoing *vertical* tensions between Member States determined to keep a firm hold over their individual foreign policies, the force exerted by EU institutions and the horizontal clashes spilling out into key external policies (Bretherton and Vogler, 2013). Like the first edition, the second edition joins this particular area of enquiry, in examining the consequences of having an increasingly wide number of policies categorised as 'external' and their uneven distribution across exclusive, shared and parallel areas promoting unworkably wide types of cooperation (Bretherton and Vogler, 2013: 382–383). Accordingly, debates about the differential spread of competences between the EU and its Member States highlight related questions as to whether the political principle of sovereignty has itself been eroded or merely transformed, and whether such trends should be interpreted as regressive or progressive. Thought-provoking areas on this topic that emerged a decade ago examined the shifting logics at work between a sovereign and post-sovereign era and will undoubtedly re-emerge to capture precisely these dynamics, highlighted by trends from the politics of crisis to the rise of European populism (see Caporaso, 1996 or Cooper, 1996). Much exists in this emergent discourse to delight the devotees of interdisciplinarity (itself a particularly abundant fruit of EU studies), for its arguments pit sovereignty's persistent and redoubtable attributes against a range of integrationist onslaughts. This has provided food for thought for lawyers and political scientists alike, torn between the EU's use of traditional principles like sovereignty in distinctly untraditional ways, and accepting that, in the process, the very definition of sovereignty is redefined, if not absolutely superseded (Waever, 1995).

(iv)   National revanchism

Closely connected to these explorations, which now constitute one of the original methods of tackling the multilevel nature of EU governance, is a fourth area of investigation. This area takes a Member State approach to examining areas of explicitly 'national' forms of foreign policy. Such examples can operate on their own merits, alongside extant EU policies, outside the overall EU framework, or in outright opposition to a range of shared (or even supranational) EU competences. As all four of these areas touch substantively upon the overall rationale of the text, and the thrust of many of the individual chapters, a brief overview of each is instructive.

The scope for robust Member State activity increases as the areas of competence become progressively less integrated. Shared, coordinated, even supplementary competences do not generally produce the political fireworks that erupt periodically in the category of parallel, or separate competences, wherein dwells the majority of traditional foreign and security policies. As the ensuing chapters illustrate, interesting disjunctures have arisen between a variety of Member States with a well-established strategic culture, determined to retain full control over their foreign policy and keep EU approaches within acceptably national limits on the one side, and the long-standing arguments and recent pressures for concerted EU foreign and security policy on the other (Edwards, 2013).

The June 2016 European Union Global Strategy entitled 'Shared vision, common action: A stronger Europe' attempts to square the circle, suggesting that Europe's national security cultures together present an effective collective response to external threats: '[I]n challenging times, a strong Union is one that thinks strategically, shares a vision and acts together' (European Union, 2016: 3). The reality however is not that simple. Member State action can be at once effective (French interventions in Mali in 2013), divisive (attitudes over Libya in the same year) or pioneering, in paving the way to EU action (CSDP forces in Mali in 2014). Getting to grips with the national value-sets by which Member States continue to fashion their foreign policy, before they calibrate it to the use of EU-specific goals, is therefore the first goal of this text and comprises the majority of findings in Part I.

The chapters in Part II then explore whether the sum total of such options equates to an enhanced capacity for EU actorness, or whether the duality at the heart of its foreign policy structure, along with the spate of recent crises within and beyond the EU itself presages the gradual erosion of EU foreign policy effectiveness (Bretherton and Vogler, 2013).

Enlargement and European foreign policy: catalyst or catastrophe?

Lauded as the EU's most successful foreign policy, enlargement policy has constituted the primary source of widening geopolitical footprint and the driver of deepened institutionalisation. Yet the consequences of a union that so rapidly absorbed the political, economic and cultural dimensions of post-Cold War turmoil continue to be felt in the struggle to find a common voice abroad and a legitimate stance at home.

Enlargement criteria both determined the conditions of membership for states in terms of their European identity and obligations of Union membership. Enlargement has also established a key part of the EU's internal political identity and the attributes of its gradually expanding externalities. In dual fashion, enlargement policy stimulated a broadening of the policies and practices of EU foreign policy and obliged new members to recalibrate their domestic political identities and foreign policy preferences to this same developing framework of EU actorness.

Widening the Union however has signally failed to deepen it in terms of integrative foreign policy-making. Broadened geopolitical presence has not necessarily produced more extensive strategies or more influence. As recently argued:

> The EU and its member states have given an inordinate amount of attention to the development of institutions and decision-making processes for the CFSP and the CSDP through successive treaty amendments. . . . However, they have been unable to devise a clear grand strategy identifying the range of capabilities that would be necessary to give the EU optimal power and influence within international relations.
>
> (Stokes and Whitman, 2013: 1097)

National preferences preserved

The two significant challenges that preceded enlargement have arguably been worsened by it. First, the increasing number of EU-level external policies, collective EU positions can, and are, easily thwarted. Second, large areas of foreign policy remain defiantly ringfenced by the national interests of the EU's twenty-eight sovereign Member States. Although EU positions are regularly forged on key 'high politics' issues, these still echo the national preferences of many Member States and of the larger states in particular. As demonstrated in attitudes to Iraq, Libya, Syria and the Sahel, as well as the migratory crises of 2015 onwards, attempts to recalibrate entrenched national foreign policy preferences, even on issues deemed to be of strategic interest to the Union as a whole, fail frequently, swiftly and publicly. There are exceptions of course, including the shift in traditional German foreign policy attitudes to Russia that permitted a collective EU sanctions policy after the Russian annexation of Crimea and ongoing violence across the Ukraine, as well as some collective responsibility in tackling the migration crisis.

The irony is acute indeed. Enlargement represents the foreign policy by which the EU has emerged as a regional and arguably global actor; but it has not provided a reliable template regarding the overall effectiveness of the EU's enhanced composition. Instead, enlargement continues to dictate both the substantive equivalence and the regulatory harmonisation between the EU and third parties in major policy areas, as well as providing the form for the most ambitious of its proximate foreign policies – the neighbourhood policy. As Bretherton and Vogler have argued, the *presence* entailed in an enlargement-oriented actor like the EU establishes both 'the international reputation of the EU and associated third-party expectations of EU action' (2013: 376), yet enlargement itself has failed to be the catalyst for a common foreign and security policy constructed across all members, old and new, that is greater than the sum of its parts. A reliable foreign and security policy – whether traditional or hybrid – still requires a few basic elements to be effective. It needs to be visible by external parties, viable in terms of implementation, representative of the *vox populi* of its EU constituents (both Member State governments and national communities), regarded as necessary by its recipients and represent an operable framework by which Member States can over time attune the national means of their individual foreign policy profiles to EU ends. A good example here is that of EU humanitarian aid policy, which operates as a shared competence under Article 4 of the Treaty on the Functioning of the European Union (TFEU). In this area, while Member States are free to undertake their own form of humanitarian aid, they are also obliged to cooperate in the production of an EU-level policy. EU humanitarian aid has a solid reputation globally for effectively responding in major crisis areas around the world, as well as having improved its ability to react to unforeseen disasters. It also has strong credibility within the EU. Actor coherence here is key. The European Commission's Humanitarian Aid and Civil Protection department (ECHO) manages EU-funded relief effectively between itself and upwards of 200 host agencies, reflecting not only the EU approach to dealing with crises but the Europeanised method that has itself been downloaded effectively into the aid and civil protection mindset of the Member States as a whole.

Not all policies work so well. Despite the broad range of areas that constitute the 'common foreign and security policy' heading (e.g. peace and security, diplomacy and partnership, peacekeeping missions, the European Neighbourhood Policy, regional bilaterals, and the multiple activities led by the European External Action Service), the area is hampered because of the overall weakness of its integration as a policy area. With the possible exception of some areas of Freedom, Security and Justice, there is no clear and robust obligation upon Member States within the TFEU requiring them to coordinate their foreign and security policies in a way that is either recognizably collective in its means, or Europeanised in its ends.

Absent a firm treaty base by which to ensure Member State cooperation in a systematic rather than superficial method, and spurred by a slew of crises that have undermined the EU's actorness since 2008, a range of anti-integrationist foreign policies have emerged from key national capitals, which in our view has restricted the EU's ability to deploy its *capabilities*, foreclosed on key *opportunities* and ultimately weakened its overall *presence*. Changes have occurred of course. The domain of Freedom, Security and Justice illustrates areas of genuine EU-level collaboration, key diplomatic structures have emerged and been consolidated and improvements evident in key bilateral relations. Elsewhere, however, in the policies of enlargement, energy security, and neighbourhood and migration, there has been little major or permanent change in terms of competences or decision-making to move the EU as a whole beyond the voluntarism of the Lisbon Treaty, and push Member States beyond lip service to 'solidarity' in terms of collective foreign policy. The same is true for security and defence: 'despite Europe's Common Security and Defence Policy (CSDP), nascent structures for aggregating capabilities and deepening institutional power continue to remain highly fragmentary, with differential contributions overdetermined by national interests' (Stokes and Whitman, 2013: 1093).

Reaching the limit of EU capabilities?

Will the EU's ambition to improve its capacities ironically incapacitate it in terms of genuine engagement? A number of responses are on offer, beginning with the possibility of the EU unravelling as a foreign policy actor. The geopolitical *variety* that initially inspired both EU unity and governance perhaps is itself proving too *varied* and, indeed, *variable*. The fundamental differences in national contexts, primarily in terms of identities, preferences and pre-determined policy blueprints still function according to national path-dependency, rather than as Europeanised activity in strategic, sovereign or even sensitive policy areas. This in turn undermines policy coherences and jeopardises its implementation. As our contributors explore, the 'worlds of compliance' between national and European jurisdictions – portrayed by the earliest Union architects as complementary – have proven to be not merely discordant but wholly incommensurate (Falkner and Treib, 2008).

From this perspective, as Bretherton and Vogler suggest, the EU's heyday was the decade between the 1993 Treaty on European Union and the first wave of enlargement which saw 'a significant increase in EU actorness and effectiveness' (2013: 376). However, a series of internal knocks (the failure of the Constitutional Treaty) and external shocks (the onset of the global financial crisis) 'focused attention upon the internal problems of Member States and threatened the cohesion, even the continuing existence, of the Union itself' (2013: 376). Significant problems regarding the practical implications of EU membership among key states also conspired to undermine the construction a viable foreign EU foreign policy. As a result of the partial presence, unexploited opportunities and constrained capabilities that together comprise the totality of EU actorness, observers of EU externality have from the mid-2000 onwards witnessed a process of 'actorness in decline' (2013: 376).

Recent events appear to confirm these misgivings. In December 2013, the EU stood accused of having suffered 'its biggest defeat since the end of the Cold War' with the defection of Ukraine in December 2013 to the Moscow stable over trade and gas concessions, leaving the Association Agreement in tatters (James Brooke, 2013). EU attempts via the Minsk Agreements to repatriate Kiev produced a regional impasse at best followed by prolonged local volatilities. The EU–Russia–Ukraine situation however is not an anomaly but typical of other foreign policy mishaps. The EU's transformative power failed to resuscitate the Union of the Mediterranean (pithily described by Barber as 'all desert and no oasis', 2014). The UfM was strategically unable to react to the 2011 Arab uprising in 'its Mediterranean' and spectacularly unprepared in terms of collective or national responses to the 2015 migration crisis. The Mediterranean component of the European Neighbourhood Policy has suffered from an absence of practical crisis-specific implementation, while the Eastern Partnership has failed to provide reliable signals to its members regarding the EU's ultimate objectives and prevented the EU from resolute actions beyond sanctions in dealing with Russia.

Member States are generally at the heart of criticisms of EU foreign policy. As this text explores, the EU contains a host of individuated national presences, which are both capable of working collectively and innovatively, and in other ways unevenly, and who as a group are unreliably absorbed into the contours of EU strategic thinking. Despite twenty years of developing a socialised European foreign policy reflex since the Treaty of Maastricht first institutionalised the CFSP, both Member State and third-party perceptions of it – and a variety of newer external affairs – remains skeptical. The overall result is a protracted 'absence of clear foreign objectives' amongst the twenty-eight Member States as a whole, increasing the likelihood that Europe itself 'will stumble from one humiliation to the next' (De Gruyter, 2013).

Equally however, the EU in its external actions has, and will continue to evolve, charting a path between hard-fought national preferences and hard-won EU-level innovations. While it may be afflicted by protracted existential questions regarding its internal identity and the *sui generis* nature of external clout, the EU remains a polyvalent polity, with an exceptional ability to support the widest series of external affairs of any international organisation. It also has a track record of progress in key areas including development, humanitarian aid and crisis management, and a reputation for tackling both regional and global issues, from climate policy to European defence development. With such varied perspectives regarding its foreign policy inputs and outputs, the geopolitical map of the EU remains a veritable contrast and an inviting area for scholarship.

Roadmap to the text

The tension between these two positions is the focal point of this text. At its simplest, we survey the foreign policy stances of the EU Member States, including policies that are largely within the purview of the EU and those still within the remit of the state itself. To do so however, we need to examine the impact of EU membership on the national role conceptions and the national foreign policy-making of its constituent states. In simple terms, we ask first what explains the attitudes of European states *as Union members* in either providing support for, or fuelling opposition against, EU external relations? Second, in terms of identifiable change, adaptation and policy action, why do some Member States operate on the basis of foreign policy attitudes that fundamentally support EU external affairs, whilst others oppose the integrationist implications, the EU-level approach or the policy itself, producing stances that run at odds to EU attempts?

To provide insightful responses to such challenging questions, our text is necessarily somewhat different than others of its kind. While we aim to provide the reader with a comprehensive understanding of the internal and external construction of EU foreign policy, the chief objective is to engage with the distinct foreign policies of EU Member States as they emerge from their respective geopolitical value-sets, as found in Part I, and subsequently to explore the construction of various EU-level foreign policies, as found in Part II. We feel that this approach provides an essential balance between the composition of twenty-eight national foreign policies and preferences, the structure and objectives of EU policy-making and the nature and consequences of their inter-relationship.

As examined in Part I, the EU contains robust intergovernmental dynamics in which its Member States – as sovereign governments – choose 'to influence or manage events outside the state's boundaries' (Smith, 1988: 15). From this perspective, Member States operate as policy architects within a classic state-centrist structure. The EU however represents a unique structure of externalities that has designated an increasingly large number of policies as not only EU-level in type but which 'nurtures the ambition of strategic autonomy for the

European Union' itself and which rests upon a complex blend of supranational and intergovernmental methods of decision-making and implementation (EU Global Strategy, 2016: 4). This requires a wider cast of analysis. To the bottom-up geopolitical preferences explored in Part I, the text adds the complementary top-down perspectives found in Part II, in which Member States operate as recipients and bearers of EU external affairs, themselves post-state-centric, neo-institutional, even continental in nature. As our contributors demonstrate, the outcome are national foreign policies containing downloaded EU objectives, some of which attenuate the sovereign instinct, while others are geared to enshrining it. The consequences of this dualism, whether evident in vertical coherence spats between Member States and EU officials, or horizontal coherence rifts typified by 'tensions between policy sectors that impede effective policy formation and implementation' are key to the current ambiguities in EU foreign policy and the uncertain role that membership itself plays regarding the extent of Member State's overall commitment to both national and Union goals (Bretherton and Vogler, 2013: 383).

The role of goal formation in foreign and security policy as a function of Union membership is the key issue that this text seeks to explore. On the one hand are traditional sovereigntist dimensions that are susceptible to remaining deeply politicised, even securitised by periodic infusions of national attitudes from key Member States. More integrated policies further up the scale of competences however allow redefinitions of sovereignty itself, and its supportive dimensions of national preferences and policies, producing genuinely collective structures which in turn render EU foreign policy as indisputably unique. As argued by Cebeci (2012), Ole Waever's 1995 observation remains instructive:

> [T]he E.U. exists as an independent political voice, an independent logic acting vis-à-vis the outside world and with its own 'Euro-logic' in relation to European affairs, where it is more than the sum of its members. That is what I have referred to as systemic post-sovereignty. But seen from the perspective of the states, they are still sovereign; there is no post-sovereignty at the unit level. . . . The E.U. emerges as something more than a pure instrument of the states (i.e. no longer to be seen as derived from sovereign states) without contesting state sovereignty . . . on the one hand, a post-sovereign unit, the E.U., takes on increasing importance and therefore, in a sense makes the system post-sovereign (since the system can no longer be described in sovereignty terms), while on the other hand, the states remain sovereign.
>
> (2012: 568; Waever, 1995: 389–431)

As our contributors illustrate, two logics vie for supremacy. EU Member States remain the sovereign constituent units of a post-sovereign entity, itself capable of transforming the system. Traditional foreign policy-making structures underwrite key Member State preferences, while the EU itself operates as both a unique derivative of those preferences, capable of transforming both them and itself, in the process.

Both the historical and geopolitical contours of states examined in Part I and the tensions they encounter between national and EU-level policy-making in Part II revolve around the legal boundaries that simultaneously *preserve* national sovereign competences and *permit* EU foreign policy-making. TFEU Articles 3 through 6 indicate the degree to which Member States are obliged to work with, alongside, or independent of, the EU (TFEU, 2008). The lack of foreign policy coherence amongst EU Member States arises in most cases from 'the *location of competence* and the degree of Member State sensitivity concerning policy transfer to the Union level or the extent to which the Commission should be involved in the

Table 0.1 Categories and areas of Union competence

Article 2.4: **Parallel Competence**: to define and implement a common foreign and security policy, including the progressive framing of a common defence policy, in accordance with the provisions of the Treaty on European Union.

Article 3: **Exclusive EU competences**: extend to trade, competition and monetary policies, and for conservation of marine biological resources.

Article 4: **Shared Competences**

• A **'core' of shared competence** domains: internal market, energy, cohesion (economic, social and territorial), transport, agriculture, fisheries, freedom-justice-security, environment, consumer protection, and aspects of social and public health (Article 4.2).

• A secondary category of **parallel competences** for research and development policies where the Member States have more substantial competences (Article 4.3–4).

Article 5: **Policies requiring coordination** between the EU and the Member States (a loose sub-category of the shared competences): economic, employment and social policies.

Article 6: **Policies where the EU may engage in actions supplementary** to the predominant Member States competences, as for industry, culture, tourism, education, civil protection and public health.

Source: TFEU (2008: 50–53) and European Commission (2016).

policy process. 'Sensitive' areas tend to be those of greatest importance – they include, inter alia, fiscal policy, energy policy and foreign and security policy' (Bretherton and Vogler, 2013: 382, emphasis added). This is a vital, and yet frequently under-analysed point. As illustrated in Table 0.1, Articles 3–6 (TFEU) list the EU's categories of competences, best understood from the perspective of vertical coherence that 'denotes the extent to which the bilateral external policies of the Member States are *consistent with each other* and *complementary to those of the EU*. Hence, it is a measure of Member State political commitment to common policies' (Bretherton and Vogler, 2013: 382, emphasis added). As illustrated in Part II, **exclusive** competences like trade produce high degrees of coherence which can translate successfully into global leadership. **Shared** competences can produce relatively positive outcomes in which national role conceptions of leaders and laggards are features of differing national commitments but general consensus or negative policy outcomes fuelled by internal spats over the required degree of convergence regarding regulatory methods, or appropriate modes of EU representation within international forums. **Parallel** policies offer the greatest scope for differential approaches, leading to a general 'failure to coordinate the various policies, which are often competing or overlapping' (Bretherton and Vogler, 2013: 382, emphasis added). All too frequently however, relational positions splinter into oppositional preferences, and the gap between pre-established agreements and national preferences widens beyond the boundaries of a workable outcome.

Policies with external dimensions feature in Articles 2.4, 3–5 and 6 and vary widely between an exclusive, shared, coordinated, supplementary and parallel division of competences. As such, there exists an operable, but not always clearly understood spectrum in which the EU exercises strong policy control over exclusive competences and proportionately weaker policy control over shared, coordinated and parallel competences, with Member States exercising what remains in tandem with, or in the absence of, the EU.

Assessing *where* Member States retain national control is determined by legal competence. Consequently, 'the approach to analysis of the national foreign policies of EU Member States ought to vary according to the policy area under study' (Larsen, 2009: 537). The area of greatest potential for disconnects between *modes of Europeanisation* and *modes of nationalisation* will therefore be policy areas included within Article 2.4 (TFEU) which are determined by Member States, either in parallel with or separate to the EU. The study is thus in broad agreement with approaches like that of Larsen in suggesting that 'rather than inquiring into the assumed general effect of the EU on national foreign policy, the *extent* to which national foreign policy is conducted within the EU in particular policy areas is taken as the point of departure' (Larsen, 2009: 538, emphasis added).

However, this study also strives to be rather clearer on the latter point. Simply because EU Member State policies are framed by both the depth of the *acquis* and extent of a policy's institutionalisation, their national foreign policy will not necessarily be conducted *within* the EU, but in parallel, separate from or in direct opposition to the EU. The central logic of the text is therefore to pay particular attention to the *foreign policy changes* registered across the interface of assumed forces of Europeanisation and under-explored national imperatives, and the consequent forms of *foreign policy action* undertaken in fora embedded within, parallel to or autonomous from the EU.

The risk with parallel policy areas like the CFSP and CSDP is the lack of a formal requirement to coordinate foreign policies and the ensuing gap between Member State foreign policies and strategic capabilities, and EU institutions with a clear mandate to formulate common positions on the other. This gap has frequently hardened into a permanent source of difference that remains the severest test to decent vertical coherence. Decision-making structures operating on the basis of Qualified Majority Voting (QMV) provide a source of majoritarian strength for producing consensus in most shared and parallel policies, yet require unanimity voting on issues where no EU competence exists and yet where the strategic need for a collective approach is greatest. This in turn produces only enhanced, rather than coordinated national preferences: in other words a superficial aligning of differences that do not of themselves obtain as a Union-wide identity but still reflect 'historical traditions and commitments' arising from particularist geopolitical sensitivities (Bretherton and Vogler, 2013: 383). Thus, while the EU has done well in improving its 'joined-up' global policy', particularly in multilateral forums like the UN and the WTO, the sheer range of so many different types of external action across so many varieties of competence, managed by a variety of decision-making modes and individual EU institutions leaves both their formulation and implementation open to incoherence at home and 'bilateral agreements that do not follow the EU line' abroad (Stokes and Whitman, 2013: 1102).

The text undertakes these various goals in the following ways. First, it constructs an innovative method of organisation, in which state profiles emerge via dominant foreign policy orientations both in terms of their specific geographical location in Europe (their 'geographic orientations' of Part I) and in terms of their policy-specific orientations (or the 'policy dimensions' of Part II), rather than an A–Z encyclical. This in turn requires examining the precise way in which states themselves are grouped within these themes, allowing an analysis of both well-established preferences and lesser-known orientations. Second, the analysis empirically and comparatively charts the extent to which Europeanisation has or has not produced categoric forms of foreign policy *change* in the foreign policy composition of key EU Member States, as found across the 'strong-weak competence spectrum' and, on this basis, explores the extent to which the resulting foreign policy *action* is similarly transformed, as found within the four key modes. We suggest that Europeanisation (i.e. the use of EU norms and instruments) is neither the dominant policy-making mode of all EU Member States nor a process that affects all policy areas.

As laid out in Part I, and demonstrated via key policies in Part II, despite the tenacious institutional influence of the dynamics of Europeanisation and its impact upon the external affairs of states and national societies, traditional foreign policy forces, foregrounded in pragmatism, cost-benefit analysis, strategic requirements and interest-driven instrumentalism, continue to shape the ideational motivations (input) and the strategic behaviour (output) of all Member States. Whilst Europeanisation has a role to play in determining the long-term *ends* of the EU, the demands of national decision-makers to ensure sovereign imperatives in as many areas as possible still informs the foreign policy *means* of most states, in most instances. Our contributors responded by deciding whether these preferences produce an uneasy but workable corpus of compromise-driven European foreign policies or whether 'too many member states are too exclusively focused on their national foreign policies and do not invest sufficiently in making the collective EU instruments and institutions (that they have themselves created) work' (Biscop, 2013: 1128).

Drawn against the strong/weak competence spectrum outlined earlier in this chapter, Member States produce **policy change**, in both limited and substantial ways, in terms of their engagement with national and Europeanised stances, as exemplified in Part I. At the level of EU policy-making, our contributors have given examples in Part II of policy **action** across a four-mode spectrum. Policy **action** is widely drawn, operating as the full range of official outputs flowing from Member States, both relative to their external environment, and within the EU itself. To simplify the enormous range of outputs, these foreign policy actions are organised within a **four-mode spectrum** that indicates the degree of EU versus national content within a given policy mode:

- **Mode I**: Member State foreign policy operating within established EU frameworks in a deeply institutionalised, integrated, potentially supranational fashion.
- **Mode II**: Member State foreign policy operating within the established EU frameworks, according to intergovernmental mechanisms.
- **Mode III**: Member State foreign policy conducted bilaterally or multilaterally between EU Member States, but outside established EU frameworks and/or the EU *acquis*.
- **Mode IV**: Member State foreign policy conducted between EU and non-EU Member States.

Accordingly, policy changes that operate according to the integrative dynamics that are the hallmark of Europeanised foreign policy (Mode I) are actioned by a visible use of Europeanising norms, values, processes and instruments. Taken together, these components take deep and permanent effect via a procedural and substantive recalibration of policy areas that formerly had a distinctly national profile, possibly to the point of producing a form of European strategic culture (Biava, Drent and Herd, 2011). Policy changes which use intergovernmental mechanics to strike a balance between EU-level and national demands (Mode II) enable Member States to coordinate, and operate supportively within, EU structures while retaining distinct national preferences. Mode II policies thus generally obtain due to a perceived a 'goodness of fit' between national imperatives and EU goals.

Modes I and II represent the two most Europeanised facets of the competence spectrum, while Modes III and IV represent preferences for singular or independent national foreign policy-making alongside, or possibly in opposition to, EU policies. Policy change via Mode III is typified by cooperation between Member States that can initially operate outside EU structures, while still remaining broadly supportive of EU-level goals. Policy action from this perspective is thus supportive of strategic EU ends as long-term goals, but which routinely favour the use of national means and approaches to achieve these goals in the short-term. Mode IV policy changes can emerge from national strategies that have been redefined subsequent to EU accession, or from enduring or historical attitudes that prioritise state goals above or in opposition to perceived EU goals (Mode IV).

Modes I and II are indicative of strongly integrated foreign policy-making that reinforces Europeanisation; Mode II may also represent foreign policy-making that can reinforce national policy-making preferences but does so commensurate to EU policy objectives. Modes III and IV are indicative of less integrated foreign policy-making that prioritises national preferences, possibly at the expense of Europeanised policy objectives. Equally, Modes II, III and IV can illustrate instances of Member States finding ways in which to assert national agendas in EU structures rather than actively seeking to undo the process of integration or alternatively seeking to 'de-Europeanise' their concept of Union membership.

Moving beyond the collective value-sets established in Part I, the chapters in Part II provide a current and we hope innovative survey of the most well-established and also distinct areas of EU foreign policy. These chapters also provide insights on three key questions: the initial objectives of a given EU-level policy (e.g. neighbourhood); the nature of key Member State contributions to a given EU-level policy relative to their own foreign policy orientations and objectives and operationalised as *changes to the input* of given policy stances; and the current composition of a given EU-level policy, arising from the combination of EU-level and Member State foreign policy dynamics and operationalised in the *action of policy outputs*.

Authors and editors alike have had to tread carefully with such an ambitious approach. There is for instance an inherent difficulty in empirically separating the processes of downloading from uploading (even if we understand the need to do so analytically); likewise the categories of policy change and action, and inputs and outputs. With external policies falling across ever-wider aspects of the competence spectrum, EU foreign policy-making emerges as an aggregate competence and an intrinsically **shared exercise**. Member States must necessarily negotiate between their national domains and an EU forum dominated by attempts to construct shared EU interests. They must then decide on the basis of their abiding national interest *and* their perceptions of what is entailed in Union membership on the degree to which they want to participate.

Some policies remain comprehensively EU in nature, like external trade, in which the key challenge is 'strategic agenda-setting' alongside identifying areas of enhanced effectiveness in terms of regional representation and global impact (Elsig, 2013: 325). Other areas suggest that Member States can display few misgivings, for instance in 'instrumentalising enlargement [policy] for domestic political gains', demonstrating in the process that 'EU Member State-building policy . . . [as] increasingly dominated, if not held hostage, by national agendas' (Hillion, 2010: 6). It is thus deceptively easy to use only an operative spectrum of modes to denote preferences. It is tougher, but infinitely more requisite and necessary, to analyse the national rationales behind these preferences and to comment upon the impact these preferences have on the EU's overall foreign policy actorness. As will be seen, the pull of primary and secondary EU law, the generational expansion of Treaty iterations, are balanced against abiding national attitudes and much *ad hoc* practice in constructing shared Member State perspectives regarding their immediate, and proximate, neighbourhood, regardless of where a given EU border lies. In an increasing number of policies, both revanchist Council edicts and reactive bottom-up 'adjustments have entailed a strengthened control by the Member States' in which not only the policies are challenged but more broadly 'the rules of the game', pitting the centripetal pull of an integrated EU centre against increasing instances of 'national dérive' (Hillion, 2010: 7–8). In the area of foreign policy, outcomes can be frustratingly wide: from an EU whose Member States converge in their interpretations of a given crisis (as with Iran in 2013) to uneasy balances between regional allegiances (e.g. with the US or Russia), to results in which 'Member States' interpretations diverge[d] beyond a common 'ideational space' due to due irreconcilable national strategic cultures, and where ongoing 'dissonance will be the probable outcome' (Kienzle, 2013: 424).

This volume thus endeavours to move from identifying the 'who' and 'what' of EU foreign policy that characterised the EU and its sovereign units at the turn of the twentieth century, to examining the 'hows' and 'whys' that have arisen in the wake of 2004, 2007 and 2013 enlargements; the slew of internal crises and external challenges; and where possible, the consequences of the June 2016 UK Referendum to leave the EU. The ultimate goal is therefore to provide a clear and current overview of the value-set motivations (FP inputs) and preference-based outcomes (FP outputs) of Member States regarding their foreign policy-making within and beyond the EU. While a text of this sort is always hostage to changing national and European fortunes, we feel it to be empirically timely and conceptually necessary, in order to engage with theoretic developments and policy changes alike in this endlessly rich area.

Note

1 "Kneaded in equanimity, human beings, my neighbours, eat their daily bread. None wants to be ashes." *My Neighbours*, Huchel, 1984.

Bibliography

Ashton, C., (2010), 'Presenting the New EU Diplomatic Service', July 27th, *The Wall Street Journal*. Available at: http://www.wsj.com/articles/SB10001424052748703700904575391090464445532.
Barber, T., (2014), 'Debt Crises and Coups Blunt EU's Foreign Policy Tools', *Financial Times*, 14 January 2014. Available at: http://www.ft.com/intl/cms/s/0/53281190-7d17-11e3-a579-00144feabdc0.html?siteedition=uk#axzz2tUOz0HZi. Accessed: 10 October 2016.
Biava, A., Drent, M. and Herd, G.P., (2011), 'Characterizing the European Union's Strategic Culture: An Analytical Framework', *Journal of Common Market Studies*, Vol. 49, No. 6, pp. 1227–1248.
Biscop, S., (2013), 'Peace without Money, War without Americans: Challenges for European Strategy', *International Affairs*, Vol. 89, No. 5, pp. 1125–1142.
Bretherton, C. and Vogler, J., (2013), 'A Global Actor Past Its Peak?', *International Relations*, Vol. 27, No. 3, pp. 375–390.
Bretherton, C. and Vogler, J., (2012), *The European Union as a Global Actor*, 2nd Edition, London: Routledge.
Bretherton, C. and Vogler, J., (1999), *The European Union as a Global Actor*, 1st Edition, London: Routledge.
Brooke, J., (2013), 'Russia's Putin uses political karate to keep Ukraine from moving West', The Voice of America. Available at: http://blogs.voanews.com/russia-watch/2013/11/25/russias-putin-uses-political-karate-to-keep-ukraine-from-moving-west/. Accessed: 10 October 2016.
Bull, H., (1982), 'Civilian Power Europe: A Contradiction in Terms?', *Journal of Common Market Studies*, Vol. 21, No. 2, pp. 149–164.
Caporaso, J., (1996), 'The European Union and Forms of State: Westphalian, Regulatory or Post-Modern?', *Journal of Common Market Studies*, Vol. 34, No. 1, pp. 29–52, 45–48.
Carlsnaes, W., Sjursen, H. and White, B., (eds.) (2004), *Contemporary European Foreign Policy*, Sage Publications.

Carlsnaes, W. and Smith, S., (eds.) (1994), *European Foreign Policy: The EC and the Changing Perspectives in Europe*, Sage Publications.

Cebeci, M. (2012), 'European Foreign Policy Research Reconsidered: Constructing an 'Ideal Power' Europe through Theory?', *Millennium Journal of International Studies*, Vol. 40, No. 3, pp. 563–583.

Chaban, N. and Holland, M., (2014), 'Introduction: The Evolution of EU Perceptions: From Single Studies to Systematic Research', in Chaban, N. and Holland, M. (eds.), *Communicating Europe in Times of Crisis: External Perceptions of the European Union*, Basingstoke: Palgrave Macmillan, pp. 1–23.

Cooper, R., (1996), *The Post-Modern State and the World Order*, London: Demos, p. 31.

Dannreuther, R., (ed.) (2004), *European Union Foreign and Security Policy*, London: Routledge.

De Gruyter, C., (2013), 'Europe, not much of a card sharp', Amsterdam, Eastern Partnership, Available at: http://www.presseurop.eu/en/content/article/4353961-europe-not-much-card-sharp.

Duchêne, F., (1972), 'Europe in World Peace', in R. Mayane (ed.), *Europe Tomorrow: Sixteen Europeans Look Ahead*, London: Fontana, pp. 32–47.

Dür, A. and Manfred, E., (eds.) (2011), *The European Union's Foreign Economic Policies*, London: Routledge.

Edwards, G., (2013), 'The EU's Foreign Policy and the Search for Effect', *International Relations*, Vol. 27, No. 3, p. 287.

Elsig, M., (2013), 'The EU as an Effective Trade Power? Strategic Choice of Judicial Candidates in the Context of the World Trade Organization', *International Relations*, Vol. 27, No. 3, pp. 325–340.

Elsig, M., (2002), *The EU's Common Commercial Policy: Institutions, Interests and Ideas*, Hampshire: Ashgate.

European Commission, (2016), 'EU competences', Available at: http://ec.europa.eu/citizens-initiative/public/competences/faq.

European Union, (2016), 'Shared vision, common action: A stronger Europe: A global strategy for the European Union's foreign and security policy', Brussels, June, 2016, Available at: http://europa.eu/globalstrategy/sites/globalstrategy/files/eugs_review_web.pdf.

Falkner, G. and Treib, O., (2008), 'Three Worlds of Compliance or Four? The EU-15 Compared to New Member States', *Journal of Common Market Studies*, Vol. 46, No. 2, pp. 293–313.

Gower, J. and Timmins, G., (eds.) (2011), *The European Union, Russia and the Shared Neighbourhood*, London: Routledge.

Groen, L. and Niemann, A., (2013), 'The European Union at the Copenhagen Climate Negotiations: A Case of Contested EU Actorness and Effectiveness', *International Relations*, Vol. 27, No. 3, pp. 308–324.

Hettne, B., (2008), 'EU as a global actor: An anatomy of actorship'. Paper at the EU in International Affairs 2008 Conference, Vrije Universiteit, Brussel.

Hill, C., (1998), 'Closing the Capability-Expectations Gap', in J. Peterson and H. Sjursen (eds.), *A Common Foreign Policy for Europe?*, London: Routledge, pp. 18–36.

Hill, C., (ed.) (1996), *The Actors in Europe's Foreign Policy*, London: Routledge.

Hill, C. and Smith, M., (eds.) (2005), *International Relations and the European Union*, Oxford: Oxford University Press.

Hillion, C., (2010), *The Creeping Nationalisation of the EU Enlargement Policy*. Report No. 6, SIEPS. Available at: http://www.sieps.se/sites/default/files/2010_6_.pdf. Accessed: 10 November 2016.

Holsti, K.J., (1970), 'National Role Conceptions in the Study of Foreign Policy', *International Studies Quarterly*, Vol. 14, No. 3, pp. 233–309.

Huchel, P., (1984), 'Die Nachbarn', *Peter Huchel Gesammelte Werke*, Volume I: Gedichte. Suhrkamp, Frankfurt (am Main), p. 203.

Jupille, J. and Caporaso, J., (1998), 'States, Agency, and Rules: The European Union in Global Environmental Politics', in Rhodes, C., (ed.) *The European Union in the World Community*, Boulder, CO: Lynne Rienner, pp. 213–229.

Keukeleire, S. and MacNaughtan, J., (2008), *The Foreign Policy of the European Union*, Basingstoke: Palgrave Macmillan.

Kienzle, B., (2013), 'The Role of Ideas in EU Responses to International Crises: Comparing the Cases of Iraq and Iran', *Cooperation and Conflict*, Vol. 48, No. 3, pp. 424–443.

Koops, J., (2011), *The European Union as an Integrative Power?*, Brussels: VUB Press.

Larsen, H., (2009), 'A Distinct FPA for Europe? Towards a Comprehensive Framework for Analysing the Foreign Policy of EU Member States', *European Journal of International Relations*, Vol. 15, No. 3, pp. 537–566.

Lucarelli, S. and Manners, I., (eds.) (2006) *Values and Principles in European Union Foreign Policy*, London: Routledge.

Manners, I., (2002), 'Normative Power Europe: A Contradiction in Terms?', *Journal of Common Market Studies*, Vol. 40, No. 2, pp. 235–258.

Manners, I. and Whitman, R., (eds.) (2000), *The Foreign Policies of the European Union Member States*, Manchester: Manchester University Press.

Mayer, H. and Vogt, H., (eds.) (2006), *A Responsible Europe? Ethical Foundations of EU External Affairs*, Houndmills, Basingstoke: Palgrave Macmillan.

McCormick, J., (2007), *The European Superpower*, Basingstoke: Palgrave Macmillan.

Meunier, S. and Nicolaïdis, K., (2006), 'The European Union as a Conflicted Trade Power', *Journal of European Public Policy*, Vol. 13, No. 6, pp. 906–925.

Moravcsik, A., (2009), 'Quiet Superpower', *French Politics*, Vol. 7, Nos. 3/4, pp. 403–422.

Niemann, A. and Bretherton, C., (2013), 'Introduction: EU External Policy at the Crossroads: The Challenges of Actorness and Effectiveness', *International Relations*, Vol. 27, No. 3, pp. 261–275.

Rosamond, B., (2005), 'Conceptualising the EU Model of Governance in World Politics', *European Foreign Affairs Review*, Vol. 10, No. 4, pp. 463–478.

Rosecrance, R., (1998), 'The European Union: A New Type of International Actor', in Jan Zielonka (ed.), *Paradoxes of European Foreign Policy*, The Hague: Kluwer Law International, pp. 15–25.

Ruggie, J.G., (1998), *Constructing the World Polity: Essays on International Institutionalization*, London: Routledge.

Smith, K., (2003), *EU Foreign Policy in a Changing World*, London: Polity Press.

Smith, K., (1998), 'The Instruments of European Foreign Policy', in J. Zielonka (ed.), *Paradoxes of European Foreign Policy*, The Hague: Kluwer Law International, pp. 67–86.

Smith, M., (2004), 'Toward a Theory of EU Foreign Policy-Making: Multi-Level Governance, Domestic Politics, and National Adaptation to Europe's Common Foreign and Security Policy', *Journal of European Public Policy*, Vol. 11, No. 4, pp. 740–758.

Smith, S., (1988), 'Foreign Policy Analysis and International Relations', *Millennium: Journal of International Studies*, Vol. 16, No. 2, pp. 345–348.

Smith, S., Hadfield, A. and Dunne, T., (eds.) (2016), *Foreign Policy: Theories, Actors, Cases*. 3rd Edition. Oxford: Oxford University Press.

Stokes, D. and Whitman, R.G., (2013), 'Transatlantic Triage? European and UK "Grand Strategy" after the US Rebalance to Asia', *International Affairs*, Vol. 89, No. 5, pp. 1087–1107.

Telo, Mario, (2007), 'The EU as an Incipient Civilian Power: A Systemic Approach', *Politique Européenne*, Vol. 22, pp. 35–54.

Toje, A., (2011), 'The European Union as a Small Power', *Journal of Common Market Studies*, Vol. 49, No. 1, pp. 43–60.

Treaty on the Functioning of the European Union, Consolidated Version of the (TFEU) (2008), *Official Journal of the European Union*. O.J. C 326/47. 26/10/2012 P. 0001 - 0390 Available at: http://eur-lex.europa.eu/legal-content/EN/TXT/?uri=CELEX%3A12012E%2FTXT. Accessed: 15 September 2016.

Waever, O., (1995), 'Identity, Integration and Security: Solving the Sovereignty Puzzle in E.U. Studies', *Journal of International Affairs*, Vol. 48, No. 2, pp. 389–431, 430–431.

Wallace, W. and Paterson, W.E., (eds.) (1978), *Foreign Policy Making in Western Europe: A Comparative Approach*, Farnborough: Saxon House.

Wunderlich, U., (2008), 'The EU: A Post-Westphalian Actor in a Neo-Westphalian World?' Paper for presentation at the UACES Annual/Research Conference, University of Edinburgh.

Young, A.R. and Peterson, J., (2014), *Parochial Global Europe: 21st Century Trade Politics*, Croydon: Oxford University Press.

Young, O., (1972), 'The Actors in World Politics', in J.N. Rosenau, V. Davis and M.A. East (eds.), *The Analysis of International Politics*, New York: Free Press, pp. 125–144.

Part I

Geographic orientations/ geopolitics

1 The Northern European Member States

Hiski Haukkala, Tobias Etzold and Kristi Raik

Introduction[1]

In the EU debates, it is commonplace to lump the three Nordic (Denmark, Finland and Sweden) and three Baltic (Estonia, Latvia and Lithuania) Member States together and assume a high degree of commonality within and even between these two groupings. To a degree, this is understandable as the countries are indeed bound together by deep ties stemming from geographical and cultural proximity. They have also undertaken attempts at developing cooperation on the regional and EU levels. However, all six have different historical experiences; have to a degree varying economic and societal models; and, as Table 1.1 summarizes, have also adopted differing foreign and security policy orientations during the post-Cold War era.

Therefore, instead of assuming a high level of natural commonality between the Northern European Member States, this chapter sets out to analytically map out core areas of potential commonality as well as differentiation between the countries. The role of geography and cultural and economic closeness are all factors that suggest that potential for commonality does exist (see Miles, 2000; Smith et al., 2002; Ingebritsen, 2006). However, there are also significant differences that in fact inhibit the emergence of a fully shared perspective on foreign policy throughout the region. Being all small states, even in the EU context, external factors and events obviously play the key role in their foreign and security policies. But at the same time they all have their own national histories, attitudes, traditions and consequent roles and reflexes in the external domain. None can afford the luxury of a fully indigenous policy formation, but their responses are not a mere function of their external environment either (Elman, 1995). For the past two decades, Europeanisation has played a strong role in shaping these countries' foreign policy, but more recently, the development of Russia has once again risen to the fore in shaping their attitudes.

Table 1.1 The basic security policy orientations of the Northern European EU Member States

Country	Role in the CSDP	Relationship with NATO
Denmark	Opt-out	Member
Estonia	Participant	Member
Finland	Participant	'Enhanced' partner
Latvia	Participant	Member
Lithuania	Participant	Member
Sweden	Participant	'Enhanced' partner

This chapter will look at how the countries in the region pursue their foreign policies individually as well as how they interact within the EU context to gauge to what extent true commonality – or potential for that – actually exists in the North. It is divided into three parts. First, key changes and continuations in the individual foreign policies of the Northern European Member States are discussed. This is then followed by a case-study concerning the roles the Northern Europeans have played in the formation of the EU's policies towards the East. It is argued that an analysis concerning Russia, EU enlargement, the European Neighbourhood Policy (ENP) and Eastern Partnership (EaP) shows both the potential as well as the limits of joint approaches between the Northern Member States. The chapter ends with some conclusions that ponder the degree and likely future trajectory of foreign and security policy commonality at the regional level and within the EU context. These conclusions also discuss the roles and modes the countries have adopted and are indeed likely to adopt in the future.

Changes and continuities in foreign policies of Northern European Member States

The defining feature of the post-Cold War era for Northern European Member States has been constant change. In this respect, the dissolution of the Soviet Union in 1991 was merely a starting point in a process that still continues. The big issue with clear geopolitical ramifications was the dual enlargement(s) of the EU and NATO in 2004. Also the development of Russia and its role in Northern European security is a key in understanding the foreign policies of the countries in question as they all are either direct neighbours or located in Russia's immediate neighbourhood.

Finland had a fairly well-established identity as a neutral country, stemming from the Cold War. Although during the post-Cold War era the notion of neutrality was quickly replaced with military non-alignment a certain hesitance towards the issue still remained (Ojanen, 2002). This is perhaps best exemplified by the difficult relationship Finland has enjoyed with NATO: while Finland has become a keen Partnership for Peace (PfP) member and provider of troops for crisis management, it seems to have a very limited appetite for becoming a full member of the Alliance in the foreseeable future. The same hesitance has been visible in Finland's take on the development of the ESDP/CSDP: the Finnish eagerness to push the project forward has only been matched by the certain awkwardness the country has signalled when more ambitious – and potentially binding – forms of solidarity and perhaps even security guarantees have been discussed in the EU context (Ojanen, 2008).

A good deal of the Finnish sitting on the fence becomes understandable only by bringing the Russia factor into the equation. A well-respected retired Finnish diplomat, Jaakko Blomberg has characterized the leitmotif of Finnish foreign policy as 'yearning for stability' (Blomberg, 2011). Indeed, one way to interpret the variance in Finnish activism concerning EU-level foreign and security policy is to interpret it against this background. Therefore, at the beginning of the 1990s, there was certain hesitance towards the project, which was then replaced by a willingness to develop the policy and become more Europeanised. More recently, a growing disillusionment with the prospects of genuinely common European foreign policy could be detected, entailing a return to a more national take on Finnish foreign policy, giving grounds to envisaging Finnish foreign policy as being in a pendulum swing in slow motion (Haukkala and Ojanen, 2011). That said, in conjunction with the Ukraine conflict, some noises have been made by Finland suggesting that the pendulum could be swinging more in the European direction once again. For example, President Sauli Niinistö has repeatedly called for enhanced cooperation on the EU level in tackling the potential hybrid threat from Russia (Niinistö, 2015).

Although for Finland the EU has become the key multilateral forum in terms of foreign and security policy, it is not the only one. In fact, a multilateral reflex is still important for Finland (Ministry for Foreign Affairs of Finland, 2012a). For example, Finland sought, although unsuccessfully, the UN Security Council membership for 2013–14, a process that nevertheless had the beneficial outcome of 'forcing' Finland to re-think and develop its UN agenda (Gowan, 2015). Finland has also continued to emphasize the role of the OSCE in the field of security in Europe. All in all, Finnish foreign policy can be seen as deeply enmeshed with EU and other multilateral structures in Europe and even globally.

For Sweden, too, joining the EU in 1995 shortly after the termination of the Cold War was a major change in the country's foreign policy. Before, owing to its policy of neutrality and proximity to the Soviet Union, membership was regarded as impossible (Wedin, 2008: 38). However, after joining, Sweden has revealed a certain EU-scepticism. It did not negotiate any opt-outs from the Maastricht Treaty but did not join the euro-zone although formally the country would have been obliged to. In the accession negotiations, Sweden also reserved its right not to participate in any future EU defence alliance. Like Finland, Sweden pursues a policy of military non-alignment but supports international cooperation in response to threats against peace and security. In this respect, Sweden puts a special emphasis on international issues such as disarmament, arms control and nuclear non-proliferation and contributes to UN- and NATO-led peacekeeping missions. Sweden has a privileged position amongst NATO's partners; it is regarded as security provider and operational partner and even considered a closer ally and a more reliable contributor to NATO than several of its members (Dahl, 2012: 1). The Ukraine conflict and related tensions with Russia even triggered a debate on joining NATO, which had been almost unthinkable until then but in 2014 found a majority of voters for the first time. Yet an accession will not be a quick fix. Instead, Swedish cooperation with NATO as well as bilateral security arrangements with neighbouring countries and multilateral Nordic and Nordic–Baltic defence cooperation became even closer since 2014.

Sweden is also supporting a common European foreign and security policy that safeguards respect for human rights, democracy and the principles of the rule of law (Bildt, 2012: 2). Sweden also wishes to take a pro-active role in strengthening the EU's capacity in civilian and military crisis management and even assumed a leadership role in the Nordic Battlegroup (Bildt, 2011: 3). Jointly with his Finnish counterpart, then Swedish Foreign Minister Carl Bildt launched an initiative supporting EU peace mediation in 2010. They proposed to establish the 'European Institute for Peace' as an independent body for conflict resolution, peace mediation and related training. Despite not being willing to participate in any future EU defence alliance, for Sweden, EU membership also implies to being part of a political alliance and taking its share of responsibility for Europe's security in the spirit of solidarity (Bildt, 2012: 3).

During the early 1990s, Sweden was occupied with negotiating and preparing EU membership. Shortly after joining, Sweden, owing to its aforementioned scepticism towards the EU, has looked for alternative arenas in which it could become active and even take on a lead role. As the Baltic Sea Region (BSR) forms a central element of Swedish regional and foreign policies, Sweden became one of the lead countries in the Council of the Baltic Sea States (CBSS). At a later stage, Sweden has also strongly supported the EU's Northern

Dimension (ND) policy, which was originally initiated by Finland. The regional dimension, in particular the Baltic Sea area, is still important for Sweden, not so much within traditional regional institutional formats such as the CBSS but increasingly more within the EU context, as exemplified by the European Union Strategy for the Baltic Sea Region (EUSBSR), being the first-ever macro-regional strategy of the EU. Sweden had pushed the elaboration of the strategy which was adopted by the European Council under Swedish EU Presidency in October 2009. Denmark and Finland have put a smaller emphasis on the strategy than Sweden and the Baltic states.

Turning to Denmark, since the end of the Cold War, its traditional 'adaptive foreign policy', which was rather pragmatic and reactive (Brun Pedersen, 2012: 334), has been changed into an 'active foreign policy' in which human rights, democracy and other values are defended and supported actively (Royal Danish Ministry of Foreign Affairs, 2007: 1). This active foreign policy rests on a European and an Atlantic pillar (Rahbek-Clemmensen, 2011: 1). Denmark has been in the EU since 1973 but is overall perceived as one of the more EU-sceptic members. This scepticism has been reflected in the four opt-outs Denmark negotiated from the Maastricht Treaty in the fields of the European Monetary Union (EMU), ESDP/CSDP, certain aspects of the Justice and Home Affairs (JHA) cooperation and EU citizenship.

Despite this background, Denmark has in fact played an important constructive role in finalizing the negotiations over EU enlargement during its EU Presidency in the second half of 2002, and it has also strongly and actively supported the ENP since its inception. The social-democratic-led government of 2011 until 2015 was overall more pro-EU and more pro-active in European affairs than the previous liberal/conservative governments. The government even considered abolishing the CSDP and JHA opt-outs, arguing that they actually stood against Danish interests but stepped back from its initial plans due to low popular support. It conducted a fairly active and constructive EU Council Presidency in the first half of 2012. Since the conservative liberal *Venstre* of Prime Minister Lars Løkke Rasmussen regained power forming a small minority government supported by the right-wing populist and EU-sceptic Danish People's Party in the Parliament in July 2015, Denmark has returned to the path of a rather EU-sceptic country leaning more towards Great Britain than the core of the EU. Indeed, a referendum on turning the JHA opt-out into an opt-in in December 2015 failed.

For Denmark as a founding member, NATO continues to be the cornerstone of its defence and security policy. From a Danish point of view, NATO still forms the guarantee of Danish and wider European security (Royal Danish Ministry of Foreign Affairs, 2007: 8). Denmark has even played an active role in defining NATO's future orientation and activities and in putting a more pro-active approach to civil-military cooperation on NATO's agenda. Under previous liberal/conservative governments, Denmark followed a value-based foreign policy that entailed active Danish participation in military interventions, promoting democracy and freedom (Jensen, 2012: 3). Denmark did so mostly on the side of the US and was one of those few EU members that actively backed the US in their military campaign in Iraq. In particular, the former Prime Minister Anders Fogh Rasmussen (2001–9) showed a strong and active trans-Atlanticist approach (Brun Pedersen, 2012: 331). The social-democratic-led government followed a slightly different approach and put a smaller emphasis on military interventions while promoting classic peacekeeping and security missions instead. Considerable cuts of the defence budget also allowed fewer military actions abroad (Jensen, 2012: 3). Instead the government intended to more strongly promote democracy, rule of law and human rights by civilian means and to tackle climate change, amongst others (Jensen, 2012: 3), thus bringing Denmark potentially closer to the lines of other Nordics. Furthermore, the Arctic region remains an important part of Denmark's foreign policies. Of all the Northern European EU members, Denmark has the greatest stake and interest in the Arctic region due to Greenland, which still is a part of the Danish realm. Owing to its national interest in the region, Denmark is interested in a stronger EU role in the Arctic and therefore pushes for an EU Arctic policy.

For the Baltic states, the EU, US/NATO and Russia constitute the three main dimensions of their foreign and security policies that account for a strong degree of continuity. After regaining independence in 1991, the foreign (and domestic) policies of the three Baltic states were dominated by efforts to 'return to the West', above all to become full members of the EU and NATO. Belonging to the trans-Atlantic community and making an active contribution to the preservation of that community continue to be an overarching issue for the Baltics (cf. Kuus, 2002). The other side of the coin was and remains an existential concern about national security, with Russia perceived as a latent threat (see Aalto, 2003; Mälksoo, 2006; Berg and Ehin, 2009). Therefore, the Baltic foreign policy conceptions are dominated by a traditional realist view of the surrounding world, coupled with an emphasis on value-based integration as the best security guarantee for a small state.

Accession to the EU and NATO in 2004 has been characterized as a moment of 'zero gravity' for the Baltic states (Jakniunaite, 2009: 123). For years, the Baltic foreign policy elites had been using most of their time and energy striving for these two goals. Membership in the EU opened up space for new activity, but it also created the need to develop policies and positions on a whole range of global issues where they had never been active before. As members, they faced the question of what to do with the membership, i.e. how to define their priorities and pursue them in the complex EU machinery. The surplus of diplomatic resources created by EU accession was harnessed above all to the EU's Eastern neighbourhood, which became a major priority for all three Baltic states. At the same time, the Europeanising effect of the first years of membership made them realize that perhaps being active on specific national priorities was not the main challenge. Even more importantly, one had to engage constructively in addressing whatever issues were high on the EU agenda (Maasikas, 2012).

The EU and NATO accession was thus about passing major goalposts but only to continue the game in a higher league, as members of the strongest possible team. The EU changed from a foreign policy goal to an instrument, and the framework of EU foreign policy became increasingly important in defining national positions. At the same time, the process of integration continued, with Schengen and the euro as the next goals. In 2011, having adopted the euro, Estonia could proudly declare itself 'the most integrated state in northern Europe' (Ilves, 2010). In spite of the deep crisis of the euro-zone, Latvia followed suit in adopting the euro in 2014 and Lithuania in 2015. Adoption of the euro meant strengthening their membership in the club and was thus 'an essential factor in ensuring the nation's security' (Paet, 2011). This assessment reflects a shift in the Baltic perceptions of the significance of the EU for national security. For example, a 'strong presence in the European Union' has become 'one of the main ways of ensuring national security' for Lithuania (Government of Lithuania, 2008). There has also been a general change, in particular in the case of Estonia, which was initially the most euro-sceptic among the three, towards a more pro-integrationist outlook. At the same time, the Balts have consistently supported further enlargement of the EU.

Upon their accession to the EU and NATO, the Baltic states were rather sceptical towards the CFSP and the ESDP/CSDP, although not willing to undermine these policies nor to choose between a European or Atlanticist orientation (Raik and Palosaari, 2004). NATO continues to be *the* provider of hard security guarantees for the Baltics, and the US remains the most important security ally, which explains for example the strong contribution of Estonia in particular to the NATO-led ISAF operation in Afghanistan during 2003–14. However, the strong Atlanticism of the Baltic states has been softened by the Europeanising effects of membership in the EU (EU-internal factors) as well as by changes in the trans-Atlantic relationship (EU-external factors). The Ukraine crisis reconfirmed the indispensable role of NATO in national defence, but this did not come at the cost of the perceived importance of the EU for national and European security. On the contrary, the need for a united EU foreign policy became ever more strongly underlined by the three Baltic states.

Being small countries with limited resources, the Baltic states share an anxiety about whether they are acknowledged as fully equal partners in the EU. While they support the strengthening of the CFSP and have been constructive towards the EEAS, they are sensitive about national sovereignty and stress the intergovernmental nature of EU foreign policy – positions that are quite similar to some Nordic countries (Raik, 2015). Bilateral diplomacy both inside and outside the EU remains important and is not seen as something that could be replaced by common European institutions. For the Baltics, regained sovereignty has intrinsic value, and it is not to be shared or given up lightly.

In addition to varying national perspectives, the shared Nordic–Baltic links merit discussion as well. The 1990s witnessed a certain waning in the importance of Nordic cooperation (Mouritzen, 1995; Browning, 2007). Yet the Nordic role in Baltic foreign policies has been far from insignificant, and the Nordic–Baltic cooperation has been gaining in importance in the 2000s (Schouenborg, 2013: 160–161). During the 1990s, the Nordic countries were perhaps the strongest supporters of the Baltic states' independence as well as their integration into key Western structures (Archer, 1999). To date, they still remain a key reference group especially for Estonia and Latvia, somewhat less for Lithuania. The Balts have been keen to learn from the Nordic experiences of promoting one's interests and positions in the EU. Obviously, the Nordic countries offer different role models, with their varying degrees of and positions on integration. More recently, the relationship has become more balanced where, in addition to being recipients of political and economic support, even downright aid, the Baltic states have increasingly come to their own. This is increasingly the case in the field of foreign and security policy as well which has resulted in a situation where the six have started to develop cooperation and coordination on more equal grounds. For example in the EU context, the six Nordic and Baltic EU members (the so-called NB6) have the practice to meet and coordinate their positions before every European Council and Foreign Affairs Council. Another example of practical foreign policy cooperation extended from the Nordic to the Baltic group are co-location arrangements of diplomatic missions. The Nordic countries, including the non-EU-members Norway and Iceland, are currently sharing diplomatic premises abroad in close to thirty locations (in different configurations, in most cases among two countries). This practice has been recently extended to the Baltic states. Although this is a purely practical arrangement with a cost-saving purpose, with no linkage to the substance of foreign policy, it does require a certain level of trust and sense of community.

One cannot argue that the Northern European Member States would present a united front, but they are aware of the existence of joint interests and are looking for ways to identify, expand and promote them better together. Interestingly, regional cooperation has been picking up speed even in the field of defence. Under the auspices of Nordic Defence Cooperation (NORDEFCO), Denmark, Finland, Norway and Sweden have developed cooperation in terms of procurement and training (see http://www.nordefco.org/). Also with the Baltic states, the Nordics have sought closer ties in defence matters since 2014. Bilaterally, Finland and Sweden have taken cooperation even further, including intensive joint training and starting to develop plans and even capabilities for joint operations in terms of territorial defence, although shying away from forming a formal alliance (Salonius-Pasternak, 2014).

The potential and limits of Northern European commonality in foreign policy actions – a case-study

In this section, we discuss a case-study that highlights both the amount of commonality as well as lack thereof between the Northern Europeans in the field of foreign policy. The case to be discussed deals with the EU's policies towards the East. Although the EU's Eastern policies have operated on three parallel, even separate tracks of enlargement, neighbourhood and Russia policies, for the Member States the close linkages and interdependence between these issues have, for both good and for ill, been self-evident. In general, we may note certain variegation in Member State attitudes concerning these issues. The relations with Russia bring some of the long-standing differences between the six perhaps to the sharpest relief with the countries having pursued largely different, and at times even entirely incommensurable, policies vis-à-vis Russia. That said, there are signs that on the level of overall threat perceptions Russia's actions in the Ukraine conflict have increased commonality inside the grouping, although the eventual policy conclusions may nevertheless continue to diverge for the foreseeable future. By contrast, other issues on the Eastern agenda, the EU's enlargement as well as its ENP and EaP, have portrayed a much larger degree of commonality throughout the region.

Finland has devoted a somewhat unequal amount of attention on the different parts of the Eastern portfolio. Russia has clearly been a priority with a great deal of attention to fostering positive relations with Moscow. Yet below the surface, some disagreements and problems have been brewing, even before the dramatic events in Ukraine (Etzold and Haukkala, 2013). Also the trauma of Finlandization during the Cold War has not fully disappeared, and one of the mainstays of Finnish foreign policy during the post-Cold War era has been attempts to multilateralize its relations with Russia – and keep them that way (Vaahtoranta and Forsberg, 1998). As a consequence, a good deal of Finnish foreign policy activism concerning Russia has been devoted to the development and promotion of EU level policies towards the country.

On the regional level, Finland has sought the role of a lead state with the initiative for the Northern Dimension. When it comes to overall EU–Russia relations, a more accurate characterization might be a support state where Finland has shown support to the pragmatic engagement policy developed and spearheaded by Germany. In addition, there seems to be a certain shift in Finnish EU policy from the activism of the late 1990s and early 2000s to a more passive stance more recently. To a degree, this is simply a reflection of the growing malaise in EU–Russia relations (see Forsberg and Haukkala, 2016) that has diminished the scope for initiatives and activism also on the part of Finland. The Ukraine conflict has also resulted in a re-think in Finland concerning the very foundations of its foreign and security policy. It is noteworthy that, in the Ukraine conflict, Finland has situated itself squarely in the Russia critical camp of the Union and has taken part in all EU sanctions against Russia. It has also accentuated the debate about the relative merits of national defence, the emerging consensus being that, at least for the time being, joining NATO is not the best option for Finland.

The other items on the Eastern agenda have received much less Finnish attention. In early 2000s, Finland assumed a positive stance concerning the enlargement of the EU and has supported keeping the perspective open for countries of Eastern Europe and Turkey as a matter of principle. Finland has also paid lip service to supporting the ENP/EaP but has refrained from taking significant steps in actively supporting them. This brings an almost laggard dimension to its role concerning the wider Eastern neighbourhood. At the same time, there are also some more recent signs indicating an increased Finnish activity concerning the EU's Eastern neighbourhood. The Finnish Wider Europe Initiative for Eastern Europe and Central Asia 2009–14 was a case in point. It was aimed at channelling Finland's Official Development Aid funds to Eastern Europe and Central Asia. The initiative included all the CIS countries apart from Russia, and its onus was put on low-political technical assistance with the view of strengthening stability and security across the region (Ministry for Foreign Affairs of Finland, 2012b: 6). This activism was flanked with the opening of a Finnish Embassy in Kazakhstan, Finland's first in Central Asia, as well as a smaller Liaison Office in Belarus. To a degree, the increased Finnish activism in 'Wider Europe' can be interpreted as a response to the ENP/EaP and as an attempt to lessen the Russo-centric qualities of Finnish Eastern policies. All in all, Finland's increased activism shows that the emergence of new EU policies does exert pressure on Member States to re-align their foreign policy priorities. It also shows that there is an increasing level of commonality among the Nordic–Baltic Member States concerning the EU's Eastern policies.

For both Denmark and Sweden, Russia is an important element of their foreign policies and their neighbourhood that gives them potentially an important position in EU efforts to develop a joint approach towards the country. However, several thorny subjects, such as the wars in Chechnya and Georgia, Kaliningrad, the democratic development of Russia and the Baltic Sea gas pipeline *Nord Stream*, all managed to sour bilateral relations between Denmark and Sweden and Russia during the 2000s. As a consequence, the Danish and Swedish impact on the EU level has remained fairly modest, and both of them can, to a degree, be characterized as laggards. That said, until 2014, Danish and Swedish bilateral relations with Russia started to improve while the economic and political ties became somewhat stronger. In the Ukraine conflict, both countries supported the EU's policies towards Russia, including the sanctions. Especially Sweden's relations to Russia became increasingly tense mainly due to ongoing debates concerning the possibility of joining NATO.

Sweden and Denmark have been active supporters of EU enlargement. They strongly supported the Baltic states' bid for accession especially but also welcomed the other countries. They have been supportive of further EU enlargement (even Turkey) and have encouraged and supported Iceland in its EU membership bid. Since their accession, the Baltic states have also consistently supported further enlargement and were particularly active in pushing for a membership perspective to Ukraine after the 2004 Orange revolution as well as highlighting Georgia's European credentials.

Sweden and Denmark have also attached great importance to the promotion of democracy and political stability in Eastern Europe and the Caucasus. Denmark was one of the EU members that initiated the launch of the ENP in 2002. That said, the countries to the East of the new EU Member States never had the same significance in political and economic respect as the countries that joined in 2004 and therefore caught less attention and interest from the Danish side (Jensen, 2012: 3). Sweden played a key role in the EU by co-initiating the Eastern Partnership with Poland in 2009 and has actively promoted and supported the policy ever since.

The Baltic states have showcased an entirely different dynamic within the EU concerning Russia. Upon their entry to the EU, they had some hopes that the Union would help them build 'equal and mutually advantageous relations with Russia' (Government of the Republic of Latvia, 2010). Yet the Baltic–Russian relations have remained tense. The Baltic states' activity in promoting closer relations between the EU and its Eastern neighbours, above all Ukraine and Georgia, has contributed to a confrontational atmosphere. Overall, both Brussels and Moscow tended to see the Baltic states as 'troublemakers' or 'agenda-spoilers' in the EU–Russia relationship (Kononenko, 2006; Galbreath and Lasas, 2011). However, the worsening of the EU–Russia relationship and a modest degree of improvement of the EU's unity vis-à-vis Russia over the past few years have pushed the Baltic states to a more marginal place on the EU–Russia agenda – which can be seen as a normalization of sorts.

The Baltic states, above all Lithuania, have also taken actions to shape EU–Russia relations. Lithuania tried to block EU–Russia negotiations on a new agreement twice in 2008. First, in spring 2008, it posed several conditions to the adoption of an EU negotiation mandate, calling for a tougher stance of the EU on energy security and on the protracted conflicts of Georgia and Moldova. Second, after the Russo–Georgian war of August 2008 the EU suspended negotiations but resumed them in November, with only Lithuania opposing on the grounds that Russia did not fully meet the commitments it had taken under the ceasefire agreement. Yet this issue was not subject to formal vote, so Lithuania could not block the resumption of talks. In recent years, Estonia and Lithuania have been among the most active Member States promoting a stronger EU policy on energy relations with Russia, which reflects their vital interest to reduce their dependence on Russian energy.

On the positive side, the Baltic states have experienced that their concerns with regard to Russia are increasingly understood and taken seriously in Brussels and other European capitals. For the Estonians, the so-called Bronze Soldier Crisis of spring 2007 was the most significant proof that 'political solidarity inside the EU is not just empty words' (Lepassaar, 2011). The crisis was provoked by the relocation of a Second World War monument by the Estonian government and involved extensive cyberattacks, harassment of Estonian diplomats in Moscow and unofficial economic sanctions by Russia (see Brüggemann and Kasekamp, 2009). The EU's unity in backing Estonia came as a surprise to both the Estonians and Russians.

Ever since their accession to the EU, the Baltic states have been active supporters of both the ENP and the Eastern Partnership. Their support to European-oriented reforms in the East has served a double purpose: first, addressing geopolitical concerns over Russia's dominance in the post-Soviet region and, second, finding a niche in EU foreign policy where the Baltic states could make use of their own transition experience (cf. Made, 2011). There is a tension between these two motives, however. The geopolitical motive represents continuity in the old existential security problem, addressed in a new way (Kesa, 2011) whereas the EU-oriented motive emphasizes European values and can be seen as an attempt to translate national security concerns into a normative EU agenda. The difficulty to merge the two motives has been reflected in an ambivalent position of the Balts on authoritarian tendencies in Ukraine during 2010–13 and their willingness to engage Belarus in spite of the authoritarian nature of the regime. Controversial interplay of security and values is not, however, a peculiar feature of the Baltic positions but characterizes the EU's Eastern Partnership policy at large (Christou, 2010).

The Eastern Partnership was a priority of both Lithuania's (2013) and Latvia's (2015) first EU Council presidencies. Lithuania was among the key players actively pushing for the signature of the EU-Ukraine Association Agreement in late 2013, seeing this above all as a matter of preventing Ukraine's fall under Russian sphere of influence. The Agreement, which was eventually signed in June 2014, triggered the worst crisis between Russia and the

EU since the end of the Cold War. In the changed, tense geopolitical context, the Latvian presidency of 2015 aimed to secure the EU's continued commitment to the region and to 'reaffirm the sovereign right of each partner freely to choose the level of ambition and the goals to which it aspires in its relations with the European Union' (Council of the European Union, 2015). Support to Ukraine thus became an ever more crucial matter for the Baltic states, as it was now tied to defending the European security order and the sovereignty of Russia's neighbours in the post-Soviet space.

Taken together, this discussion highlights a long-standing lack of genuine commonality between the Northern Europeans with regards to Russia. The range of bilateral relations with Russia have varied from friendly to pragmatic and openly frosty. This has been a factor inhibiting the development of cooperation on the regional level and it is one that undoubtedly played a negative role in the development and cohesion of a coherent Russia policy on the EU level as well (for a fuller analysis and discussion, see David, Gower and Haukkala, 2013). At the same time, the conflict in Ukraine has resulted in a certain convergence in terms of threat perceptions concerning Russia. Although it is too early to arrive at a definitive judgement, it seems clear that, although the conflict in Ukraine has increased commonality inside the grouping, the actual policy conclusions may nevertheless continue to diverge for the foreseeable future. NATO members are increasingly accentuating the role of the formal security guarantees provided by the Alliance while the non-aligned Sweden and perhaps to a slightly lesser extent Finland continue to ponder the relative merits of joining the Alliance. Also many Northern Europeans, in particular but not solely the Baltic states, advocate a 'tough' response to Russia while Finland in particular is still navigating the difficult waters between confrontation and engagement with Russia. Taken together, there is no compelling evidence that would suggest that the six would see eye-to-eye in terms of how best to deal with the potential Russia threat.

Turning to enlargement and the development of the ENP/EaP, on these issues, the interests of the Northern Europeans have been more similar or at least compatible. Hence, all the Northern Europeans (albeit to varying degrees) have been actively engaged and have sought joint appearances and policy coordination on the EU level. In the context of the Ukraine conflict, all of them have given their strong backing to the EU's increased support to the beleaguered Ukraine and have actively taken part in the formation and implementation of economic sanctions against Russia.

Conclusions

This chapter has analysed the foreign policies of the six Northern European Member States in the EU context. Although the notion of a 'Northern European caucus' inside the EU is tempting, one should not assume that any substantial or stable commonality necessarily exists throughout the region. Yet this does not imply that there is no commonality at all or that the prospects for increased commonality in the future are necessarily totally bleak. On the contrary, it is fair to conclude that there is at least a modicum of commonality between the Northern Europeans in the field of foreign policy. However, as shown in Table 1.2, there are also certain differences, in particular concerning the question whether in those selected areas of foreign policies within the EU context the countries act as lead state, support state or laggard. The existence of such variance in the roles throughout the region suggests some caution when drawing a conclusion that the basic commonality in foreign policy outlooks shared by the Northern Europeans could somehow self-evidently be developed into a more coherent and effective joint policies or appearances in the EU context in the future.

Table 1.2 The roles of the Northern European EU Member States in the light of two case-studies

Country	Role in Russia relations	Role in enlargement	Role in Eastern neighbourhood
Denmark	Laggard	Lead	Support
Estonia	Laggard	Support	Support
Finland	Lead/support*	Lead/support*	Laggard
Latvia	Laggard	Support	Support/lead
Lithuania	Veto	Support	Support/lead
Sweden	Laggard	Lead	Lead

* This variance indicates a certain shift in Finnish EU policy from the activism of late 1990s and early 2000s to the more passive stance more recently.

For example, since accession, most of the Finnish foreign policy actions have been nested in the EU framework. Even prior to accession Finland acquired a reputation of a 'Musterknaben' (cf. Mouritzen, 1993). At the beginning of its membership, Finland played the role of a support state in particular to Germany and in the EU's Russia policy. More recently, the role of a support state has been carried on in foreign policy but perhaps less with an accent on Germany and more overall to the common EU foreign policies. For example, Finland has been one of the most vocal supporters of the former High Representative Ashton and the new EEAS (Beneš and Raik, 2015). The recent financial crisis has revealed, however, a different Finland, more assertive of its interests. It will be interesting to see whether this will spill over into the field of foreign policy.

Denmark and Sweden are countries with partly similar priorities, similar in style and tactics. They both use a critical constructive and pragmatic approach in their foreign policies. Traditionally, both countries are not known for a particular EU enthusiasm, but this does not mean that they do not take their share of responsibility within the EU seriously. Their EU presidencies have always been very professional and thorough, pushing certain items on the agenda forward. Thus, in both countries, elements of both support and laggard states are present, depending on issue areas, with an overall tendency towards the former. For both countries, intra-EU cooperation on the intergovernmental level (rather than intra-EU integration) seems to be the dominant mode in their foreign policies, while elements of traditional national foreign policies and foreign policy elements outside an EU framework (most prominently, Nordic cooperation) remain.

The Baltic states share largely similar foreign policy priorities due to their shared history and geography. It has been important for them, however, to seek stronger partners in the EU and fade the perception of a distinct Baltic group. The strengthening of a Nordic–Baltic, Northern European and/or Baltic Sea cooperation and even shared identity is thus probably more important for the Balts than other countries in the region. That said, there are notable differences in foreign policy style and tactics among the three. All mostly perform as support states in EU foreign policy, but Lithuania has been more outspoken and self-assured, whereas Estonia and Latvia have adopted a more pragmatic approach and tendency to avoid confrontations, although sometimes acting as 'laggards'. When it comes to the different approaches of the Nordic and Baltic states to Russia and the Eastern neighbourhood, Estonia and Latvia have to some degree learned from the Finnish pragmatism, while also appreciating Sweden's and Denmark's more outspoken and critical approach. They have made a conscious effort to disprove the image of 'agenda-spoilers' in EU–Russia relations by accommodating to widely shared positions. Lithuania, by contrast, has aimed to be among the lead states on Russia, pushing for a more critical EU approach and, on the Eastern neighbourhood, promoting stronger EU support to the region. At the same time, it has not stopped short of acting as a veto state if it has seen its vital interests being in danger. In case of future multispeed developments in the field of EU foreign policy, all three would have a strong instinct to be included in the 'avant-garde' because of their security concerns, but they are unlikely to promote differentiated integration.

In conclusion, the scope for commonality is not vast, but it does exist. To a degree, it stems from the fact that the countries share, by and large, a similar structural position in the EU: they all are small and fairly peripheral Member States on the fringes of Europe, and their chances of being heard are vastly improved if they act in concert. On top of this, there seems to be a natural, largely cultural affinity, a 'we-feeling' emerging where the Nordics and Baltics alike engage each other in an ongoing conversation and increasingly perceive each other as friends. Too much should not be made out of this basic propensity – as the six often disagree in substance – but it should not be belittled either as such is what eventual deeper and more penetrating forms of cooperation and even integration are made of.

Too much should not be made out of the disagreements, either. More often, the issue is that of different and therefore not necessarily overlapping foreign political priorities. The fact that Finland emphasizes North-Western parts of Russia, Sweden the Baltic Sea, Denmark the Arctic and the Baltic states the Eastern neighbourhood does not make for a fierce battle between the countries. In fact, the countries simply do not have a joint agenda to promote and/or fight over. This means for the EU level that the Northern European Member States often are a sum that is less than their parts. Moreover, in the face of increasing problems on the EU level, recourse to national foreign policies is hardly an option. Therefore increased and re-strengthened Nordic/Nordic–Baltic/Baltic Sea/Northern European cooperation including some form of coordination of EU-related matters within these regional configurations (for example NB6) seems to be one of the trends of today. However, this speaks more about the perceived weaknesses and problems of EU policies rather than of some innate strength of Northern European cooperation in the field of foreign policy. The need to balance or somehow otherwise manage Russia's regional security challenge plays also into this. In the future, the space to watch is to what extent the Northern Europeans can surpass their differences and build more common approaches in the EU or whether they are increasingly pushed for makeshift regional arrangements to fill the gaps created by the problems and shortcomings of EU policies.

Note

1   This chapter is part of the 'Reimagining Futures in the European North at the End of the Cold War' project, funded by the Academy of Finland (decision number 2501268650). The Academy's support is gratefully acknowledged.

Bibliography

Aalto, P. (2003) *Constructing Post-Soviet Geopolitics in Estonia*, London and New York: Routledge.
Archer, C. (1999) 'Nordic Swans and Baltic Cygnets', *Cooperation and Conflict*, Vol. 34, No. 1, 47–71.
Beneš, V. and Raik, K. (2015) 'The Czech Republic, Estonia and Finland: European Vocation Re-Confirmed?', in R. Balfour, C. Carta and K. Raik (eds.) *The European External Action Service and National Foreign Ministries: Convergence or Divergence?*, Farnham: Ashgate, 181–194.

Berg, E. and Ehin, P. (eds.) (2009) *Identity and Foreign Policy: Baltic-Russian Relations and European Integration*, Aldershot: Ashgate.

Bildt, C. (2011) *Statement of Government Policy*, in the Parliamentary Debate on Foreign Affairs, Wednesday, 16 February 2011, http://www.sweden.gov.se/sb/d/2059/a/161173, date accessed 10 October 2012.

Bildt, C. (2012) *Statement of Government Policy*, in the Parliamentary Debate on Foreign Affairs, Wednesday, 12 February 2012, http://www.sweden.gov.se/sb/d/5304/a/186282, date accessed 10 October 2012.

Blomberg, J. (2011) *Vakauden kaipuu. Kylmän sodan loppu ja Suomi*, Helsinki: WSOY.

Browning, C. (2007) 'Branding Nordicity: Models, Identity and the Decline of Exceptionalism', *Cooperation and Conflict*, Vol. 42, No. 1, 27–51.

Brüggemann, K. and Kasekamp, A. (2009) 'Identity Politics and Contested Histories in Divided Societies: The Case of Estonian War Monuments', in E. Berg and P. Ehit (eds.) *Identity and Foreign Policy: Baltic-Russian Relations and European Integration*, Aldershot: Ashgate, 51–64.

Brun Pedersen, R. (2012) 'Danish Foreign Policy Activism: Differences in Kind or Degree?', *Cooperation and Conflict*, Vol. 47, No. 3, 331–349.

Christou, G. (2010) 'European Union Security Logics to the East: The European Neighbourhood Policy and the Eastern Partnership', *European Security*, Vol. 19, No. 3, 413–430.

Council of the European Union (2015) *Joint Declaration of the Eastern Partnership Summit: Eastern Partnership: the way ahead Riga. 28–29 November 2013*, http://www.consilium.europa.eu/uedocs/cms_data/docs/pressdata/EN/foraff/139765.pdf, date accessed 11 April 2017.

Dahl, A. (2012) *Partner Number One or NATO Ally Twenty-Nine? Sweden an NATO Post-Libya*, Research Paper, Research Division, NATO Defense College, Rome, No. 82, September 2012.

Danish Presidency of the Council of the EU (2012a) *Europe at Work: Programme of the Danish Presidency of the Council of the European Union 2012*, http://eu2012.dk/en/EU-and-the-Presidency/About-the-Presidency/Program-og-prioriteter, date accessed 10 October 2012.

Danish Presidency of the Council of the EU (2012b) *Europe at Work: The Results of the Danish Presidency*, http://eu2012.dk/en/NewsList/Juni/Uge-26/The-Presidencys-achievements, date accessed 10 October 2012.

David, M., Gower, J. and Haukkala, H. (eds.) (2013) *The National Perspectives on Russia: European Foreign Policy in the Making?*, London and New York: Routledge.

Elman, M. F. (1995) 'The Foreign Policies of Small States: Challenging Neorealism in Its Own Backyard', *British Journal of Political Science*, Vol. 25, No. 2, 171–217.

Etzold, T. and Haukkala, H., (2013) 'Denmark, Finland and Sweden', in David, M., Gower, J. and Haukkala, H. (eds.) *National Perspectives on Russia: European Foreign Policy in the Making?*, London and New York: Routledge, 132–148. European Council (2015) *Joint Declaration of the Eastern Partnership Summit*, Riga, 21–22 May.

European Voice (2010) 'Lithuania is discovering the value of pragmatism', *European Voice*, 25 March 2010, http://www.europeanvoice.com/article/imported/lithuania-is-discovering-the-value-of-pragmatism/67505.aspx, date accessed 5 November 2012.

Forsberg, T. and Haukkala, H. (2016) *EU-Russia Relations: The Partnership That Failed*, London: Palgrave Macmillan.

Galbreath, D. and Lasas, A. (2011) 'The "Baltic" Factor in EU-Russian Relations: In Search of Coherence and Co-operation in an Era of Complexity', *Journal of Contemporary European Studies*, Vol. 19, No. 2, 261–272.

Government of Lithuania (2008) *Programme of the Government of the Republic of Lithuania*, adopted on 9 December 2008.

Government of the Republic of Latvia (2010) *Declaration of the Intended Activities of the Cabinet of Ministers*, adopted on 3 November 2010.

Gowan, R. (2015) *Finland and the United Nations: In Defence of the National Interest*, Paper commissioned by the Ministry for Foreign Affairs of Finland, 7 December 2015, http://formin.finland.fi/public/default.aspx?contentid=338747&nodeid=49540&contentlan=2&culture=en-US, date accessed 20 January 2016.

Haukkala, H. and Ojanen, H. (2011) 'The Europeanization of Finnish Foreign Policy: Pendulum Swings in Slow Motion', in R. Wong and C. Hill (eds.) *National and European Foreign Policies: Towards Europeanization*, London and New York: Routledge, 149–166.

Ilves, T. H. (2010) *Speech by the President of Estonia at the Official Independence Day Concert*, Vanemuine Theatre, Tartu, 24 February 2010.

Ingebritsen, C. (2006) *Scandinavia in World Politics*, Lanham: Rowman & Littlefield.

Jakniunaite, D. (2009) 'Neighbourhood Politics of Baltic States: Between the EU and Russia', in E. Berg and P. Ehin (eds.) *Identity and Foreign Policy: Baltic-Russian Relations and European Integration*, Aldershot: Ashgate, 117–132.

Jensen, P. M. (2012) *The Eastern Partnership and the Danish EU Presidency: Caught between Realism and Disillusion*, Policy Paper Otwarta Europa Open Europe, Batory Foundation, Warsaw, March 2012, http://www.batory.org.pl/upload/files/Programy%20operacyjne/Otwarta%20Europa/EaP_and_EU_Danish_Presidency.pdf, date accessed 5 November 2012.

Kesa, K. (2011) 'Latvian and Lithuanian Policy in the Eastern Neighbourhood: Between Solidarity and Self-Promotion', *Perspectives*, Vol. 19, No. 2, 81–100.

Kononenko, V. (2006) '"Normal Neighbours" or "Troublemakers"? The Baltic States in the Context of Russia-EU Relations', in A. Kasekamp (ed.) *Estonian Foreign Policy Yearbook 2006*, Tallinn: Estonian Foreign Policy Institute, 69–84.

Kuus, M. (2002) 'Toward Cooperative Security? International Integration and the Construction of Security in Estonia', *Millennium: Journal of International Studies*, Vol. 31, No. 2, 297–317.

Lepassaar, J. (2011) 'Eesti Euroopa Liidu poliitika', *Diplomaatia*, No. 99, November 2011.

Maasikas, M. (2012) 'On Estonian Topics in the European Union, Once Again', in *Yearbook 2012*, Tallinn: Estonian Ministry of Foreign Affairs, http://www.vm.ee/en/estonian-topics-european-union-once-again, date accessed 5 November 2012.

Made, V. (2011) 'Shining in Brussels? The Eastern Partnership in Estonia's Foreign Policy', *Perspectives*, Vol. 19, No. 2, 67–80.

Mälksoo, M. (2006) 'From Existential Politics towards Normal Politics? The Baltic States in the Enlarged Europe', *Security Dialogue*, Vol. 37, No. 3, 275–297.

Miles, L. (2000) 'Sweden and Finland', in I. Manners and R. G. Whitman (eds.) *The Foreign Policies of European Union Member States*, Manchester and New York: Manchester University Press, 181–203.

Ministry for Foreign Affairs of Finland (2012a) *Foreign Minister Tuomioja at the Annual Meeting of Finnish Heads of Mission: Multilateralism Will Come to the Fore in Foreign Policy*, Press release 184/2012, 20 August 2012, http://formin.finland.fi/public/default.aspx?contentid=255543, date accessed 2 October 2012.

Ministry for Foreign Affairs of Finland (2012b) *Mid-Term Evaluation of the Wider Europe Initiative*, Final Report, September 2012, http://formin.finland.fi/public/download.aspx?ID=102864&GUID={FCE42EA0–6031–4A99–8717–4EE7DB5301ED}, date accessed 1 November 2012.

Mouritzen, H. (1993) 'The Two Musterknaben and the Naughty Boy: Sweden, Finland and Denmark in the Process of European Integration', *Cooperation and Conflict*, Vol. 28, No. 1, 373–402.

Mouritzen, H. (1995) 'The Nordic Model as a Foreign Policy Instrument: Its Rise and Fall', *Journal of Peace Research*, Vol. 32, No. 1, 9–21.

Niinistö, S. (2015) *Speech by President of the Republic Sauli Niinistö at the Ambassador Seminar*, Helsinki, 25 August 2015, http://www.tpk.fi/public/default.aspx?contentid=333284&culture=en-US, date accessed 20 January 2016.

Ojanen, H. (2002) 'Sweden and Finland: What Difference Does It Make to Be Non-Aligned?', in N. Græger, H. Larsen and H. Ojanen (eds.) *The ESDP and the Nordic Countries: Four Variations on a Theme*. Programme on the Northern Dimension of the CFSP No. 16, Helsinki and Berlin: The Finnish Institute of International Affairs and Institut für Europäische Politik, 154–217.

Ojanen, H. (2008) 'Finland and the ESDP: "Obliquely Forwards"?', in C. Archer (ed.) *New Security Issues in Northern Europe: The Nordic and Baltic States and the ESDP*, London and New York: Routledge, 56–77.

Paet, U. (2011) *Address by Foreign Minister Urmas Paet to the Riigikogu on behalf of the Government of Estonia*, 8 February 2011. Available at: http://www.vm.ee/en/news/address-foreign-minister-urmas-paet-riigikogu-behalf-government-estonia-8-february-2011.

Rahbek-Clemmensen, J. (2011) 'Denmark in the Arctic: Bowing to Three Masters', *Atlantisch Perspectijef*, No. 3, http://www.atlcom.nl/upload/AP%202011%20No_%203%20Rahbek-Clemmensen.pdf, date accessed 5 November 2012.

Raik, K. (2015) 'Renaissance of Realism, a New Stage of Europeanization, or Both? Estonia, Finland and EU Foreign Policy', *Cooperation and Conflict*, Vol. 50, No. 4, 440–456.

Raik, K. and Palosaari, T. (2004) *It's the Taking Part That Counts: The New Member States Adapt to EU Foreign and Security Policy*, FIIA Report 10/2004, November 2004, Helsinki: Finnish Institute of International Affairs.

Royal Danish Ministry of Foreign Affairs (2007) *Factsheet Denmark: Foreign Policy*, http://www.netpublikationer.dk/um/8466/html/entire_publication.htm, date accessed 10 October 2012.

Salonius-Pasternak, C. (2014) *Deeper Defence Cooperation: Finland and Sweden Together Again?*, FIIA Briefing Paper 163, December 2014, Helsinki: The Finnish Institute of International Affairs, http://www.fiia.fi/fi/publication/459/deeper_defence_cooperation/, date accessed 20 January 2016.

Schouenborg, L. (2013) *The Scandinavian International Society: Primary Institutions and Binding Forces, 1815–2010*, London and New York: Routledge.

Smith, D., Pabriks, A., Purs, A. and Lane, T. (2002) *The Baltic States: Estonia, Latvia and Lithuania*, London and New York: Routledge.

Vaahtoranta, T. and Forsberg, T. (1998) 'Finland's Three Security Strategies', in M. Jopp and S. Arnswald (eds.) *The European Union and the Baltic States: Visions, Interests and Strategies for the Baltic Sea Region*. Programme on the Northern Dimension of the CFSP No. 2, Helsinki and Bonn: The Finnish Institute of International Affairs and Institut für Europäische Politik, 191–211.

Wedin, L. (2008) 'Northern Europe and the ESDP: The Case of Sweden', in C. Archer (ed.) *New Security Issues in Northern Europe: The Nordic and Baltic States and the ESDP*, London and New York: Routledge, 38–55.

2 Western EU Member States foreign policy geo-orientations

UK, Ireland and the Benelux

Richard G. Whitman and Ben Tonra

Introduction

Western EU Member States represent a collection of countries which are less regularly grouped together than other configurations such as Nordic or Baltic Member States, where there is assumed to be a high degree of commonality of foreign policy. The Western Member States are drawn together more by geography than any other factor. The Benelux countries are distinctive for their geographical and cultural proximity and their cooperation as a Benelux Union, which predates the wider European integration process of the European Union. The UK and the Republic of Ireland have a separable but intertwined history and have maintained an economic, political and cultural inter-relationship with a unique institutional architecture.

This chapter approaches these Western European countries by demonstrating that the EU framework of cooperation has created areas of commonality but there has also been the preservation of differentiation between the countries. These differences illustrate that a 'Western EU' perspective on foreign policy needs to be heavily qualified. A key distinction also needs to be drawn between the UK, as one of the EU's 'big three' alongside the UK, and the remaining states which are small states. Each of the latter have their own national histories and traditions which give rise to highly differentiated roles and positions on foreign policy issues. Furthermore, Europeanisation processes have had an impact on shaping all Western European countries' foreign policy but to differing degrees.

This chapter is organised to examine how the Western European countries in the region pursue their foreign policies as individual states alongside their interaction within the EU to assess the extent to which they exhibit areas of commonality. The chapter first assesses the key changes and elements of continuity in the individual foreign policies of the West European Member States. This is then followed by an examination of the roles and actions that West Europeans have undertaken through the collective foreign policy of the EU and separately as national foreign policy. The chapter concludes by assessing the potential of Western European Member States as a coherent grouping. The chapter ends with some conclusions that ponder the degree and likely future trajectory of foreign and security policy commonality at the regional level and within the EU context in the context of the UK decision to seek exit from the EU. It also discusses the roles and modes the countries have adopted and are indeed likely to adopt in future.

Changes and continuities in foreign policies of Western European Member States

As a grouping, the West European Member States diverge significantly across several axes: NATO versus non-NATO membership (Republic of Ireland), Atlantic versus European geostrategic orientation, middle versus minor power status, former colonial powers versus former colonies. To that end, these states represent a fascinating microcosm within the project of creating a visible, credible and effective foreign policy on the part of the European Union.

A common question of assessment is the extent to which, if at all, these states (the UK, the Republic of Ireland, Belgium, Luxembourg and the Netherlands) have adapted to the exigencies of a common European policy, whether there are shared patterns in that adaptation which characterise the shape of that adaptation and its embeddedness within policy-making structures. This runs alongside the resilience of 'national interest' discourses within national policy construction of these states and which have significance for the European project as a whole.

Despite the apparently obvious differences in size, scale and scope for foreign policy, the Western European states are currently experiencing a common set of change processes. The early twenty-first century has been a period of change and transition in international relations to which Western European states are still adjusting. Individually and collectively, Western European states face foreign policy challenges in connection with the forging of relations with other key global powers such as the United States and the 'rising powers'. These relations are developing in the context of an ongoing process of globalisation, alongside the *relative* decline of the US as the Asia-Pacific region accounts for a greater share of global economic activity, levels of US indebtedness increase, and US military power appears diminished as a consequence of the difficulties encountered by interventions in Iraq and Afghanistan.

Against this challenging backdrop, Western European Union Member States have preserved national foreign policies while creating enhanced arrangements for collective diplomacy through the EU. However, notwithstanding the organisational significance of the Lisbon Treaty reforms, European collective foreign policy remains substantively in the hands of the Member State governments.

Consequently, there is a shared set of contemporary contextual challenges for the Western European states. This can be expressed in terms of 'outside in' challenges facing national and European Union diplomacy: the fragmentation of contemporary international relations as well as the 'inside out' challenge of the preservation of national foreign policies alongside the emergent EU diplomatic system.

During the decades of the Cold War, West European states' foreign policies were heavily conditioned by where they stood along the Cold War divide: alignment, non-alignment or formal neutrality. The situation was transformed after the fall of the Berlin Wall in 1989 and the dissolution of the USSR in 1991. As argued by Christopher Hill, the removal of the ideological 'straitjacket' of the Cold War, which had constrained the foreign policies of European states for many decades, led to dramatic changes in both the domestic and foreign policies of states (Hill, 2003). Immediate post-Cold War Europe was characterised by economic and political disparity between the wealthy West (underpinned by institutional membership of the European Union (EU) and the North Atlantic Treaty Organisation (NATO) and the struggling new democratic states in the East. European integration acted as a new conditioning factor on states' foreign policies by transforming intra-European states' relations through the progressive enlargement of the EU and by the attempt to build a collective foreign policy through the EU.

For the Western European Member States of the EU, their post-Cold War national foreign policies are characterised by intensive bilateral and multilateral relationships with other EU Member States and cover a wide range of issues that straddle domestic and international politics, a variety of national and European institutions, sectoral ministries and sub-national actors. Whether this *intra-EU* diplomacy has now gone beyond diplomacy as relationships between Member States have been 'domesticated' is a matter of debate (Hocking, 2004). But alongside this *intra-EU* diplomacy European states continue to pursue international politics individually, but also increasingly collectively, beyond the EU. As for the other states analysed in this volume, the political and economic policies of the EU impact significantly on their national foreign policies.

Western European national foreign policies

All Western European states retain the foreign policy-making and diplomatic infrastructure to pursue national foreign policies in international politics. States do, however, have differing resources at their disposal and differing levels of ambition in international relations. The 'Large' Western European state, the UK, is more comparable to France, with extensive diplomatic networks and foreign policy-making infrastructure. It pursues foreign policies which are global in extent and aspires to be a first-order international actor active on all issues on the international agenda. The UK is distinctive as a permanent European member of the UN Security Council (an anachronism that reflects the balance of power in 1945 rather than in 2016) in possession of nuclear weapons. For the UK, the EU is more often perceived as a constriction on national foreign policy or simply as a means to amplify national foreign policy. The UK, alongside France and Germany has been a member of an informal EU foreign policy *directoire* between whom there needs to be agreement in areas of foreign policy if the EU is to have a coherent collective position. The agreement between this EU3 successfully driving EU policy towards Iran's uranium enrichment programme has been contrasted with their disagreements over the war in Iraq and, consequently, for the failure of the EU Member States to agree a common position there.

By contrast, the other Western European states demonstrate a preference for working through the EU to make a distinctive contribution to international politics. And in some policy areas, this can be a preference to defer foreign policy prerogatives to the Union. This can be because the EU presents an opportunity within which to hide difficult decisions (a preference that the UK has also exercised) or the absence of any abiding foreign policy interest in the region or issue under discussion. Within this pattern of external relations are two types of West European states – states without the capacity or desire to engage in extensive external relations, and states which, for historical reasons, wish to enmesh themselves in a European rather than national system of foreign policy-making. The examples of the 'European' state are Belgium and Luxembourg, both of whom find EU solutions a first-order preference. An important additional point here is whether the EU can provide a balance between 'Europeanist' or 'Atlanticist' foreign policy trends which satisfy internal tensions. As has been the case for the Netherlands and Ireland, this second pattern of foreign policy can be viewed as a solution to the tensions between pro-European (read 'EU' or 'anti-US') and pro-American (read 'NATO' or 'anti-EU') forces within these countries. Clearly in this pattern of external relations, the EU is more often perceived as an opportunity for foreign policy action (or perhaps as an excuse for national foreign policy inaction).

Ireland also demonstrates a distinctive pattern of behaviour related to the post-colonial and Cold War experience of a country with a strong preference for multilateral foreign policy orientation especially through the UN system. In this type of pattern, EU membership represents, not so much an opportunity or a constriction, but merely another forum for its foreign policy.

For the EU Member States, participation in the Union represents a mixed blessing for their foreign policy activities. On the one hand, it forces them to confront the rigidity or flexibility in their foreign policy-making within a European framework, while on the other hand it tends to underline the paramount role which non-traditional foreign policy (external or economic relations) has come to assume in the twenty-first century.

What is clear is that EU membership involves asking some difficult questions of Western European foreign policy practices, or the absence of them. The challenges and responses this presents can be considered through looking at notions of the 're'-formulation of foreign policy in terms of 'remove', 'rescue', 'retreat' and 'renationalise' (Manners and Whitman, 2000). The first response is the attempt by Member States to 'remove' many of the activities of foreign policy-making from state capitals to Brussels. It is important to note that this 'Brusselisation' of foreign policy does not mean the wholesale communitarisation of foreign policy-making and implementation within the European Union. Rather, it has been argued, the Brusselisation of foreign policy-making is facilitated by the 'steady enhancement of Brussels-based decision-making bodies' such as the Political and Security Committee of the Council of Ministers, although some might wish to include decision-making within the NATO Headquarters also located in Brussels (Allen, 1998).

The second response goes further than simple 'removal' by attempting to 'rescue' the foreign policies of Member States by using membership of the EU as 'the means by which member states made their positions less rather than more vulnerable' (Allen, 1996). In broad terms, this second strategy goes far beyond the strategy of simple removal by Europeanising a Member State's foreign policy in an attempt to improve or strengthen its relations. From this perspective, the European Union is often presented as an intergovernmental mechanism for rescuing and strengthening the state and its foreign policy (Laffan, O'Donnell and Smith, 2000). However, as has been made clear by other commentators, the extent to which Europeanisation can 'rescue' foreign policy from the pressures of the supra-national, the sub-national and the transnational needs to be questioned (Spence, 1999).

Another response to any perceived 'retreat' of states' foreign policies is more recent and for some reflects the crisis moments for CFSP, particularly in light of the embarrassing failures in the Balkans and over the Iraq War. This response would appear to be the 'renationalisation' of foreign policy as a means of dealing with the 'failure to progress' through the reassertion of 'traditional national foreign policies' (Hill, 1998). It is important to note, as they do, that even though 'renationalisation' is 'freely discussed' and a 'drift apart' has been noticed by some, 'vested interest' in the still early stages of CFSP makes this argument questionable.

The contrasting benefits of 'removal', 'rescue' or 'renationalisation' in response to a perceived 'retreat' depend on the viewpoints of those engaged in the foreign policy processes under discussion. For post-colonial states such as the UK, the Netherlands and Belgium, the use of development policy and external relations provides a convenient conduit for a 'rescue' of these relationships in the guise of a less historically 'loaded' EU policy. For Ireland, the EU can represent a rescue of their non-security policies, but the pressure to 'remove' security interests to Brussels is fiercely resisted whilst also seeing the human rights and development policies of the EU as a means for rescuing, or at least advancing, these issues on a larger stage.

In several respects, Belgium, Ireland and Luxembourg are exemplifiers in demonstrating Europeanisation. A contrast can, however, be drawn between Ireland and the other two states (Tonra, 2001, 2006) where a small, comparatively poor and peripheral west European state took every possible advantage from its EU membership so as to create a modern, successful and prosperous state at the heart of European construction. Notwithstanding residual issues related to military neutrality and a handful of sensitive socio-cultural issues, the dominant narrative has been one of a textbook illustration of 'successful' European engagement and Europeanisation. Over the last decade, however, that dominant narrative has come under severe pressure in both the domestic and the foreign policy realms. There is no doubt that Ireland remains subject to the pressures of 'Europeanisation', defined as the 'domestic implications of European integration' (Lynggaard, 2011: 18). What is striking, however, especially over the last decade, is the extent to which those pressures have given rise to significant counter-pressures as the realm of the 'European' has extended further and deeper into the Irish body politic and most especially in the context of the Irish economic and fiscal crisis from 2008.

Arguably, the foreign policy realm is the least likely place to identify these counter-pressures. With the exception of policy towards Northern Ireland, Irish foreign policy-makers have modest ambitions and certainly no problematic pretensions as to the state's international role. In general terms, Ireland is presented as a progressive Northern European state, anxious to contribute to the strength of legitimate multilateral institutions, with a broad and holistic concept of security and an historical experience which gives rise to a profile on issues of development, human rights and disarmament. These are then pursued with some diplomatic ambition but with an acknowledgement that resources are few (and diminishing) and that there is rarely any domestic political gain to be made from high-profile forays into foreign policy. To that extent then, Irish foreign policy falls largely within a comfortable mainstream of EU foreign policy – perhaps to be found in the vanguard group on some of the aforementioned thematic issues – but rarely, if ever, defined as being either a 'leader' or a 'blocker' within collective EU foreign policy-making (ECFR, 2015).

Strikingly, however, there is a somewhat unique nexus in the Irish case between the domestic and the foreign policy realms where the pressures and counter-pressures of Europeanisation and (re)nationalisation become starkly visible. Due to a quirk of judicial interpretation and the subsequent path-dependency of Irish political leadership, all proposals for EU treaty change to date have been placed before the Irish electorate for their consideration. Twice, the Irish electorate has rejected such treaty change (Nice in 2001 and Lisbon in 2008), and twice, the electorate has been convinced/induced to reconsider and then approve such treaty change (Nice again in 2002 and Lisbon in 2009).

Western European foreign policy: national policies in action

UK

Within the EU, the UK is also one of the EU's 'Big 3' – alongside France and Germany – by size of population and economy. It is one of the EU's major diplomatic and military powers, accounting for, according to SIPRI, 20.8 per cent of the EU Member States' total military expenditure, compared to 21.4 per cent for France and 16 per cent for Germany. (SIPRI, 2015) As one of the EU's two permanent members of the UN Security Council, and also as both a G8 and G20 member, it is at the centre of a number of internationally significant organisations. It is also a founding member of NATO and a nuclear armed state. The UK is the EU's largest provider of overseas development assistance (ODA), second only to the United States internationally, retaining its commitment of 0.7 per cent of GDP expenditure despite austerity over the last five years. Britain also retains one of the EU Member States' most extensive diplomatic networks (with slightly fewer embassies than France and slightly more than Germany) and increasing the total number of its embassies in recent years. The UK also possesses a network of soft power resources utilising its linguistic and cultural power through the Commonwealth and British Council.

As the 2013 joint French-led and British-backed intervention in Mali (following the 2011 intervention in Libya) underscored, Europe currently has only two main strategic powers, France and the UK, with many other European militaries increasingly resembling so-called 'bonsai armies' (Missiroli, 2013: 12). Given its traditional role as interlocutor between Europe and the United States, the UK has been presented as a key player in helping to map out this nascent European grand strategy and how it relates to a now rebalancing United States. The UK's ambition to maintain itself as a globally significant player has been demonstrated by its most recent Strategic Defence and Security Review (SDSR) and the National Security Strategy (NSS) (HM Government, 2010).[1] These both, however, with their absence of substantive references to the EU, also demonstrated that the UK has not viewed the EU's foreign, security and defence policy ambitions as central to the British national ambitions (Whitman, 2016a). Further, the 2016 referendum on UK EU membership raises fundamental questions about the future relationship between the UK and the EU's foreign, security and defence policies.

The UK has the most fraught relationship with 'Europe' of any of the West European states, and as such its broader political economy relations with Europe may well influence the future direction of its strategic relations. The UK has also traditionally enjoyed a role as interlocutor between the US and the EU. As Thomas de Maizière, Germany's Defence Minister, argued in the context of a potential British exit from the EU:

> I think it is part of the British tradition that Britain has to play a role in the world. . . . We in Germany would lose a strong partner for a pro-Atlantic co-operation with America and a pragmatic British way to deal with security issues.
>
> (Hopkins, 2013)

As such, the UK's grand strategy, developing against the background of austerity and deep shifts in world politics, has the capacity to radically alter the EU debate and has done this by seeking to exit the EU.

This may well play to the UK's capacity for strategic institution-building, given its status as a leading military power in Europe and its historic role as interlocutor between the United States and Europe, as well as helping to legitimate action. However, in any attempt to leverage its power in a developing European debate, its strategic relations are now complicated by its uncertain position vis-à-vis integration within the EU political economy. If the UK were to move more definitively out of Europe's orbit, its options would be likely to diminish along with its capacity to shape architectures and mould priorities. As contingencies emerge that require coordinated responses, particularly in the context of austerity, and as centripetal forces gather strength, a significant institutional reorientation that sees the UK's position shift from being 'in' to being 'out' could also undermine its opportunities for a broader strategic voice in Europe as well as potentially change the balance of calculation of key powers within world politics.

For example, in the context of US–UK bilateral relations, it is arguable that the UK's broader leverage is increased as a result of its institutional power as both a shaper of, and a participant in, pan-European structures. This was made plain by Philip H. Gordon, US assistant secretary in the Bureau of European and Eurasian Affairs, when, articulating the position of the Obama administration during the 2016 referendum debate, he argued that a UK outside the European Union would be markedly less relevant to US interests and that such a move would severely weaken the 'special relationship'. Gordon stated that:

> A strong British voice in [the] European Union . . . is in the American interest . . . for the UK to be a part of that stronger, more important voice in the world is something I know a lot of British people welcome, and from an American perspective we certainly welcome the British voice in that EU.
>
> (Pickard, 2013)

One immediate impact of the referendum vote to leave the EU is to throw the UK–Ireland relationship into some potential turmoil. The UK is Ireland's most important trading partner, and the UK exports more to Ireland than it does to China, India and Brazil, combined. The two states also share a passport-free Common Travel Area, and in the context of the Northern Ireland peace process, the two states have institutionalised relationships between governments on the island of Ireland and between the two islands – including the devolved governments in Scotland and Wales. Other key bilateral relationships will also be complicated by the UK's withdrawal from the EU. The 2010 Lancaster House treaties created a new Anglo-French defence relationship rooted in collaboration on nuclear weapons technology and increased interoperability of armed forces within the EU. The treaties are premised on closer cooperation between the UK and France to facilitate greater burden-sharing in the EU and NATO. The rationale for closer links between the UK and France could now diminish.

Netherlands

The Netherlands is the EU's middle power *par excellence*. It has sought to preserve an EU in which the largest Member States are not in a position to pursue foreign policy-making as a *directoire* while also seeking to preserve national autonomy in foreign policy-making in a different manner from that of Belgium and Luxembourg outlined in the next section. The Netherlands has also maintained a strong commitment to NATO and transatlantic relations and has US nuclear weapons based on its territory. Its strong transatlanticism has had support across Dutch political parties but has also faced extra-parliamentary public opposition especially on the second Gulf War (which the Dutch government supported politically but did not send armed forces), involvement in Afghanistan under a deployment with ISAF (from which the Dutch government fell in February 2010 on the issue of extending the duration of the country's military mission) and more recently opposition to Transatlantic Trade and Investment Partnership (TTIP).

The Netherlands was originally tepid in its support for the development of a European defence policy. This position has been modified in recent years. Christian Democrat and progressive parties in the Netherlands became more enthusiastic towards EU defence policy as the US and the UK became more supportive of its development. Conservatives in Dutch politics retain a stronger commitment to NATO than the CSDP. Dutch interest in the development of the CSDP has, however, also been conditioned by a declining national defence budget and diminishing national military capabilities.

As a post-colonial state, the Netherlands emulates some aspects of the UK's foreign policy in remaining formally responsible for overseas territories situated outside Europe, with its dependencies in the Caribbean, and acting as leading overseas aid donor meeting the UN's ODI target of 0.7% of GNI. With a long-standing centre of international law in The

Hague, the Netherlands has also been a consistent advocate for a strengthening of the rule of international law through the EU.

A key recurring tension in Dutch foreign policy is between the *dominee* and the *koopman*, or between the minister and the merchant. That is defined as the balance between economic and security imperatives with a rights-based foreign policy focusing on developmental aid and the promotion of human rights. A preference for security was given a substantial boost by the shooting down of the Malaysia Airlines Flight 17 over Eastern Ukraine in the summer of 2014 to the cost of the lives of 193 Dutch citizens. A direct consequence has been a commitment to increased defence and intelligence service budgets. It has also given rise to a Dutch interest in strengthening the EU's diplomatic and foreign policy capabilities as a consequence of a deteriorating security environment to the South and East of the EU.

Belgium and Luxembourg

Of the West European countries, Belgium represents the most reflexively EU-orientated country. Its default position on foreign policy challenges is to seek to use the EU as the vehicle for implementing a response. It has been one of the EU's most consistent supporters of the deepening of the EU's foreign, security and defence policies.

Belgium sees the EU both the primary venue for pursuing Belgian national foreign policy interests as well as the strengthening of the EU as the key objective for its national foreign policy. The pro-EU position is also reflective of a values-based view that a European political, economic and social model can be exercised as a distinctive form of soft power influence for Belgium.

While the Netherlands has increasingly exhibited a more EU-critical stance and a diminished support for European integration, Belgium has remained consistent in its foreign policy actions. The capacity for leadership on key initiatives has, however, been diminished in recent years due to a series of domestic political crises including the formation of governments following elections. Further, diminishing resources have been allocated to foreign policy and deference expenditure, which have reduced Belgium's capacity for influence.

Belgium was a strong supporter of the Lisbon Treaty reforms and been consistently supportive of the European External Action Service most notably in third countries where the EEAS delegations operate alongside those of other EU Member States.

Belgium has also been notable in uploading national policy preferences in seeking to lead in the development of a number of EU foreign policy initiatives on antipersonnel mines, crisis management in Belgium's former colony of the Democratic Republic of Congo and the pursuit of perpetrators of crimes against humanity.

Where Belgium is distinctive from other West European states is in the decision-making architecture of its foreign policy. The Belgium state has gone through a series of constitutional revisions since 1970 which have elaborated the powers of six federal and federated region including in the area of external relations. This multilayered system of government has led to ongoing disputes on the separations of powers and complicating Belgian diplomacy by allowing for constitutionally mandated rights for the sub-national community and regional governments to engage in separate sets of diplomatic relations.

The Grand Duchy of Luxembourg is generally assessed as a country which has exercised considerable influence disproportionate to its size as consequence of its EU influence. The consequence of Luxembourg's limited personnel and financial resources is that its policy has been targeted at gaining key leadership and initiative seeking roles within the EU. Providing

Commission Presidents and conducting EU Presidencies (on twelve occasions) have been two of vehicles through which the Grand Duchy has been able to exercise influence. Luxembourg, alongside Belgium, has been the staunchest supporter of the deepening of the EU's foreign, security and defence policies.

Luxembourg's foreign policy has, by necessity, been focused on a small number of issue areas and predominantly influenced by the needs of its strongly export-oriented economy. The Grand Duchy's position as a financial services hub has created foreign policy complications especially on the issue of banking secrecy, which generated considerable pressure for reform from outsiders including other Member States and the European Commission. Luxembourg has also been less enthusiastic in its application of financial sanctions on Russia following the invasion of Crimea and Eastern Ukraine (in significant contrast to the Netherlands) as it functions as a major centre for Russian investors, banks and inward investment to Russia. It does however use its wealth in development policy objectives and is notably compliant with the UN's Millennium Development Goals by dedicating 1 per cent of GNI to development aid.

Luxembourg's foreign policy has undergone a substantive evolution over the last decade. The Second Gulf War represented a turning point in being in opposition to the US and adopting the same position as Belgium, France and Germany on the war in Iraq. And there has been an ongoing convergence with France and Germany since that period.

Ireland

As noted earlier in this chapter, Ireland's foreign policy actions can be said to exist pretty comfortably within a European mainstream, albeit with a handful of thematic issues on which Ireland sees itself as standing within something of a vanguard group (Tonra, Kennedy, Doyle and Dorr, 2012).

Within most core EU foreign policy positions, Ireland is best described as a follower or policy-taker rather than policy-maker. Whether on China, relations with Russia, on Iran, climate change, frozen conflicts etc., Irish policy-makers are diligent partners, working in close coordination within well-established policy lines or coalescing towards, and contributing to, EU policy development (ECFR, 2010–2016). At the same time, certain themes are readily visible within each of these portfolios: a commitment to the centrality of the UN, a focus on human rights and human rights defenders, an interest in – and dedication of scarce resources to – development, particularly poverty eradication and health issues. There is little by way of grandstanding and plenty of solid engagement.

In one established EU foreign policy realm, however, Ireland, if not correctly described as 'blocking', is at least seen as a long-term straggler. In the realm of security and defence, Ireland's well-known policy of military neutrality is an ongoing challenge. It would be fair to say, however, that Irish foreign policy-makers have worked assiduously to ensure that Irish sensitivities are reflected and respected within EU texts without compromising or qualifying EU consensus. To a large degree, this sophisticated balancing act has been facilitated by the fact that there remains such a breadth of policy difference between the core Member States. To that extent, therefore, hard choices have not been presented and Irish policy has nestled – if not always comfortably – within the interstices of Atlanticist and neo-Gaullist models of EU security and defence. Moreover, in the absence of any formalised variable geometry within the Union (such as through Permanent Structured Cooperation), the exceptional Irish position has not had to be institutionalised, as has been that of Denmark. Irish statutory requirements under the so-called 'triple-lock' arrangement which, inter alia, requires formal

UN sanction for the overseas deployment of Irish troops, has not forestalled Irish participation in either EU battle groups or EU military deployments: Operation Concordia in the Republic of Macedonia (2003) being the single exception.

Indeed, it might be argued that some significant Europeanising movement is visible here. With all of the political qualifications and treaty addenda underlining the particular position of Ireland as regards security and defence cooperation, it is perhaps surprising to note that Irish participation therein has been so wholehearted. Ireland allocated up to 150 troops to both the Nordic and the Austrian/German EU battle groups. There has also been a 75 per cent Irish participation rate in EU military missions, and in terms of the size of its defence forces, Ireland is a well above-average contributor to EU military operations. In 2011, Irish engagement was further reinforced with the participation of the Irish Defence Forces in two EDA research projects: maritime surveillance and in chemical, biological, radiological and nuclear protection. This high participation level has also been reflected in staff appointments within CSDP, namely the appointment in 2007 of Lt General Pat Nash as operational commander of the EUFOR mission in Chad and the appointment of an Irish Officer to command the EU Training Mission (EUTM) in Somalia.

Outside the well-established lines of agreed EU foreign policy, the profile of Irish foreign policy actions is somewhat more variable, and we do witness more 'traditional' foreign policy orientations.

The 2003 Iraq War is perhaps emblematic of the pressures faced within Irish foreign policy. In the latter half of 2002, Ireland served as an elected member of the Security Council. On the emerging Iraqi crisis and in concert with well-established Irish foreign policy lines, ministers and officials worked assiduously to strengthen the UN's position and to press the Iraqi government on its compliance with outstanding UN resolutions. When the locus of debate shifted in early 2003 towards the question of formal UN authorisation for an invasion of Iraq, the Irish government found itself untethered from its usual foreign policy moorings. With the EU Member States riven with dissention and with reinforcing legal advice from the US and UK, the Irish insisted that while a formal UN resolution was certainly desirable, they could not make a judgement as to whether or not it was necessary. In the midst of vigorous public debate and in the light of more than 100,000 demonstrators in central Dublin protesting at the prospect of an invasion in early February 2003, Irish government ministers repeatedly insisted that Irish ties to both the US and UK were critical, that the legal arguments at the UN were complex and that any move actively to frustrate US policy (through, for example the withdrawal of over-flight or landing rights for US military and charter aircraft at Shannon Airport) was impossible. US government sources also suggested that Ireland was included in their list of 'coalition' countries but that, for political reasons, it was one of those that preferred not to be specified in public. Thus, in this case, while there could hardly be a Europeanised context for a foreign policy decision which divided EU Member States almost down the middle, it is significant that Irish policy-makers reverted to an 'Anglo-Saxon' position, far removed from obvious popular sentiment.

Irish foreign policy actions in the realm of disarmament are also apposite. Nuclear non-proliferation and disarmament are long-standing areas of Irish foreign policy interest dating back to the 'Irish Resolution' which ultimately led to the 1968 Nuclear Non-Proliferation Treaty (NPT). Ireland's interest in the NPT regime has been consistent and ongoing. At the 2010 NPT Review Conference in New York, the Irish delegation – in concert with its allies in the Vienna Group of Ten (VG10: Australia, Austria, Canada, Denmark, Finland, Ireland, Netherlands, New Zealand, Norway and Sweden,) and the 1998 New Agenda Coalition (NAC: Brazil, Egypt, Ireland, Mexico, New Zealand, South Africa and Sweden) – had to overcome a variety of obstacles to a successful conclusion. On one of the thorniest issues – that of an 'effectively verifiable Middle East zone free of weapons of mass destruction' – Irish diplomacy played a leading role in negotiations which led to the 2012 regional conference and the appointment of a dedicated facilitator to support implementation. The failure of the 2015 NPT review conference to agree an implementation plan was a signal disappointment.

Similarly, Ireland has pursued with vigour other disarmament initiatives. Ireland joined with other like-minded states, UN agencies, NGOs and humanitarian organisations in 2007 to address the problem of cluster munitions and the pursuit of a legally binding international instrument to prohibit the use, production, transfer and stockpiling of these weapons. Following a series of preparatory conferences, delegates from 111 states and 21 organisations gathered in Dublin over 10 days in May 2008 to discuss a draft convention on the elimination of these weapons. Several major UN Member States – including EU Member States – had issues with either the principle and/or the detail of the proposed convention. In the end, the Dublin Diplomatic Conference on Cluster Munitions adopted a comprehensive new treaty banning cluster munitions. No exceptions and no transition periods were provided and the treaty was opened for signature in Oslo in December 2008 with over a hundred subsequent signatories and ratifications.

Finally, outside the realm of agreed EU foreign policy, Irish foreign policy has pursued the UN's negotiation of a multilateral Arms Trade Treaty. Irish policy dedicated itself to such a treaty as a means to agree common standards for the import, export and transfer of arms across borders and in 2006 Ireland submitted its call for an international, legally binding treaty in this realm. Ireland was among the first 66 states to sign the ATT in 2013 and has vigorously supported its full implementation since it came into operation at the end of 2014.

Conclusion

Western European states are inseparable from the international environment that impacts upon their foreign policies and through which they seek to have influence individually and collectively. European states face significant foreign policy challenges in the face of early twenty-first-century international developments. Like the US, the global financial crisis has also impacted upon Europe's international relations. Ongoing problems in its political economy have served to put the European project under severe strain with potential sovereign defaults and mismatches between its monetary and fiscal integration amplifying centrifugal forces.

The 'outside in' impinges heavily on the contemporary practice of diplomacy. Each of these countries are adjusting themselves to broader developments within international relations and the implications for their own national interests. Shrinking resources for diplomacy and defence have been a shared problem for the majority of Western European states.

The preservation of the means to conduct national foreign policies alongside the evolving collective EU foreign policy arrangements also creates an 'inside out' challenge for Western European states. For the analyst of EU Member State foreign policy, there is the need to understand developments within, across and between European states diplomacies if the role of these Western European states in the European Union and the consequent implications for Europe's global role is to be fully comprehended – the most significant development in this area being the 2016 UK referendum decision to leave the EU.

In the cases of the Netherlands and Ireland, there are certainly no signs of any comprehensive advancing Europeanisation. Both of these states are well settled within existing policy arrangements which allow for the preservation in national action in foreign policy.

There is, however, a divergence within these three states on the development of the CFSP and the CSDP and with each state evolving a more supportive perspective on EU policy development. Even prior to the UK referendum vote, the British remained less persuaded as to the value of EU foreign and security policy and maintained a national foreign and security policy which does not see EU foreign policy as a key prerogative. In contrast, Belgium and Luxembourg have taken a consistent position in favour of a deepening of integration to strengthen institutions and instruments of collective foreign policy. This view, however, does not automatically translate into the unequivocal acceptance of all EU foreign policy initiatives.

In some instances, there is also evidence of a shift towards a renationalisation of foreign policy. In the context of Ireland's economic crisis, there was a renewed focus on the bilateralisation of Irish foreign policy, most especially vis-à-vis the United States and China. While the first is certainly an extension of a long-standing bilateral interest, the development of an explicitly China-focused 'Asia Strategy' is of some significance and may prove to be illustrative of a longer-term trend. The UK looks set to pursue an extreme variant of renationalisation with its exit from the EU. Its diplomacy will, however, be inevitably heavily focused on the EU even after its withdrawal (Whitman, 2016b).

Consequently, while the foreign policies of EU Member States are distinctive because of the additional impact of the structures and processes of European integration, it is clear that the CFSP does not always constrain national foreign policy-making when national interests or alliances are at stake. Further integration in Europe could result in the emergence of a true common and collective foreign policy, but on the basis of the majority position across Western European states, the retention of national control over foreign and defence policies in a wider, rather than a deeper, EU is a trend that looks likely to continue in the foreseeable future.

The collective diplomacy of European Union Member States is still a work in progress. The reforms introduced by the Lisbon Treaty have created new capabilities and capacity, but these have not replaced national arrangements for diplomacy. For each of the Western European states, there is no evidence that there is retreat from maintaining the national capacity for foreign, security and defence policy. There is, however, an ongoing process of Member State accommodation to the development of the CFSP and CSDP where Western European states are adjusting the pursuit of national foreign and security policies primarily to upload or amplify national foreign policy objectives. However, both EU and national diplomatic systems are confronted with a common set of challenges in the practice of diplomacy in the second decade of the twenty-first century. In addressing these challenges, a key issue is whether national and EU-level responses are complementary or convergent.

Note

1   See also HM Government, *Securing Britain in an Age of Uncertainty: The Strategic Defence and Security Review* (London: TSO, 2010).

Bibliography

Allen, D. (1996) 'Conclusions: The European Rescue of National Foreign Policy?', in C. Hill (ed.) *The Actors in Europe's Foreign Policy*. London: Routledge, pp. 288–304.
Allen, D. (1998) '"Who Speaks for Europe?" The Search for an Effective and Coherent External Policy', in John Peterson and Helene Sjursen (eds.) *A Common Foreign Policy for Europe?* London: Routledge, pp. 41–58.

ECFR (2010–2016) *Foreign Policy Scorecard*. London: ECFR. Available at: http://www.ecfr.eu/scorecard (Accessed 25 November 2016).

Hill, C. (1998) 'Convergence, Divergence and Dialectics: National Foreign Policies and the CSFP', in Jan Zielonka (ed.), *Paradoxes of European Foreign Policy*, The Hague: Kluwer Law International, pp. 35–52.

Hill, C. (2003) *The Changing Politics of Foreign Policy*. Basingstoke: Palgrave Macmillan.

HM Government (2010) *A Strong Britain in an Age of Uncertainty: The National Security Strategy*. London: The Stationery Office, October 2010, p. 15.

Hocking, B. (2004) 'Diplomacy', in Walter Carlsnaes, Helen Sjursen and Brian White (eds.) *Contemporary European Foreign Policy*. London: Sage, pp. 91–109.

Hopkins, N. (2013) 'UK would jeopardise military standing by leaving EU, says German minister', *Guardian*, 22 April 2013. Available at: http://www.guardian.co.uk/world/2013/apr/22/uk-military-eu-german-minister (Accessed 31 July 2013).

Laffan, B., O'Donnell, R. and Smith, M. (2000) *Europe's Experimental Union: Rethinking Integration*. London: Routledge.

Lynggaard, K. (2011) 'Domestic Change in the Face of European Integration and Globalization: Methodological Pitfalls and Pathways'. *Comparative European Politics* Vol. 9, No. 1, pp. 18–37.

Manners, I. and Whitman, R. (eds.) (2000) *The Foreign Policies of European Union Member States*. Manchester: Manchester University Press.

Missiroli, A. (2013) *Enabling the Future European Military Capabilities 2013–2025: Challenges and Avenues*. Paris: European Union Institute for Security Studies, May 2013.

Pickard, J. (2013) 'What Obama's Europe Adviser Actually Said about the UK in the EU', *Financial Times*, 10 January 2013. Available at: http://blogs.ft.com/westminster/2013/01/what-exactly-did-obamas-europe-adviser-say-about-uk-in-eu/ (Accessed 31 July 2016).

SIPRI (Stockholm International Peace Research Institute) (2015) *SIPRI: Armaments, Disarmament and International Security Yearbook 2015*. London: SIPRI.

Spence, D. (1999) 'Foreign Ministries in National and European Context', in B. Hocking (ed.) *Foreign Ministries: Change and Adaptation*. Houndmills: Macmillan, pp. 247–268.

Tonra, B. (2001) *Europeanisation of National Foreign Policy: Dutch Danish and Irish Foreign Policies in CFSP*. London: Ashgate.

Tonra, B. (2006) *From Global Citizen and European Republic: Irish Foreign Policy in Transition*. Manchester: Manchester University Press.

Tonra, B., Kennedy, M., Doyle, J. and Dorr, N. (2012) *Irish Foreign Policy*. Dublin: Gill and Macmillan and the Royal Irish Academy.

Whitman, R. (2016a) 'The UK and EU Foreign and Security Policy: An Optional Extra'. *Political Quarterly*, Special issue: Britain and the European Union Vol. 87, No. 2 (April–June 2016), pp. 254–261.

Whitman, R. (2016b) 'Brexit or Bremain: What Future for the UK's European Diplomatic Strategy?' *International Affairs* Vol. 92, No. 3 (May 2016), pp. 509–529.

3 Foreign policies of Eastern EU states

Karolina Pomorska

Introduction

The aim of this chapter is to analyse Europeanisation in eight Eastern EU Member States, namely in Austria, Bulgaria, Czech Republic, Hungary, Poland, Slovakia, Slovenia and Romania. Most of them describe their geographic position as Central European (see e.g. Wagrowska, 2009), which in the past served as a way of distancing themselves from the former Soviet bloc or the Balkans and of showing willingness to join Western political structures, such as NATO or the EU.[1] The choice to group them together was based on geopolitical assumptions and consequently, as outlined in the Introduction to the book, the chapter seeks to check whether it is possible to identify any common foreign policy values or principles on the basis of belonging to one geographical region. Out of the eight countries, only one, Austria, featured in the previous edition to this book, edited by Manners and Whitman in 2000. Seven others are post-communist countries; for this reason, we could expect they may share a similar heritage. They joined the EU in the two rounds of enlargements, in 2004 and 2007, when Austria has already been a member for a decade, having joined in 1995. Most of them share the relative lack of experience in modern foreign policy-making and (multilateral) diplomacy, due to decades spent in the zone of Soviet dominance. Countries like Slovakia or Slovenia needed to arrange their foreign policies and diplomatic structures in the 1990s almost from 'scratch', very much like the Baltic states.

Several factors need to be taken into account when looking for Europeanisation trends in the region. First, if geography indeed plays a role in relation to the Eastern European states, it may prove to be a factor for divergence, rather than for convergence, of interests. However, it is likely to determine the geographical 'hot spots' on the Member States' political radar. The main dividing line in the European Union, in the foreign and security realm, lies between the North and the South. Among the states discussed here, only Poland could be classified as a 'Northern' state. Together with Slovakia and the Czech Republic, Poland has been active in the EU's policy towards Eastern neighbours (even though in the case of the Czech Republic only from the mid-2000s; Tulmets, 2008; Weiss, 2011), while for Austria, Hungary, Slovenia, Bulgaria and Romania it was the region of the Balkans and relations with Turkey that came to the fore. After the initial interest, EU diplomats reported that Poland became withdrawn and largely uninterested in active involvement in that region, focusing its efforts on the creation of Eastern Partnership (EaP). The EU's relations with the Southern neighbourhood were initially perceived by its diplomats as a competition to the idea of Eastern Dimension and later only as of secondary importance.

Second, the existing literature on Europeanisation suggests that the size of the Member State matters. In this respect, Poland is the odd one in the group, aspiring to be counted among the influential, or 'big', Member States. These ambitions have direct impact on the self-perceived role in the European Foreign Policy, a topic which will be discussed throughout the chapter. Third, Austria is another odd case here: it did not belong to the Soviet bloc; it is also the only one pursuing its neutrality status. It does, of course, share to a large extent its history with Hungary, who had also embedded the idea of neutrality in its national identity, even though it was never officially reached (Juhász, 2003: 52; Kovács and Wodak, 2003). Including it in the analysis has its advantages, as it allows for observation whether geography and possibly similar geopolitical interest result in similar adaptational patterns in foreign policy.

There are a few multilateral platforms for foreign policy co-operation in the region of Eastern Europe, none of them, however, is inclusive of all the states discussed here (except the European Union itself). In 1988, the Central European Initiative (CEI) was created, first called Pentagonale and then Hexagonale, including Italy, Hungary, Austria, Yugoslavia and later Czechoslovakia (now the Czech Republic and Slovakia) and Poland. It has lost much of its importance after the Visegrad Group was formed in 1990, and after the transition processes in the region ended (Fitzmaurice, 1998: 183). The so-called V4 is now composed of the Czech Republic, Slovakia, Hungary and Poland, with Slovenia often participating in the meetings. The group has listed explicitly as its aim the contribution to the development of the CFSP, especially in the area of Eastern Partnership and Western Balkans (for more on V4, see Dangerfield, 2009). The Group raised its public profile after Orban came to power in Hungary and after Law and Justice (PiS) won elections in Poland in 2015. In spite of the high density of meetings within the Visegrad Group, at different levels (from Heads of States summits to national diplomats in the Council of the EU) and at different levels of formality (from formal summits to informal 'V4 energy lunches' in Brussels), it is hard to determine the level of influence the group had on EU's Common Foreign and Security Policy. As this chapter will show, foreign policy preferences among the participants are so diverse that, on many occasions, it proved impossible to arrive at common positions, such as in the immediate follow-up to the crisis in Georgia. Starkly diverging positions on Russia make any meaningful co-operation in foreign policy difficult.

The chapter proceeds as follows: it first looks separately at the different states, starting with Poland, the Czech Republic and Slovakia, followed by Hungary and Austria, and finally Slovenia, Romania and Bulgaria. It pays special attention to the role-conception each country holds of its participation in the CFSP, the areas when it has had greatest ambitions to change the European Foreign Policy as well as the 'special relationships' and sensitive issues. Finally, the concluding part aims at teasing out any potential trends in the Europeanisation processes and tensions between nationalisation versus Europeanisation throughout the region. The analytical emphasis is on the Member States themselves and on the way in which they responded to the pressures of European integration. In particular, the chapter analyses how they responded to the participation in the Common Foreign and Security Policy.

Czech Republic, Poland and Slovakia

Czech Republic, Poland and Slovakia have all been busy reinventing their relations with Russia and vitally interested in developing EU's relations with its neighbours to the East. Together with the Baltic states (called the B3 in the Brussels jargon), they have been active within the Baltic Sea Region Co-operation. At the same time, the three hold different self-images concerning the role they would like to play in CFSP. Since the accession to the EU, Poland has considered itself as a mid-sized or even a big Member State, which should be able to express positions on all aspects of European foreign policy and take the lead on the EU's relations with Eastern neighbours. It has aspired to be a 'bridge' between the 'Big Three' and the smaller Member States in the region, after disillusionment about becoming a new 'bridge' between the United States and the EU. This approach has initially not been appreciated by its partners, but with time, and after the Polish presidency in the Council of the EU (second part of 2011), the relations in the region had improved. Polish diplomats and politicians have repeatedly emphasised that Poland joined the Union to be a 'leader not a follower'. This position has been softened with time, once the consensus-oriented nature of the decision-making in the CFSP was understood. The Czech Republic and Slovakia generally see themselves as rather vulnerable and small countries that need alliances in order to be protected from the big players in the region (such as Russia) (Kořan, 2013). Still, they have also expressed ambitions to be among the 'shapers' of some policies, concerning for example human rights or enlargement. At the same time, there is a large degree of frustration among their diplomats delegated to Brussels, who complain that their ideas were not given enough attention due to the small size of the country (one diplomat went as far as to say, '[G]enerally big Member States don't listen to you', Interview 2011).

It has been a shared perception among the Poles, Czechs and the Slovaks that, due to their deep understanding of the countries to the East (i.e. more nuanced that the one held by the 'old' Member States), it is they who should be in the lead of the Union's policy towards Eastern neighbours (see e.g. Kořan, 2013; Pomorska, 2011). However, there is an understanding that, while the Czech Republic and Slovakia are able to offer ideas, they have only very few resources or power to back them up.[2] The perceptions on how the policy should be shaped differ among the three neighbours. Polish diplomats would probably name Eastern Partnership (EaP) as their greatest success of policy 'uploading'. This initiative, branded together with Sweden, was endorsed by foreign ministers at the Council meeting in May 2008. Even though the countries from the region were consulted beforehand, also in the V4 format, the initiative was not promoted as their collective effort. This sparked some minor antagonisms, especially between Poland and the Czech Republic.

It is apparent that most of the foreign policies are conducted through or with the EU. There are a number of areas that are considered of special national importance for the three states and could possibly result in what Manners and Whitman (2000) called 'ring-fencing' in the previous edition of this volume. Such was the move by Poland, which brought up the situation of Polish minority in Belarus to the Council Conclusions. However, in most cases, the states decided to act through the EU even when their vital national (security) interests were concerned. An early sign that these new Member States would not attempt to 'ring-fence' parts of its Eastern policies was Polish engagement in the Orange Revolution in Ukraine (at the end of 2004). The Polish President, together with Javier Solana, then Special Representative for CFSP and the Lithuanian President, acted as brokers in the crisis. A decade later, Polish Minister of Foreign Affairs, Radek Sikorski, became engaged in mediation during the so-called 'Euromaidan' events in 2014.

There seems to be an implicit understanding among the Visegrad states that Polish relationship with Russia 'verges on the obsessional' and is of a different nature than of the other, smaller, Visegrad partners (Dangerfield, 2012: 970). This perception became even more acute after the PiS government was installed in 2015. For a long time, Poland was among the laggards of the EU's policy towards Russia and did not present any substantial constructive proposals. However, with Radek Sikorski as a Foreign Minister, Polish diplomacy began a more pragmatic approach linked with close co-operation with Germany on the policy towards Russia and Belarus (ECFR, 2012). This came after a period of a more radical approach under the rule of the Kaczynski brothers' Law and Justice Party (PiS) between 2005 and 2007 and changed again back with their return to power in 2015. The relations with Germany worsened, which made any common initiatives difficult to imagine. Such policy resulted in Poland vetoing the mandate for the European Commission to negotiate a new EU–Russia agreement in 2006, caused by a bilateral dispute between Poland and Russia over meat exports. Even more stark is the difference with the next governments' policy, which put Poland among the countries considered as 'leaders' of the EU's policy towards Russia (ECFR, 2012). Poland remained on the forefront of discussions when it came to the response to Russian actions in Ukraine and pushed for the sanctions to be implemented.

This example shows that the Europeanisation of foreign policy has been a patchy process that may well experience setbacks, an experience of de-Europeanisation. Both Czech and Slovak policies on Russia were less confrontational, not least due to the energy dependence. Polish sources reported that it was impossible to achieve an early Visegrad statement on the Georgian conflict in 2008 due to lack of Czech support. Slovak diplomats, on their part, claimed that there has been an internal shift in the policy and they would speak more 'bluntly' about Russian policies than before, while others claimed there was still a dose of 'pragmatism' in Bratislava's policy towards Russia. This is an example of a shift in foreign policy with the change of government and shows that Europeanisation of foreign policy is a subject to many internal political factors.

The issue on which many expect divergence in national foreign policies in the region and which has been a top priority of every country discussed in this chapter is energy security. In this regard, Slovakia is one of the most vulnerable countries. Heavily dependent on Russian gas, coal and oil, it experienced a near-to-blackout situation in winter 2009 (Bátora and Pulišová, 2013). Since then, it has been particularly interested in having dispute settlement mechanisms included in agreements with countries like Russia or Ukraine.[3] Together with the Czech Republic, Slovakia initiated the European Nuclear Energy Forum to discuss the use of nuclear energy in the EU and pushed for including nuclear energy among the 'clean' energy sources (Bilcik, 2010). Both Czech (2009) and Polish (2011) presidencies in the Council of the EU treated energy policy as one of its priorities and worked towards Europeanisation of energy security. In the Czech case, this followed from an idea that as a 'small, resource-poor and landlocked European country' (Kořan, 2013: 97), it needed a strong European approach to secure its interests. Poland on its part, in the light of its sensitive relations with Russia, has been interested in pushing for a new energy strategy.

A good example of a circular nature of Europeanisation in foreign policy is Polish policy towards Belarus. Already before the accession, Polish officials and academics pointed out that it would be a mistake if the policy towards Belarus would be simply a function of Member States' stance on Russia. At the time of enlargement, Poland had no choice but to adapt its policy to be in line with the EU. This meant for example abandoning all official contacts with Belarusian officials at the ministerial level. As soon as Poland became a member though, it intensified its efforts to 'upload' its policy preferences to the EU level. It argued for 'minimising' rather than 'abolishing' the official contacts (see GAERC Conclusions from November 2004) or including the hardships of Polish minority in Belarus on the Council agenda (see GAERC Conclusions from January 2005). Opening up for more relations with

Belarus was also a vital part of the Eastern Partnership concept. This shows how the initial national adaptation to the policies of the Union is followed by the process of policy uploading and attempts to project one's policy goals onto the EU level.

All three countries are also vitally interested in the transatlantic relations. Some observers have argued that the historical experiences, through shaping the notions of sovereignty, statehood and security, have resulted in emergence of a distinctive 'Atlanticist 'security culture' or, in other words, 'instinctive Atlanticism' (Longhurst and Zaborowski, 2007: 5, 11). Poland, even before becoming a member of the EU, has frequently spoken against duplicating NATO structures when institutionalising ESDP (later CSDP), echoing the voice of the United Kingdom. A general pro-Atlanticist attitude remains a common policy trend for most of the analysed Member States. The reasons for the broad support of the United States can be traced to the perceived role of the US in bringing communism down and enlarging NATO. In some cases we could go even further in history, for example in the case of Poland and the support of American President Wilson for the independent Polish state after World War I or in the case of the Czech Republic, the memories of 1939 and 1968 (Weiss, 2011). The almost unconditional support became apparent in the widespread backing of the US-led invasion of Iraq in 2003.[4] The same year, Donald Rumsfeld labelled the countries in the region as 'New Europe', providing support over the war in Iraq, as opposed to the 'old Europe' of Germany and France. This would suggest that we could treat them as a somewhat homogeneous bloc when it comes to transatlantic relationship. However, even within this group, attitudes towards the United States vary and have undergone change (see e.g. Kavalski and Zolkos, 2007).

The choice between the US and the EU has been highly avoided in most of Eastern Europe (Edwards, 2006: 145). According to a Polish MFA official, in the 1990s, the EU and the United States acted for Poland as a 'mother and a father figure' (Wiśniewski, 2011). The pro-American attitude has been sometimes even understood in terms of a 'moral commitment' (Rotfeld, 2006). The Czech Republic has always prioritised its relationship with NATO as regards security, and the pro-American orientation in foreign policy has remained even after the development of CSDP (Weiss, 2011). At least one policy 'action' related to the transatlantic relationship after the membership caused frustration of the other Member States. Poland and the Czech Republic insisted that the potential installation of the anti-missile defence shield had nothing to do with CDSP and the EU and was a domain of their bilateral relations with the US. Nevertheless, the relations with the United States are being revisited in the light of the waning attention of the US in Europe, especially under the first Obama administration and its so-called 'reset policy' in relations with Russia (Kořan, 2013). A pragmatic approach has evolved in Poland under Foreign Minister Radosław Sikorski, who had repeatedly emphasised the value of co-operation with Germany and within the European Union (BBC HARDTALK, 2012). This policy was later revised by the PiS government.

The communist heritage is often mentioned by diplomats from Eastern Europe when they talk about their country's engagement in the protection of human rights. The analysts point out that the whole identity of foreign policy in Czech Republic and Slovakia was built on the notion of human rights protection (Kořan, 2013; Weiss, 2011) and that there is a strong element of the dissident tradition (Waisová and Piknerová, 2012). This is the case of Czech's policy towards Cuba or Slovak's recent stance on Belarus and Iran (earlier also on Libya), both states on the radical side of the positions in the Council. In 2008, Czech Republic was opposed to lifting the sanctions against Belarus, amid the improvement in the human rights record, arguing that these were only minor and temporary. Another example is Czech policy towards Cuba, when Prague argued in the Council that sanctions should be lifted only conditionally and the Union should provide support to Cuban dissidents (Waisová and Piknerová, 2012: 173).

The notion of 'solidarity' frequently enters the foreign policy discourse of the three countries, not only with regards to foreign and security policies. For example, in the case of Czech foreign policy, political and financial expressions of solidarity have recently increased (Weiss, 2011), while the Slovak President advocated Union's solidarity as a 'key value of European integration' (Gašparovič, 2011: 12). Slovakia has expressed its willingness to share the experiences in its democratic transformation process with Moldova. Slovak diplomats insisted there were many similarities between the two countries, and hence their country's assistance had potentially more added value than in the case of other countries (Interviews, 2011). In a similar vein, the Czech diplomats claim their country has been focusing their assistance on Georgia. Poland has become recently engaged in humanitarian assistance and training to officials in Libya and Egypt, aiming to foster the democratic change. The calls for solidarity are also aimed at other Member States, for example when it comes to EU's relations with Russia and the United States. The new Member States exceptionally used to act as a bloc and called for support in their talk with the United States over lifting the visa requirement for their citizens. Poland has argued that there was ample field to express solidarity in the field of energy security, where any country experiences problems with energy deliveries should be helped by the others (Bilcik, 2010: 5).

As for other areas of special interest, while Poland clearly became less interested in the policy towards Western Balkans as one of its priority areas, both the Czech Republic and Slovakia remain vitally involved in the region. The Slovaks have been keen advocates of the EU membership for Croatia and opening the negotiations with Serbia. Between 1999 and 2000, the Slovak government worked with anti-Milošević opposition. In 2011, Slovak MFA supported the launch of National Conventions on the EU in Croatia and Montenegro (Bátora and Pulišová, 2013). Still, Slovakia had been one of the EU countries that did not recognise Kosovo's independence, unlike most of the Member States, but continued to work with the UN mission (UNMIK) (Bátora and Pulišová, 2013). It could be understood as lack of Europeanisation, if one assumes that there is one EU position which can serve as a template (or as an independent variable in the analysis). Another example is the Czech Republic, which has been taking a rather radical position on a couple of foreign policy issues. It took a pro-Israeli position in the Council, in opposition to most other Member States (together with the Netherlands). Arguably, this had a detrimental effect on its ability to represent the EU during the conflict in Gaza, taking place during the Czech presidency in 2009 (Beneš and Karlas, 2010: 76). The explanations for this vary, from a traditional pro-Israeli orientation of dissident elites in Prague to the willingness to delimit the Czech policy from what it was like during the communist Czechoslovakia (pro-Palestine) (Interviews in Brussels, 2011). From another perspective, Kořan (2013: 93) has argued that Europeanisation of Czech foreign policy can be well seen in the way in which the EU accession had a significant impact on the Czech policy towards Germany and led to a general improvement of the relations and overcoming historical resentments.

Hungary and Austria

As mentioned in the introduction to this chapter, Austria is an odd case in the group: it did not belong to the Soviet bloc, it is also the only one pursuing its neutrality status, but it shares to a large extent its history with Hungary. Austria's self-image is one of a state in a 'balancing mediatory position', a diplomatic host, active in conflict resolution processes, or in other words, it plays 'the role of an imaginary political first-aid man' (Vajda quoted in Liebhart, 2003: 27). It has also been pursuing a very multilateral approach in its foreign policy, somewhat similar to what the EU had tried to promote for example through its European Security Strategy. Since its accession in 1995, there were hardly any instances when Austria would block a compromise on CFSP issues (Alecu De Flers, 2012: 81). An exception was when Austria presented a radical position in the Council in 2005, with regards to opening accession negotiations with Turkey, calling for inclusion of the so-called 'absorption capacity' clause and insisting that Tukey was offered arrangements alternative to the EU membership (Alecu De Flers, 2012: 82). It was speculated that the final agreement on the Austrian side was secured through a 'package deal' and an almost simultaneous opening of accession negotiations with Croatia.

Austria certainly stands out with regards to the security policy, as since 1955 it has adopted a neutral status. This did not prevent it from getting involved in the CFSP and claim its full support at the time when it joined the EU in 1995 (Phinnemore, 2000: 205)[5] and to sign Partnership for Peace (PfP) with NATO the same year. In effect, Austrian status at the moment is no longer that of a neutral state but rather 'an alliance-free' one (Hauser, 2006: 211) and an active supporter of a common security policy of the EU. For example, Austria has been participating in two battlegroups: one with Germany, the Czech Republic and Ireland (with Croatia and Macedonia) and another one with Netherlands, Germany, Finland and Lithuania. In this sense, Europeanisation meant a redefinition of some significant national myths, for example the consensus among the political elites that the status of neutrality was incompatible with the membership of a supranational organisation (Liebhart, 2003: 29). Finally, after 2000, neutrality was questioned officially by the government coalition (Liebhart, 2003: 41), and as convincingly shown by Benke (2003), discourse analysis concerning Austrian identity has been undergoing a profound change. The new security doctrine from 2011, where neutrality is retained, emphasises that Austria will show solidarity with the EU Member States in crisis management operations and 'military contributions to the security policy of the EU' (Alecu De Flers, 2012: 99).

Considering Austria's attempts to influence the CFSP, it has always been a keen promoter of human rights, establishing the ban on landmines and promotion of the rights of children (Phinnemore, 2000: 217). Starting from a position in the minority of the Member States that supported an international convention for a total ban on anti-personnel mines, it successfully advocated the issue in the EU and saw the joint action adopted, based on an Austrian draft in 1997 (Alecu De Flers, 2012: 92). Austria has also been very active in promoting the European perspective for the Western Balkan states, which was one of the key priorities for its presidency in 2006. It has brought the Balkans back on the agenda, in particular through raising the issue of security co-operation. Despite the relatively low public support for further enlargement (29 per cent), with the support of Hungary and Slovenia, it secured a so-called 'Salzburg Declaration' on 11 March 2006, mentioning the future membership of Serbia, Montenegro, Macedonia, Albania and Bosnia and Herzegovina (Pollak and Puntscher Riekmann, 2007: 11). The document was later endorsed by the European Council. It is also worth noting that an Austrian politician, Benita Ferrero-Waldner, held a post of Commissioner responsible for External Relations and European Neighbourhood Policy in the European Commission from 2004–9.

A strong element of Hungarian foreign policy is what is defined as 'responsibility for minorities living abroad', dominating policies towards countries such as Slovakia, Ukraine and Romania (Racz, 2011). This reflects on Hungarian involvement in CFSP, for example it has been pushing for the EU agenda issues related to the collective minority rights, for example the Serbian minority in Kosovo. Both Hungary and Austria are engaged in the EU's policy towards Western Balkans, as the key area of their interest within the CFSP. During the Hungarian presidency in the first half of 2011, the EU finalised the accession negotiations with Croatia and held a Western Balkan Forum in Luxembourg, in spite of the initial reluctance on the part of the European External Action Service (Interviews, 2012).

As was the case in other countries in the region, the dominating trend in the Hungarian political discourse was its support of the NATO membership, which would secure Hungarian independence and potentially provide protection from Russia (Kovács and Wodak, 2003: 18). This was coupled with Atlanticism as 'a determining factor' in Hungarian foreign policy (Varga, 2009: 50). Still, even here, there are differences what 'Atlanticism' meant for Hungary and other states in the region. For example, while modernising the air-forces in 2001, the Hungarians decided to opt for the Swedish SAAB Grippen planes instead of the American F-16s (Varga, 2009), which were chosen by Poland in 2003. Even though Hungary signed the 'Letter of Eight' in 2003, mentioned earlier in the chapter, the Prime Minister was openly criticised by the opposition (Varga, 2009).

Energy security plays a central role in Hungary's foreign policy, including its involvement in the EU. Its dependence on the Russian gas reaches 80–85 per cent (Kałan, 2012) and the import takes place through one country, Ukraine, and through one pipeline (Varga, 2009: 52). Therefore, Hungary has concentrated its 'uploading' efforts on promoting the North-South gas route, which would ensure diversification of its own gas supplies and also those to Croatia. Hungary has also been involved in promoting harmonisation and creating a coherent EU strategy for the Danube region in policies such as energy, development, environment and transport (Bátora, 2012). Hungary's policy towards Russia has been more restrained than that of its Visegrad partners. An example of this is the fact that Hungary did not sign an open letter of the NATO members, including other Visegrad states, addressed to the NATO secretary general and supporting Ukrainian and Georgian Membership Action Plan (MAP) (Varga, 2009: 53). In line with this, the Eastern Neighbourhood in general is of a lesser importance to Hungary than other priorities listed here, with the exception of Ukraine, Moldova and Azerbaijan. It was even argued elsewhere that, unlike in the case of Poland, there are practically 'no shared meanings of history, constitutional practices and institutions between Hungary and this region' (Racz, 2011: 146).

Finally, since the rise to power of the Prime Minister Viktor Orban, the relationship with Russia became even closer and a thorn of disagreement in Hungary's relations with other countries described here. Even though, following the German position, Hungary supported EU sanctions against Russia, in place since 2014, Viktor Orban continued his visits to Moscow and agreed on an increase in gas supplies to Hungary as well as on Russia's involvement in the development of the Hungarian power plant.

Slovenia, Romania and Bulgaria

Slovenia, Bulgaria and Romania are all most interested in developing the EU's policy towards Western Balkans, and this remains their top priority in CFSP. Having said that, their individual approaches differ from one another, which will be shown in this section. Slovenia has been particularly active with its efforts to retain Western Balkans on the EU agenda during its presidency in 2008, when the EU experienced a sort of 'Balkan fatigue' (Kajnč, 2011: 204–205). While being a staunch supporter of further enlargement to the Balkans, Slovenia also used the EU to gain leverage over Croatia in its bilateral dispute with the neighbour when it threatened to block further accession talks because of the border dispute (Kajnč, 2011: 205). Bulgaria, on its part, has been very supportive of Serbia's perspective to join the EU and did not directly condition its support on Belgrade's treatment of ethnic minorities. Such a condition was made in March 2012 by Romania, who threatened to veto granting Serbia candidate status if it did not grant rights to Romanian speakers (Bechev, 2013).

Like in the case of many other small Member States, Slovenia's contribution to CFSP has been limited due to scarcity of the resources (Bátora, 2012), for example its professional army counts around 7,500 active soldiers. Still, it has tried to present itself as a committed European and 'a normative power contributor' that can fulfil the role of a 'bridge between the EU and the Western Balkans' (Zupančič, 2011). Slovenia was the first country among the newcomers from 2004 enlargement to host the presidency in the Council of the EU in the first half of 2008, and it was widely proclaimed as successful. The top priority was to assist the Western Balkans on their road to the EU membership and specifically to conclude the Stabilization and Association Agreements (SAA) and to start a dialogue on visa liberalisation (Kajnč, 2009). Despite that, Slovenia's policy towards Western Balkans has not always been seen as a representation of the EU's position, and it has been called for more coordination with its EU partners. Zupančič (2011: 72) gives an example of the conference on Western Balkans in Brno in March 2010, as a case in point, when EU officials cancelled their participation. Having this in mind, Slovenia's foreign policy towards Eastern Europe and the rest of the world has been almost entirely conducted through the European Union (Żornaczuk, 2012). An exception took place in February 2012 when Slovenia initially protested against including one of the Belarusian businessman on the 'visa-ban' blacklist. This was after a Slovenian company was awarded an investment contract in Minsk, with participation of the businessman in question. Slovenian diplomats had expressed concerns that the Eastern Partnership initiative should not be conducted with a disadvantage to Union's policy towards its Southern neighbourhood and the Western Balkans (Żornaczuk, 2012).

For both Bulgaria and Romania, transatlantic relationship has been a crucial element of foreign and security policies, but their approach has not been the same. Romania has run into trouble with the EU in 2002, during the negotiation processes, when it became the first country to sign a bilateral agreement with the US, granting the Americans immunity from the International Criminal Court in the Hague (Micu, 2011: 54). It was argued that such decision resulted from the belief of Romanian elites that national security interests came before any norms or practices developed in the course of EU's political co-operation (Micu, 2011: 56). Both supported the US-led intervention in Afghanistan and later in Iraq where they took part in the 'coalition of the willing' under Polish command (Linden, 2009: 273). This pro-American stance has been less challenged in Romania then it was in Bulgaria, which has a traditionally more pro-Russian attitude (Katsikas, 2012; Linden, 2009: 275). In 2006, both signed agreements with the Bush administration on establishing US military bases on their territories (Bechev, 2013). Bulgarian government has for a long time pursued a 'NATO-first' policy in the region, with its Embassy in Tbilisi serving as a NATO contact point in 2005–9 (Bechev, 2013).

Romania and Bulgaria have been engaged in promoting initiatives in a Black Sea area (and later also the EU's initiative called the Black Sea Synergy, BSS), a policy that, at least at the beginning, was seen as competitor to the Swedish/Polish idea of Eastern Dimension. Romania has been particularly active in attempts to raise its profile, taking the lead on the Black Sea Border Initiative on proliferation in 2004 and hosting a Black Sea Forum in 2006 and earning a praise from the United States (Linden, 2009: 277). Since Russia remains a key player in the Black Sea region, Romanian government made attempts to mend the relations with Russia, which has only led to the opposite effect of worsening the strained relationship (Anglescu, 2011). In 2014, Romania was among those states that were pushing for the sanctions against Russia. With Moscow being cautious about any EU's policies in the region, Bulgarian position has been less active than the Romanian one (Linden, 2009: 278). Bulgaria has on its part made an attempt to become more active in Georgia and secured the position of Head of EU Delegation in September 2010 (Bechev, 2013). Bulgarian Foreign Minister Mladenov acted as an intermediary between the EU and the Belarussian President in August 2011 in relation with release of political detainees (Bechev, 2013), which showed it is also an active participant of CFSP in areas other than Western Balkans.

There also areas of special interests, which fall outside of the prevalent position among the other Member States. Even though for both countries Kosovo poses potential problems, only Romania has been among five EU members that did not recognise the independence of Kosovo. The decision is often linked to the fears of establishing a precedent that potentially could lead to the break-up of Moldova, if the rule was applied to the eastern region of Transdniestria with whom Romania has had a complex relationship with a central issue of potential reunification. The dual citizenship law adopted by Romania allowed for free movement between the two countries but also meant that Moldovans could travel visa-free to the Schengen area, an issue that sparked protests from other Member States (Anglescu, 2011: 132). The recognition of Kosovo has also been worrying the Romanian government because of the Hungarian minority, 1.9 million inhabitants mostly in Transylvania. Their representatives announced in 2008 that they would hold a referendum on autonomy and forward the results to the Council of Europe and the European Parliament (Linden, 2009: 288). Those two issues allow for understanding why the Romanian government decided to take a different position on Kosovo than most of its EU partners. Kosovo's independence was also reason for some concern in Bulgaria, as it could provide encouragement to the Albanians living in western Macedonia (Linden, 2009: 288). Still, the government decided to recognise Kosovo, despite the fact that the move was very unpopular (74 per cent of the population opposed) (Linden, 2009: 289).

Bulgaria has threatened to use its veto on Montenegro's Association Agreement due to a dispute in Brussels on how to spell 'EURO' in Cyrillic and supported Greece in its dispute with Skopje over the name of the country (Bechev, 2013). Being in a potentially vulnerable position with regards to gas supplies (85 per cent dependence on the Russian gas), it has also pursued bilateral relations with Azerbaijan and Central Asia, outside of the EU framework (Bechev, 2013). While Romania is generally supportive of Turkish accession in the EU and so is officially the government on Sofia, the issue is much more sensitive in Bulgaria, where the public support for the Turkish membership is very low (Linden, 2009: 285). All in all, despite many commonalities and shared history, it would be a mistake to assume that Romanian and Bulgarian foreign policies are largely similar. Both countries differ with their approach towards Russia, towards the Turkish membership in the EU, in the extent of their support for the United States' global policy and in their activism regarding Black Sea Synergy.

Conclusions: what type of change in the region?

One of the greatest changes to most East European countries was the gained stability after the period of Cold War and the subsequent years in the 'grey zone of insecurity'. In this respect, the last two decades was called an era of 'blessed boredom' (Michta, 2011), which allowed for gradual learning and understanding of the ways in which policies are made in Brussels. Most political and diplomatic attention was paid to the direct neighbours, both in the East and in the Western Balkans. The relatively quiet times finished abruptly with the Russian intervention in Crimea and in the Eastern Ukraine. This security crisis is now a main concern of all countries described in this chapter, even though, their assessment of the situation and the most effective response differ.

What becomes apparent from this analysis is that all countries generally conduct their foreign policy with or through the EU, rather than on a bilateral basis (with some exceptions mentioned in this chapter). This is then the first sign of Europeanisation, which manifests itself in changing the co-operation patterns and the intensity of consultation with other EU Member States. Scholars studying foreign policy in the region note that national foreign policy goals are now established in a changed context, when the positions of partners from the EU matter. Most of the states have expressed aspirations to lead selected policies of the EU, but a few only lived up to these self-set expectations. Most states analysed in the chapter do not have the resources needed to become the 'drivers' behind foreign and security policy. Still, there are two regions in particular towards which they claim expertise and know-how that they wish were appreciated by their EU partners: Eastern Europe and the Western Balkans. The arguments are similar in the case of both: shared history, cultural and linguistic similarities, deep understanding of political driving forces in their neighbouring states.

If we look for trends in the way foreign policies were adapted to the CFSP, there is a clear difference between the smallest states in the region and larger countries, like Poland. For the small countries the initial adaptation meant 'mimicking' of the EU foreign policies, such as the case in Slovakia or Slovenia (Bátora and Pulišová, 2013). In the case of Austria, membership in the EU has arguably led to a debate and a subsequent redefinition of the county's neutral status. At the same time, EU membership enlarged the scope of interests in foreign policies of the smaller Member States, where the rhythm of work was often determined by the schedules and agendas in Brussels. The diplomats from those states also believed that their countries needed to make concessions in Brussels and align to positions that did not always reflect their initial foreign policy. This, in turn, is also an element of Europeanisation and learning that CFSP is a result of concessions.

As for the trends in the content of foreign policies, there has not been any apparent convergence towards one common approach in any of the considered areas. This is hardly surprising, having in mind the relatively less advanced level of European integration in the foreign and security field. In spite of the high ambitions of regional groupings such as the V4, the region has not established itself as an effective and coherent force inside of the EU, capable of championing its original projects. The 'shadow' of Russia is very present in the region, and all countries are interested in developing a clearer policy of the Union towards its Eastern neighbour. The divisions manifested themselves most strikingly when the EU discussed sanctions towards Russia in 2014, when Poland and Romania were amongst those arguing in favour, while Hungary and Slovakia argued against.

Still, even in this matter, there are differences as to the details, which were showed throughout this chapter. Undoubtedly though, it was due to the 2004 enlargement that countries like Belarus, Ukraine or Moldova appeared firmly on the EU's political radar. The majority of the countries has also pushed for an 'open door' policy regarding future enlargements towards the neighbours, whether those to the East or to the South (but even here there are exceptions, such as the complex stance of Bulgaria towards the Turkish accession). It is worth mentioning that, historically and politically, Poland has been probably more closely related to its neighbouring Lithuania than to any other country discussed in this chapter. This is despite the ongoing disagreements related to the rights of Polish minority.

While the relationship with the United States is considered as 'special' and 'strategic' throughout the region, it is done so in most European capitals. Hence, this *per se* is nothing distinctive about Eastern Europe, or as Donald Rumsfeld would have it, the 'New Europe' and the transatlantic relationship. What is apparent in the case of post-communist states is the reluctance to face the situation when a choice is to be made between the EU and the United States. Most of them have pursued a 'NATO-first' policy when security was concerned. Still, after the 2004 enlargement, some had argued that Central and Eastern Europe begun to 'fall out of love with the United States' (Wiśniewski, 2011) and show more commitment to working with the partners from the EU, even in security-related matters. A good example is Poland, which went a long way from being considered a potential 'laggard' in ESDP when it was joining the EU to the staunch advocate of creating a joint headquarters for CSDP in Brussels, during its presidency in 2011.

In a similar vein, most of the states have been active in the field of energy security, which often was listed among their priorities for the presidency period. In parallel, they also acted outside of the EU framework. A good example is Bulgaria or Hungary, working towards a closer cooperation with Russia. Still, there is no common EU policy in the field, and as Linden (2009: 282) put it, the actions of the Member States studied in this chapter do not 'put them out of step with the behaviour – as opposed to the declared policy – of the EU's dominant actors'.

Almost equally homogeneous is the cautious, or even suspicious, attitude towards Russia, albeit here the differences in the group have recently become more pronounced in the wake of the Ukrainian crisis. For many East European states, the 'return to Europe' after 1989 meant, not only re-aligning with the Western structures, but also building up independent, critical and often difficult relationship with Russia. For countries like Poland and the Czech Republic, the post-1989 period was marked by strong delimitation from the post-Soviet Russia (Kořan, 2013). This was not exactly the case for Bulgaria, as observed by Katsikas (2012: 88), where Russia had a positive image in the public opinion due to the economic benefits and status it held in the times of the Soviet Union. At the time of the accession, as noticed by Edwards, there was 'an element of despair at the lack of any coherent EU position towards Russia' (Edwards, 2006: 146). Nowadays, it is difficult to perceive the region as a bloc. The differences may be subscribed to the dependence on Russian oil and gas, such as in the case of Slovakia, Romania or Bulgaria. But even here, we see different tendencies, as in the case of Romania's rather critical approach and Bulgaria seeking more co-operation with Russia. As Bechev observed, in relations with Russia, one can observe a 'Europeanization deficit' (Bechev, 2013), as they are mainly conducted bilaterally and not through the EU.

The conclusions of the chapter echo those reached by the authors in the chapter on Northern Member States: it should not be assumed that there are shared commonalities throughout the region. Different theoretical schools may be useful when trying to explain this change: some can see it as a result of different material and security interests, while others would rather point to the varying historical traditions and societal norms. Still, there are considerable overlaps when it comes to areas of interests and issues that the countries mentioned would like to keep high on the EU agenda. Europeanisation effects, understood as change due to participation in the CFSP (and not simply as policy convergence), are clearly observable in all analysed states. The EU became a solid part of reference and focus in foreign policy-making.

Notes

1 In fact, in some countries, the concept of Eastern Europe is based on the assumption that it is 'different' from 'us' Central Europeans (e.g. Racz, 2011: 147).
2 The author would like to thank Vladimir Bilcik for making this point.
3 In the words of one diplomat following the disruption in gas deliveries in 2009, which reflect well the feelings in the region: 'we don't care whose fault it was, we wanted the gas we paid for!' (Interviews, 2011).
4 The support was expressed inter alia in the famous 'Letter of Eight', including Poland, Czech Republic and Hungary, published in various newspapers on 30 January 2003 (for the text see BBC online: http://news.bbc.co.uk/1/hi/world/europe/2708877.stm), later followed by the 'Vilnius Letter' (6 February 2003), signed by Albania, Bulgaria, Croatia, Czech Republic, Estonia, Latvia, Lithuania, Macedonia, Romania and Slovakia) in support of US military intervention in Iraq.
5 At that time, Austria redefined its neutrality and reduced it to three major points: non-participating in any war, non-participating in military alliance and no foreign military basis on Austrian territories (Phinnemore, 2000: 207).

Bibliography

Alecu De Flers, N. (2012) *EU Foreign Policy and the Europeanization of Neutral States: Comparing Irish and Austrian Foreign Policy*, London: Routledge.

Anglescu, I. (2011) 'New Eastern Perspectives? A Critical Analysis of Romania's Relations with Moldova, Ukraine and Black Sea Region', *Perspectives*, Vol. 19, No. 2, 123–142.

Armitage, D., Zaborowski, M., Mitchell, W. and Kron, R. (2011) *Translating Opportunity into Impact: Central Europe in the European Union, 2010–2020*, Washington, DC: Center for European Policy Analysis.

Bátora, J. (2012) 'Europeanization of Foreign Policy: Whither Central Europe?', in Z. Šabič and P. Drulák (eds.) *Central Europe in Regional and International Relations*, Basingstoke: Palgrave, 219–238.

Bátora, J. and V. Pulišová (2013) 'Slovakia: Learning to Add Value to EU Foreign Policy', in M. Baun and D. Marek (eds.) *The New Member States and the European Union: Foreign Policy and Europeanization*, London: Routledge, 68–83.

Baun, M. and Marek, D. (2010) 'Czech Foreign Policy and EU Integration: European and Domestic Sources', *Perspectives on European Politics and Society*, Vol. 11, No. 1, 2–21.

BBC HARDTALK (2012) 'Radoslaw Sikorski – Foreign Minister of Poland', 14 November 2012. Available at: http://www.bbc.co.uk/programmes/b01nvpcz. Accessed: 10 November 2016.

Bechev, D. (2013) 'Bulgaria: The Travails of Europeanization', in M. Baun and D. Marek (eds.) *The New Member States and the European Union: Foreign Policy and Europeanization*, London: Routledge, 190–205.

Beneš, V. and Karlas, J. (2010) 'The Czech Presidency', *Journal of Common Market Studies*, Vol. 48 (Annual Review), 69–80.

Benke, G. (2003) 'From Prices and Prizes to Outmoded Things: Neutrality and Identity in the Speeches of Austrian Presidents on the National Holiday (26.10) in the Second Republic', in A. Kovács and R. Wodak (eds.) *NATO, Neutrality and National Identity: The Case of Austria and Hungary*, Vienna: Böhlau Verlag, 103–146.

Bilcik, V. (2010) 'Foreign Policy in Post-Communist EU', *International Issues and Slovak Foreign Policy Affairs*, Vol. 19, No. 4, 3–17.

Dangerfield, M. (2012) 'Visegrad Group Co-Operation and Russia', *Journal of Common Market Studies*, Vol. 50, No. 6, 958–974.

Dangerfield, M. (2009) The Visegrad Group and the European Union's Eastern Dimension, *Paper presented at the EUSA Biennial Conference*, Los Angeles, 2009.

Dimitrova-Grajzl, V. (2011) 'Trust, Path Dependence and Historical Legacy: The Second Decade after Transition', in N. Hayoz, L. Jesień and D. Koleva (eds), *20 Years after the Collapse of Communism: Expectations, Achievements and Disillusions of 1989*, Berlin: Peter Lang, 143–166.

ECFR (2012) *European Foreign Policy Scorecard 2012*, London: ECFR.

Edwards, G. (2006) 'The New Member States and the Making of EU Foreign Policy', *European Foreign Affairs Review*, Vol. 11, No. 2, 143–162.

Fitzmaurice, John (1998) *Politics and Government in the Visegrad Countries: Poland, Hungary, the Czech Republic and Slovakia*, London: Macmillan.

Gašparovič, I. (2011) 'Slovak Foreign Policy in 2010 as Seen by the President of the Slovak Republic', *Yearbook of Slovakia's Foreign Policy*, Vol. 1, 9–18.

Hauser, G. (2006) 'ESDP and Austria: Security Policy between Engagement and Neutrality', in G. Bischof, B. Bischof, A. Pelinka and M. Gehler (eds.) *Austrian Foreign Policy in Historical Context*, London: Transaction Publishers, 207–245.

Juhász, B. (2003) 'Neutrality in the 1956 Hungarian Revolution', in A. Kovács and R. Wodak (eds.) *NATO, Neutrality and National Identity: The Case of Austria and Hungary*, Vienna: Böhlau Verlag, 51–74.

Kajnč, S. (2011) 'Slovenia: Searching for a Foreign Policy Identity via the EU', in R. Wong and C. Hill (eds.) *National and European Foreign Policies: Toward Europeanization*, London: Routledge, 189–209.

Kajnč, S. (2009) 'The Slovenian Presidency: Meeting Symbolic and Substantive Challenges', *Journal of Common Market Studies*, Vol. 47 (Annual Review), 89–98.

Kałan, D. (2012) 'Polityka środkowoeuropejska Węgier', *Biuletyn Polskiego Instytutu Spraw Międzynarodowych*, No. 57(922), 12 June 2012, 2690–2691.

Katsikas, Stefanos (2012) *Negotiating Diplomacy in the New Europe: Foreign Policy in Post-Communist Bulgaria*, London: Tauris.

Kavalski, E. and Zolkos, M. (2007) 'The Hoax of Was: The Foreign Policy Discourses of Poland and Bulgaria on Iraq, 2003–2005', *Journal of Contemporary European Studies*, Vol. 15, No. 3, 377–393.

Kořan, Michal (2013) 'Coloring It Europe? The Europeanization of Czech Foreign Policy', in M. Baun and D. Marek (eds.) *The New Member States and the European Union: Foreign Policy and Europeanization*, London: Routledge, 53–67.

Kovács, A. and Wodak, R. (2003) 'Preface', in A. Kovács and R. Wodak (eds.) *NATO, Neutrality and National Identity: The Case of Austria and Hungary*, Vienna: Böhlau Verlag, 7–22.

Král, D. (2011) 'Between East and South: Balancing Central Europe's New Approach to the Neighbourhood', *CEPA Issue Brief No. 121*, Washington, DC: Center for European Policy Analysis.

Liebhart, K. (2003) 'Austrian Neutrality: Historical Development and Semantic Change', in A. Kovács and R. Wodak (eds.) *NATO, Neutrality and National Identity: The Case of Austria and Hungary*, Vienna: Böhlau Verlag, 23–50.

Linden, R. (2009) 'The Burden of Belonging: Romanian and Bulgarian Foreign Policy in New Era', *Journal of Balkan and Near Eastern Studies*, Vol. 11, No. 3, 269–291.

Longhurst, K. and Zaborowski, M. (2007) *The New Atlanticist: Poland's Foreign and Security Policy Priorities*, London: The Royal Institute of International Affairs.

Manners, I. and Whitman, R. (2000) *The Foreign Policies of the European Union Member States*, Manchester: Manchester University Press.

Maresceau, M. (ed.) (1997) *Enlarging the European Union: Relations between the EU and Central and Eastern Europe*, London: Longman.

Michta, A. (2011) 'Central Europe: Will Boundaries Become Fault Lines?', in A.W. Mitchell, J.J. Grygiel and R. Kron (eds.) *Building the New Normal: US-Central European Relations 2010–2020*, Washington, DC: Centre for European Policy Analysis, 16–22.

Micu, M. (2011) 'The Europeanization of Romanian Foreign Policy: Mitigating European and National "Misfits" in the International Criminal Court and Kosovo Cases', *Romanian Journal of European Affairs*, Vol. 11, No. 4, 50–65.

Mitchell, A.W., Grygiel, J.J. and Kron, R. (eds.) (2010) *Building the New Normal: U.S.-Central European Relations 2010–2020*, Washington, DC: Center for European Policy Analysis.

Phinnemore, D. (2000) 'Austria', in I. Manners and R. Whitman (eds.) *The Foreign Policies of European Union Member States*, Manchester: Manchester University Press, 204–223.

Pollak, J. and Puntscher Riekmann, S. (2007) 'The Austrian Presidency: Pragmatic Management', *Journal of Common Market Studies*, Vol. 45 (Annual Review), 7–16.

Pomorska, K. (2011) 'Poland: Learning the Brussels Game', in R. Wong and C. Hill (eds.) *National and European Foreign Policies: Toward Europeanization*, London: Routledge, 167–188.

Pomorska, K. and Vanhoonacker, S. (2012) 'Poland in the Driving Seat: A Mature Presidency in Turbulent Times', *Journal of Common Market Studies*, Vol. 50, Special Issue No. 2, 76–84.

Racz, A. (2011) 'A Limited Priority: Hungary and the Eastern Neighbourhood', *Perspectives*, Vol. 19, No. 2, 143–164.

Rotfeld, D.A. (2006) *Polska w niepewnym świecie*, Warsaw: Polish Institute of International Affairs.

Tulmets, E. (2008) 'Preparing the EU Presidency: The Czech Contribution to the Project of "Eastern Partmership"', *The Polish Quarterly of International Affairs*, Vol. 4, 79–98.

Varga, G. (2009) 'Central European Security Identity and Transatlanticism: A Hungarian Perspective', *International Issues and Slovak Policy Affairs*, Vol. 18, No. 4, 44–56.

Wagrowska, M. (2009) 'Visegrad Security Policy: How to Consolidate Its Own Identity', *International Issues and Slovak Foreign Policy Affairs*, Vol. 18, No. 4, 31–42.

Waisová, S. and Piknerová, L. (2012) 'Twenty Years After: Dissident Tradition in Czech Foreign Policy Matters', *East European Politics and Societies*, Vol. 26, No. 1, 162–188.

Weiss, T. (2011) 'Projecting the Re-Discovered: Czech Policy towards Eastern Europe', *Perspectives: Central European Review of International Affairs*, Vol. 19, No. 2, 27–44.

Wiśniewski, J. (2011) 'Toward a New Central European Geopolitical Environment', in A.W. Mitchell, J.J. Grygiel and R. Kron (eds.) *Building the New Normal: US-Central European Relations 2010–2020*, Washington, DC: Centre for European Policy Analysis, 5–9.

Zaborowski, M. (2004) 'From America's Protégé to Constructive European: Polish Security Policy in Twenty-First Century', *Occasional Paper No. 56*, Paris: Institute for Security Studies.

Zaborowski, M. and Dunn, D. (eds.) (2003) *Poland: A New Power in Transatlantic Security*, London: Frank Cass.

Żornaczuk, T. (2012) 'Sąsiedztwo wschodnie UE w polityce zagranicznej Słowenii', *Biuletyn Polskiego Instytutu Spraw Międzynarodowych*, No. 27(892), 16 March 2012, 2630–2631.

Zupančič, R. (2011) 'Normative Power as a Means of a Small State in International Relations: The Role of Slovenia within the "EU Concert" of Normative Power', *Lithuanian Foreign Policy Review*, Vol. 25, 56–76.

4 France and Germany

The European Union's 'central' Member States

Luis Simón

Introduction

In a book that utilizes geography to make sense of the foreign policies of the EU Member States, it is legitimate to wonder to what extent France and Germany should really be cobbled together. Admittedly, these two countries present important similarities: they are both 'continental' powers, and regional/European dynamics are central to their geostrategic calculations. However, the geopolitical foundations underpinning their foreign and security policies are actually notably different. France's are very much informed by the country's 'hybrid' geostrategic predicament: partly continental and partly maritime, partly European and partly 'extra-regional'. Germany, for its part, is perhaps one of the purest examples of a continental power, for it is in Europe where most of its foreign and security policy energies concentrate.

No less controversial is the decision to refer to these two countries as 'Central' Europe, a label that, apparently, distinguishes them from 'western', 'eastern', 'northern' and 'southern' Europe. From a geographical viewpoint, Central Europe could be loosely defined as the space delimited by the Rhine River in the west, the Vistula in the east, the Alps and Carpathian Mountains in the south and the Baltic Sea in the north. Geopolitically speaking, its insertion within the broader 'North European' plain makes Central Europe an inherently porous space. These considerations notwithstanding, it would be hard to dispute Germany's place in Central Europe.

Applying the 'Central European' label to France is certainly more problematic. Geopolitically, France is really situated in 'Western' Europe, although it reaches into both 'Central' and 'Southern' Europe, as reflected in a geostrategy that gravitates around three main geographical axes: the 'Atlantic', the 'Mediterranean' and 'Europe'. While, there is a 'Central European' dimension to French power and geostrategy, reducing France to 'Central Europe' is too far a stretch – historically, politically, culturally and geographically.

Politically speaking, France and Germany are both 'central' to 'Europe', as best illustrated by their historical role as the 'engine' of the European integration process. Moreover, they have both placed European integration at the very centre of their national geostrategies. During the Cold War, both countries saw 'Europe' as an alternative to the 'Western' and 'Eastern' blocs. In this important sense, their geostrategies were somewhat inspired by the notion of 'centrality'. Their interest in developing Europe as an autonomous ('central'?) political reality had largely to do with the fact that both France and, to a greater extent, (West) Germany occupied a rather peripheral position in the geostrategic hierarchy of the Western system, largely engineered and managed by the Americans and, to a lesser extent, the British. Their conception of Europe was geopolitical as much as it was ideological. In contrast to America's excessive economic liberalism and the Soviet Union's communist dictatorship, France and Germany identified Europe with the promise of reconciling individual freedom and social justice. Therefore, when applying the lens of 'Central Europe' to France and Germany, this chapter does so based on these broader geopolitical and ideological considerations.

This chapter examines how geostrategic considerations have shaped the foreign and security policies of France and Germany. It starts by discussing the geostrategic underpinnings of French and German power and examines their impact upon those countries' conceptions of European integration and their evolving attitudes towards European cooperation in foreign, security and defence policy. Special emphasis is placed on the relationship between a dynamic international geopolitical environment and patterns of change, adaptation and policy action in France and Germany. Reflecting upon these changes, the conclusions question whether it is still possible to refer today to France and Germany jointly as 'Central Europe'.

France as a hybrid and 'extra-regional' power

From a geostrategic viewpoint, France constitutes one of the best examples of a 'hybrid' power (Braudel, 1990; Pritchard, 2012). While the 'continental' aspect of France's persona translates into a strong emphasis on Europe, its 'maritime' orientation manifests itself in a strong interest in extra-European, and even global, affairs (Wusten and Dijink, 2002). However, it is perhaps useful to break down France's maritime identity into its 'blue water' (Atlantic) and 'brown water' (Mediterranean) components and refer to the Atlantic, the Mediterranean and Europe as the 'three axes' of French geostrategy (Dufourcq, 2002).

The fact that the Mediterranean, 'brown water' element played such a prominent role in French geostrategy during the 'second colonial empire', from 1815 to 1920, allows us to conceptualize France more as an 'extra-regional' power than a truly 'global' one – in the British or American sense. Admittedly, France did have its own 'blue water' experience. However, the Seven Years' War (1756–63) and the Napoleonic Wars (1803–15) represented important historical setbacks to France's 'global' position and reach (Kennedy, 1987). From the late nineteenth century onwards, the unification and subsequent rise of Germany, served to further underscore the geographical shrinking of French power and presided over a substantial reorientation of French economic and strategic resources from the Atlantic onto the European continent and its immediate neighbourhood (Néré, 2002). This process reached a high point in the Second World War, being perhaps immortalized by France's withdrawal from Indochina following a long and resource-draining engagement between 1945 and 1954.

The aspiration to play a global role continues to feature prominently in French foreign and security policy narrative to this day. And indeed, the country's permanent seat in the UNSC; its far-reaching diplomatic and intelligence networks; and its possession of blue-water naval capabilities, overseas sovereign territories and military installations help substantiate such aspiration. Even today, its sovereign possessions in the Pacific may well prove to be an important European gateway into what promises to be an increasingly Asian-centred century (Rogers and Simón, 2009). However, as an 'extra-regional' power, France's geostrategic attention concentrates primarily on Europe, and its extra-European experience is largely confined to the so-called southern 'axis of strategic priority' (French Ministry of Defence, 2008: 41–42, 72, 136, 202, 302). This southern 'axis of strategic priority' irradiates from the Mediterranean Sea southwards and westwards towards the Maghreb-Sahel area, Africa's western seaboard and the Great Lakes region in Central Africa and eastwards towards the Levant and, via the Red Sea, the Persian Gulf and the Western Indian Ocean (see Figure 4.1).

Figure 4.1 Directions for French geostrategy

The importance attached to this southern 'axis of strategic priority' captures most elo-quently France's hybrid, 'brown water' and 'extra-regional' character. Particularly illustra-tive in this regard is France's geostrategic conception of the Mediterranean Sea as a stopgap on its route to the Levant and Africa. Admittedly, the Atlantic and, to a lesser extent, the Indian Ocean, have historically played an important role in linking France with parts of its African empire. However, their main geostrategic purpose was to cement the links between metropolitan France and an immense swath of land in the African continent and to a lesser extent to assist France's maritime and global mobility.

The foundations of French geostrategy after
the Second World War

The Second World War and its aftermath presided over the ascendancy of the US and Soviet Russia as Europe's pre-eminent strategic powers (Kennedy, 1987), marking Britain's rel-egation to the second rung of global power as well as the political division and external occupation of Germany. This led to a series of structural adaptations in French foreign and security policy, whereby France came to see European integration as the only viable path to economic prosperity and political autonomy from the Soviet and American superpowers. Moreover, a united Europe would underscore France's pivotal geostrategic position between 'maritime' Britain and 'continental' Germany.

Ever since the end of the Second World War, France's attitude towards European integration has been informed by its attempt to strike the right balance between its European, Atlantic and Mediterranean axes. France's attempt to adapt to a dynamic geopolitical environment has determined its specific oscillation between its 'continental' and 'maritime' personas. In particular, the evolution of the positions and power of the US and Germany (and not so much that of the USSR) have been critical in shaping France's geostrategic calculations.

The dynamic geopolitical environment of the Cold War largely accounted for patterns of change, adaptation and action in French foreign and security policy. Whenever Germany showed signs of greater independence or flirted with neutrality, France clung to its relationship with the US and proved to be the staunchest *Atlanticist* (Lellouche, 1983/4). In turn, whenever the shadow of a hegemonic US loomed large, France embraced its German partner. Through a permanent act of adaptation and balancing, France sought to mitigate its security dependence on the 'West' and reduce its vulnerability to the east. Its inferiority vis-à-vis both 'west' and 'east' only served to underscore France's special attachment with its 'brown water' persona, embodied by its southern geostrategic axis, conceived of as a reservoir of resources, influence and status (Simón, 2013).

Throughout the Cold War, a substantial US–NATO military presence in (West) Germany helped to balance against the Soviet threat to Central and Western Europe. Perhaps more importantly for France, such presence also served to ensure Bonn's strategic subordination to the West and paved the way for its political and economic integration in Western Europe. By effectively neutralizing the Soviet threat and the German 'challenge', the US and NATO created the structural conditions for French security and 'freed up' French strategic resources, which could be devoted to developing military strategic excellence or building up its influence in the southern axis. These circumstances allowed France to claim political leadership over the European Community (EC), which in turn was instrumental in strengthening the country's political standing and influence in the southern axis.

The Cold War, France and European foreign, security and defence cooperation

Throughout the Cold War, France sought to use the structures of the EC to secure preferential treatment to its former colonies (Hanrieder, 1989; Moravcsik, 2000). It also promoted a number of (intergovernmental) schemes for European foreign policy and defence cooperation, including most notably European Political Cooperation (EPC), the European Defence Community (EDC) and the Fouchet Plans I and II (Sutton, 2011).

From 1970 onwards, EPC consolidated as a useful mechanism for intergovernmental European foreign policy cooperation (Nuttall, 1992). However, in line with French designs, it was a rather modest and informal endeavour. Beyond EPC, France's reluctance to transcend intergovernmentalism and ongoing European reservations about French leadership are largely responsible for the failure of European defence cooperation during the Cold War (Furdson, 1980). Any attempt to transcend intergovernmentalism, either through a supranational European defence structure or some sort of Franco-German sharing arrangement over

France's nuclear deterrent, would have eliminated France's edge in Europe and paved the way for German leadership.

Despite its strong rhetoric about European defence and autonomy or its public criticism of NATO and the US, France was a *status quo* power during the Cold War. It was comfortable with a Soviet Union that was strong enough to keep US and German power at bay, but not so strong as to bend the West. It was also comfortable with a US that was strong enough so as to contain the spectrum of a potential Soviet run on Europe and to keep West Germany strategically subordinated to the West. However, it did not want a US that was strong enough to turn France and Western Europe into its political satellites. Similarly, France welcomed a (West) Germany that was weak and dependent enough to accept French political and strategic leadership in the framework of the EC. Yet, it needed (West) Germany to be strong enough to underpin European economic growth and prosperity and to avoid any temptations of geopolitical neutrality that could endanger the West as a whole. Finally, France wanted Britain to be 'far enough' so it would not challenge its own leadership over the EC, yet close enough to keep (West) German influence in Western Europe at bay.

The end of the Cold War and French geostrategy

With the collapse of the Soviet Empire, France's Cold War geostrategic equation was shattered. Suddenly, Germany was reunified and faced no existential threat to its east. Additionally, the absence of the Soviet counterbalance meant the US enjoyed a hegemonic strategic position. Washington was intent on taking up such a historical window of opportunity by adopting an increasingly expansive geostrategy. This led to a series of significant changes and adaptations in French foreign policy. Throughout the 1990s, the French tried to build bridges with Russia and implicate Moscow in any discussions about a post-Cold War European security architecture (Lequesne, 2008); repeatedly resisted US calls for NATO's geographical and functional expansion (Andréani, 1999); and advocated for greater European economic integration and foreign and security policy cooperation (Douin, 1997).

Critically, the French came to see European integration as the best solution to their post-Cold War puzzles. An integrated and strategically autonomous Europe would help to both 'lock' a reunified Germany within a multilateral political framework as well as reduce the prospect of unchecked US power in Europe and beyond. Given its excellence in the realm of military strategic assets and its condition of geopolitical 'middle man' between 'maritime' Britain and 'continental' Germany, France would be in an ideal position to act as the 'framework nation' of a politically integrated and strategically autonomous Europe.

For Paris, a politically united and strategically autonomous EU depended upon two main factors: Economic and Monetary Union (EMU) and a Common Foreign, Security and Defence policy. EMU was intended to help France mitigate the influence of the *Deutsche Bundesbank* over its own monetary policy, as well as to reduce the hegemonic position of the US dollar in the international monetary system (Howarth, 2000). In turn, greater European cooperation on foreign and security matters would serve to keep Germany strategically close and to mitigate the spectrum of excessive US power.

Throughout the post-Cold War period, France advocated continuously for greater European cooperation in foreign, security and defence policy. In the context of the 1993 Treaty of Maastricht, Paris was the driving force behind the adoption of Common Foreign and Security Policy (CFSP), which aimed to formalize European foreign policy cooperation through the figures of Joint Actions and Common Positions, and was founded on 'the eventual framing of a common defence policy' (Article 17, Title V, Treaty on European Union).

France and Germany actually tried to get the EU to adopt a common defence policy in 1992 and proposed to that end a merger between the Western European Union (WEU) and the EU. However, their proposal was vetoed by Britain both at Maastricht and during the 1997 Treaty of Amsterdam negotiations (Whitman, 1999). In the context of the Amsterdam Treaty negotiations, France and Germany also agreed to further develop CFSP through the creation of a new legal figure (Common Strategy) and the position of a High Representative.

Four years after Amsterdam, France approached Germany to introduce the figure of enhanced cooperation in the area of CFSP, a change brought about by the 2001 Nice Treaty. This would allow a reduced group of countries to cooperate closely in certain foreign policy matters under the legal and political aegis of the EU. It was also France and Germany who pushed through the last major institutional push in the area of CFSP during the 2002–3 Convention on the Future of Europe. This included the strengthening of the position of the High Representative for CFSP and the creation of a European External Action Service (EEAS), changes that would be implemented along with the Lisbon Treaty's entry into force in December 2009.

France's main CFSP priority has been the development of a common European defence policy to allow the EU to play an autonomous foreign policy role. For Paris, an effective European defence policy would be premised upon three factors: reversing Europe's demilitarization and strengthening its expeditionary military capabilities; creating strong European political institutions in the area of defence policy; and developing strategic military assets and structures at the EU level – such as an Operational Headquarters for the planning and conduct of European military operations and a European Armaments Agency.

In order to stimulate the development of European expeditionary military capabilities, France shelved its commitment to collective European defence and joined forces with Britain. At the 1998 Saint-Malo Summit, the two countries agreed on a common vision for a Common Security and Defense Policy around external crisis management (Howorth, 2000). In doing so, France and Britain prioritized the need to reverse Europe's pacifist and 'introvert' instincts in the area of foreign policy (Cornish and Edwards, 2001 and Heisbourg, 2000) and develop more expeditionary military capabilities. In that same spirit, the two countries would later join forces to push for the 2003 and 2010 Headline Goals, aimed at promoting the development of more expeditionary concepts and capabilities in Europe

Whereas Britain saw capability development as a means to strengthen the transatlantic relationship, France perceived it as a means to strengthen the EU as a foreign and security policy actor. Thus, at the June 1999 Cologne European Council, France joined forces with Berlin in support of strong political institutions that guaranteed the EU's political ownership of CSDP, chiefly the Political and Security Committee and the EU Military Committee (Andréani, 2000).

Finally, France would receive little support from either Germany or Britain when it came to establishing the foundations of EU strategic autonomy either operationally or industrially. Ever since CSDP was established in 1999, France made it its top priorities to create a permanent EU Operational Headquarters (OHQ) for the planning and conduct of military operations (Simón, 2010) and a European Armaments Agency to spearhead armaments and industrial cooperation at the European level. Paris was also behind all autonomous EU military operations launched to date, all of which have concentrated on France's southern axis of geostrategic priority.

11 September, the Iraq War and French grand strategy

The post-11 September years presided over a period of French animosity towards the US and the UK, which peaked in the run up to the 2003 Iraq War and during its immediate aftermath. Washington's so-called War on Terror and its unilateral decision to invade Iraq in 2003 offered France a golden opportunity to rally a number of European countries (most notably Germany) against US unilateralism. Thus, in 2003, a European Draft Constitutional Treaty that promised to make important headway in CFSP and CSDP, a strong Franco-German opposition to the Iraq War and the adoption of the first European Security Strategy seemed to convene around the same theme: a more autonomous Europe was needed to mitigate the excesses of US unilateralism. However, it would not take long for France to swing from 'anti-Americanism' to 'Atlanticism' (Serfaty, 2005).

As the costs of the Afghanistan and Iraq interventions ate into Washington's political capital at home and abroad, the US began to retreat from its post-11 September unilateral and militaristic manners around late 2004/early 2005 (Gaddis, 2005 and Haass, 2005). The difficulties to achieve political stability in Iraq following the toppling of the Saddam Hussein regime was a reminder of the limitations inherent to unilateral military force and of US/Western hegemony. For many scholars, this even signalled the transition towards a more multipolar global order (Calleo, 2009; Cox, 2007; Gray, 2005 and Layne, 2006). In any event, the very notion of a weakening America and a weakened West was problematic for France. Whereas excessive US power had been a recurring concern throughout the Cold War and post-Cold War years, Paris remained aware that its security was ultimately tied to the future of the US-led Western system. That system guaranteed a balance of power in Europe, in the European neighbourhood and globally. In other words, while US overreaching represented a concern for France, a weakened West was a serious strategic liability. That very prospect led to yet another important process of change and adaptation in French foreign policy.

Accordingly, from 2005 onwards, Washington's adoption of an increasingly multilateral approach to foreign policy and its accommodation of European and French views (Serfaty, 2005 and Zaborowski, 2006) cleared the way for a Franco-American rapprochement. Such rapprochement was further animated by France's perception that most European countries were 'overlearning' the lessons from Iraq, as they further encroached onto their pacifist and 'civilian power' mentality and turned further away from military force (Simón, 2013). A clear manifestation of this fact was CSDP's turn towards civilian crisis management and civ-mil coordination from the mid-2000s (Simón, 2012). This trend represented an important obstacle to the development of military CSDP and to France's ambitions of European strategic autonomy. This was partly offset by France's progressive engagement in NATO, which culminated with its official re-integration into the Alliance's military structure as of April 2009 (Howorth, 2010).

From mid-2008, a global financial, economic and fiscal crisis engulfed the US and Europe through 2011 and reinforced the perception that Asia (and, more particularly, China) was on the rise. In turn, from 2011 onwards, the US began to 'rebalance' its political priorities inwards (towards domestic economic recovery) and eastwards (towards the Asia-Pacific region), away from Europe. The effects of the global financial crisis proved detrimental to France's position and interests in Europe, not least as they highlighted Germany's leadership within the EU (Simón and Fiott, 2014) and further aggravated the continent's trend towards demilitarization (Mölling, 2011). Against the backdrop of economic crisis, defence budgetary cuts and a dwindling political position in Europe, France looked westwards again. In November 2010,

France and Britain signed at Lancaster House (London) two ambitious military agreements, whose political significance was underscored by the leading operational and diplomatic role played by the two countries in toppling Gadaffi's regime in Libya in 2011 (Mueen and Turnbull, 2011).

Overall, the mid-2000s presided over a process of significant change and adaptation in French foreign and security policy, eliciting a more 'Atlantic' direction. This process was initiated by a rapprochement to the US and culminated with France's return to NATO's military structure in 2009 and the signing of the Lancaster House military agreements with the UK in 2010. The West and NATO were becoming more attractive for France; a more confident and assertive Germany and an increasingly 'civilian' Europe were becoming less attractive. While the image of a politically and strategically autonomous Europe underscored French leadership, a 'civilian power Europe' emphasized Germany's increasing influence over the direction of European foreign policy.

To be sure, France has not quite given up on the EU's CSDP. In fact, the November 2015 terrorist attacks in Paris led France to invoke Article 42.7 of the Treaty on European Union, a mutual assistance clause. This allowed Paris to advocate for greater intelligence cooperation at the EU level and demand greater security assistance from its European partners (Biscop, 2015). However, France's recent efforts to fight terrorism abroad have been conducted primarily on a unilateral basis (e.g. Mali) or as part of an international coalition of the willing and in close cooperation with the US and UK (e.g. Syria, Iraq).

Based on these considerations, it could be argued that French expectations about CSDP have been lowered. The French have realized that persisting differences amongst the EU's key partners means the CSDP is unlikely to lead to the consolidation of the EU as a truly unified and autonomous political and strategic actor. However, the CSDP can prove a valuable mechanism for supporting and reinforcing national strategic and operational initiatives, primarily in the so-called southern axis of strategic priority. In this regard, it is clear that a dynamic strategic environment has triggered a process of significant adaptation in French foreign policy, having led France to undertake important efforts to diversify away from its hitherto excessive concentration on European integration and its special relationship with Germany.

Germany's continental destiny: towards a stable pan-European settlement

Germany's geostrategic destiny is characteristically continental: the achievement of a politically and economically integrated Europe. *Mittellage* (its central geographical position in Europe) is a central theme in Germany's strategic and foreign policy narrative. Its large population, a topography that is apt for agile communications and trade (characterized by short distances, plain soil and a dense and navigable river system) and its geographical location make Germany the natural leader of *Mitteleuropa*, and the geoeconomic and geopolitical hub of the European plain (Ash, 1993). *Mittellage*, however, is also a source of vulnerability. Its size, central location and economic and industrial potential mean that a unified and independent Germany represents a challenge to the autonomy of other European powers – and to the very existence of a balance of power in the European continent (Calleo, 1978).

The image of Germany being outflanked by an alliance of European powers wary of its potential is a recurring one in German strategic debates (Calleo, 1978 and Simms, 1998). So is the need for Germany to exercise strategic restraint and reassure its European neighbours

Figure 4.2 Germany's geostrategic predicament

about its commitment to the *status quo* (Calleo, 1978 and Simms, 1998). Given its vulnerable geopolitical position (see Figure 4.2), diplomacy and economic cooperation are the safest paths for Germany to realize its destiny of an integrated and stable pan-European settlement. Germany's resort to overt military power and failure to exercise restraint gave way to two world wars that resulted in a substantial loss of German power – and Germany's division and external penetration after the Second World War (Behnke, 2006).

The core tenets of (West) German grand strategy have remained fairly stable since the end of the Second World War. Ever since, (West) Germany's chief geostrategic referent has been the achievement of a stable pan-European political and economic settlement – with a reunified Germany at its centre. Germany has been patient in its pursuit of that goal, as illustrated by its emphasis on restraint and multilateralism. While Germany's geostrategic objectives have remained fairly stable, a dynamic geopolitical context has had an important impact upon the way in which such objectives have been articulated, pursued and prioritized, having triggered successive patterns of change and adaptation in German foreign and security policy.

During the Cold War, Germany attached a supreme value to its strategic alliance with the US and the need to remain a loyal NATO ally (Haftendorn, 2006), consistently joined forces with France to further European economic and political integration and sought to build bridges to the East, via *Ostpolitik*. Reconciling those objectives proved next to impossible. For one thing, the bipolar nature of the Cold War geopolitical context translated in a strong antagonism between West and East, thwarting the prospects of German reunification – let alone a stable and integrated pan-European settlement 'from the Urals to the Atlantic'. For another, its own 'battleground' status meant Germany was strategically vulnerable and dependent, and its political room of manoeuvre was very limited.

West Germany and European foreign, security and defence policy cooperation

Throughout the Cold War, European integration served (West) German interests in a number of important ways. By spearheading economic integration and political stability in (Western) Europe, the EC offered Europeans the promise of progressively overcoming the polarization of the Cold War, setting the foundations for overcoming Europe's division – as well as Germany's. Relatedly, Bonn saw the very process of European integration as an opportunity to mitigate its own dependence on the US and the NATO framework. Last but not least, the EC served as a key transmission belt for Franco-German reconciliation, a prerequisite for West German political credibility in Europe and in the broader West. This often translated in Bonn's acceptance of French leadership in the EC framework. Despite its own preference for supranationalism, Bonn came to accept that working closely with Paris in an intergovernmental setting was the only way to establish European cooperation in foreign and security policy (Nuttall, 1992).

Insofar as European defence cooperation is concerned, (West) Germany was less keen to give in to French demands. In the early 1950s, Bonn embraced France's EDC project. West Germany's main priorities were to ensure the EDC would have a supranational orientation and would remain inserted within the broader NATO framework – perceived by Bonn as critical to balancing the Soviet military threat. However, Bonn was soon disappointed by France's backtracking onto a more 'intergovernmental' vision during the EDC negotiations – and its eventual failure to ratify a watered down the EDC Treaty in 1954 (Furdson, 1980). A similar dynamic unfolded when France proposed the Fouchet Plans I and II, in 1961 and 1962 respectively. Aware that the Fouchet plans would only serve to strengthen French leadership over the EC process and could jeopardize NATO, West Germany rejected both plans (Nuttall, 1992). As long as European defence was not built along supranational lines, maintaining a balance between NATO and the US link on the one hand and France and the EC on the other was the best path to security and autonomy for (West) Germany.

German grand strategy after the Cold War

With the end of the Cold War and the collapse of the USSR, the US became the indisputable European and global hegemon. However, the absence of an immediate strategic threat gave Western Europeans a degree of breathing space they had not enjoyed since the Second World War. This was particularly the case for a reunified Germany, which suddenly could regain the *Mittellage* that the Cold War divisions had denied it (Bach and Peters, 2002 and Schwarz, 1994). Thus, the end of the Cold War gave Germany increasing freedom of action and influence in Europe (Mead, 1990).

According to the 1994 German Defense White Paper, Germany had 'gained most from the revolutionary political changes in Europe' (White Paper, 1994: 207). Its critical mass, economic and industrial might and the lack of constraints in the east, meant a (re)united Germany was set to reap many of the benefits that resulted from the end of the Cold War, as it evolved from a 'state with a seriously restricted autonomy to a great power of European, or even global, significance' (Peters, 2001: 13). All of a sudden, the notion of a stable pan-European political and economic settlement with a strong and secure Germany as its geopolitical hub had become a realizable possibility (White Paper, 1994: 201). This settlement would depend on three conditions: continued integration within the Euro-Atlantic framework, support for democratic and market reforms in central and Eastern Europe, and a strengthening in relations with Russia (especially) and Ukraine (White Paper, 1994: 312–315).

The end of the Cold War also brought important geostrategic challenges for Germany (Baring, 1994) and required a series of adaptations in German foreign policy. A unified, more secure and less dependent Germany meant a more confident Germany. And the idea of a more confident Germany with the opportunity to expand its economic and political influence in Central and Eastern Europe was one that generated certain uneasiness among its various neighbours (Banchoff, 1999). Hence, Germany's emphasis on reinvigorating its commitment to multilateralism and to the Euro-Atlantic structures (White Paper, 1994). Perhaps most importantly, that meant addressing the concerns of its American and French allies.

In a post-Cold War context, the realization of Germany's geostrategic objectives required reaching beyond the West (Thies, quoted in Behnke, 2006: 408). The preservation of a stable environment in Central and Eastern Europe was central to the security and influence of Germany. In that spirit, Berlin championed NATO and EU enlargement to Central and Eastern Europe throughout the 1990s as it sought to strengthen its bilateral economic and political ties to Russia and stimulate a dialogue between Moscow and Europe's multilateral institutions (NATO and the EU).

Germany's geostrategic vision for post-Cold War Europe was riddled with important contradictions. For one thing, Berlin's interests in bringing Central and Eastern Europe into the Western fold clashed with its intent to build bridges to Russia. Moscow still considered much of Eastern Europe as part of its rightful sphere of influence and perceived NATO's expansion there as a threat. Additionally, Berlin's championing of EU enlargement to Central and Eastern Europe caused uneasiness in Paris, who understood that an eastwards shift in Europe's economic and political centre of gravity meant a diminishing influence for France and more autonomy for Germany. Finally, Germany's efforts to remain in good terms with Russia was a source of ongoing suspicion for Washington (Szabo, 2009).

Germany's post-Cold War geostrategic puzzle was how to strengthen its economic and political position in Central and Eastern Europe, develop an amicable and predictable relationship with Russia and maintain its privileged links with Washington, Paris and the Euro-Atlantic structures. Striking the right balance between those aims was key to both the preservation and thriving of a stable pan-European settlement and Germany's own security and influence. It is against the backdrop of these partly contradictory aims that we must understand Berlin's clinging to a 'civilian power' narrative (Harnisch and Maull, 2001; Maull, 1990) centred on multilateralism, trade and economic cooperation.

To some extent, Germany's constant but growing emphasis on 'civilian power' and multilateralism signalled its progressive emancipation from its former condition of strategic subordination to the West. During the Cold War, multilateralism was understood in a 'narrow' sense, that is as an unwavering commitment to the Euro-Atlantic structures and to the post-war *status quo* (Haftendorn, 2006). With the end of the Cold War, Germany developed a broader understanding of multilateralism, one that transcended the former Euro-Atlantic space. This can be appreciated in the references made by the 1994 German Defence White Paper to the importance of the UN (1994: 215, 222, 401–403) and the OSCE (1994: 215, 222, 401, 408–409), its emphasis to dialogue, diplomacy, development and a culture of prevention (1994: 212–215), economics and trade (1994: 213) and an increasingly vocal rejection of military force aimed at propping up 'a certain image of neutrality' (interview with US official, 19 February 2009).

Germany's appeal to a broader sense of multilateralism would be most instrumental to communicate with Russia. And that was a top priority for Berlin. Moscow was a key political stakeholder in Central, Eastern and Southeastern Europe and controlled vast energy resources and minerals that Germany needed and lacked (Crawford, 2007: 45). Accordingly, it was key to the political viability of a stable pan-European settlement (White Paper, 1994: 313) and to the development of Germany's industrial and economic potential. Beyond Europe, a narrative of geostrategic eclecticism would allow Germany to communicate with *status quo*, revisionist and neutral powers alike, and thereby clear the way for German trade and exports in established as well as emerging markets. This strategy fed into the country's potential as a global economic and trade superpower, and served to further dilute its economic and political dependence on the Euro-Atlantic space.

Germany, CFSP and CSDP

Ever since the end of the Cold War, Germany has striven to reconcile its ongoing allegiance to the US and the transatlantic community, its renewed commitment to European integration and special relationship with France and a broader vision of multilateralism and increasing emphasis on 'civilian power'. Those priorities have largely oriented the country's attitude towards European foreign, security and defence policy cooperation.

By supporting CFSP and CSDP and focusing on their institutional development, Germany managed to advance the cause of European cooperation in foreign and security matters and showcase its special relationship with France, without substantially damaging either the transatlantic relationship or compromising its own civilian power credentials. Germany has also made it a priority to strengthen the political, economic and institutional links between the EU and Russia. Berlin was one of the driving forces of the EU-Russia Partnership and Cooperation Agreement, signed in 1994, and has remained one of the strongest advocates of EU–Russia cooperation ever since (interview with German official, 1 April 2008).

Germany has also supported the EU's expansion into the realm of collective defence. This policy was consistent with Germany's broader geostrategic priorities for two reasons: a common defence policy would represent a key step in the process of European political integration, and an emphasis on defence would be less damaging to the EU's (Germany's) civilian power profile than an emphasis on expeditionary warfare. Having pushed for an EU–WEU merger at Maastricht (1993) and Amsterdam (1997), Berlin was 'disappointed' to learn that the French 'swapped teams' at the December 1998 Saint-Malo Summit and decided to side with the British to design the EU's CSDP around external crisis management (interview with German official, 2 April 2008). French and British pushes for 'external crisis management, an inherently pro-active and 'strategically extrovert' (Heisbourg, 2000) concept, endangered the aspiration of civilian power Europe Germany held so dear. However, Berlin's own commitment to military transformation within the NATO framework and its political interest in remaining a constructive partner counselled against a strong resistance to the Franco-British CSDP initiative.

The Franco-British Saint-Malo summit on CSDP in December 1998 had caught Germany relatively unprepared. However, its double EU/WEU Presidency in the first semester of 1999 would allow Berlin to have an important input over the CSDP process. During its EU

Presidency, Germany sought to shift the CSDP debate from expeditionary military capabilities towards institutional development, downplaying those elements of the Franco-British vision that smacked of militarism. Germany partnered with France to promote the creation of political institutions that would oversee the CSDP process, insisted the EU should contemplate the use of force only as a very last resort, concentrate primarily on 'low end peacekeeping tasks' and be availed by the UN (interview with German official, 2 April 2008). Moreover, Germany insisted on the importance of developing a civilian operational component to the CSDP process. To this end, it joined forces with Sweden to create a Committee for the Civilian Aspects of Crisis Management, established in May 2000, and the adoption of a Civilian Headline Goal in 2000 (Heisbourg, 2000).

Berlin has been the main political sponsor of 'civilian CSDP'. Its contribution to civilian CSDP missions been second to none in terms of money spent and personnel deployed (Grevi, Helly and Keohane, 2009), and it has been behind every effort to strengthen civilian CSDP institutionally and place 'civ-mil' integration at the centre of CSDP doctrine. In that process, Germany found an unexpected partner in Britain, who from the mid-2000s onwards expressed an increasing interest in civilian CSDP and civ-mil integration (Simón, 2012). The two countries joined forces to push for the creation of the Civ-Military Cell in late 2003, the Civilian Planning and Conduct Capability in 2005 or the Crisis Management Planning and Conduct Directorate in 2008.

Finally, in its attitude towards the question of an EU military planning and conduct capability, an EU armaments cooperation and CSDP military operations, Germany has been notoriously contradictory. It has tried to reconcile its relationship with France in support for European integration, its commitment to transatlantic coherence and its interest in preserving the EU's 'civilian power' *acquis*. Against this backdrop, Berlin has expressed some support to French calls for an autonomous EU military planning and conduct capability and greater armaments and defence-industrial cooperation at the EU level. It has also supported diplomatically and operationally French-led CSDP military operations, for example EUFOR DRC, EUNAVFOR Atalanta and EUCAP Sahel Mali. Having said this, Germany's Atlanticism and allegiance to 'civilian power' have resulted in important caveats. While Germany has lent France political support in its attempt to strengthen the EU's military planning and conduct capability, it has repeatedly insisted that the emphasis should be placed on integrated civ-mil planning, not least to avoid duplicating structures already existing within the NATO framework. In a similar spirit, Germany's contribution to French-led CSDP operations has usually come at the price of lowering the ambitions of such missions (both quantitatively and qualitatively), as was the case with EUFOR DRC and EUNAVFOR Atalanta.

Germany and European foreign policy after Crimea

The resurgence of a revisionist Russia in Eastern Europe has re-ignited the contradictions that animate German grand strategy. Ever since Russia's annexation of Crimea in March 2014, Germany has faced some difficult and long-averted foreign policy choices. In fact, Chancellor Merkel played a key diplomatic role in putting together a rather tight EU-wide sanctions regime against Russia, leading to a worsening in EU-Russian and German-Russian relations (Speck, 2015).

However, Germany has also been careful not to push too far against Russia and has insisted on the need not to burn all bridges. Thus, Germany spearheaded a diplomatic effort aimed at achieving a ceasefire and political settlement in Eastern Ukraine, culminating in the so-called Minsk II agreements (Speck, 2015). Furthermore, Berlin has resisted calls for the permanent deployment of NATO forces in Central and Eastern Europe and has opposed efforts to provide lethal weapons to Ukraine in its fight against Russian-backed separatists in the Donbass region. More recently, Germany and Russia have agreed on the setup of Nord-Stream 2, a project aimed at bringing Russian gas into Germany bypassing Berlin's Eastern European partners (Dempsey, 2016). As these cases show, while there has been a significant geopolitical fallout between Germany and Russia over the past two years, not all bridges have been burnt.

How 'central' are France and Germany?

The image of 'Charlemagne Europe' perhaps best evokes the notion of Europe as an autonomous political reality, with France and Germany at its core. Indeed, the 'Charlemagne' image played an important role in the history of European integration during the Cold War, by helping create the myth of a Europe that was geopolitically and ideologically discernible from the US and Soviet superpowers. However, Europe's strategic insertion within the broader West represented an obvious limitation to the operationalization of that myth. In fact, the end of the Cold War marked the political climax of the myth of 'Charlemagne Europe'.

From the early 1990s until about 2004–5, France and Germany were more 'central' than ever. This was partly explained by their shared feeling that the US had just become too powerful for their taste. Without the Soviet balance, US hegemony was unbalanced – both geopolitically and ideologically. Franco-German uneasiness about US hegemony and their interest in ensuring the newly unified Germany would be bound by a commitment to multilateralism, presided over the 'Golden Age' of European integration. This period ran from the 1992 Maastricht Treaty to the mid-2000s, with eastern enlargement (2004–7) and the failure of the Constitutional Treaty (2005) symbolizing respectively a growing gap between France and Germany and a crisis of political Europe. Between 1992 and 2005, France and Germany were very close to each other and very 'Central', but that period seems to have come to an end.

The 1992–2005 years represented the peak of Franco-German togetherness and the 'centrality' of the Franco-German engine in European politics. Then came eastern enlargement, which strengthened Germany's strategic position in Europe and weakened France politically; the rejection of the EU Constitutional Treaty by French (and Dutch) voters in 2005; France's return to NATO and its strategic rapprochement to the US and UK; a Euro-debt crisis that evidenced political tensions at the heart of Europe; and the Franco-German split over the War in Libya in 2011. All in all, Germany's increasing influence and leadership in the EU and France's 'Atlanticist' shift have presided over an important crisis of the idea of 'Charlemagne Europe'.

As Germany has become increasingly more 'central' than France to the development of the European integration process, French foreign and security policy has engaged in a process of significant change and adaptation. In recent years, France has sought to reinvigorate its 'Western' and 'Atlantic' persona and to look 'South' to make up for its progressive loss of centrality in European affairs. Against this backdrop, it is unlikely that the Franco-German engine will become 'central' in the way it was at Maastricht, or when both countries publicly opposed Washington's decision to invade Iraq in 2003 – claiming to speak for the whole of Europe.

Bibliography

Andréani, G. (1999) 'France and NATO after the Cold War: Old French Problem– or New Transatlantic Debate?', *The RUSI Journal*, Vol. 144, No. 1, 20–24.

Andréani, G. (2000) 'Why Institutions Matter', *Survival*, Vol. 42, No. 2, 81–95.

Ash, T.G. (1993) *In Europe's Name: Germany and the Divided Continent*. New York: Random House.

Bach, J. and Peters, S. (2002) 'The New Spirit of German Geopolitics', *Geopolitics*, Vol. 7, No. 3, 1–18.

Banchoff, T. (1999) *The German Problem Transformed*. Ann Arbor: University of Michigan Press.

Baring, A. (ed.) (1994) *Germany's New Position in Europe: Problems and Perspectives*. Oxford: Berg Publishers.

Behnke, T. (2006) 'The Politics of *Geopolitik* in Post-Cold War Germany', *Geopolitics*, Vol. 11, No. 3, 396–419.

Biscop, S. (2015) 'Can European Strategy Cope ?', *European Geostrategy*, 16 December 2015. Available at: http://www.europeangeostrategy.org/2015/12/can-european-strategy-cope/. Accessed: 10 October 2016.

Bozo, F. (2008) 'Alliance atlantique: la fin de l'exception française?', *Document du travail*, Fondation pour l'Innovation Politique, February.

Braudel, F. (1990) *L'identité de la France: Espace et Histoire*, Tome 1, Paris: Flammarion.

Calleo, D. (1978) *The German Problem Reconsidered*. Cambridge: Cambridge University Press.

Calleo, D. (2009) *Follies of Power: America's Unipolar Fantasy*. Cambridge: Cambridge University Press.

Cornish, P. and Edwards, G. (2001) 'Beyond the EU/NATO Dichotomy: The Beginnings of a European Strategic Culture', *International Affairs*, Vol. 77, No. 3, 587–603.

Cox, M. (2007) 'Is the United States in Decline – Again? An Essay', *International Affairs*, Vol. 83, No. 4, 643–653.

Crawford, B. (2007) *Power and German Foreign Policy: Embedded Hegemony in Europe*. New York: Palgrave Macmillan.

Dempsey, J. (2016) 'Germany, Dump Nord Stream 2', *Carnegie Europe*, 25 January 2016. Available at: http://carnegieeurope.eu/strategiceurope/?fa=62567. Accessed September 20th 2016.

Douin, A.J.P. (1997) 'Adapting French Defence to the New Geostrategic Context', *The RUSI Journal*, Vol. 142, No. 4, 1–5.

Dufourcq, J. (2002) 'A la charnière', *Politique Etrangère*, Vol. 2, 471–486.

French Ministry of Defence (2008) *French White Paper on Defence and National Security*, http://www.defense.gouv.fr/content/download/215253/2394121/file/White%20paper%20on%20defense%25, date accessed 11 April 2017.

French Presidency (2008) *French White Paper on Defence and National Security*. Paris: Documentation Française.

Furdson, E. (1980) *The European Defence Community: A History*. London: Macmillan.

Gaddis, J.L. (2005) *The Cold War: A New History*. London: Penguin Books.

German Ministry of Defense (1994) *White Paper on the Security of the Federal Republic of Germany and the Situation and Future of the Bundeswehr*, Bonn, 5 April.

Gray, C. (2005) *Transformation and Strategic Surprise*. Washington, DC: Strategic Studies Institute.

Grevi, G., Helly, D. and Keohane, D. (eds.) (2009) *European Security and Defence Policy: The First Ten Years* (1999–2009). The European Union Institute for Security Studies. EUISS: Condé-sur-Noireau (France).

Haass, R. (2005) *The Opportunity: America's Moment to Alter History's Course*. New York: Public Affairs.

Haftendorn, H. (2006) *Coming of Age: German Foreign Policy since 1945*. Lanham: Rowman and Littlefield.

Hanrieder, W. (1989) *Germany, America, Europe: Forty Years of German Foreign Policy*. New Haven: Yale University Press.

Harnisch, S. and Maull, H.W. (eds.) (2001) *Germany as a Civilian Power? The Foreign Policy of the Berlin Republic*. Manchester: Manchester University Press.

Heisbourg, F. (2000) 'Europe's Strategic Ambitions: The Limits of Ambiguity', *Survival*, Vol. 42, No. 2, 5–15.

Howarth, D. (2000) *The French Road to European Monetary Union*. New York: Palgrave Macmillan.

Howorth, J. (2000) 'Britain, France and the European Defence Initiative', *Survival*, Vol. 42, No. 2, 33–55.

Howorth, J. (2010) 'Prodigal Son or Trojan Horse: What's in It for France?', *European Security*, Vol. 19, No. 1, 11–28.

Kennedy, P. (1987) *The Rise and Fall of the Great Powers*. New York: Random House.

Layne, C. (2006) 'The Unipolar Illusion Revisited', *International Security*, Vol. 31, No. 29, 7–41.

Lellouche, P. (1983/4) 'France and the Euromissiles', *Foreign Affairs*, Vol. 62, No. 2, 318–334.

Lequesne, C. (2008) *La France dans la Nouvelle Europe: Assurer le changement d'échelle*. Paris: Presses de Sciences Po.

Maull, H.W. (1990) 'Germany and Japan: The New Civilian Powers', *Foreign Affairs*, Vol. 69, No. 5, 91–106.

Mead, W.R. (1990) 'The Once and Future Reich', *World Policy Journal*, Vol. 7, No. 4, 593–638.

Mölling, C. (2011) 'Europe without Defense', *SWP Comments*, Vol. 38, November 2011. Available at: https://www.swp-berlin.org/en/publication/europe-without-defence/. Accessed: 8 October 2016.

Moravcsik, A. (2000) 'De Gaulle between Grain and Grandeur: The Political Economy of French EC Policy 1958–1970 (Part 1)', *Journal of Cold War Studies*, Vol. 2, No. 2, 3–43.

Mueen, S. and Turnbull, G. (2011) 'Accidental Heroes: Britain, France and the Libya Operation', *An Interim RUSI Campaign Report*, September 2011.

Néré, J. (2002) *The Foreign Policy of France from 1914 to 1945*. London: Routledge.

Nuttall, S.J. (1992) *European Political Co-Operation*. Oxford: Oxford University Press.

Peters, D. (2001) 'The Debate about a New German Foreign Policy after Unification', in Rittberger, V. (ed.), *German Foreign Policy since Unification: Theories and Case Studies*. Manchester: Manchester University Press, 11–37.

Pritchard, J. (2012) 'France: Maritime Empire, Continental Commitment', in Erickson, A., Goldstein, L. and Lord, C. (eds.), *China Goes to Sea: Maritime Transformation in a Comparative Historical Perspective*. Annapolis: Naval Institute Press, 123–144.

Rogers, J. and Simón, L. (2009) 'The Status and Location of the Military Installations of the Member States of the European Union and Their Potential Role for the European Security and Defence Policy (ESDP)', *Briefing Paper for the Security and Defence Sub-Committee of the European Parliament*, 19 February, Brussels. Available at: http://www.europarl.europa.eu/meetdocs/2004_2009/documents/dv/sede300309studype407004_/SEDE300309StudyPE407004_en.pdf. Accessed: 10 October 2016.

Schwarz, H.P. (1994) 'Germany's National and European Interests', in Baring, A. (ed.), *Germany's New Position in Europe: Problems and Perspectives*. Providence: Berg Publishers, 107–130.

Serfaty, S. (2005) 'Terms of Estrangement: French-American Relations in Perspective', *Survival*, Vol. 47, No. 3, 73–92.

Simms, B. (1998) *The Struggle for Mastery in Germany, 1779–1850*. London: Macmillan.

Simón, L. (2010) 'Command and Control? Planning for EU Military Operations', *Occasional Paper* 81, EU Institute for Security Studies. Available at: http://www.iss.europa.eu/uploads/media/Planning_for_EU_military_operations.pdf. Accessed: 10 October 2016.

Simón, L. (2012) 'CSDP, Strategy and Crisis Management: Out of Area or Out of Business?', *The International Spectator*, Vol. 47, No. 3, 100–115.

Simón, L. (2013) 'The Spider in Europe's Web? French Grand Strategy from Iraq to Libya', *Geopolitics*, Vol. 18, No. 2, 403–434.

Simón, L. and Fiott, D. (2014) 'Europe after the U.S. Pivot', *Orbis: A Journal of World Affairs*, Vol. 58, No. 3, 413–428.

Smith, M.A. (2000) *NATO in the First Decade after the Cold War*. Norwell: Kluver Academic Publishers.

Speck, Ulrich (2015) 'German Power and the Ukraine Conflict', *Carnegie Europe*, 26 March 2015. Available at: http://carnegieeurope.eu/2015/03/26/german-power-and-ukraine-conflict-pub-59501. Accessed: 10 October 2016.

Sutton, M. (2011) *France and the Construction of Europe, 1944–2007: The Geopolitical Imperative*. New York, NY: Berghahn Books.

Szabo, S.F. (2009) 'Can Berlin and Washington Agree on Russia?', *The Washington Quarterly*, Vol. 32, No. 4, 23–41.

Whitman, R.G. (1999) 'Amsterdam's Unfinished Business? The Blair Government's Initiative and the Future of the Western European Union', *Occasional Paper* 7, WEU Institute for Security Studies. Available at: https://peacepalacelibrary.nl/ebooks/files/occ07.pdf. Accessed: 10 October 2016.

Wusten (van der), H. and Dijink, G. (2002) 'German, British and French Geopolitics: The Enduring Differences', *Geopolitics*, Vol. 7, No. 3, 19–38.

Zaborowski, M. (ed.) (2006) *Friends again? EU-US Relations after the Crisis*. Paris: EU Institute for Security Studies.

5   Southern Europe

Portugal, Spain, Italy, Malta, Greece, Cyprus[1]

*Madalina Dobrescu, Tobias Schumacher
and Stelios Stavridis*

Introduction

Southern European EU Member States differ in size, population, political and economic strength and foreign policy tradition, with Italy and Spain often being referred to as 'middle powers' (Wood, 1987; Giacomello and Verbeeck, 2011) and with Portugal and Greece, and Cyprus and Malta, considered to be 'small states' and 'micro-states' respectively (Magone, 2000; Pace, 2002, 2005; Tsardanidis and Stavridis, 2011). Comparative analysis is also affected by diachronic factors: it may be difficult to engage in comparing Europeanisation given that both Maltese and Cypriot actors have not yet become firmly established in the EU context, as opposed to, say, their Italian counterparts, who are operating in the circles for fifty years. However, longer membership does not guarantee better adaptation to EU rules and principles as the cases of Greece or even Portugal have shown (in the former case, an 'enfant terrible' not only of EU integration but also over foreign policy issues, let alone economic and financial disciplines, in the latter especially during the first years of the 2008 crisis).

Any classification/categorization contains, therefore, limitations and weaknesses, as well as of course strengths and advantages: for instance the editors' preference for a Southern European space as opposed to a Mediterranean one allows for an exploration of the region's positioning at the European periphery and the associated challenges of occupying the Southern fringe of the EU's external borders. Traditionally conceived of as, not only the EU's geographic, but also economic periphery, the four 'old' south European Member States – Italy, Spain, Portugal and Greece – evolved as a socio-economic entity that shared a reliance on EU structural and cohesion funds and more recently huge public indebtedness in the context of the Eurozone crisis (Bull, 2012: 283–286). The EU's enlargement in 2004 to include Cyprus and Malta, together with migratory pressures emerging from North Africa and the Middle East following the Arab uprisings of 2011 and in particular the consequences of the ongoing conflict in Syria since the summer of 2015, have contributed to the expansion and further morphing of this space into the EU's southern 'gateway'. This reinterpretation of a Southern European role within the European Union has conferred a certain cohesion of purpose to the region while at the same time deepening previously existing, as well as refashioning new, intra-EU divisions. A focus on Southern Europe, in this context, seems highly relevant.

Geographically located around or in close vicinity to the Mediterranean, all six states under study, except Italy, which is a founding member, eventually joined through the then European Community southern enlargements in the 1980s or in one of the EU's most recent enlargement rounds. Moreover, and more importantly, there is broad consensus in the literature that they are examples of considerably successful Europeanisation processes (for Portugal see Magone, 2000; for Spain see Torreblanca, 2001; for Italy see Walston, 2011; for Malta see Fiott, 2010; for Cyprus see Sepos, 2008; for Greece see Economides, 2005) even if these vary in terms of depth and scope.[2] Among the issues that have been singled out as evidence of a successful Europeanisation process are the less prominent pro-Arab positions of some Southern European governments, the recognition of Israel by Spain on its EEC accession and by Greece after some years as an EEC member, the more varied positions on issues related to US foreign policy than in the past, a more common approach towards the disintegration of Yugoslavia and the appearance of other new states following the end of the Cold War and even a clearer 'pro-European' stance on security and defence issues, including industrial weapons procurement programmes (an area traditionally dominated by 'national champions').

These claims however relate mainly to the top-down dimension and thus to 'the adaptation of national structures and processes to the various demands of the EU' (Chapter 6) or to what Lynngaard coins the 'domestic implications of European integration' (Lynggaard, 2011). Moreover, one recent comparative study of the Europeanisation of foreign policies (Wong and Hill, 2011) contains a number of critical analyses which – while not as sceptical as some of the more unfavourable accounts of the concept of Europeanisation (Moumoutzis, 2011) – show the limits of such a process, especially vis-à-vis Germany, *Italy* and *Greece* (see Daehnhardt, 2011; Brighi, 2011; Tsardanidis and Stavridis, 2011, respectively). At the same time, however, the six Member States also, on different occasions and either alone or even in close coordination with one another, regularly embarked on an 'uploading' of their interests, ideas and policies to the EU level. This happened – and continues to happen – to project their national preferences in an attempt to influence the positions of other Member States ('negative impact') or with a view to contribute positively to the shaping of an existing common European stance, thereby contributing to the strengthening of the overall influence of EU external action ('positive impact'). A fourth reason underpinning these 'uploading' attempts, discernible in all six cases, is the opportunity structure that 'Europe' has regularly offered to national decision-makers to use 'Brussels' as an excuse for the implementation of decisions that otherwise would not have been acceptable to domestic electorates and/or national parliaments.[3]

Although it has been argued that it is easier to establish causal links between the EU level and Member States public policies – and thus identify uploading dynamics – in contrast to the impact of 'Europe' on national polities and Member States foreign policy through downloading mechanisms (Radaelli, 2004; Smith, 2008), this chapter aims at providing a comparative overview of bottom-up processes in the area of foreign policy in recent years in the six countries under study. The main reason for doing so relates to the fact, now well established in the literature, that to upload national problems does not necessarily amount to successful Europeanisation (see also distinction made earlier in this chapter between 'negative' and 'positive' impacts). In addition, the chapter traces the foreign policy action of the six Member States since the signing of the Nice Treaty in 2001 and enquires into the extent to which specific foreign policy action is coherent with EU policies in the sector in question, or – where a common EU policy does not exist – the ability of Member States' uploading attempts to contribute to EU-wide policy formation.

The chapter is based on the assumption that, although the foreign policies of all six states have embarked upon, or have been exposed to, processes of Europeanisation in recent years, this does not necessarily justify the excessively positive reading of a 'successful'

Europeanisation *tout court* that can predominantly be found in the literature. This is the case, as will be shown, because all too often policy changes and/or Europeanisation occurred in form but not in substance.

Southern Europe's foreign policy since 2001: bottom-up Europeanisation at work?

Of all uploading attempts that the governments of all six southern European Member States engaged in during the past fifteen years, those that were destined to influence the positions of other EU Member States and to influence EU decision-making directly were most prominent. This can be observed for example in policy areas such as the CSDP, conflict resolution, immigration and in the field of external relations, mainly with respect to North Africa, the Middle East and the Balkans. As a rule, governments used, or tried to make use of, the EU Presidency although the latter was equally often preceded by statements such as the one made by Cypriot President Demetris Christofias shortly before Cyprus took over the EU Presidency during the second half of 2012, who announced that Cyprus 'will not use [its] position as president of the council for the promotion of national positions' (Hürriyet Daily News, 2012).

An additional way of influencing EU foreign policy decision-making has been used by all six southern European Member States, as they have been consistently engaging in efforts to assign key positions in EU institutions to their nationals. However, these efforts have generated different results. Shortly before the European External Action Service (EEAS) became operational, Cyprus and Malta were represented in the Commission's DG RELEX and DG RELEX DEL only with two and one officials respectively, substantially lagging behind Spanish (197) and Italian representation (168) (Formuszewicz and Kumoch, 2010: 12). Up until June 2010, Italy also had the highest number of nationals (16) representing the EU abroad as heads of delegations (HoDs), followed by Spain (10) (Formuszewicz and Kumoch, 2010: 12). Nonetheless, over the last few years, this situation has been balanced by the ability of both Portugal and Greece to secure diplomatic posts within the EU's representations abroad. As of February 2016, Portugal counted six HoD posts – amongst others to the United Nations – while Greek nationals held three HoD positions and two posts as EU Special Representative for Human Rights and the Horn of Africa respectively.[4] In light of the general low percentage of Portuguese and Greek representation in EU external services, this suggests that Portugal's and Greece's lobbying has been relatively successful. The 'jewel in the crown' is of course the appointment of Federica Mogherini to the joint post of High Representative of the European Union for Foreign Affairs and Security Policy and of Vice-President of the European Commission in the Juncker Commission since November 2014, thus adding a Mediterranean flavour that was missing in the previous top EU posts.

CSDP and conflict resolution

All six southern European states during the last decade have formally subscribed to further integration steps in the field of security and defence, irrespective of whether centre-right or centre-left governments were in power. Spain and Portugal were among the frontrunners as regards joint efforts to build common institutions for the CSDP and to establish a common European defence industry. So was Italy, even though during Berlusconi's second term in office (2001–5), the Italian government withdrew its participation in the development of the military transporter Airbus A400M as a result of an intra-government split over the issue (Walston, 2011: 71). Due to Article 1 (3) of its constitution, stipulating Malta's neutrality, the country's Europeanisation efforts were comparatively more limited (Fiott, 2010: 111), although it is now clear that it is no longer a formal obstacle. Following its accession to the EU, Cyprus gave up membership in the Non-Aligned Movement in May 2004, which it had helped found in the 1960s. Nonetheless, its attempts to join NATO are blocked by Turkey thus limiting any real impact on EU–NATO security and defence collaboration, a situation tolerated by most EU states, including those who claim to be more Europeanised. As for Greece, it re-joined the NATO Military Command once it had shown its condemnation of the US role in the 1974 Cyprus invasion and collaborates fully with NATO and EU military missions, particularly those that include Turkish troops as witnessed in the Balkans.

The six southern European Member States have been consistent and active contributors to CSDP military and civilian missions, with Italy, Spain, Portugal and Greece among the most prolific providers of personnel for EU operations, and even Cyprus and Malta – both of them disposing of very limited, if any, deployable land forces – participating to the extent allowed by their modest capabilities. Apart from the latter, all five countries also participated in a number of rotating EU Battlegroups, though Italy, Greece and Portugal, mainly due to budgetary constraints and inappropriate military capabilities (Melo Palma, 2009: 11), for some time were at the bottom as far as the proportion of active forces pledged are concerned (Giegerich and Wallace, 2004: 173–174).[5] This is complemented by Spain's, Italy's and Portugal's permanent participation in long-standing CSDP-linked multinational forces such as Eurofor (now dissolved); Euromarfor; the Italian-French initiated Eurogendfor; and Spain's, Italy's and Greece's contribution to the Strasbourg-based Eurocorps. While the relatively low contributions in terms of capabilities to EU Battlegroups, for example by Italy, Greece and Portugal, are seen rather as the result of structural domestic problems in the respective defence apparatus than as unwillingness to support the achievement of the (lapsed) European Headline Goal 2010 as such, it is remarkable however that none of the six countries has acted as the initiator of a CSDP mission so far.

This supports the notion that involvement in CSDP affairs is a function of clear foreign policy considerations serving the purpose of avoiding marginalization at the EU level – an aspect common to Portugal, Greece, Cyprus and Malta – and/or to ensure that individual foreign policy interests requiring a military component are not affected by the growing international commitments and decreasing defence budgets.

As defence budget cuts have become unavoidable during the current financial crisis,[6] Cyprus, which traditionally has good relations with Russia, turned towards it in 2011 and 2012, asking for loans totalling EUR 7.5 billion amid the country's lock-out of international debt markets and concerns over its domestic banks.[7] In an effort to diversify its external relations, this was complemented by talks over financial assistance with Beijing and a recent decision to cooperate closely with Israel on gas exploration in the Mediterranean. A similar argument can be made with the Tsipras government, at least during its first months in office, in the first half of 2015.[8] Given Russia's and China's reluctance in the UN Security Council to step up the pressure on the Syrian regime to end the bloodshed in Syria, these foreign policy decisions by the Cypriot government have been regarded in Brussels with scepticism and have contributed to undermining the Europeanisation of this EU foreign policy issue. Considered to be signs of what Baun and Marek (2013) describe as 'ring fencing', they exemplify – also in the case of other southern European EU Member States – that Europeanisation often amounted to formal dynamics but not necessarily to substantive processes and thus greater communitarization. At the same time, they raise important questions about the concept of Europeanisation itself: if it only amounts to uploading national interests, then it would not lead to too much. If on the other hand it means respecting, promoting and defending specific principles and values, then such uploading will have to be consistent and selective and, as such, promote a truly European voice in the world (see also "Conclusions" in this chapter), as stipulated by the Lisbon Treaty.

This was particularly evident with respect to Turkey and the Cyprus question, Kosovo as well as the Macedonian question, the Parsley Island conflict and the Western Sahara issue. The most prominent incident, where not even a formal communitarization of national foreign policies was possible, occurred however in the context of the US-led invasion of Iraq in 2003. In spite of the fact that their involvement in the CSDP's operational sub-structures has been marked by a high degree of commitment and continuity throughout the years, Spanish, Portuguese and to some extent Italian foreign policy displayed strong Atlanticist traits in early 2003, when Spanish Prime Minister Aznar and Portuguese Prime Minister Barroso openly supported the US-led invasion of Iraq. Opposing any Franco-German-inspired Europeanisation efforts of the matter, Barroso and Aznar participated in the Azores Summit of 16 March 2003, at the end of which they joined their American and British counterparts and signed the Azores Declaration, which acted as an accelerant of the war dynamics and deepened the split within the EU.[9] In contrast, Italy's foreign policy course was more ambiguous (Davidson, 2008). After Prime Minister Berlusconi had originally declared his support for military action in the fall of 2002, Italy did not participate directly in the initial phase of the invasion. Due to the Italian public's strong opposition to the war, it provided logistical support thereby trying to portray itself as a bridge-builder between what US Defense Secretary Rumsfeld had coined 'old Europe' and 'New Europe'.[10] While the Greek and Maltese governments strongly rejected any military action that was not backed by a UNSC resolution, thus joining the anti-war camp within the EU, the Cypriot government, in spite of a Parliament resolution of 13 March 2003 stressing the need to respect the sovereignty and territorial integrity of Iraq, secretly granted the use of Cypriot airspace and port facilities to British and American forces (Hummel, 2007), thereby contradicting its official rejectionist stance. Eventually, Spain and Portugal, and even Italy once the initial fighting had wound down, including a UN resolution that somewhat 'legitimized' the intervention after the fact,[11] deployed troops, and although these were gradually withdrawn again following the electoral success of the more pro-European socialist parties in Spain and Portugal in 2004 and 2005, and of the Italian Left in 2006 respectively as a result of campaign pledges, the three countries' foreign policy action contributed substantially to one of the worst ever splits within the EU. This action, as well as Cyprus' indirect support, undermined the declared principles and values of the CFSP, represented clear attempts to re-nationalize EU foreign policy, and ignored the overwhelmingly negative public opinion of societies in all four countries.[12]

As far as the Cyprus conflict is concerned, Greece was successful in uploading the issue to the EU level, thereby ensuring that the island's division was not an impediment to its EU accession, and it even succeeded in shifting the position of other Member States (Tsardanidis and Stavridis, 2011: 119). In contrast, Cyprus, whose pre-accession objective was to use EU support to resolve the Cyprus problem, did, *sensu stricto*, Europeanise the issue through its accession but did not manage to fundamentally change the EU's policy towards the conflict and therefore towards Turkey. However, together with Greece and other Member States, in 2005, Cyprus pushed through that the recognition of the Republic of Cyprus becomes an integral part of Turkey's accession negotiations, and in 2007, it left a strong imprint when Nicosia together with Paris forced the EU to suspend negotiations of the chapters dealing with external trade and full membership due to Turkey's intransigent position. Recently, in the context of negotiations over the EU–Turkey migration deal and despite enormous pressure to reach an agreement with Ankara aimed at stymieing migratory flows to Europe, Cyprus reasserted its opposition to opening up the chapters it had blocked and effectively succeeded – with the broad support of the other Member States – to ensure that Turkey's EU membership and the resolution of the conflict continue to remain interlinked (Kades, 2016). While EU membership unavoidably provided Cypriot foreign policy with a new forum for conflict resolution, thus changing the context in which it had dealt with the problem before, it could not use the EU level to either change the Buffer Zone's grey area status – this being a long-standing objective of Cyprus – or to change the EU's practice of rhetorically supporting Nicosia, but *de facto* tolerated Turkish occupation of northern Cyprus (Stavridis and Kassimeris, 2013).

Another example where southern EU Member States continued to maintain national foreign policy preferences in spite of a different position of the majority of EU Member States is the Kosovo question. Spain, Greece and Cyprus – together with Romania and Slovakia – refused to recognize Kosovo and its declaration of independence from Serbia issued in February 2008. Although government representatives repeatedly rejected the notion that non-recognition was a function of contentious domestic issues,[13] their respective foreign policy action at, as well as outside, the EU level clearly reflected similar concerns. While Greece, whose Alternate Foreign Minister Dimitris Droutsas attempted to broker a solution between Serbia and Kosovo in August 2010 following the advisory opinion of the International Court of Justice on Kosovo in July 2010, has upheld its opposition in view of its close relations with Serbia, nationalism and separatist tendencies have been fuelling Spanish foreign policy towards Kosovo both under Socialist Prime Minister Zapatero and his conservative successor, Mariano Rajoy. Similarly, Cyprus has consistently been placing sovereignty and territorial integrity at the centre of its approach, thereby trying to prevent Kosovo from becoming a precedent that could possibly be seen as compromising a just and viable solution of the Cyprus problem in the future. In fact, all three countries have securitized the matter, made it an indisputable issue of national importance and have since followed a nationalist foreign policy stance that unavoidably generates a mutually reinforcing dynamic between public opinion and the government (Kavakas, 2000: 150). The Kosovo issue is extremely relevant because the EEC was upgraded into the EU at the time of the disintegration of Yugoslavia with the EU self-appointed Badinter Commission that had called for the recognition of Slovenia and the Former Yugoslav Republic of Macedonia (FYROM) but not Croatia. Due to domestic pressures, Germany had recognized *solo* the Slovenian and Croatian Independence Declarations, two weeks before the EU-agreed deadline, thus leading to strong criticisms at the time (see Crawford, 1996).

In the case of FYROM, Greece managed to successfully upload its national concerns by vetoing any recognition under the name of 'Republic of Macedonia' not only as far as the EU was concerned but also within NATO. (President Bush recognized it under that name a few weeks before leaving office.) But it was a pyrrhic victory as a number of EU Member States also recognized the Republic under its preferred name. In fact, the real issue at stake regarding FYROM is one of crossloading, as the popular opposition in Greece in general, but in Northern Greece in particular (the Greek regions that bear the name of Macedonia: Western, Central and Eastern), shows that there is a substantial problem regarding any future Europeanisation of the issue. The Greek veto in 2008, opposing FYROM's bid for NATO membership, clearly showed that the problem would not simply disappear over time. The current gap between Greek public opinion and the rest of Europe is exacerbated by the growth of neo-fascist and neo-Nazi extreme political groupings following in part the economic, financial, social and political crisis in the past few years.[14] What remains equally puzzling is the lack of interest by other EU Member States and societies to even try and understand some of the Greek demands over that issue, when for instance, in part due to the 1994–5 Greek economic embargo over FYROM, the latter's government did alter some of its initial constitutional articles and other national symbols, thereby confirming that not all of Greece's demands are unfounded. Since the lifting of that embargo in 1995, Greece has become FYROM's most important business partner. However, in the meantime, the government in Skopje has continued to expand its use of 'Macedonian history' (with the re-naming of its main airport and the construction of a huge statue of Alexander the Great), thus ignoring attempts at downplaying the tension and finding a solution to the problem. To date, and in spite of Greek efforts, the EU has not reacted to this development, thus substantiating the absence of a common European stance on the matter.

A similar dynamic was also at play in the context of the confrontation between Spain and Morocco over the islet of Parsley (*Perejil* in Spanish and *Laila* in Arabic) in 2002. Motivated by broad societal support to respond to Morocco's invasion of the islet on 11 July 2002 in a hawkish fashion, but also in view of the potential repercussions of tolerating the Moroccan occupation with respect to Spain's two disputed North African enclaves Ceuta and Melilla, the Partido Popular-led government of Prime Minister Aznar considered the issue to be a matter of national interest. In parallel to the initial pursuit of the bilateral Spanish-Moroccan track, which was severely impeded by the interference of the Moroccan Royal Palace and the King's shadow cabinet, Spain at first attempted to upload the issue onto the EU level, thereby acknowledging existing EU cooperation frameworks, such as the Euro-Mediterranean Partnership. The Danish EU Presidency responded to this request by sending a communiqué to Rabat while Commission President Romano Prodi engaged in direct contact with Moroccan Prime Minister Abderrahmane Yussoufi.[15] As these efforts did not bear any fruit and most of all after France, with the support of Portugal, blocked the adoption of a common EU statement denouncing the occupation during a meeting of EU ambassadors in the Comité des Représentants Permanents (COREPER), the Committee of Permanent Representatives in the European Union, Spain felt compelled to re-nationalize the matter. As a consequence, and in contrast to the government's original intention to seek a diplomatic solution, Defence Minister Federico Trillo ordered the Spanish military to end the occupation and on 17 July 2002 the islet was recaptured (Gillespie, 2006). The subsequent critique voiced by other EU Member States over what was widely perceived as a disproportionate and potentially bellicose move reinforced the re-nationalization dynamics of the matter even further. The Spanish government, still interested in a return to the pre-occupation status as quickly as possible and aware that it could not factor in the EU as a potential mediator (Monar, 2002), turned towards the US, and eventually accepted a Spanish-Moroccan accord, brokered by US Secretary of State Colin Powell, in which both parties agreed on the withdrawal of Spanish forces and the absence of all personnel and symbols of sovereignty in the future.[16]

A conceptual challenge raised by the dynamics of uploading processes relates to the fact that it cannot always be determined whether a Member State Europeanises or re-nationalizes its foreign policy, simply because the EU's position itself is sometimes shifting or imprecise. This applies, for example, to the Western Sahara conflict, where the positions of the European Parliament (EP) on the one hand and the Commission and the Council on the other hand occasionally diverge. This was most notably the case on 14 December 2011 when the EP voted for the first time ever in favour of terminating the Fisheries Partnership Agreement with Morocco, dating back to 2005 and granting licenses to 119 EU vessels – predominantly Spanish – to fish in Moroccan and thus Western Sahara waters. For years, the Commission and the Council followed a pro-Moroccan policy, thereby accepting Morocco's *de facto* occupation of Western Sahara and treating its fishing grounds as an integral part of Morocco, whereas the EP since the mid-1980s pursued a more critical approach (Vaquer, 2004). Regardless of whether the agreement's marginal profitability or considerations of international legality motivated the EP, its decision is important as it acknowledges the unresolved legal status of Western Sahara and thus breaks with the EU's past policy of silently ignoring the matter. Strictly speaking, this example does unavoidably raise the question what precisely a Europeanised foreign policy towards the conflict means and whose position is regarded as the ultimate benchmark: the EP's or the Council's and the Commission's?

This problem is further underlined by the ambiguous foreign policy action of Spain, Portugal, Italy, Greece, Cyprus and Malta. While the governments of all six Member States have in common that throughout the last decade they repeatedly acknowledged the Sahrawis' right to self-determination,[17] they have in practice moved closer to Morocco's preference of resolving the conflict by offering the Sahrawis' only an autonomous status. While Cyprus – due to its own conflict – had been a staunch defender of the Sahrawis' claims for Western Sahara, since it joined the EU it gradually intensified its cooperation with Morocco in the field of investment, tourism, and visa abolition, thereby increasingly turning a blind eye to Moroccan occupation and the concerns of the EP.[18] Similarly, successive National Party-led Maltese governments expanded the country's bilateral diplomatic and economic relations,[19] accompanied by the continuous efforts of both Socialist and Conservative Greek governments to deepen bilateral ties in areas such as industry, customs, trade, business, tax cooperation and energy. Portuguese foreign policy toward Morocco also stands in the tradition of past policy actions, as it continued to prioritize commercial and energy issues at the expense of working towards a fair and just resolution of the Western Sahara conflict, as demanded by the EP. In fact, following the announcement of Socialist Prime Minister Socrates in Algiers in 2007 that the Maghreb had become a Portuguese foreign policy priority (Noivo, 2011), Portugal concluded a multitude of agreements and memoranda of understanding with Morocco, Algeria and Tunisia, in the field of trade, energy, culture and even security and defence. During its EU Presidency in the second half of 2007, it succeeded in uploading its newly found geostrategic interest onto the EU level and initiated the first-ever held EU Troika meeting with the Arab Maghreb Union at which, however, it carefully avoided any discussion on the resolution of the Western Sahara conflict yet again.[20] Such a practice was also in the interest of Spain and Italy. Hosting some of the very few international representation offices of the Frente Polisario, the Saharawi rebel national movement working for the independence of Western Sahara, Spanish and Italian governments – regardless of the party in power – consistently ignored both the EP's critical stance and their own societies' predominantly pro-independence position. While the Italian government of Prime Minister Prodi even rejected a motion by the lower chamber of the Italian Parliament during the summer 2007 to officially recognize the Polisario, the Spanish *Partido Socialista*, after it had assumed power in 2004, undertook a complete U-turn and abandoned its pro-Sahrawi attitude held since Spain had ended its colonization of the Western Sahara. In March 2010, Prime Minister Zapatero used the Spanish EU Presidency to hold the first ever EU–Morocco summit in Granada with a view to single out Morocco as a reform champion and key EU ally in the Mediterranean.[21] Although some measured joint statement was adopted that referred to the Western Sahara,[22] it was not an issue that was pushed by the Spanish socialist government and its conservative successor has continued to strictly adhere to the Commission's and Council's pro-Moroccan line.[23]

Immigration

Although it is widely claimed – perhaps unjustifiably given for example Israel's considerable and rather unique impact on regional and global politics – that small states have limited influence on international agenda-setting, with Tonra referring to small states as the 'flotsam and jetsam of the international system or as "make-weights" for realist-inspired bandwagoning coalitions' (Tonra, 2000: 224), immigration turned out to be a policy sector in which Greece, Cyprus and Malta, all considered to be small states, together with Italy, through their Interior Ministries and the Ministries of Foreign Affairs have become highly pro-active and influential on the EU level since 2008. In the wake of the adoption of the French-inspired European Pact on Immigration and Asylum in mid-October 2008, the Maltese Interior Ministry and the Foreign Ministry feared that the attention given to migration issues in the context of the French EU Presidency would lose momentum during the then upcoming Czech EU Presidency and decided to engage in coalition-building with other EU Member States. This was done with a view to increasing the chances of going beyond the Pact and, more importantly, the Dublin II regulation of 2003. As the latter stipulates that immigrants have to reside in the country they first arrive in and given Malta's exposure to large flows of irregular migration from across the Mediterranean, it had throughout the years become a highly contentious issue for the successive Nationalist Party-led Maltese governments and even a part of Malta's foreign policy.[24]

In the second half of 2008, Maltese Minister of Interior Carmelo Mifsud therefore undertook to transcend the boundaries of domestic politics and turned to Greece, Cyprus and Italy, societies which are equally exposed to an uncontrolled inflow of undocumented migrants and overwhelmingly share the conviction that the number of asylum-seekers needs to be allocated more equally across Member States and that the EU should provide more assistance to the latter to handle irregular migration.[25] The Maltese proposal to develop a common position on the issue of burden-sharing was welcomed instantly by the three governments, and it was decided that the self-proclaimed Quadro Group would henceforth not only coordinate efforts but also present a 'common front within the EU' (The Malta Independent, 2008) in the JHA Council and, if need be, in the General Affairs Council. The quartet met both on the technical and ministerial level on several occasions in Malta and Italy throughout the winter months of 2008–9 and eventually tabled a paper entitled 'Combating Illegal Immigration in the Mediterranean' at the informal meeting of JHA ministers in Prague on 15 January 2009. Emphasizing that 'the Mediterranean region is becoming a transit area for drug and other illicit trafficking from Africa and the East' and stressing the need to be provided with more resources and support to cope with the 'systematic influx of illegal migrants,' the four governments' demands mainly revolved around amending the Dublin II regulation 'to ensure a more equitable allocation of responsibility for the examination of asylum applications' (Council of the EU, 2009a). While this would lead to a more formalized approach to intra-EU reallocation of irregular immigrants and a mainstreaming of the EU's external relations, they also stressed the need to enforce as soon as possible the implementation of intra-EU reallocation under existing agreements. And in those cases, where the latter would not allow for or impede readmission, they announced their intention to go back to past practices and conclude jointly and separately agreements with other countries of origin and transit. At first, the Quadro Group's initiative was welcomed as valuable input for the preparation of the then upcoming Stockholm programme.[26] As a direct consequence of the efforts of the Group and consistent lobbying, particularly by the Maltese government, among other Member States governments, the European Council of June 2009 therefore took up the four countries' concerns. It called for 'the coordination of voluntary measures for internal reallocation of beneficiaries of international protection' (Council of the EU, 2009b) and decided to set up a pilot project for Malta, the so-called EUREMA project in which Portugal also participated,[27] which – following yet another joint effort by the Group in April 2011 – was replaced by EUREMA II in 2012.

Although the EU stopped short of adopting a formalized approach to intra-EU reallocation of beneficiaries and mainstream its external relations in this regard, the governments of the Quadro Group acted as policy entrepreneurs to the extent that their uploading efforts led to the setting-in motion of an intense debate on the EU level during late 2008 and 2011, the setting-up of EUREMA and EUREMA II,[28] and to an anchoring of at least some of their national preferences in the field of migration in the 'New Response to a Changing Neighbourhood'[29] – the EU's strategic response to the Arab Spring. For all five countries – Spain joined the Group in April 2011 – establishing and participating in the Quadro Group and intersecting domestic with foreign policy objectives did signify a change with past practices. It was an attempt to re-nationalize not only EU immigration policies but also all those dimensions of EU external relations that contain an immigration element, as a result of growing concerns in the five countries' domestic constituencies over the uncontrolled flow of irregular migrants and the putatively negative impact it may have on both national identity and socio-economic perspectives in times of financial crisis. For all five, and in particular for Malta and Cyprus, which prior to accession simply relied on bilateral readmission agreements with transit and/or sending countries, it was seen as a possibility to re-introduce the past practice of sending away irregular migrants either directly or through a different mechanism and thus to renege on Dublin II – a regulation they had all subscribed to in the past.

Attempts at re-nationalizing migration, asylum, border and visa policies continued following the refugee and migratory pressures resulting from the Arab uprisings. Faced with an increase in asylum applications from Tunisian nationals and anticipating a large-scale influx of Libyan refugees, Italy's Interior Minister Roberto Maroni warned his European counterparts of what was perceived in Rome as a looming 'invasion', at the same time requesting a substantial financial package to support Southern European Member States of first entry and the activation of Directive 2001/55/EC which could have provided for a mechanism of burden-sharing (Monar, 2012: 117; 122). Italy's proposals encountered little support in the Council where its assessment of the situation was not shared by the majority of Member States – only Greece and Spain lent their support – and its threat perception was deemed as overly dramatic. This perceived lack of solidarity of fellow Member States unravelled the introduction of a series of national measures that put under serious threat the functioning of the Schengen border system. 'Deeply offended', Italy decided to start issuing – on humanitarian grounds – temporary residence permits to Tunisian nationals as of early April 2011, which also granted the beneficiaries the right to travel within the Schengen zone (Pascouau, 2013). In response to what was perceived as on open invitation to cross into its territory, France introduced checks at the border with Italy, which resulted in refusing entry to hundreds of migrants and even blocking several trains from Ventimiglia, located only kilometres away from the French border. The 'Franco-Italian affair' outlined the failure of both Italy and France to comply with EU border law and the Schengen regime more generally, pointing not only to the difficulties of downloading EU norms but to a more worrying trend towards 'a "race to the bottom" by two Schengen members . . . as regards the principles of solidarity, mutual respect, loyal cooperation and fundamental rights protection' (Carrera et al., 2011).

The tensions between Italy and France signalled the sharpening of an intra-EU division between Southern European frontline states, such as Greece, Italy and Malta, and Member States, which, while not located at the EU's external borders, feel threatened by the relentless influx of migrants and their tenacious attempts at reaching deep into the heart of Europe. Notable among the latter group are France and most of the new Central and Eastern European Member States, but also Spain where high levels of unemployment have hardened the government's position against immigration. The reactions triggered by the European Commission's proposed European Agenda on Migration in the spring of 2015 aptly illustrate this growing rift cutting through Europe's underbelly. The document put forward two main proposals: a resettlement scheme for 20,000 refugees coming directly from conflict-ridden regions to be distributed across the 28 Member States under a quota system over a two-year period and, second, the relocation of 40,000 refugees from Italy and Greece according to a fixed distribution scheme. The envisioned measures generated a wide range of responses: 'Hungary and the Czech Republic found fault with the lack of geographic balance'; 'Luxembourg was astonished'; 'Poland called for compliance with the voluntary principle'; Lithuania, Estonia, Slovakia and Romania objected to 'imposed' solidarity (Fichtner et al., 2015); France expressed its opposition to the introduction of quotas (Maurice, 2015). Southern European Member States themselves presented a rather fragmented front with Spain indicating that it would not comply with the plan (Lledó, 2015); Cyprus, Malta and Portugal appealed to solidarity, and Italy threatened to resort to a 'Plan B' similar to its 2011 initiative which would see the Italian government refusing to register new arrivals and potentially granting them Schengen visas that would allow migrants to move further north towards Austria, Germany and France (Fichtner et al., 2015). Despite Prime Minister Matteo Renzi's efforts at uploading Italy's – and by extension the Southern European 'gateway' states' – interests onto the European level, which on this occasion went beyond lobbying attempts and reached the level of direct threats, the deep split between Member States undermined the concept of mandatory redistribution quotas. Instead, a new plan was devised that turned the objectives of the initial Agenda on their head by shifting the focus back on the countries of first entry who were expected to strengthen their capacity to identify, screen and register migrants with the help of Commission assistance (European Commission, 2015).

Conclusions

This chapter has shown that although Southern European Member States have been eager to contribute to further integration of the EU's common security and defence policy – through, for example, participation in civilian and military missions – their uploading of national preferences onto the EU level is indicative of strong (re)nationalized modes of foreign policy action. This, in turn, cannot be said to constitute a bottom-up Europeanisation process for at least two reasons. First, the uploading attempts of the six Southern European states examined here reflect long-standing national foreign policy priorities and concerns which have failed to produce consensus within the EU. To the extent that the process of uploading their distinctly national interests onto the EU arena allowed individual Member States to conduct their foreign policy in a new and expanded arena, and occasionally garner support for their positions from other Member States, this was a far cry from shaping a coherent and common European stance. Thus, despite both Greece and Cyprus being relatively successful in uploading the Cyprus conflict on the EU level – by altering the positions of some of the Member States and even conditioning Turkey's EU accession on Cyprus's recognition – the EU has continued to tacitly accept the occupation of Northern Cyprus. As far as the name dispute over FYROM is concerned, Greece's uploading attempts merely came down to obstructing Skopje's EU and NATO membership, failing to produce a unified EU stance on the matter if we are to consider the large number of Member States which have recognized the 'Republic of Macedonia'. An even starker example of quashed uploading attempts is provided by Spain's unsuccessful bid for an EU common statement in the context of its conflict with Morocco over the Parsley islet. Not only did an EU position fail to materialize, but it also pushed Spain towards renational-izing and ultimately escalating the issue by opting for a military intervention. More recently, the refugee crisis confronting Europe has highlighted the inability of the Member States form-ing the EU's Southernmost periphery to upload their policy preferences – notably in favour of mandatory distribution quotas – on the EU level, signalling one of the most extraordinary instances of intra-EU fragmentation and national entrenchment in the history of the Union.

Second, in addition to failing to produce common European foreign policies, upload-ing processes by Southern European Member States have also occasionally undermined the values and principles underpinning the Union's Common Foreign Security and Defence Policy. The debacle that surrounded the US-led invasion of Iraq is without doubt one of the most prominent examples of re-nationalized foreign policy action as far as at least some of the six Member States scrutinized here are concerned. What makes this instance even more remarkable is the ease with which Member States such as Spain and Portugal and – to some extent – Italy were able to gloss over fundamental principles of EU foreign policy, such as respect for international law, and adopt an interventionist foreign policy. In addition to bringing into sharp focus the deep divisions between Member States, the challenge of migra-tory pressures from the Mediterranean has also underlined the subordination of fundamental European values such as solidarity, cooperation and protection of human rights to nationally driven imperatives to enforce different variants of 'fortress Europe'. Italy's attempts at forc-ing '"European solidarity" through the back door' by enticing Tunisian migrants to cross the border into France can be interpreted as subverting the principle of sincere and loyal cooperation (Carrera et al., 2011), while Spain's resistance to the uploading attempts of its fellow Southern European neighbours with respect to refugee quotas is a grim reminder of the limits of genuine solidarity.

Given that Southern European Member States' uploading attempts have not contributed to the EU's ability to speak with one voice on a number of relevant foreign policy issues, nor have they advanced common EU foreign policy values and norms, it cannot be argued that such uploading dynamics amount to successful bottom-up Europeanisation. Rather, they illustrate deeply national foreign policy stances which, when transferred and advocated onto the European level, do more to strengthen than coordinate national preferences. What results from these uploading processes is often weakened EU actorness and diminishing effective-ness of EU foreign policy action.

Notes

1 The authors wish to thank Mattia Filippin at the College of Europe (Natolin campus) for his sup-port and comments.
2 There is some discrepancy with this approach, however: on Italy see Brighi (2011); on Greece see Tsardanidis and Stavridis (2005, 2011); on Spain see Stavridis (2013).

3 This function has traditionally been referred to as an 'alibi' function in the literature, starting with EPC (European Political Cooperation, the CFSP's predecessor) back in the early 1970s (Hill, 1983: 10).

4 Greek nationals Alexander Rondos and Stavros Lambrinidis are the EU Special Representative to the Horn of Africa and the EU Special Representative for Human Rights, respectively.

5 See also Melo Palma (2009) who provides a good overview of Portugal's role in EU Battlegroups and CSDP missions.

6 Although there were reductions prior to the crisis as no 'peace dividend' actually materialized at the end of the Cold War. See also DG for External Policies, April 2011, at http://www.europarl. europa.eu/document/activities/cont/201106/20110623ATT22406/20110623ATT22406EN.pdf

7 See *Wall Street Journal*, 6 July 2012 at http://online.wsj.com/article/SB10001424052702303962 304577510243907446000.html. On the wider implications of the crisis for its foreign policy, see Christou and Kyris (2015).

8 For a general review of the impact of the financial and economic crisis on the Europeanisation of Greek foreign policy, see Tsardanidis (2015).

9 See *New York Times*, 17 March 2003 at http://www.nytimes.com/2003/03/17/international/17FTEX. html

10 US Secretary of Defense Donald Rumsfeld made this remark at the Foreign Press Center in Washington on 22 March 2003. See also http://www.rferl.org/content/article/1102012.html

11 Moreover, the UN headquarters in Baghdad were a target of a terrorist attack in August 2003 killing several officials of that organization including the UN's chief envoy to Iraq, Sergio Vieira de Mello.

12 See for example Hummel (2007) and Davidson (2008).

13 See for example the statement made by Spanish Deputy Prime Minister Maria Teresa Fernandez de la Vega shortly after the release of the International Court of Justice's advisory opinion. See http://www.novinite.com/view_news.php?id=118450

14 The extreme far-right "Golden Dawn" party came fifth with nearly 7 per cent of the June 2012 vote and obtained 7 per cent also in the general elections in September 2015. In contrast, in Spain, the far-left Podemos Party obtained 20.7 per cent in the parliamentary elections in December 2015.

15 See *New York Times*, 14 July 2002 at http://www.nytimes.com/2002/07/15/world/europeans-urge-morocco-to-withdraw-from-spanish-island.html and http://news.bbc.co.uk/2/hi/europe/2137407. stm

16 See *The Guardian*, 23 July 2002 at http://www.theguardian.com/world/2002/jul/23/spain.gilestremlett

17 See for example the statement of Spanish Secretary of State for Foreign Affairs, Ignacio Ibanez, in February 2016 at http://www.aps.dz/en/world/10996-spain-supports-un-efforts-allowing-sahrawi-people-exercise-right-to-self-determination and the statement made by Portuguese Prime Minister Socrates in June 2010 at http://www.sahara-news.org/index.php?option=com_content&view=arti cle&id=116:western-sahara-portugal-in-favour-of-a-l-political-solution-r-&catid=1.

18 For Cyprus, see http://www.mfa.gov.cy/mfa/mfa2006.nsf/All/A7FAF913E17722A3C22579EA00 33FBB0?OpenDocument

19 See for example http://www.foreign.gov.mt/default.aspx?MDIS=21&NWID=1469.

20 See http://www.eu2007.pt/ue/ven/noticias_documentos/20071105amadouma.html

21 See Kausch 2010 at http://www.neurope.eu/blog/morocco-needs-tougher-talk-sweeter-carrots.

22 See Council of the European Union, Joint Statement European Union-Morocco Summit Granada, 7 March 2010.

23 A similar case could be made regarding Cuba, whose own geopolitical changes also reflect wider global developments such as the Obama initiative of December 2014, which to some extent reduced the role played by Europe.

24 According to a Eurobarometer survey, 55 per cent of all Maltese think that immigration does not enrich Malta culturally or economically. See Special Eurobarometer 380, June 2012.

25 See ibid. In Cyprus 96 per cent and in Malta and Greece 95 per cent of all respondents are most likely to agree that the EU should provide more assistance to Member States to cope with undocumented migration.

26 The Stockholm programme defines the EU's priorities for the period 2010–14 in the area of justice, freedom and security.

27 The main objective of EUREMA was to implement the principle of solidarity, as called for by the European Council of June 2009. The other Member States are France, Germany, Hungary, Luxembourg, Poland, Romania, Slovakia, Slovenia and the United Kingdom.

28 On 21 April 2011, the European Commission decided to extend EUREMA and finance it through the European Refugee Fund (ERF).
29 See European Commission and European Union External Action, 25 May 2011, 'A New Response to a Changing Neighbourhood. A Review of European Neighbourhood Policy', COM (2011) 303.

Bibliography

Baun, M. and Marek, D. (eds.) (2013) *The New Member States and the European Union: Foreign Policy and Europeanization*, London: Routledge.
Börzel, T. (2002) 'Pace-Setting, Foot-Dragging, and Fence-Sitting: Member State Responses to Europeanization', *Journal of Common Market Studies*, Vol. 40, No. 2, pp. 193–214.
Brighi, E. (2011) 'Resisting Europe? The Case of Italy's Foreign Policy', in Reuben Wong and Christopher Hill (eds.), *National and European Foreign Policies: Towards Europeanization*, London: Routledge, pp. 57–71.
Bull, M. J. (2012) 'Southern Europe and the "Trade Off": Architects of European Disunion?', in Jack Hayward and Rüdiger Wurzel (eds.), *European Disunion: Between Sovereignty and Solidarity*, Basingstoke; New York: Palgrave Macmillan, pp. 283–297.
Carrera, S., Guild, E., Merlino, M. and Parkin, J. (2011) *A Race against Solidarity: The Schengen Regime and the Franco-Italian Affair*, Centre for European Policy Studies. Available at: https://www.ceps.eu/system/files/book/2011/04/The%20Franco-Italian%20Affair.pdf. Accessed: 15 August 2016.
Christou, G. and Kyris, G. (2015) 'The Financial Crisis and Cypriot Foreign Policy: Re-Europeanization?', *Hellenic Studies/Etudes Helleniques*. Vol. 23, No. 1, pp. 39–58.
COM (European Commission) (2011) 'A New Response to a Changing Neighbourhood', Brussels, 25/05/2011 COM(2011) 303. Available at: https://eeas.europa.eu/enp/pdf/pdf/com_11_303_en.pdf. Accessed: 10 September 2016.
Council of the EU (2009a) *Note from the Cyprus, Greek, Italian and Maltese Delegations to: Delegations, Subject: Combating Illegal Immigration in the Mediterranean* (5689/09 JAI 39 ASIM 9). Brussels, 23 January. Available at: http://register.consilium.europa.eu/doc/srv?l=EN&f=ST%205689%202009%20INIT. Accessed: 15 August 2016.
Council of the EU (2009b) Brussels European Council Presidency Conclusions (11225/09, Brussels, 19 June 2009). Available at: http://europa.eu/rapid/press-release_DOC-09-2_en.htm?locale=en. Accessed: 15 August 2016.
Crawford, B. (1996) 'Explaining Defection from International Cooperation: Germany's Unilateral Recognition of Croatia', *World Politics*, Vol. 48, No. 4, pp. 482–521.
Daehnhardt, P. (2011) 'Germany in the European Union', in Reuben Wong and Christopher Hill (eds.), *National and European Foreign Policies: Towards Europeanization*, London: Routledge, pp. 35–56.
Davidson, J. W. (2008) 'In and Out of Iraq: A Vote-Seeking Explanation of Berlusconi's Iraq Policy', *Modern Italy*, Vol. 13, No. 1, pp. 37–50.
Economides, S. (2005) 'The Europeanisation of Greek Foreign Policy', *West European Politics*, Vol. 28, No. 2, pp. 471–491.
European Commission (2015) *A European Agenda on Migration*, COM (2015) 240, 13 May 2015, Brussels.
Fichtner, U., Popp, M., Schult, C. and Smoltczyk, A. (2015) 'The EU's Shipwrecked Refugee Plan', *Spiegel Online*, 23 June 2015. Available at: http://www.spiegel.de/international/europe/how-eu-promises-to-introduce-refugee-quotas-failed-a-1040226.html. Accessed: 10 September 2016.
Fiott, D. (2010) 'How Europeanized Has Maltese Foreign Policy Become?', *Mediterranean Quarterly*, Vol. 21, No. 3, pp. 104–118.
Formuszewicz, R. and Kumoch, J. (2010) *The Practice of Appointing the Heads of EU Delegation in the Wake of Council Decision on the European External Action Service*, Warsaw. Report of the Polish Institute of International Affairs, Warsaw. Available at: http://www.pism.pl/zalaczniki/PISM_Report_HoD.pdf. Accessed: 10 September 2016.

Giacomello, G. and Verbeeck, B. (2011) *Italy's Foreign Policy in the 21st Century. The New Assertiveness of an Aspiring Middle Power*, Lanham: Lexington.

Giegerich, B. and Wallace, W. (2004) 'Not Such a Softpower: The External Deployment of European Forces', *Survival*, Vol. 46, No. 2, pp. 163–182.

Gillespie, R. (2006) 'This "Stupid Little Island": A Neighbourhood Confrontation in the Western Mediterranean', *International Politics*, Vol. 41, No. 1, pp. 110–132.

Hill, C. (ed.) (1983) *National Foreign Policies and European Political Cooperation*, London: George Allen and Unwin.

Hummel, H. (2007) *A Survey of Involvement of 10 European States in the Iraq War 2003*, paks (Parlamentarische Kontrolle von Sicherheitspolitik) Working paper 9.

Hürriyet Daily News (2012) 'Greek Cyprus Vows to Be Neutral at EU Post', *Hürriyet Daily News*, 4 June. Available at: http://www.hurriyetdailynews.com/greek-cyprus-vows-to-be-neutral-at-eu-post. aspx?pageID=238&nID=22310&NewsCatID=351.

Kades, A. (2016) 'More Pressure on Cyprus Predicted in Wake of EU-Turkey Deal', *Cyprus Mail*, 19 March. Available at: http://cyprus-mail.com/2016/03/19/more-pressure-on-cyprus-predicted -in-wake-of-eu-turkey-deal/.

Kavakas, D. (2000) 'Greece', in Ian Manners and Richard G. Whitman (eds.), *The Foreign Policies of European Union Member States*, Manchester: MUP, pp. 144–161.

Lledó, E. (2015) 'Spanish Foreign Policy Monitor: April–June 2015', Policy Brief No 207, *FRIDE*.

Lynggaard, K. (2011) 'Domestic Change in the Face of European Integration and Globalization: Methodological Pitfalls and Pathways', *Comparative European Politics*, Vol. 9, No. 1, pp. 18–37.

Magone, J. (2000) 'Portugal', in Ian Manners and Richard G. Whitman (eds.), *The Foreign Policies of European Union Member States*, Manchester: MUP, pp. 162–180.

The Malta Independent (2008) 'Quadro Group Technical Experts Meet in Nicosia', *The Malta Independent*, 21 December. Available at: http://www.independent.com.mt/articles/2008-12-21/local-news/Quadro-Group-Technical-experts-meet-in-Nicosia-217872.

Maurice, E. (2015) 'France Opposes EU Migrant Quotas', *EUobserver*, 18 May 2015. Available at https://euobserver.com/political/128730.

Melo Palma de, H. (2009) 'European by Force and by Will: Portugal and the European Security and Defence Policy', *College of Europe EU Diplomacy Papers 7*.

Monar, J. (2002) 'The CFSP and the Leila/Perejil Island Incident: The Nemesis of Solidarity and Leadership', *European Foreign Affairs Review*, Vol. 7, No. 3, pp. 251–255.

Monar, J. (2012) 'Justice and Home Affairs', *Journal of Common Market Studies*, Vol. 50 Annual Review, pp. 116–131.

Moumoutzis, K. (2011) 'Still Fashionale Yet Useless? Addressing Problems with Research on the Europeanization of Foreign Policy', *Journal of Common Market Studies*, Vol. 49, No. 3, pp. 607–629.

Noivo, D. (2011) 'Portugal and the Maghreb: Time to Renew the Vows', *IPRIS Lusophone Countries Bulletin*, 16.

Pace, R. (2002) 'A Small State and the European Union: Malta's EU Accession Experience', *South European Society and Politics*, Vol. 7, No. 1, pp. 24–42.

Pace, R. (2005) 'Cyprus in the EU: A Small State Perspective', in Constantin Stefanou (ed.), *Cyprus and the EU: The Road to Accession*, Aldershot: Ashgate, pp. 238–254.

Pascouau, Y. (2013) 'The Schengen Governance Package: The Subtle Balance between Community Method and Intergovernmental Approach', *European Policy Centre Discussion Paper*. Available at: http://www.epc.eu/pub_details.php?cat_id=1&pub_id=4011. Accessed: 1 September 2016.

Radaelli, C. M. (2004) 'Europeanisation: Solution or Problem?', *European Integration Online Papers*, Vol. 8, No. 16, pp. 1–23.

Sepos, A. (2008) *The Europeanization of Cyprus: Polity, Policies, and Politics*, New York: Palgrave.

Smith, K. E. (2008) *The EU in the World: Future Research Agendas*, Working Papers 1, London: European Foreign Policy Unit.

Stavridis, S. (2013) 'Re-Assessing the Claim of a "Successful Europeanization" of Spanish Foreign Policy: Conceptual and Empirical Criticisms', in C. Blanco Sío-López and S. Muñoz (eds.), *Converging Pathways: Spain and the European Integration Process/Itinerarios Cruzados: España y el proceso de construcción europea*, Brussels: P.I.E Peter Lang, pp. 393–419.

Stavridis, S. and Kassimeris, C. (2013) 'Cyprus: The Limits of European Solidarity with a Small Member State', in M. Baun and D. Marek (eds.), *The New Member States and the European Union: Foreign Policy and Europeanization*, London: Routledge, pp. 142–158.

Tonra, B. (2000) 'Denmark and Ireland', in Ian Manners and Richard G. Whitman (eds.), *The Foreign Policies of European Union Member States, Manchester*, Manchester: MUP, pp. 224–242.

Torreblanca, J. (2001) 'La europeización de la política exterior española', in C. Closa (ed.), *La europeización del sistema político español*, Madrid: Istmo, pp. 483–511.

Tsardanidis, C. (2015) 'Greek Foreign Policy: The De-Europeanization Impact of the Economic Crisis', *Hellenic Studies/Etudes Helleniques*, Vol. 23, No. 1, pp. 59–81.

Tsardanidis, C. and Stavridis, S. (2005) 'The Europeanisation of Greek Foreign Policy: A Critical Appraisal', *Journal of European Integration/Revue d'Intégration Européenne*, Vol. 27, No. 2, pp. 217–239.

Tsardanidis, C. and Stavridis, S. (2011) 'Greece: From Special Case to Limited Europeanization', in R. Wong and C. Hill (eds.), *National and European Foreign Policies: Towards Europeanization*, London: Routledge, pp. 111–130.

Vaquer, J. (2004) 'The European Union and Western Sahara', *European Foreign Affairs Review*, Vol. 9, No. 1, pp. 93–111.

Walston, J. (2011) 'Italy as a Foreign Policy Actor: The Interplay of Domestic and International Factors', in Maurizio Carbone (ed.), *Italy in the Post-Cold War Order: Adaptation, Bipartisanship, Visibility*, Lanham: Lexington, pp. 65–80.

Wong, R. and Hill, C. (eds.) (2011) *National and European Foreign Policies: Towards Europeanization*, London: Routledge.

Wood, B. (1987) *Middle Powers in the International System: A Preliminary Assessment of Potential*, UNU-WIDER Working paper 11.

Part II

Foreign policy dimensions

6   Foreign policy and diplomacy

Simon Duke

Context: the times they are a-changin'

One of the more notable changes since the last Manners and Whitman (2000) volume has been that of the international system itself. The last volume appeared soon after the end of the Cold War in a period of relative strategic unconsciousness on the part of the EU and its Member States. It was the era of Francis Fukuyama's (1989) 'End of History' in which the universalization of Western liberal democracy had become the final form of human government. Although his thesis generated considerable discussion and disagreement, it contributed to the assumption that the EU would just have to continue being what it was, an exemplar of post-modern civility and normative advocacy. As the pinnacle of Western liberal democracy, the EU was decidedly post-modern and an example that the modern, and even pre modern, worlds would want to emulate (Cooper, 2003). These assumptions informed much of the EU's external actions, ranging from enlargement (where the message was quite explicit), to the European Neighbourhood Policy, launched in 2004, and the negotiation of a flurry of trade agreements during the course of the decade and a half. It also implied that, for much of this period. the EU was largely unaware of external perceptions of its own actions, as well as the lack of a clearly identifiable foreign *policy* persona.

There were, however, a number of potential wake-up calls that should have called the EU and its members to strategic consciousness. One such was the disagreements over military intervention in Iraq in 2003 provoked major divisions within the EU as well as across the Atlantic. Efforts were made to reach a shared view of the world, based largely (and deliberately) on the then applicable US National Security Strategy. This led to the 2003 *European Security Strategy* (ESS) which was notable for its lack of strategy which could have guided foreign policy – preferring, instead, to present a *tour d'horizon* with no real priorities or benchmarks (European Council, 2003). Other events which should have prompted more concern, such as the Russian intervention in Georgia in 2008, did little to change the continuation of policies and, importantly, the underlying assumptions about the surrounding world.

At other times between 2000 and the present, foreign policy assumed the back seat, especially the period 2008–14, which was also a time of spectacular global change. The period commenced with an attempt to revaluate the ESS that did little to correct the fundamental lack of strategic content but did add a number of new threats to the list. Overshadowing this was the onset of the global financial crisis and, soon thereafter, the EU's sovereign debt crisis. The resultant economic austerity across Europe removed foreign and security policy from the front of the EU's consciousness and that of its members. It was only in late 2013 that the European Council turned its attention back to security and, the following year, to foreign policy with the Russian annexation of Crimea in March 2014 and increased tensions in the Donbas region. The same year saw the emergence of Islamic State (IS) who, in June 2014, called for the establishment of a caliphate.

If there was a year of 'strategic consciousness' for the EU, and perhaps many of its members, it was 2014. Much of the focus was on events to the immediate east, in Ukraine, and to the south (IS), but the ongoing results (and disputes) over austerity, those over irregular migrants and refugees who often made perilous crossings of the Mediterranean, also cast doubt on some of the fundamentals of European integration. The events of 2014 in particular prompted soul searching in the EU institutions and, over a decade after the adoption of the ESS, recognition that there was need for more serious thought about the international system and the EU's role therein. The following year saw the appearance of a *Strategic Review* which noted that the world is now 'more connected, contested and complex' (EEAS, 2015). Tellingly, the Review also noted that 'we need a clear sense of direction. We need to agree our priorities, our goals and the means required to achieve them. . . . We need a common, comprehensive and consistent EU global strategy' (EEAS, 2015: 20).

The change in context between 2000 and the present is, in short, remarkable. The EU's role in the changing global constellations is far more uncertain than when the last volume appeared, as is that of its members, most of whom are unable to influence or shape the international system by themselves. At the same time, the foreign policy and diplomacy of the EU, which was based upon a strong normative message, revolving around democracy, multilateralism and the rule of law, was challenged by the rise of illiberal regimes, like China and Russia, who offered different models of engagement, many of which appear to have less strings attached than the highly bureaucratic and normatively laden approach of the EU. It has become a world where some of the EU's main trade partners are illiberal, where some of these same regimes have lifted millions out of poverty and one where the principal post-war multilateral structures are contested in terms of their representativeness and legitimacy.

In security terms, the fastest military growth is in Asia, as are many of the potential international flashpoints, like the South China Seas – where the EU and its members enjoy little ability to exert military pressure. The EU and its members continue to look nervously across the Atlantic following the 'pivot' or rebalance to Asia under the Obama administration, as well as the early days of the Trump administration – one of the implications being that the European allies would now have to assume more responsibility for security in their region at a time when austerity continues to ravage budgets throughout the EU. The Union also became ensnared in an increasingly delicate minuet with the US-designed Trans Pacific Partnership (TPP), which was signed in February 2016 but was not ratified due to US withdrawal from the agreement, and the Transatlantic Trade and Investment Partnership (TTIP). Both appeared to Beijing to be American-inspired containment policies, especially TPP from which China was excluded. The ongoing territorial disputes in the South East China seas, where the US is conducting 'freedom of navigation' passages by sea and air also threaten to escalate tensions between the world's main actors. The EU risks being caught in the middle.

Hence, it is against a more 'connected, contested and complex' world that we have to view the EU's foreign policy and diplomacy and that of its members.

The Member States: welcome to the jungle

The introductory chapter already noted that the enlargement of the EU is one of the main reasons for this new volume. In terms of foreign policy and diplomacy it has of course changed many of the procedural details and necessitated modernization of the institutions but has not necessarily altered some of the fundamentals outlined in the 2000 version of this volume. In this context, the post-2004 enlargement saw the addition of mainly smaller, post-Soviet states, who had not known the luxury of independent foreign policies until their independence. Poland was an exception as the largest of the newer EU entrants, as were the two Mediterranean members, Cyprus and Malta, who had developed non-aligned foreign policies since independence in the early 1960s.

In practical terms, the enlargement of the EU meant that, initially, they did not add notably to the wider experience of the older and larger Member States, or the EU generally, in large parts of the world such as Asia, Africa or Latin America, where they had between themselves little experience or representation. Estonia only has two embassies in Africa (Egypt and Morocco), Lithuania one (Egypt) and Latvia none. Slovenia and Cyprus both only have one embassy in Latin America (Argentina and Mexico respectively). Medium-sized diplomatic services, like the Czech Republic, offer slightly more representation but are still modest compared to the larger EU members. However, local experience tended to count for more, with Bulgaria's long experience in the Western Balkans, Romania's close relations with Moldova, Poland's long and often painful experience with Russia and its close relations with the Baltic states, all serving as beneficial examples of the accrual of knowledge and experience at the European level.

One of the more immediate benefits of EU membership for the newer members, especially following the introduction of the Lisbon institutional reforms, is that it represented considerable benefits in terms of deepening the knowledge and experience of *national* diplomats, which may otherwise not have been possible through the experience offered in their diplomatic services. Brian Hocking and David Spence (2005: 277) observed soon after enlargement that some foreign ministries 'have been strengthened by European integration', thus reminding us that relations between the national foreign ministries and the EU are rarely zero-sum games.

More generally, the newer Member States did little to change the patterns of intergovernmentalism and supranationalism established prior to the 2004 and 2007 enlargements. France, Germany and the United Kingdom continued to steer much of the CFSP and, in the cases of France and the United Kingdom, the CSDP. As in foreign policy, the newer members did not bring significant forces or equipment to the table, although in some cases there were valuable niche capabilities. It is hard to determine whether the travails of reaching agreement at twenty-eight, rather than fifteen, has led to more flexible forms of consultation and action. One example of this has been the growing use of 'minilateralism' where smaller groups, such as the 3+1 negotiating on Iran; the Weimar group (France, Germany and Poland) on Ukraine; or the Normandy Group (France, Germany and Russia) on the Minsk II Agreements are assumed to be negotiating in the interests of a wider group of members (see Balfour, 2015). There is, however, insufficient evidence to make a direct link between minilateralism and enlargement.

As with the older EU members, the impact of EU membership upon diplomacy has been dramatic for thirteen post-2004 members. One of the consequences of EU membership is far greater emphasis on *intra*-EU diplomacy, often with corresponding diversion or resources and manpower. It also had structural consequences, such as the heavy presence of embassies of one EU member to another member, European offices within foreign ministries and even central government offices for European affairs, as well as an increase in the exchange of information via the Correspondence Européenne (COREU) network (Bicchi & Carta, 2011). As an illustration of this the Czech Republic, with a medium-sized diplomatic service, maintains forty-one embassies or consulates in Europe, including one to every EU Member State. Even the smaller diplomatic services, like that of the Republic of Cyprus, maintain eighteen embassies to other EU countries. The need to consult, to coordinate, to refine national positions, to identify trade-offs and so forth have made considerable demands upon national foreign ministries and diplomatic services. This has led Karle Paschke of the German Foreign Office to suggest that 'over the past few years there has developed alongside bilateral and multilateral diplomacy a new type of "European diplomacy" with its own functions and characteristics that should be reflected also in the organization and functioning of our embassies *in* Europe' (Paschke, 2000).

The demands befalling national foreign ministries to coordinate their policies at the European-level are not of course a new phenomenon. This was evident in what Simon Nutall referred to as the emergence of a 'coordination reflex' in the context of European Political Cooperation (CFSP's precursor) (Nuttall, 1992: 56). The potential influence of any such reflex will be conditioned by practical considerations, such as the size of the foreign ministry, its diplomatic staff and the number of embassies and consulates. This, in turn, will have a bearing on the extent to which a Member State can pursue national foreign policy priorities that might be distinct from the EU level. The EU members with larger foreign ministries (France, Germany, Italy, Spain and the United Kingdom) might appear to have an advantage in this regard whereas, as has been suggested, the smaller to medium-sized EU members have to put a relatively higher emphasis upon intra-EU diplomatic representation, to the possible detriment of the number of diplomats in the field beyond Brussels.

Over time, the 'coordination reflex' has assumed different guises. With the growth of EU-level diplomacy, represented by those aspects of EU external action where the Union has either exclusive or shared competences, there is the constant need to take into account EU positions on a wide variety of topics, regions and countries in the formulation of national priorities and perspectives. This has made the routine meetings and information exchanges between national ambassadors and EU the heads of missions of considerable importance. Theoretically, this is a two-way street since it is equally important that the EU delegation staff are informed of emerging national positions and priorities, even if in practice the street is more one-way. This may slowly change, however, with the introduction of more secure communication networks in between the delegations and the local EU diplomatic representations. More importantly, there may also be gradual changes in mindsets as a result of a latter-day variant of Nuttall's coordination reflex.

In spite of this, there are still evident red lines regarding the parameters of national foreign policy that surface from time to time, which reminds us that the balance between the national and European levels of foreign policy is in constant flux. Obvious examples of red lines include Greek sensitivities over the name Macedonia, Germany's premature recognition of the sovereignty of Croatia and Slovenia, differences over Iraq, Franco-Spanish sensitivities over Perejil or the non-recognition of the independence of Kosovo by five EU members.

The arguments so far suggest that the coordination demands emanating from the European level have had a significant effect upon diplomatic practice at the national level. Most notably, they have influenced resource and manpower issues leading to a remarkable concentration of diplomatic representation between the EU Member States. What is less clear is whether the sum parts of this 'reflex' actually suggest the emergence of a distinctive European foreign policy, let alone common diplomacy? Put rather more provocatively, there seems to be acknowledgement of some form of Europeanisation, without a clear idea of what it is that is *Europeanising*. Is it a bottom-up process (as the coordination reflex implies), or is there evidence of a top-down (policy-inspired) variant of Europeanisation?

Policy and institutional change: musical chairs and standing foreign ministers

The Lisbon Treaty came into force on 1 December 2009. Most of the major changes introduced by the revised treaties (the Treaty on European Union and the Treaty on the Functioning of the European Union) related to the external relations of the EU. This followed expressions of concern, voiced at the Convention on the Future of Europe, at the beginning of the decade that the Union was not as coherent, effective or visible on the world stage as it could be.

One of the most notable changes was the introduction of the position of High Representative for Foreign Affairs and Security Policy, who was also made a Vice President in the Commission (henceforth HR/VP). This was intended to bridge the gap between the former Commissioner for External Relations and the High Representative for CFSP who had represented the *communautaire* and intergovernmental domains of EU external relations respectively. The HR/VP also wore an important third hat, that of chair of the Foreign Affairs Council (FAC).

Prior to the Lisbon Treaty, the relevant Council had been the General Affairs and External Relations Council (GAERC) but, largely due to complaints of overload from the foreign ministers of the Member States, was split into a General Affairs Council (GAC) and the FAC. The chairing of the FAC was also moved to the HR/VP instead of the rotating Presidency who nevertheless continued to chair the GAC. The bridging role of the HR/VP also serves as an important reminder that, even if CFSP remains rather distinct in the treaty itself, it remains heavily dependent upon the financial resources of the EU (i.e. the Commission's various external instruments).

The ongoing development of the GAC and FAC illustrates the ambivalent relationship between the two variants of the Council with, according to Piotr Kaczynski and Andrew Byrne, declining participation and prestige being attached to the GAC. Their analysis suggests that one of the main reasons for this is the introduction of a permanent chair of the European Council which severed the former link between the chairing of the European Council and the rotating Presidency of the Council. In the former system, 'the minister chairing GAERC played a key deputising and horizontal role for their head of state or government in the European Council' (Kaczyński & Byrne, 2011). The official website of the 2011 Hungarian Presidency commented:

> The role of the rotating Presidency has decreased significantly in the aspects of external relations with the adoption of the Lisbon Treaty, in the field of common security and defence policy, as well as common security and defence policy the tasks will be taken over by the High Representative and the European External Action Service.

In terms of national diplomacy, the advent of the HR/VP and the FAC and the evolution of the former delegations of the European Commission into EU delegations diminished the role of foreign ministers and foreign ministries, whilst also posing fresh coordination challenges for the national capitals. The introduction of the FAC, falling under HR/VP, meant that the chairing of the external relations preparatory groups is split between the rotating Presidency (GAC) and representatives of the HR/VP (FAC), following a Council decision on 1 December 2009. Although the Member States continue to be represented in the Council working groups, the reduction in the previous role of the rotating Presidency implies that the ability to steer, cajole or form coalitions has now slipped largely into the hands of the European External Action Service (EEAS) and the HR/VPs representatives. Although there are certain deputizing roles allocated to the rotating Presidency in external relations (such as representing the HR/VP to the European Parliament or its committees in the event that she is unavailable), the defenestration of the rotating Presidency in external relations has removed a significant source of national prestige and influence from EU external relations.

The introduction of the EEAS constitutes a further dramatic change. The Council decision of 26 July 2010 establishing the EEAS notes that the support role of the EEAS extends, not only to the HR role, but to her VP role as well and, beyond that, it shall also 'assist the President of the European Council, the President of the Commission, and the Commission in the exercise of their respective functions in the area of external relations' (European Council, 2010b, Art. 2(2)). The EEAS also has a significant role through its contributions 'to the programming and management cycle' of a number of significant financial instruments, including most of the main development instruments where most of the EU external relations budget is to be found (European Council, 2010b, Art. 6(9)). Although decisions on most of the financial instruments ultimately lie with the Commission (and the European Parliament), the involvement of the EEAS in the first three stages of the programming cycle (country allocations, country and regional strategy papers and national and regional indicative programmes) gives the Service considerable influence through the ability to link policies more closely with financial instruments.

When fully constituted (at the end of 2013) the total number of staff at all ranks including locally engaged staff in the delegations, numbered around 3,500 (of which the largest group are local agents, who number just over 1,000, and most of them are employed in delegations). This compares with around 10,000 for France, Germany and the United Kingdom; around 6,000 for Spain; 4,500 for Poland; and Belgium and the Netherlands around 3,000 each (Euractiv, 2010). But, for most of the post-2004 entrants, the Service is significantly larger than their diplomatic services.

The advent of full EU delegations, rather than Commission delegations, marked a further significant change. The EEAS consists of a central administration (the headquarters, in effect) and the 'Union delegations to third countries and to international organisations' (Council Decision, 2010, Art. 1 (4)). Since the Lisbon Treaty attributes legal personality to the EU (as opposed to just the EC), the delegations now represent *all* of the interests of the Union and its external relations – including CFSP (Council Decision, 2010, Art. 221 (1)). One of the immediate effects of this was the demand for experienced diplomats who had experience working on foreign and security portfolios (tasks normally associated with political officers). Due to the restricted competences of the former Commission delegations, there was relatively little preparation, quite aside from experience, in such roles. This is where national diplomats serving in the EEAS are making an important and perhaps groundbreaking contribution.

From the EEAS's inception in 2011, when it first opened its doors, it has featured national diplomats working on temporary assignment. Although national diplomats had served in EU prior to this, they had never done so in the numbers represented in the EEAS and in a manner that blurs the line between national and European levels of diplomacy to the same extent. Up to one-third of the staff at AD (senior administrative) level now come from the Member States in the form of temporarily assigned national diplomats, serving from 4 to 8 years in the headquarters or the delegations. In practical terms, this means around 300 national diplomats serve in the EEAS at the AD (administrative) level. In percentage terms, at the AD level, 33 per cent of Member State diplomats working in the EEAS staff were national diplomats, while they represented 45 per cent of AD posts in delegations and 25 per cent of AD posts at headquarters. Nationals of the post-2004 EU membership countries constitute around 20 per cent of staff at the AD level and 31 per cent of the diplomats recruited to the EEAS are from these thirteen Member States (EEAS, 2014).

What do these figures tell us? Perhaps unsurprisingly, national diplomats prefer to serve in delegations rather than the headquarters. This is where their skills as professional diplomats can be best harnessed. Whatever the merits of the former Commission and Council Secretariat staff, their primary qualifications lay in the ability to administer of complex funding programmes and a variety of support roles. They were not, in the general sense, trained to be diplomats. Skills, such as political reporting, consular protection, media relations or mediation, which are stock-in-trade for national diplomats, had to be learned by many officials who came from the Commission and Council Secretariat.

It is equally true that national diplomats entering the Service are often not sure of how the EU works, its procedures and practices. The working arrangements between the Commission services and the EEAS in relation to external relations issues alone, now reaches forty pages (European Commission Secretariat-General, 2012). Seasoned former Commission or Council Secretariats official can obviously complement the national diplomats in this regard. There is therefore a balance of skills and, at a certain level, 'Europeanisation' in the sense that skills and knowledge are acquired from one another. There is also an element of competition due to the fact that, since 1 July 2013, applications for posts are open to EEAS staff members, those of the EU institutions as well as Member States. Competition for positions is intense, although the initial years saw conspicuous efforts to ensure that at least every Member State had a national as a head of delegation and the role or women was actively promoted since, as with many national foreign ministries, they tended to be under-represented at the higher levels.

The overall result of the Lisbon Treaty changes was, according to David Spence, to lead to a 'major reassertion of bureaucratic politics, destined to keep Westphalian diplomacy alive and to produce even more turf battles and complexity' (Spence, 2012). It was precisely the impression that the changes being introduced by the Lisbon Treaty would introduce more assertive and stronger European-level foreign policy and diplomatic practices, at the expense of the Member States, that led to the adoption of two rather similarly worded declarations attached to the Final Act of the Lisbon Treaty, the second of which reads:

> [T]he provisions covering the Common Foreign and Security Policy including in relation to the High Representative of the Union for Foreign Affairs and Security Policy and the External Action Service will not affect the existing legal basis, responsibilities, and powers of each Member State in relation to the formulation and conduct of its foreign policy, its national diplomatic service, relations with third countries and participation in international organisations, including a Member State's membership of the Security Council of the United Nations.
>
> (Treaty on European Union: Declaration 14)

The wording of the declaration was inspired by the United Kingdom, who has detailed scrutiny in place in case of 'competence creep'. The British have been the most vociferous in terms of guarding against incursions against Westphalian diplomacy, but their position was not always supported. For instance, Austria expressed interest in strengthening the role of the delegations in consular protection and crisis management. A joint discussion paper from the Benelux countries supported a greater role in consular protection and a coordinating role for the EEAS in emergency evacuation or sheltering of EU nationals (Vogel, 2011).

This, however, was not a one-way street with criticism emanating from EU institutional quarters about national foreign policy, as well as about the possible effects of a greater national presence in the newly created EEAS. On the former, the then Commissioner for Enlargement and the European Neighbourhood Policy (ENP), Stefan Füle, noted with reference to the Arab Spring that, 'The difference between the Member States making bilateral deals and action by the European Union needs to be a lesson that we learn' (House of Lords, 2011). The clear implication of this statement is that the Member States generally pursue foreign policies that are motivated by narrow self-interest, while the EU intends to conduct a more normatively informed brand of external relations. On the latter point, Elmar Brok, one of the most influential MEP's in foreign policy circles, insisted that (EEAS) civil servants will have to be paid from the Community budget and that seconded staff from the Member States should be limited, 'Otherwise the Service would be flooded with national staff and would not represent the Union any more' and 'Member States would have the impression that the EEAS is their property' (Brok, 2010). This essentially rationalist approach suggests that the Lisbon changes represent a clear opportunity for foreign ministries to access more capabilities, information and expertise at the European level. This, in turn, will provide a bulwark against the erosion of the relative influence of foreign ministries and national diplomats portrayed earlier in this chapter.

At the more formal legal levels, attempts were made to try and clarify duties and expectations at the European level for diplomats joining the Service, under the admonishment that all EEAS personnel 'shall neither seek nor take instructions from any government, authority, organisation or person outside the EEAS or from anybody or person other than the High Representative' (Council Decision, 2010).

Action and change: more a case of dumping?

The advent of the EEAS created anticipation that the battle lines between the national and European levels of foreign policy and diplomacy were now drawn. Expectations were rife that the post-Lisbon changes would prove a venue for 'uploading' of national preferences to the European level or, conversely, of 'downloading' European agendas to the national level. Others suggested that the EU's hybrid variant of diplomacy is driven by competing preferences, logics and interests, as well as by shared goals and values, with the result that inherent contradictions, as well as complementarities, would restrict as well as foster blurring of lines between the national and European levels (Thomas & Tonra, 2012). Michael Smith observed that the 'EU seems fated to pursue a kind of rootless diplomacy, without the basis in concrete interests or material resources that might give it a harder core'. When combined with the 'sovereigntist diplomacy' of the Member States, we are left with what Smith aptly calls an 'uneasy coexistence' (Smith, 2011). Another popular theory, going back to Nuttall's 'coordination reflex', was that the interaction of national diplomats with the European-level of diplomacy will lead to increased socialization and bureaucratic adaptation at the national level (Pomorska, 2007). From this perspective, the issue would be the *extent* of any EU-inspired socialization of the national foreign ministries, their styles of operating and communication (Hill & Wallace, 1996).

What transpired was a good deal less exciting and nuanced than these suggestions, since there were often elements of both 'uploading' and 'downloading', as well as some evidence of socialization, along with evident difficulties in generating an *esprit de corps* for the new EEAS (Börzel, 2002: 193). One example would be the well-known interest of Portugal and Spain in Latin America, which could be seen superficially as a form of uploading. But, by the same token the EEAS delegations have benefitted from the experience of these countries in the region. It is also true that the newer Member States, who may have little experience in Latin America, have reaped national benefits for their diplomatic services from and through exposure via temporary assignment to the delegations, diplomats from many of the newer Member States who may have little experience (or even representation) in Latin America will reap national benefits for their diplomatic services from their exposure to the nominally European-level of diplomacy. Similar examples could be chosen in Africa, with the French experience, or parts of the Middle East, with the British experience.

Another form of diplomatic exchange, which could be misconstrued as 'uploading', might in fact constitute a form of diplomatic 'dumping'. This realist interpretation of socialization posits that states are ultimately driven by a balance-of-power logic. When primary interests (national security and bilateral trade for instance) clash with secondary interests (those that are not motivated purely by security and power maximization), states will always sacrifice the latter. It is in the interests of members to upload or dump issues on the Union's plate when there is a reluctance to address them at the national level. This would apply, in particular, to many normative issues such as minority rights, human rights, the treatment of women and so forth, especially as these issues threatened to traverse the first-level interests of Member States. A more sophisticated interpretation of dumping was forwarded by Christopher Bickerton (2011: 35) who suggested that 'EU foreign policy functions as a way of legitimizing Europe's retreat from power politics. Lying behind this retreat is the decline of distinctive national foreign policy strategies, which Member States offset by turning to Europe'.

The EU's delegations tend to enjoy more weight with the Member States in those locations where the Union already has a substantial role and presence, such as the Western Balkans or Addis Ababa (the seat of the African Union). In some areas, like trade, many Member States are reluctant (see Balfour & Raik, 2013) to transfer tasks to the EEAS, especially given the growing involvement of national diplomats in national trade promotion. In most other non-CFSP areas, 'alignment among Union Delegations and Member States' embassies occurs almost spontaneously and no real coordination is necessary' (Wouters *et al.*, 2013: 70). There are, nevertheless, some traditional no-go areas like consular affairs (with the slight exception of specific aspects of consular protection) where there is generally strong resistance to any enhanced role for the EU. This is not, though, a role that the Service has sought for itself and the former High Representative Catherine Ashton was commendably frank when she observed that 'this is an area for which the Service has very limited resources in headquarters (concentrating on coordinating crisis response) and no resources or expertise in delegations' (EEAS Review, 2013: 12).

National diplomats serving in the EEAS are not, as was suspected in the early days of the Service, Trojan horses intent on uploading national preferences. By the same token, former Commission officials serving in the EEAS are not ideologues intent on imposing federalist mindsets on their hapless national counterparts. Instead, a more subtle middle ground of diplomacy is emerging that is neither purely European nor national in character – described earlier as a *European level* of foreign policy which implies that it is accessible and mouldable by both. It is, however, important to note that foreign policy in the national context is far from static and is undergoing its own existential crisis. Foreign ministers and, with them, their ministries have been in decline for decades since many items appearing on national external agendas are shaped by powerful external forces that are beyond the ability of any single institution to influence. As Stefan Lehne (2015: 3) observed, 'The constituency for influencing foreign policy has broadened, and many more governmental and non-governmental stakeholders have emerged, while the traditional foreign policy elites have lost influence'. The weakening of the influence of hitherto powerful foreign ministries, with the possible exceptions of France, Germany and the United Kingdom, has reduced their role increasingly to that of coordination of the various ministries, governmental and non-governmental organizations, involved in the international agenda.

The possibility of subtle forms of socialization taking place, along with equally refined versions of uploading and downloading, is better reflected in the idea of modified intergovernmentalism or transgovernmentalism (Duke & Vahnoonacker, 2006: 181; Balfour & Raik, 2013: 164). The key concept behind transgovernmentalism is that there are 'direct interactions among sub-units of different governments that are not controlled or closely guided by the policies of cabinets or chief executives of those governments' (Keohane & Nye, 1974: 43). In distinction to simple intergovernmentalism, transgovernmental interactions occur at multiple levels and not solely at head-of-government or ministerial levels. Intergovernmentalism also tends to discount the possibility of any significant socialization leading to cooperation in foreign and security policy and the possibility that Brussels-based national officials may not always see eye-to-eye with their capital-based national counterparts and superiors. Transgovernmentalism, by way of contrast, posits that networks of officials interact at lower levels and that they can in turn shape policy outcomes (Slaughter, 2004).

Ultimately, transgovernmentalism suggests the possibility of a common European diplomatic space that is complementary, but not antagonistic, to national diplomacy. The formation of such a common diplomatic space goes beyond mere intergovernmentalism (which suggests that any such space is circumscribed by what the national elites permit or not) by indicating that the existence of networks at the European level of foreign and security policy play an integral role in shaping options and policy outcomes. In some cases, like the Sahel or the Horn of Africa, the roles played by the EU have facilitated joined-up approaches to regions that most Member States, or groupings thereof, would find it hard to replicate. The metamorphosis of national foreign ministries into coordination bodies is a process that is enhanced by budgetary and resource issues. The growing importance of joined-up approaches, going beyond foreign policy to include different aspects of external actions, is replicated at the national level to varying degrees. For example, in the case of the Netherlands, the Ministry of Foreign Affairs (*Buitenlandse Zaken*) is responsible for not only foreign relations but also European cooperation and international development. The advent of 'smart power' in the United States also stresses the need to link soft and hard power, or diplomacy, development and defence. These are all trends mirrored in the EU with the adoption of a comprehensive approach to external action at the end of 2013, with the possibility of greater engagement within and across the supranational and intergovernmental levels. In time, this may lead to growing sharing of resources and even diplomatic representation. There are already a few examples, but they remain the exception to the rule for the time being. Even if the political logic of joined-up approaches has yet to fully sink in, the possibility of continuing austerity and spending cuts, including for foreign and defence ministries, might just do the job.

Conclusions

This chapter has attempted to paint a picture showing some of the ways in which the European and national levels of foreign policy and diplomacy interact. It has rejected the notion that this is a zero-sum process since there will always be the need for national foreign policy and diplomacy to support it. The point of EU-level diplomacy, foreign and security policy, has never been to compete with or replace national policies but to complement them. It is in the grey zone between the national and supranational that contention as well as cooperation occurs. The European-level of diplomacy has been making quiet and largely unheralded progress, on the one part due to the prominence of 'global goods' in foreign policy, such as climate change, where the EU has a strong role to play, but also due to the corrosive effects of trying to do the same with less at the national and European levels. The ability to conduct foreign policy in the grey zone depends increasingly on joined-up approaches.

In diplomatic terms, the grey zone is also present in the form of the number of national diplomats who are directly engaged with the EU institutions, notably the EEAS. Member States and the EU institutions compete vigorously for positions therein and, as such, the former are clearly invested in the Service and have clear motivation for it to work – if only to avoid the opprobrium of failure that would reflect negatively upon the Member States themselves. There is little doubt that the Member States have brought necessary diplomatic skills to the Service and its delegations in particular. By the same token, EEAS officials have helped national diplomats negotiate the sometime byzantine procedures of the EU. The sheer time and energy required to coordinate and shape positions has also witnessed the growth of intra-EU foreign policy and coordination in the field between the EU delegations and the local diplomatic representation of the Member States.

The importance of knowledge of the procedures and pitfalls should not be underestimated in the EU context where diplomacy tends to be process-driven. It is often more important to demonstrate that funds were appropriately and legally dispersed of, than it is to demonstrate substantive change on the ground. Similarly, it is something of a diplomatic virility symbol to boast of the sixty-eight dialogues with China, for instance, with less emphasis upon what they actually produce. The manner of engagement with third parties and the resultant agreements also tend to be formulaic, with all of the appropriate normative elements ('essential clauses') but less subsequent attention to whether these are actually upheld, which can result in awkward forms of moral relativism.

As it stands, European-level diplomacy coexists with national diplomacy, but the impact of the financial crisis on national foreign ministries suggest that national foreign policies and diplomatic practice are in transition and contend with multiple uncertainties. The blurring of the lines between the national and European levels of foreign policy and diplomacy is further complicated by the increasing arbitrariness of any distinction the internal and external aspects of policies; border control, climate change, counter-terrorism or the fight against organized crime are neither purely external or internal matters. The blurring of levels and practices implies that it is increasingly improbable that a diplomat from any of the EU Member States can serve through his or her entire career without a knowledge of the EU's positions on certain policy areas or, increasingly, the expectation of service at the European level. It is just as true that the process of constant consultation, coordination and involvement of national diplomats at the European level has made those engaged in the Union's external actions more conscious of national interests and limits.

The EU's Member States will have to reach their own conclusions about the changing world around them and where they fit in. One of the overarching issues for the EU is a resolution to its existential crisis regarding its role on the global stage, for this has never been satisfactorily defined. More of the same, or drift, is clearly not called for in a world where the EU has only a marginal role in shaping the international system. The growing moral relativism of EU-level foreign policies goes to the core issues of self-identity, purpose and visibility. The appeal to the EU's founding myth as the common bond to motivate foreign policy and diplomacy has been challenged by internal doubts about the legitimacy and direction of European integration. The essence of this was put well, if rather unfortunately, by the previous President of the European Council, Herman van Rompuy (2010), who announced to the press, 'Until now, we had strategic partners, now we also need a strategy'. The challenge for the Member States is the extent to which they wish to encourage the emergence of the EU as a strategic actor in its own right. The next edition of this volume will be able to tell more accurately whether this challenge marked the reassertion of national control and direction of foreign policy, or whether it enabled the EU to develop a complementary but nonetheless distinct foreign policy, with the diplomatic skills to support it.

Bibliography

Balfour, R. (2015) 'Europe's Patchwork Foreign Policy Needs More Than a Few New Stitches', *Policy Brief*, Vol. 2, No. 6 (July), German Marshall Fund of the United States, available at www.gmfus.org/file/6336/download, date accessed 5 August 2016.

Balfour, R. & Raik, K. (2013) 'The EEAS and National Diplomacies', *EPC Issue Paper No. 73*, March, available at http://www.epc.eu/documents/uploads/pub_3385_the_eeas_and_national_diplomacies.pdf, date accessed 5 August 2016.

Bicchi, F. & Carta, C. (2011) 'The EU as a Community of Practice: Foreign Policy Communications in the COREU Network', *Journal of European Public Policy*, Vol. 18, No. 8, 1115–1132.

Bickerton, C.J. (2011) *European Foreign Policy: From Effectiveness to Functionality* (Basingstoke: Palgrave-Macmillan).

Börzel, T.A. (2002) 'Pace-Setting, Foot-Dragging, and Fence-Sitting: Member State Responses to Europeanization', *Journal of Common Market Studies*, Vol. 40, No. 2, 193–214.

Brok, Elmar (2010) 'EEAS: clarify staff issue before starting formal negotiations', quoted in European Parliament Press Release, 4 May 2010 REF 201005031PR74031, available at http://www.europarl.europa.eu/sides/getDoc.do?pubRef=-%2F%2FEP%2F%2FNONSGML%2BIM-PRESS%2B20100503IPR74031%2B0%2BDOC%2BPDF%2BV0%2F%2FEN, date accessed 5 August 2016.

Cooper, R. (2003) *The Breaking of Nations: Order and Chaos in the Twenty-First Century* (London: Atlantic Books).

Council Decision (2010) *Council Decision Establishing the Organisation and Functioning of the European External Action Service*, Council of the European Union, (11665/1/10 REV 1, Brussels, 20 July 2010), available at http://register.consilium.europa.eu/pdf/en/10/st11/st11665-re01.en10.pdf, date accessed 28 November 2010.

Duke, S. & Vahnoonacker, S. (2006) 'Administrative Governance in the CFSP: Development and Practice', *European Foreign Affairs Review*, Vol. 11, 163–182.

EEAS (2014) *EEAS Human Resources Report 2014*. EEAS.MDR.C.1 - HR Policy and Coordination, available at https://eeas.europa.eu/sites/eeas/files/hr_report_2014_final_en.pdf, date accessed 25 July 2016.

EEAS (2015) *The European Union in a Changing Global Environment: A More Connected, Contested and Complex World* (Brussels: European External Action Service), available at http://www.eeas.europa.eu/top_stories/2015/150627_eu_global_strategy_en.htm, date accessed 28 November 2015.

EEAS Review (2013) *EEAS Review*, available at http://eeas.europa.eu/library/publications/2013/3/2013_eeas_review_en.pdf.

Euractiv (2010) 'Top Officials Start Building EU Diplomatic House', 20 October 2010, available at http://www.euractiv.com/future-eu/top-officials-start-building-eu-news-499185, date accessed 1 June 2014.

European Commission (2006) *Europe in the World – Some Practical Proposals for Greater Coherence, Effectiveness and Visibility, Communication to the European Council*, COM (2006) 278 FINAL, Brussels, 8 June.

European Commission Secretariat-General (2012) *Working Arrangements between Commission Services and the European External Action Service (EEAS) in Relation to External Relations Issues*, SEC (2012) 48, 13 January.

European Council (2003) *A Secure Europe in a Better World: European Security Strategy*, Brussels, Belgium, 12 December.

European Council (2010a) 'The Challenges for Europe in a Changing World', Address by Herman van Rompuy, President of the European Council to the College of Europe, Bruges, PCE 34/10, 25 February.

European Council (2010b) 'Council Decision of 26 July 2010 Establishing the Organisation and Functioning of the European External Action Service (2010/427/EU)', *Official Journal of the European Union*, L 201/30, 3 August 2010, Art. 2(2) and Art. 6(9).

European Council (2011) *EU Statements in Multilateral Organisations*, United Kingdom Statement to the Council, 15855/11 ADD2, Brussels, 21 October.

European Union (2007) *Consolidated version of the Treaty on the Functioning of the European Union*, 13 December 2007, 2008/C 115/01, available at http://www.refworld.org/docid/4b17a07e2.html, date accessed 5 November 2014.

Fukuyama, F. (1989) 'The End of History', *The National Interest* (Summer), pp. 3–18.

Hill, C. & Wallace, W. (1996) *The Actors in Europe's Foreign Policy* (London: Routledge).

Hocking, B. & Spence, D. (2005) *Foreign Ministries in the European Union: Integrating Diplomats* (Basingstoke: Palgrave-Macmillan).

House of Lords (2011) Defence and Development Policy Inquiry on Libya, *The Select Committee on the European Union Foreign Affairs*, Evidence Session No. 2. Heard in Public. Questions 16–21, Tuesday, 15 March, Witnesses: Stefan Füle, p. 6.

Kaczyński, P.M. & Byrne, A. (2011) 'The General Affairs Council: The Key to Political Influence of Rotating Presidencies', *Centre for European Policy Studies*, No. 246, July 2011.

Keohane, R. & Nye, J. (1974) *Transnational Relations and World Politics* (Cambridge: Harvard University Press).

Lehne, S. (2015) *Are Prime Ministers taking over EU Foreign Policy?*. Carnegie Endowment for International Peace, available at http://carnegieendowment.org/files/prime_min_for_policy.pdf, date accessed 11 April 2017.

Manners, I. & Whitman, R.G. (2000) *The Foreign Policies of the European Union Member States* (Manchester: Manchester University Press).

Nuttall, S.J. (1992) *European Political Coordination* (Oxford: Clarendon Press).

Paschke, K.Th. (2000) *Report on the Special Inspection of 14 German Embassies in the Countries of the European Union* (Berlin, Germany: Federal Foreign Office, September).

Pomorska, K. (2007) 'The Impact of Enlargement: Europeanization of the Polish Foreign Policy? Tracking Adaptation and Change in the Polish Ministry for Foreign Affairs', *The Hague Journal of Diplomacy*, Vol. 2, No. 1, 25–51.

Slaughter, A. (2004) *A New World Order* (Oxford: Princeton University Press).

Smith, M. (2011) *European Responses to U.S. Diplomacy*, EUSA Conference, Boston, MA, 2–5 March.

Spence, D. (2012) 'The Early Days of the European External Action Service: A Practitioner's View', *The Hague Journal of Diplomacy*, Vol. 7, No. 1, 115–134.

Thomas, D.C. & Tonra, B. (2012) 'To What End EU Foreign Policy? Contending Approaches to the Union's Diplomatic Objectives and Representation', *The Hague Journal of Diplomacy*, Vol. 7, No. 1, 11–29.

Van Rompuy, H. (2010) *EU External Relations*, European Council, The President, Brussels, PCE 186/10, Brussels, 14 September.

Vogel, T. (2011) 'Split Emerges over Remit of EU's Diplomatic Service', *European Voice*, 26 May, available at http://www.politico.eu/article/split-emerges-over-remit-of-the-eus-diplomatic-service/.

Whitman, R. (2005) *Changing Landscape in Transatlantic Relations, New Member States and Candidate Countries between Brussels and Washington*, Prague, Czech Republic, Europeum, 23 September.

Wouters, J., Hoffmeister, F. & Ruys, T. (2007) *The United Nations and the EU: An Ever Stronger Partnership* (The Hague: TMC Asser Institute).

Wouters, J., Baere, D., Vooren, B., Raube, K., Odermatt, J. Ramopoulos, T., Sanden, T. and Tanghe, Y. (2013) *The Organisation and Functioning of the European External Action Service: Achievements, Challenges And Opportunities*. EXPO/B/AFET/2012/07, available at http://www.europarl.europa.eu/RegData/etudes/etudes/join/2013/457111/EXPO-AFET_ET(2013)457111_EN.pdf, date accessed 15 June 2016.

7 Security and defence

Ana E. Juncos

Introduction

In one of the first surveys of European Union (EU) Member States' defence policies, the authors concluded that the impact of the EU on national defence policies had been limited thus far, in particular comparing it to other pressures on national autonomy and, they added, it would probably continue to be limited in the future (Howorth and Menon, 1997). Similarly, in Manners and Whitman's volume, 'national security' was identified as one of the inner 'rings of specialness' or *domains privés,* the one policy area Member States have tried to keep at arms' length from the EU's sphere of influence. But, even in this case, it was still possible to contemplate some fluidity and change over time towards a more Europeanised policy (Manners and Whitman, 2000). A lot has changed since then, not least with the launch of the Common Security and Defence Policy.[1] Over the last fifteen years, the CSDP has been increasingly institutionalised and Brusselised and has become operational. The enlargement of the EU in 2004, 2007 and 2013 also brought with it new challenges to the EU's security and defence policy, namely regarding how to integrate new Member States' security concerns. While the Lisbon Treaty did not revolutionise this policy domain (security and defence remain firmly in the hands of national governments), it introduced reforms with a view to improving CSDP decision-making and operational capabilities which had the potential to further Europeanise this policy.

This chapters tracks changes in the EU's security and defence policy in order to determine whether national security and defence policies are becoming more 'Europeanised' or, by contrast, more 'nationalised' over time. The chapter argues that intra-EU cooperation – intergovernmental cooperation within the CSDP framework – constitutes the main mode of cooperation within this policy area, although there still remains significant bilateral cooperation with other Member States and with other security actors outside the EU (mainly the US and NATO). More recently, perceptions of heightened insecurity among the Member States have led to more pragmatism and bilateralism, all of which do not bode well with cooperation at the EU level, although Brexit and the election of President Donald Trump in the United States might reinvigorate calls for more supranational defence cooperation.

The chapter proceeds as follows. It first provides a brief overview of the main changes at the EU level that have led to the establishment of a Common Security and Defence Policy. Although the roots of these changes can be found in the post-Second World War context, since the beginning of the 2000s though, change has been rapid, accompanied by an impressive level of institutionalisation and allowing the EU to become a security actor in its own right. The rest of the chapter then examines three areas where Member States have played a key role: the institutionalisation of CSDP, the emergence of a strategic culture at the EU level and capability development.

Context and policy change: towards a common security and defence policy?

Cooperation in security and defence matters has been one of the most recent additions to the process of European integration, with the CSDP only been formally adopted at Nice (2000). Since then, this policy has developed with the 'speed of light' in the words of former High Representative Javier Solana. The CSDP has become one of the key instruments in the EU's toolbox, best exemplified by the launch of more than thirty-five missions since its establishment. This rapid development might obscure the fact that, for decades, cooperation in security and defence matters remained a taboo in European circles, especially after the failure of the European Defence Community in the 1950s. The Treaty establishing a European Defence Community (1952) sought to find a way to ensure the rearmament and re-integration of Germany to the emerging West European security framework with the creation of a supranational organisation in the field of security and defence. The rejection of this proposal by the French Assembly in 1954 and the creation of the North Atlantic Treaty Organisation (NATO) initiated a period of almost forty years where security and defence issues were excluded from the integration project.

Several developments during the 1970s and 1980s facilitated the incorporation of security and defence issues back into the EU's agenda. With the London Report (1981), the possibility of discussing issues bearing on the political aspects of security was foreseen. The Single European Act (1986) then allowed for cooperation on the political and economic aspects of security. As integration gathered speed in other areas and Europe was faced with the challenge of how to deal with the consequences of the fall of the Berlin Wall and the collapse of Yugoslavian Federation, the Maastricht Treaty (1992) stated as one of the EU's objectives 'the implementation of a common foreign and security policy including the progressive framing of a common defence policy, which might in time lead to a common defence' (Article J.4.1, TEU Maastricht). But, at that time, no common defence bodies were contemplated; only a compromise could be reached to declare the, until then, dormant Western European Union (WEU) both the 'European pillar of the Atlantic Alliance' and the 'defence arm of the EU' (*Declaration on Western European Union,* TEU Maastricht). In 1992, the WEU Ministerial Council identified the so-called Petersberg tasks including 'humanitarian and rescue tasks, peacekeeping tasks, tasks of combat forces in crisis management, including peacemaking'. Despite these initiatives, cooperation on defence issues among Member States remained almost unthinkable as security and defence continued to be perceived as a core attribute of national sovereignty.

The failure to deal with the war in Bosnia (1992–5) led to new calls for a more active role of the EU in security affairs. At the Amsterdam summit, there were plans to merge the WEU into the EU, but Britain and the neutral countries blocked them. All that could be agreed was an unspecified commitment to 'enhance cooperation' between the two organisations, but the role of the WEU in the emergence of an EU security capacity in actuality continued to be insignificant. However, by incorporating the Petersberg tasks, the Treaty reflected the operational ambitions of the EU. These developments paved the way for the incorporation of a security dimension in the integration project; but of course, they alone do not explain the move from the WEU to an *autonomous* EU defence and security policy. This step only came at the end of the 1990s as a response to the war in Kosovo.

The Kosovo crisis (1998–9) is often seen as a critical juncture in the development of an EU security and defence policy, with the Franco-British summit at Saint-Malo (1998) kicking off the process of building an autonomous EU military capacity. At Saint-Malo, the UK and France agreed that

> The Union must have the capacity for autonomous action, backed by credible military forces, the means to decide to use them, and a readiness to do so, in order to respond to international crises.

> (ISS-EU 2000)

Later developments in Kosovo created a window of opportunity to consolidate and justify what had been agreed at Saint-Malo. At the Cologne European Council (June 1999), it was decided to formally establish, within the CFSP pillar, some EU security structures: a Political and Security Committee (PSC), an EU Military Committee (EUMC) and the EU Military Staff (EUMS). For its part, on the civilian side, CIVCOM, the Committee on Civilian Aspects of Crisis Management, was established in June 2000. At the Laeken Council, in December 2001, the CSDP was declared operational.

The Iraq War can also be considered as a critical juncture for the institutional development of the CSDP. First, it served as a window of opportunity and led to the establishment of a civ/mil cell and the launch of the European Defence Agency (EDA), adding new impetus to the Brusselisation of the CSDP. Second, the *European Security Strategy* was adopted in December 2003 (see section on strategic culture), in the aftermath of the rift over the US intervention in Iraq. Since then, the CSDP has become a reality, with the EU being involved in civilian crisis management – including police missions, civilian administration, training missions and rule of law missions – but also the deployment of several military missions (for more on this, see Chapter 8 on military conflict management). More importantly, one of the EU's key strengths has been its ability to combine both civilian and military instruments and to develop a 'comprehensive approach' to conflict management.

The Lisbon Treaty did not alter this institutional path, although it led to a reorganisation of the crisis management bodies under the authority of the new position of High Representative for Foreign Affairs and Security Policy, supported by the European External Action Service (EEAS) (see Chapter 6, 'Foreign Policy and Diplomacy'). The Lisbon Treaty states that '[t]he Union's competence in matters of common foreign and security policy shall cover all areas of foreign policy and all questions relating to the Union's security, *including the progressive framing of a common defence policy that might lead to a common defence*' (Article 24.1, TEU Lisbon, emphasis added). The Treaty has expanded the Petersberg tasks to include 'joint disarmament operations, humanitarian and rescue tasks, military advice and assistance tasks, conflict prevention and peacekeeping tasks, tasks of combat forces in crisis management, including peace-making and post-conflict stabilisation' (Article 43.1, TEU Lisbon). Moreover, a solidarity clause – in the event of a terrorist attack or a natural or man-made disaster – and a mutual assistance clause have been laid down in the Treaty.

From this brief summary, one might be tempted to think that Member States have finally embraced collective defence at the EU level. But is this really the case? In order to answer this question, the following sections examine policy performance and seek to identify policy action and policy change *of* and *by* the Member States in three key areas: the institutionalisation of CSDP, the formation of a common strategic culture and capability development.

Policy performance: action and change

Institutions

The Member States have played a key role in the design of CSDP institutions by uploading their institutional preferences at the EU level. Most of the initial institutional design (the creation of a political and security committee, a military committee and an EU military staff) was done in the corridors of the ministries of defence of the 'Big Three' (UK, France and Germany), although the Nordic countries were also very active in advancing the civilian component of the CSDP, as discussed later in this section. For instance, most of the institutional engineering took place during the German Presidency that led to the Cologne European Council in 1999. For its part, the establishment of the PSC was a British proposal. The idea behind was to create an intergovernmental committee that would allow national ministries to keep firm control of the nascent CSDP. This proposal which ultimately led to the establishment of the PSC, however, resulted in the need for the Foreign and Commonwealth Office to adapt to this new structure, which provides evidence of the Europeanisation of British foreign policy (Allen and Oliver, 2006).

CSDP institutionalisation also exposes the long-standing political disagreements between the Member States regarding the role of the EU in security and defence issues, in particular, between Europeanists and Atlanticists, between NATO and non-NATO members (including neutral countries) and between Member States with different conceptions about the role civilian and military instruments should play in security issues (see next section). These divergences have shaped the institutional design of the CSDP (Howorth, 2007; Menon, 2011). For instance, the issue of a dedicated Operational Headquarters (OHQ) at the EU level has long been a matter of controversy amongst the Member States. More specifically, France has supported the creation of the Headquarters as a necessary step for an autonomous CSDP. Other support states included Poland, Belgium, Italy and Spain. For its part, the UK has been a key veto player, opposing the establishment of this facility. The UK has long argued that the creation of an autonomous OHQ would duplicate existing capabilities in NATO and in the Member States. The compromise agreed in 2003 included the establishment of an EU cell in SHAPE and liaison arrangements between the EU and NATO, as well as the establishment of a Civ-Mil Cell and an Operations Centre. The latter was to be activated at the request of the Council on a case-by-case basis. However, the establishment of an autonomous OHQ has continued to be an issue of contention in recent years (for example during the Polish Presidency of the Council in 2011), although subsequent initiatives have failed because of lack of support among some Member States and, in particular, strong opposition from the UK. The exit of the UK from the EU might provide an opportunity in this regard.

It is wrong to assume, however, that the institutionalisation of CSDP has been led only by the largest Member States. In the case of civilian crisis management, it has been the Nordic countries that have taken a leading role. Not only did they put civilian crisis management firmly on the agenda at Cologne (despite French opposition), but they have also played a key role in specific initiatives aimed at strengthening the decision-making and operational capabilities of the civilian dimension of the CSDP. For instance, the creation of a committee for civilian crisis management (CIVCOM) agreed at Helsinki (1999) was a Swedish proposal (Jakobsen, 2009: 93; Lee-Ohlsson, 2009: 129).

While uploading of Member States preferences has been an important driver of CSDP institutionalisation, one also needs to account here for the importance of learning from other international organisations. In particular, it can be argued that the EU's military structures and procedures were largely modelled on NATO's (Juncos, 2011). NATO procedures are already familiar to most of the EU Member States – twenty-two of the twenty-eight EU Member States are also NATO members and another five Member States are Partnership for Peace members. The decision-making process for the launching of a military operation follows the so-called Crisis Management Procedures (Council of the EU, 2003), which describe the procedures for the planning, implementation and evaluation of an EU crisis management operation (military or civilian in nature) and which are very similar to that of NATO. The same can be said of the EU's rules of engagement that follow closely those that are used in NATO operations. When it comes to EU institutional structures, resemblance between the EU and NATO is also striking: a politico-military body at ambassadorial level, assisted by a Military Committee composed by the representatives of the Chief of Defence and supported by a military staff. Although some differences remained – for instance the Political and Security Committee (PSC) did not originally have a permanent chair as is the case with the North Atlantic Council – ,[2] the Member States had certainly taken NATO decision-making institutions into account when establishing these structures.

Notwithstanding the role Member States have played in the institutionalisation of the CSDP, supranational elements – including the involvement of EU institutions such as the High Representative and EEAS – and the development of informal norms has meant that the Member States are no longer fully in control of this policy as an intergovernmentalist perspective might suggest. Characteristic of the institutional path followed by the CSDP is its increasing Brusselisation. According to Dave Allen (1998: 54), Brusselisation involves a physical move of the European foreign policy governance system to Brussels or, in other words, 'a gradual transfer, in the name of consistency, of foreign policy-making authority away from the national capitals to Brussels'. In other words, with the establishment of the CSDP, Ministries of Foreign Affairs and Ministries of Defence have increasingly been displaced from the core of the decision-making process by the intergovernmental bodies located in Brussels. The administrative structures created in Brussels have also taken over the planning and day-to-day implementation of CSDP operations, especially in the area of civilian crisis management. However, as far as military operations are concerned the Member States are still reluctant to give up control in this area, as exemplified by the controversy over the EU OHQ (discussed earlier in this section). Last, but by no means least, Brusselisation has facilitated processes of socialisation of national officials within CSDP institutions (Cross, 2010; Howorth, 2010; Juncos and Pomorska, 2011), which in turn has led to the Europeanisation of security and defence policies. Continuous interactions within these institutions have helped foster a common approach towards security and defence issues, as discussed in the following section.

Finally, the need to deal with an increasing security and defence network at the EU level has raised important institutional challenges for Member State organisations that had to adjust to this new multilevel context. The Europeanisation of Ministries of Foreign Affairs has been well documented elsewhere (Allen and Oliver, 2006; Hocking and Spence, 2002; Pomorska, 2007). Even Ministries of Defence, that until recently were relatively insulated from European integration processes, have had to adapt to the CSDP. Participation in CSDP operations, while voluntary, requires efficient decision-making and implementation procedures at the national level. For some Member States, this has meant the need to establish some administrative positions and coordination mechanisms anew. For instance, in the case of Belgium, although most of the structures were in place to participate in multinational military operations, some changes were required in the Ministry of Defence, including the creation of a new dedicated unit (Vanhoonacker and Jacobs, 2010: 569). More challenging was its participation in EU civilian crisis management operations, where Belgium lacked the experience and necessary institutional structures. Here, the launch of the CSDP resulted in significant administrative reforms (Vanhoonacker and Jacobs, 2010: 574–75). Even bigger Member States had to adapt to the demands of the EU security and defence policy. In the UK, new posts and responsibilities were created to deal with the CSDP, with a new Assistant Director for the EU being established. The Ministry of Defence also seconded staff to the UK Permanent Representation in Brussels to support the UK's Military Representative at the EU Military Committee (Aktipis and Oliver, 2011: 80). Defence officials are now more involved in the planning and conduct of EU operation as the UK provides one of the national operational headquarters for EU operations – the operational headquarters in Northwood has been used for Operation EU NAVFOR Atalanta, the first EU's antipiracy operation. However, as Aktipis and Oliver (2011: 81) note, despite 'the gradual adaptation of the MoD [Ministry of Defence] to the demands of EU security and defence policymaking', there remains 'a continued reluctance to establish institutional machinery or pathways completely independent of existing NATO ones'. How Brexit will affect the UK's institutional structures remains to be seen. More remarkable is the case of Denmark. According to Olsen (2011: 14), 'Europeanisation of the Danish defence administration has taken place in spite of the fact that the country has opted-out from the European defence cooperation since the adoption of the Maastricht treaty'. Despite the fact that Denmark does not participate in the implementation of EU military operations, a section within the Ministry of Defence deals with EU issues. Interestingly, almost as many officials work now on EU-related issues than on NATO's defence planning (Olsen, 2011: 22).

Overall, while CSDP institutions remain firmly intergovernmental in character, the increasing Brusselisation and socialisation processes have facilitated the Europeanisation of national institutions. Member States (in particular, the Big Three and the Nordics) have played a key role shaping the direction of the CSDP institutionalisation through the uploading of their preferences both in military and civilian crisis management, but they have not escaped unscathed from these processes. They have had to adapt their administrations to the challenge of effectively coordinating their policies at the EU level and participating in CSDP operations.

Strategic culture

Some of the problems that hinder cooperation on security and defence issues can be explained by the fact that the EU is made up of twenty-eight Member States, each with its own national interests, threat perceptions and strategic culture. Jolyon Howorth (2007: 205) notes that '[t]he emergence of an EU strategic culture is one of the greatest challenges facing ESDP'. Christoph Meyer (2005: 528) broadly defines strategic culture as 'the socially transmitted, identity-derived norms, ideas and patterns of behaviour that are shared among a broad majority of actors and social groups within a given security community, which help to shape a ranked set of options for a community's pursuit of security and defence goals'. By examining the emergence of a European strategic culture, this section seeks to detect whether there are any elements of convergence among national security and defence policies.

There are several authors that argue that the possibility of the EU developing a strategic culture remains a remote prospect (Lindley-French, 2002; Rynning, 2003). Not only the EU lacks the key attributes of nation-states, but as long as national strategic cultures remain as strong as they currently are, the Union will be unable to agree on a coherent approach to the use of force. Other authors, however, remain more optimistic. While convergence might be gradual and slow, there is evidence that the national strategic cultures of EU Member States are adapting to an emerging European strategic culture as a result of constant interaction at the EU level (Biava et al., 2011; Giegerich, 2006; Meyer, 2006). In his seminal work on this topic, Meyer argues that (2006: 11) 'strategic cultures in Europe have become more similar concerning the use of force . . . , the acceptance of the EU as an appropriate framework for security and defence policy and the de-prioritization of the partnership with the United States', but, he adds, this 'does not mean that national beliefs have become fully compatible . . . only that differences have narrowed'.

The key expression of such an embryonic strategic culture was the *European Security Strategy* (ESS) adopted by the December 2003 European Council. According to Howorth (2007: 202), the ESS 'inevitably constitutes something of a compromise between different cultures and approaches among the EU's member states'. While external events played a key role in facilitating agreement, Meyer (2006) also notes the role CSDP institutions played in promoting the convergence of Member States' strategic cultures through socialisation processes. In the aftermath of the Iraq invasion, the Member States managed to agree to a document identifying the key threats and challenges the EU was confronted with, namely terrorism, proliferation of weapons of mass destruction, regional conflicts, state failure and organised crime. The ESS calls on the EU to be a more active, more coherent and more capable international actor and to develop a 'strategic culture that fosters early, rapid, and when necessary, robust intervention'. In December 2008, the Council adopted a report on the implementation of the ESS. While the 2008 report noted some progress (e.g. the success of further enlargement, improvements in the security situation in the Balkans), the previously mentioned threats remained and new threats were identified – cybersecurity, energy security, climate change and piracy. The security context was also compounded by the shift in the balance of world power from the West to 'the rest'.

Despite the ESS providing a framework for how the EU does security, problems remained. Neither did the ESS offer a strategic vision for the EU in the twenty-first century (Howorth, 2011) nor did it rank threats according to their priority, which made it difficult to allocate resources effectively and to determine how to achieve the goals identified in the ESS. These problems together with new geopolitical realities such as the return of power politics to Europe with the crisis in Ukraine, the refugee crisis and the emergence of ISIS in the Middle East led to calls for a new EU Global Strategy. High Representative Federica Mogherini presented this new strategy to the EU Member States in June 2016.

While the ESS and the EU Global Strategy constitute steps in the right direction, there are still important divergences among the strategic cultures of the Member States. National strategic cultures have been shaped over centuries by many factors including geography (e.g. neighbours, permeability of borders); history (wars, invasions, colonial experiences); and the degree of national unity. Thus, it is not surprising that a European strategic culture might take some time to emerge as national strategic cultures might obstruct such a development. The main dichotomies in European security are between allies and neutrals, Atlanticists and Europeanists, big and small Member States and old and new Member States (see Howorth, 2002; Keukeleire and MacNaughtan, 2008; Merlingen, 2012). What is interesting, however, is that these dichotomies have not remained unchanged over time and that some of them have been eroded by Europeanisation processes. Let us examine each of these in turn.

A traditional divide in European security has been between NATO Member States and the neutral countries (Ireland, Finland, Sweden, Austria and Malta). However, not only do the neutral Member States have different concepts of neutrality, but these concepts have substantially changed since the end of the Cold War. According to Merlingen (2012: 112), '[t]hey have adapted their neutrality doctrines and reduce them to their essential core – not to join a military alliance'. Alongside changes in the post-Cold War security context, membership in the EU has also played a part in this transformation. According to Manners and Whitman (2000: 248), Finland, Austria and Sweden used EU membership to adapt from neutrality to post-neutrality. In the case of Ireland, Devine (2009: 467) shows how the positions of the main Irish political parties shifted away from 'fundamental neutrality to embrace treaty-based progress towards a maximalist EU ESDP'. She argues that part of these changes have been the result of the participation of these parties in national governments and their involvement in referendum campaigns but warns that this shift has not taken place at the level of the domestic opinion.

Initially, there were some concerns that the neutrals could hamper the development of an EU security dimension. Discussions about the integration of the WEU into the EU at Amsterdam were opposed by Finland and Sweden, which saw this as an attempt to introduce collective defence into the Treaty. Their (successful) proposal to incorporate the Petersberg tasks into the Amsterdam Treaty thus needs to be seen in this light. However, since the launch of the CSDP, the neutrals have played a positive role in its development. For instance, Sweden was a strong advocate of conflict prevention and managed to persuade other Member States to adopt an action programme for conflict prevention at the Göteborg European Council in June 2001 (Björkdahl, 2008). The neutrals have also participated in EU military crisis management. Not only have they been important contributors to CSDP operations, but they have participated in the EU Battlegroups. A Nordic Battlegroup was presented in November 2004 (Lee-Ohlsson, 2009: 131). However, the neutrals have opposed any moves towards common defence, a case in point being the mutual defence clause contained in the Lisbon Treaty.

The latter refers to another limitation that results from the divide between Atlanticists and Europeanists, which we now turn to. At the heart of the Saint-Malo Declaration lay a pragmatic compromise between the Atlanticists (represented by the UK) and the Europeanist camp (represented by France) on how to develop the military dimension of the EU. Germany has sought to mediate between these two camps by cooperating closely with France on European initiatives but, at the same time, maintaining strong relations with the US. Other Member States such as Belgium, Italy and, to some extent, Spain, have supported France in its objective to develop an autonomous European defence policy.

Ultimately, the UK and France agreed to give the EU autonomous capabilities, but for different reasons. The decision at Saint-Malo has to be explained by looking at changes in the British policy on these issues (the main brake on EU defence policy hitherto). Undoubtedly, the Bosnian experience served as a trigger for a change in the strategy of the British elites. The Kosovo crisis and the unlikely prospect of the Europeans responding to this crisis also motivated Tony Blair to take a different stance on European security and defence policy from that of his predecessors (Howorth, 2004: 221). With this initiative, Blair was also trying to maintain leadership and influence in Europe, at a time when the UK had opted for self-exclusion from the euro (Latawski and Smith, 2003). Nonetheless, Blair and his advisors did not change their standpoint about NATO and the role it should play in European security. They believed that NATO should not be weakened by the development of the EU's security and defence capabilities; on the contrary, this development should serve to revitalise the Alliance. In this way, the UK also sought to strengthen the UK's special relationship with the US, which had repeatedly asked for Europe to share its burden in the management of European security but was still suspicious of an autonomous EU defence initiative. This position differed from that of France that saw the Saint-Malo initiative as a way to develop an autonomous European defence capability. France's aim was to transform the EU into Europe's key security actor to reduce Europe's dependence on the US. As a result of this 'constructive misunderstanding' (Howorth in Bickerton et al., 2011: 3), ambiguity has surrounded the development of the CSDP since then, and there is still no agreement on the end state goal.

It is important to note, however, that France has become less reluctant to cooperate with NATO in recent years and that it has adopted a much more pragmatic attitude vis-à-vis the Alliance (Irondelle, 2008), which culminated with France's return to NATO's integrated command in 2009 during the Presidency of Nicolas Sarkozy. The participation of France in NATO's Libya mission in 2011 was also reflective of this change of attitude. The UK and France jointly led the international intervention in Libya and closely cooperated within a NATO framework, showing how the positions of the two countries have come closer in recent years. Russia's annexation of Crimea and the revival of NATO's security role in Europe has also had the unintended consequence of bridging the gap between Atlanticists and Europeanists. Increasing insecurity in the continent and beyond has led to some EU Member States (such as Spain, Italy or Sweden) to become more pragmatic (and realistic) in their approach to CSDP (Fiott, 2015). For its part, the US has increasingly supported any European capability development initiative regardless of the framework they take place in, also putting pressure on the UK to do the same. All these developments have gradually narrowed this strategic gap but have not led to more cooperation at the EU level in turn. However, Brexit and the advent of the new Donald Trump Administration in the US might increase calls for further integration in the security and defence area.

Linked to the previous dichotomy is the divide between new and old Member States. The 2004 and 2007 enlargements were seen by many as shifting the balance between Atlanticists and Europeanists in favour of the former. Some observers suggested the term 'instinctive Atlanticism' to describe the orientation of the new Member States' security and defence policies. For the new Member States, Atlanticism and close relations with the NATO were viewed as their main security guarantor against a resurgent Russia. Poland and the Baltic states have been the most committed Atlanticists, mainly owing to historical reasons and national security concerns. Despite these initial attitudes vis-à-vis the CSDP, after accession, the new Member States have eagerly participated in the development of the CSDP. The major contributors to CSDP (both civilian and military) operations have been Poland and Romania, followed by Bulgaria and Hungary. They have contributed to the EU battlegroups and to CSDP military and civilian operations, although in some cases their contribution has been mainly symbolic. Yet, there remain some disagreements with other Member States about where CSDP initiatives should focus on (the Eastern vs. the Southern neighbourhood) and NATO is still considered to be the key security organisation in Europe, particularly after the crisis in Ukraine.

A small versus large Member States divide can also be mentioned here. Given the differences in financial resources and military power between the Big Three (France, the UK and Germany) and the rest of the EU Member States, it is not surprising that the largest Member States have played a key role in shaping CSDP, especially its military component. But, as mentioned earlier, between the Big Three, there are important differences as far as national security identities are concerned: attitudes towards force projection, military instruments and relations with the US, to name but a few. This has prevented them from forming a coherent front in security and defence matters. For their part, many of the smaller EU Member States have rejected any form of *directoire* by the big Member States whether in the form of a Franco-German axis, the EU3 (France, Germany and the UK) or any other enlarged grouping (e.g. the Contact Group).

Last, EU Member States also disagree on how to use force in international relations. While some countries such as the UK and France have adopted a model of expeditionary warfare, other Member States (in particular, some of the new Member States) still perceive territorial defence as a first-order objective for their armed forces as the best way to prevent any potential invasion from Russia. Although these differences still remain, the former communist states have made significant reforms to adapt their armed forces to the requirements of participation in international peacekeeping missions, including abolishing conscription in favour of professional armed forces. However, in the eve of Russia's intervention in Ukraine, some Eastern countries are focusing again on territorial defence, with Lithuania re-introducing conscription in 2015. Germany, for its part, has traditionally rejected the use of force abroad and has been reluctant to participate in out-of-area missions (Daehnhardt, 2011). While there are some signs of change in the case of Germany, with a move towards a professional army in recent years, change is still slow – as its refusal to participate in the Libyan mission demonstrates. Member States also differ on the emphasis they put on civilian versus military instruments. While France has traditionally emphasised the role of military instruments in international security and sought to develop the military dimension of CSDP, Nordic countries have, on the other hand, stressed the importance of civilian instruments (see earlier in this chapter). As a way of compromise, the EU has developed over time a 'comprehensive approach', and the official rhetoric has sought to emphasise the EU's ability to deploy both civilian and military instruments. Finally, there still remains the issue of nuclear weapons, which has been so far kept out of the CSDP agenda by the UK and France, which are the only EU Member States with such a nuclear deterrence capacity (Howorth, 2007). To date, this remains a '*domain reservé*'.

In sum, there are still strong patterns of nationalisation in this area as a result of the legacies of national strategic cultures. Yet, a combination of external events and interactions at the EU level has facilitated a convergence among Member States' threat perceptions and have resulted in a number of changes in Member States strategic cultures, eroding some of the traditional dichotomies in European security. Whether this amounts to a 'common' European strategic culture is however a different matter. Growing security threats have meant that some Member States are opting for more pragmatic and bilateral solutions, but common European responses are still the preferred option. As far as capability development is concerned national and bilateral initiatives tend to prevail.

Capabilities

Since the end of the Cold War, European armed forces have undergone a profound transformation from an approach based on territorial defence (mass mobilisation of conscripts, reliance on artillery and tanks) to force projection or expeditionary warfare (deployable forces, strategic transport facilities, high-technology warfare). However, this has been far from an easy process, especially in the context of declining defence budgets. Although collectively the EU is the second biggest defence spender in the world with €210 billion spent in 2014 after the US (€460) (EPSC, 2015), there are still many capability gaps and shortages in EU defence. The gap between the US and the EU has continued to grow in recent years as a result of defence cuts in Europe (military spending in Europe has fallen 9 per cent since 2005) but especially in relation with other military powers (China's defence spending has increased 137 per cent in the same period). Former NATO Secretary-General Anders Fogh Rasmussen warned that 'Europe risks becoming increasingly adrift from the United States. If Europe becomes unable to make an appropriate contribution to global security, then the United States might look elsewhere for reliable defence partners' (quoted in IISS, 2012: 75). There are also important differences among the Member States, with France and the UK being the third and fourth top spenders in the world respectively, and these two countries plus Germany and Italy amounting to almost 70 per cent of the total EU defence spending; by contrast, the fifteen lowest-spending EU members states only 'account for 7.7 per cent of the 'EU budget" (Howorth, 2011: 209). Moreover, only a handful of Member States meet the 2 per cent of GDP benchmark recommended by NATO. The problem lies not only in the amount of money European states spend in defence but in the quality of their armed forces. Of a total of almost two million troops, only 10 to 20 per cent are deployable abroad (Merlingen, 2012: 80). Other shortfalls in European capabilities relate to lack of intelligence, surveillance and reconnaissance (ISR) systems, strategic air-lift and air refuelling capabilities and unmanned vehicles. While EU leaders produced ambitious plans to address these shortfalls at the European Council of December 2013, delivering on them has proved problematic.

Ultimately, the key problem results from the fact that there is no agreement among the Member States regarding the question of what kind of armed forces are required and for what purpose. National defence remains a sensitive issue because it is considered to be 'the last bastion of sovereignty' (Howorth, 2007). Member States are thus reluctant to cooperate on defence projects that might entail giving up national autonomy. It is not surprising then that defence procurement in the EU remains mostly a national affair. For instance, in 2013, 83 per cent of all procurement spending occurred at the national level (EPSC, 2015). This state of affairs is also maintained by the fact that the defence sector is excluded from the rules of the EU's single market. This situation has led to twenty-eight different national defence strategies, duplication and fragmentation in the area of capability development.

Throughout the 1990s, Europeans sought access to US assets through NATO in order to meet some of the weaknesses of European capabilities and to facilitate the deployment of European forces in crisis management operations. The Berlin Plus arrangements were first agreed at the 1996 NATO's meeting in Berlin to make NATO assets and capabilities (headquarters, communication and information systems, access to NATO's planning capabilities and intelligence) available for a possible WEU operation. A series of formal agreements for EU–NATO cooperation were adopted between December 2002 and March 2003. For instance, in Bosnia, NATO provided planning and logistical support, the Headquarters for the EUFOR Althea mission (Camp Butmir) and support for secure communications.

The real step forward was taken with the launch of the CSDP and EU Member States' commitment to develop a serious military capacity to assume responsibility for crisis management tasks. Cooperation on armaments procurement and capability development has been achieved through the so-called Headline Goals and the EDA. Hence, there is evidence of intra-EU cooperation in this area. The purpose of the Helsinki Headline Goal agreed in 1999 was to draw a 'force catalogue', from which the EU could draw appropriate resources from the Member States for future operations. However, this entirely voluntary exercise was found to be insufficient to ensure the necessary level of capabilities available to the Union. A new Headline Goal 2010 was thus adopted which put more emphasis on interoperability, deployability and sustainability rather than on the raw number of troop contributions. Part of this process was the establishment of the EDA in 2004, tasked to develop EU defence capabilities in the area of research, acquisition and armaments in order to enhance interoperability and rationalise the defence expenditure of the Member States. Since then, the focus has been on pooling and sharing projects in order to boost European capacity building. However, as noted by Batora (2009), some of the problems confronted by EDA have to do with the fact that this organisation is a 'flashpoint' of different institutional logics about how integration in the defence area should be achieved – between the logic of supranational regulation and intergovernmental networking, defence sovereignty versus defence resources, Europeanist versus a Euro-Atlanticist logic and between the logics of liberalisation and Europeanisation of the defence market. As a result, 'EU states continue to act as twenty-[eight] sovereign states rather than as a collective actor' (Merlingen, 2012: 84).

Undoubtedly, cooperation at the EU level and the need to implement CSDP operations – which require force projection capabilities – has put pressure on the Member States to modernise their armed forces. Both in the cases of Spain and Poland, Europeanisation has acted as a key driver of military reform (Barbé, 2011; Pomorska, 2011). The need to implement the Battlegroup concept also had a transformational effect on Member States armed forces, for instance, in the cases of Sweden and the Czech Republic, although prevailing ideas on defence reform determined the degree of Europeanisation (Jacoby and Jones, 2008; Lee-Ohlsson, 2009). Even Denmark might not be immune to these pressures despite the opt-out from European defence cooperation. According to Olsen (2011), the reorganisation of Danish armed forces was done in a way to ensure that Denmark was able to participate in EU operations if and when defence opt-out was lifted. However, he also admits that 'it is an open question if the reorganisation is the result of Europeanisation or if it is the result of other types of pressure as for example from globalisation or more likely from NATO' (Olsen, 2011: 20). In other cases, Member States have been slower to implement reforms. For a long time, Germany was reluctant to Europeanise in the area of capabilities, to modernise the Bundeswehr – which remained a conscript-based force – and its weapons and logistics systems, as well as to implement the Battlegroup concept (Daehnhardt, 2011: 41). This was an important obstacle to the development of strong capabilities at the EU level (Merlingen, 2012: 106). However, more recently, there have been signs of change in this regard. In 2011, Germany announced the professionalisation of its armed forces and abolished conscription.

Aside from Europeanisation pressures, when it comes to capability and doctrine development, the Member States are also subject to 'NATO-ization' (Merlingen, 2012: 96). Member States need to transform their armed forces in the context of the Prague Capabilities Commitment (2002), the Lisbon Capabilities Package (2010) and the implementation of NATO's new Strategic Concept, which was adopted in November 2010 at the Lisbon summit. NATO's operation in Libya in 2011, however, still revealed many shortcomings and, in particular, the fact that small European states do not have the capabilities to contribute to this type of operations. There is also strong cooperation between EU Member States and the US in the area of defence capabilities. The UK, for instance, benefits from close cooperation with the US in the field of research and development (Batora, 2009). Italy's FINMECCANICA group has also signed procurement projects with the US to provide the US armed forces with air-lift planes C-27J and to provide US Presidents with EH101 helicopters (Brighi, 2011: 65).

Finally, Member States have sought to cooperate bilaterally as symbolised by the Defence and Security Cooperation Treaty signed by the UK and France in 2010 and the 2014 Anglo-French Brize-Norton Summit. Other examples of joint procurement include an agreement between Sweden and Norway to develop and order self-propelled artillery systems and discussions between Romania, Bulgaria and Croatia to jointly purchase F-16s (IISS, 2012: 75).

Even though civilian crisis management developed in the shadow of EU military capabilities, soon after the launch of the CSDP, Member States pledged to further enhance the capabilities of the EU in this area. At the Feira Council (2000), the EU Member States identified four priority areas in civilian crisis management (policing, rule of law, civilian administration and civil protection) and made a commitment to provide 5,000 police personnel by 2003. EU civilian crisis management missions have become one of the most important contributions of the EU to international security. Significant improvements have also taken place in recent years with the adoption of the Civilian Headline Goal 2010 for civilian capabilities. The Lisbon Treaty also foresees the creation of a start-up fund for these operations. As mentioned earlier, in this area, the Nordic EU Member States have taken the lead. For example, Sweden was one of the Member States successfully sponsoring the previous Civilian Headline Goal 2008, and together with Germany, it launched the idea of the Civilian Response Teams (Lee-Ohlsson, 2009: 129). However, despite progress in recent years, difficulties in recruiting personnel from the Member States to meet the EU's operational needs are still a source of concern (Korski and Gowan, 2009).

In sum, since the end of the Cold War, Member States armed forces have undergone a profound transformation from their focus on territorial defence to expeditionary warfare. These changes have been propelled by transnational cooperation both within the EU and NATO. Domestic factors and the consequences of the economic and financial crisis have added pressure to these reforms and the need to find synergies and savings within an EU framework or through other bilateral or multilateral initiatives. Not even the largest Member States can afford to maintain full spectrum capabilities. Thus, pooling and sharing has become a pragmatic option for many Member States to improve their capabilities in the context of declining defence budgets. However, Member States are still reluctant to give up autonomy in exchange for capabilities and this will remain a delicate balance for Member States. Yet, European defence cooperation may well emerge as the only viable option to ensure that Member States can play a key role in international security in the years to come.

Conclusion

The aim of the chapter was to determine the extent to which Member State security and defence policies have shaped and been shaped by developments in this policy area. It has shown that the dominant mode of cooperation in this field is increasingly that of intra-EU cooperation (Europeanisation, mode II), that is, an intergovernmental mode of cooperation within the CSDP framework facilitated by processes of Brusselisation and socialisation. Within this framework, Member States have sought to upload their preferences at the EU level (whether in terms of institutions, security strategy or capabilities), but they have not been immune to the impact of European integration processes as they had to adapt their own organisations, policies and capabilities to pressures at the EU level. There are no signs, however, that Member States are going to move towards intra-EU integration any time soon. Furthermore, while cooperation at the EU level is more intense than ever before, it coexists with significant bilateral cooperation with other Member States outside the CSDP context (mode III) and with other security actors outside the EU, mainly the US and NATO (mode IV). Bilateral cooperation and an increasing role for NATO have been the result of growing security threats in the EU's Eastern and Southern neighbourhoods.

While it is fair to say that the UK and France have played a leading role in the institutionalisation of CSDP and in the area of capability development, it is also worth noting the activist role of the Nordic countries in relation to conflict prevention and civilian crisis management. Germany could be considered somewhat a laggard state because its uneasiness regarding the use of military force, although it has played a more constructive role in the development of the EU's civilian dimension. Small and medium Member States have also lagged behind regarding the development of military and civilian capabilities. Finally, the UK has used its veto to halt particular developments (such as the setup of an EU permanent Headquarters), but so did France until recently when it came to the establishment of closer relations with NATO. In principle, Brexit could thus remove a veto player in the CSDP area. While important disagreements about the use of force remain among EU Member States, future CSDP developments are more likely to be the result of pragmatic security concerns than ideological battles.

Notes

1 Prior to the Lisbon Treaty, the CSDP was referred to as the European Security and Defence Policy (ESDP); for the sake of consistency, the term CSDP is used throughout the chapter.
2 With the entry into force of the Lisbon Treaty, the PSC is chaired by a permanent representative of the High Representative (Declaration 9, TEU Lisbon).

Bibliography

Aktipis, M. and Oliver, T. (2011) 'Europeanization and British Foreign Policy', in C. Hill and R. Wong (eds.), *National and European Foreign Policies: Towards Europeanization*, London: Routledge, 72–92.
Allen, D. (1998) 'Who Speaks for Europe? The Search for an Effective and Coherent External Policy', in J. Peterson and H. Sjursen (eds.), *A Common Foreign Policy for Europe? Competing Visions of the CFSP*, London and New York: Routledge, 41–59.
Allen, D. and Oliver, T. (2006) 'The Foreign and Commonwealth Office', in I. Bache and A. Jordan (eds.), *The Europeanization of British Politics*, Basingstoke: Palgrave Macmillan, 52–66.
Barbé, E. (2011) 'Spain and Europe: Mutual Reinforcement in Foreign Policy', in C. Hill and R. Wong (eds.), *National and European Foreign Policies: Towards Europeanization*, London: Routledge, 131–49.
Batora, J. (2009) 'European Defence Agency: A Flashpoint of Institutional Logics', *West European Politics*, Vol. 32, No. 6, 1075–98.
Biava, A., Drent, M. and Herd, G. (2011) 'Characterizing the European Union's Strategic Culture: An Analytical Framework', *Journal of Common Market Studies*, Vol. 49, No. 6, 1227–48.
Bickerton, C.J., Irondelle, B. and Menon, A. (2011) 'Security Cooperation beyond the Nation State: The EU's Common Security and Defence Policy', *Journal of Common Market Studies*, Vol. 49, No. 1, 1–21.
Björkdahl, A. (2008) 'Norm Advocacy: A Small State Strategy to Influence the EU', *Journal of European Public Policy*, Vol. 15, No. 1, 135–54.
Brighi, E. (2011) 'Resisting Europe? The Case of Italy's Foreign Policy', in C. Hill and R. Wong (eds.), *National and European Foreign Policies: Towards Europeanization*, London: Routledge, 57–71.
Council of the EU (2003) Suggestions for procedures for coherent, comprehensive EU crisis management, Doc. 11127/03, 3 July, Brussels.
Cross, M.K.D. (2010) 'Cooperation by Committee: The EU Military Committee and the Committee for Civilian Crisis Management', in *Occasional Paper* 82, Paris: EU Institute for Security Studies.
Daehnhardt, P. (2011) 'Germany in the European Union', in C. Hill and R. Wong (eds.), *National and European Foreign Policies: Towards Europeanization*, London: Routledge, 35–56.
Devine, K. (2009) 'Irish Political Parties' Attitudes towards Neutrality and the Evolution of the EU's Foreign, Security and Defence Policies', *Irish Political Studies*, Vol. 24, No. 4, 467–90.
EPSC (2015) 'In Defence of Europe: Defence Integration as a Response to Europe's Strategic Moment', *EPSC Strategic Notes*, Issue 4, June 2015. Available at http://ec.europa.eu/epsc/pdf/publications/strategic_note_issue_4.pdf, last accessed 29 February 2016.
European Council (2003) *A Secure Europe in a Better World*. European Security Strategy. Report presented by the High Representative for the CFSP to the Brussels European Council, 12 December, Brussels.
Fiott, D. (ed.) (2015) 'The Common Security and Defence Policy: National Perspectives', in *Egmont Paper* 79, Brussels: Egmont Institute. Available at http://www.egmontinstitute.be/wp-content/uploads/2015/05/ep79.pdf, last accessed 29 February 2016.

Giegerich, B. (2006) *European Security and Strategic Culture*. Baden-Baden: Nomos.

Hill, C. (1993) 'The Capability-Expectations Gap, or Conceptualizing Europe's International Role', *Journal of Common Market Studies*, Vol. 31, No. 3, 305–28.

Hocking, B. and Spence, D. (eds.) (2002) *Foreign Ministries in the European Union: Integrating Diplomats*. Basingstoke: Palgrave Macmillan.

Howorth, J. (2002) 'The CESDP and the Forging of a European Security Culture', *Politique Européenne*, Vol. 8, No. 1, 88–108.

Howorth, J. (2004) 'Discourse, Ideas and Epistemic Communities in European Security and Defence Policy', *West European Politics*, Vol. 27, No. 2, 211–34.

Howorth, J. (2007) *Security and Defence Policy in the European Union*. Basingstoke: Palgrave Macmillan.

Howorth, J. (2010) 'The Political and Security Committee: A Case Study in "Supranational Intergovernmentalism"?', in *Les Cahiers Européens 01/2010*, Centre d'Etudes Européennes, Paris: Sciences Po.

Howorth, J. (2011) 'The EU's Security and Defence Policy: Towards a Strategic Approach', in C. Hill and M. Smith (eds.), *International Relations and the European Union*, 2nd ed., Oxford: Oxford University Press, 197–225.

Howorth, J. and Menon, A. (1997) *The European Union and National Defence Policy*. London: Routledge.

IISS, International Institute for Strategic Studies (2012) *The Military Balance 2012*. London: IISS.

Irondelle, B. (2008) 'European Foreign Policy: The End of French Europe?', *Journal of European Integration*, Vol. 30, No. 1, 153–68.Jacoby, W. and Jones, C. (2008) 'The EU Battle Groups in Sweden and the Czech Republic: What National Defense Reforms Tell Us about European Rapid Reaction Capabilities', *European Security*, Vol. 17, Nos. 2–3, 315–38.

ISS-EU (EU Institute for Security Studies) (2000) 'Joint Declaration Issued at the British-French Summit, Saint-Malo, France, 3–4 December 1998'. Available at: https://www.consilium.europa.eu/uedocs/cmsUpload/French-British%20Summit%20Declaration,%20Saint-Malo,%201998%20-%20EN.pdf. Accessed: 10 June 2016.

Jacoby, W. and Jones, C. (2008) 'The EU Battle Groups in Sweden and the Czech Republic: What National Defense Reforms Tell Us about European Rapid Reaction Capabilities', *European Security*, Vol. 17, No. 2, 315–38.

Jakobsen, P.V. (2009) 'Small States, Big Influence: The Overlooked Nordic Influence on the Civilian ESDP', *Journal of Common Market Studies*, Vol. 47, No. 1, 81–102.

Juncos, A.E. (2011) 'The Other Side of EU Crisis Management: A Sociological Institutionalist Analysis', in E. Gross and A.E. Juncos (eds.), *Making Sense of EU Conflict Prevention and Crisis Management: Institutions, Policies and Roles*, London: Routledge, 84–100.

Juncos, A.E. and Pomorska, K. (2011) 'Invisible and Unaccountable? National Representatives and Council Officials in EU Foreign Policy', *Journal of European Public Policy*, Vol. 18, No. 8, 1096–114.

Keukeleire, S. and MacNaughtan, J. (2008) *The Foreign Policy of the European Union*. Houndmills: Palgrave Macmillan.

Korski, D. and Gowan, R. (2009) *Can the EU Rebuild Failing States? A Review of Europe's Civilian Capacities*. London: European Council of Foreign Relations.

Latawski, P. and Smith, M.A. (2003) *The Kosovo Crisis and the Evolution of Post-Cold War European Security*. Manchester: Manchester University Press.

Lee-Ohlsson, F. (2009) 'Sweden and Development of the European Security and *Defence* Policy: A Bi-Directional Process of *Europeanization*', *Cooperation and Conflict*, Vol. 44. No. 2, 123–42.

Lindley-French, J. (2002) 'In the Shade of Locarno? Why European Defence Is Failing', *International Affairs*, Vol. 78, No. 4, 789–811.

Manners, I. and Whitman, R. (eds.) (2000) *The Foreign Policies of the European Union Member States*, Manchester: Manchester University Press.

Menon, A. (2011) 'Power, Institutions and the CSDP: The Promise of Institutionalist Theory', *Journal of Common Market Studies*, Vol. 49, No. 1, 83–100.

Merlingen, M. (2012) *EU Security Policy: What It Is, How It Works, Why It Matters*. Boulder and London: Lynne Rienner.

Meyer, C. (2005) 'Convergence towards a European Strategic Culture? A Constructivist Framework for Explaining Changing Norms', *European Journal of International Relations*, Vol. 11, No. 4, 523–549.

Meyer, C.O. (2006) *The Quest for a European Strategic Culture: Changing Norms on Security and Defence in the European Union*. London: Palgrave Macmillan.

Olsen, G.R. (2011) 'How Strong Is *Europeanisation*, Really? The Danish *Defence* Administration and the Opt-Out from the European Security and *Defence* Policy', *Perspectives on European Politics and Society*, Vol. 1, No. 1, 13–28.

Pomorska, K. (2007) 'The Impact of Enlargement: Europeanization of Polish Foreign Policy? Tracking Adaptation and Change in the Ministry of Foreign Affairs', *The Hague Journal of Diplomacy*, Vol. 2, No. 1, 25–51.

Pomorska, K. (2011) 'Poland: Learning to Play the Brussels Game', in C. Hill and R. Wong (eds.), *National and European Foreign Policies: Towards Europeanization*, London: Routledge, 167–88.

Rynning, S. (2003) 'The European Union: Towards a Strategic Culture?', *Security Dialogue*, Vol. 34, No. 4, 479–96.

Vanhoonacker, S. and Jacobs, A. (2010) 'ESDP and Institutional Change: The Case of Belgium', *Security Dialogue*, Vol. 41, No. 5, 559–81.

8 Member State policy towards EU military operations

Annemarie Peen Rodt

Context

Since 2003, the European Union (EU) has deployed military operations in Macedonia, Bosnia-Herzegovina, Democratic Republic of Congo, Central African Republic, Chad, Somalia and Mali.[1] The EU's military endeavours are particularly important to this enquiry, as they indicate a significant change in the cohort of Member States' foreign policy towards, within and beyond the Union, which until the turn of the millennium had been considered by its Member States, amongst others, a predominantly 'civilian power' (Manners, 2005; Whitman, 1998). The significance of such policy change and action merits a chapter that delves deeper into Member State foreign policy specifically related to EU military operations. The rationale for the following is thus to unpack intra-EU foreign policy and its effect on the external defence dimension of the Union, which, as argued by Duke (in Chapter 6), has been under-researched so far. This contribution takes as its starting point the conclusions from Chapters 6 and 7, which identified a series of political, diplomatic and institutional changes in European foreign, security and defence policy. These, this chapter posits, have made way for *change* and *action* of Member State foreign policy towards the EU military operations investigated in this chapter.

Foreign policy is understood in accordance with Christopher Hill's definition as 'the sum of official external relations conducted by an independent actor (usually states) in international relations' (Hill, 2003: 3). For the purpose of this endeavour, that definition is operationalized as the positioning (including participation) of individual Member States with regard to EU military operations. The volume's focus on foreign policy *action* allows one to better distinguish between rhetoric and behaviour in this highly political and at times rather contentious realm. Common Foreign and Security Policy, which includes Common Security and Defence Policy, is a 'sensitive area' of weak EU policy and strong Member State control, cf. the 'strong-weak competence spectrum' introduced in the first chapter of this volume. It is therefore expected to be 'the area of greatest potential for disconnects between modes of Europeanisation and modes of nationalization' and as such particularly important to examine.

The *range of change* identified in the next section by tracing trends in the broad direction of Member State policy towards joint military deployment confirms that expectation – for whilst the field of military operations has developed a new European dimension, the policies of individual Member States remain predominantly national in decision-making preference and persuasion. There is thus a new degree of Europeanisation with domestic implications of European integration (change) as well as a sustained reassertion of military deployment as an area of traditional national foreign policy. The chapter categorizes this as a Mode II change of foreign policy (inter)action, where intra-EU cooperation exists but remains inter-governmental in its dominant mode. Overall, Member States have had contradictory motivations rather than contradictory policy and actions, which have gone in the same overall direction now allowing for EU military deployment – albeit with different degrees of support and participation from various Member States.

Policy change

Table 8.1 illustrates Member State participation (or lack thereof) in every EU military operation from 2003 to 2013. Because this contribution seeks to evaluate Member State foreign policy specifically towards the EU's emergence as a military actor, the analysis which follows includes neither civilian nor hybrid missions; it also does not incorporate operations launched outside the EU framework. Instead, the following explores particularities regarding the various roles that different Member States (have sought to) play in EU military operations – that is, 'military operations launched under the auspices of the EU, within the framework of the Common Security and Defence Policy (CSDP)[2] and undertaken by EU forces (EUFOR) on the ground' (Peen Rodt, 2014: 13).

Operation Concordia (Macedonia)

In March 2003, the EU launched its first military operation. The operation, code-named Concordia, was authorized by United Nations Security Council Resolution 1371. The Berlin Plus agreements, completed just two weeks before its launch, allowed the EU to make use of NATO assets in the operation.[3] Operation headquarters were subsequently set up at NATO's Supreme Headquarters of Allied Powers in Europe (SHAPE) and the Deputy Supreme Allied Commander for Europe (DSACEUR) was appointed EU Operation Commander (Council of the EU, 2012; Council Joint Action 2003a/92/CFSP, 2003). Approximately 350 personnel were deployed to Macedonia and twenty-six countries took part in the operation, which took over its stabilization mission from the prior NATO deployment in the country.

All EU Member States at the time, except Denmark and Ireland, took part. Denmark could not join because of its post-Maastricht opt-out on EU defence cooperation, and Ireland declined with reference to its traditional neutrality. The otherwise full participation illustrates wide Member State support for the EU's first advance into joint military deployment. Likewise, all countries that would join the Union in 2004 and 2007, with the exceptions only of Malta and Cyprus, also took part, as did non-EU Member States: Norway, Turkey and Iceland (Hadden, 2009).

Some states proved particularly important to the operation. The United Kingdom played a crucial bridging role between Europe and the United States in the Berlin Plus negotiations, which upon completion made Concordia possible both in practical and political terms. France performed the framework nation responsibilities for the duration of the original mandate.[10] It also provided the first Force Commander, later followed by Portugal. France, Portugal and Sweden were each responsible for one of the three multinational sectors to which the twenty-two field liaison teams, which made up the force in the former crisis area, were assigned. France and Italy provided the heavy platoon reserve for the entire area of operations (Augustin, 2005; Council of the EU, 2012; Council Joint Action 2003a/92/CFSP, 2003; ICG, 2005: 48–49).

Table 8.1 European Union military operations[4]

Operation	EUFOR Operation Concordia	EUFOR Operation Artemis	EUFOR Operation Althea	EUFOR DRC	EUFOR Chad/CAR	EUNAVFOR Operation Atalanta	EUTM Somalia	EUTM Mali
Area of operations	Macedonia	Democratic Republic of Congo	Bosnia and Herzegovina	Democratic Republic of Congo	Chad and Central African Republic	Southern Red Sea, Gulf of Aden and Western Indian Ocean[5]	Somalia[6]	Mali
Deployment	2003	2003	2004	2006	2008	2008	2010	2013
Duration	8.5 months	2.5 months	Ongoing	4 months	13.5 months	Ongoing	Ongoing	Ongoing
Max strength	350	2,200	7,000	2,466[7]	3,400	1,594	206	550
Current strength (January 2014)	–	–	800	–	–	1,400	126	500
Framework responsibilities	**France**[8]	**France**	–	**Germany**	**France**	–	–	–
Operation HQ	NATO–SHAPE	**France**	NATO–SHAPE	**Germany**	**France**	UK	Uganda and Somalia	Mali
Operation commander	Feist (**Germany**)	Neveux (**France**)	Feist (**Germany**), Reith (**UK**), Shirreff (**UK**)	Viereck (**Germany**)	Nash (**Ireland**)	Jones (**UK**), Hudson (**UK**), Howes (**UK**), Potts (**UK**), Tarrant (**UK**),	–	–
Force commander	Maral (**France**), Dos Santos (EUROFOR/**Portugal**)	Thonier (**France**)	Leakey (**UK**), Chiarini (**Italy**), Villalain (**Spain**), Castagnotto (**Italy**), Bair (**Austria**), Brieger (**Austria**), Heidecker (**Austria**)	Damay (**France**)	Ganascia (**France**)	Manso (**Spain**), Jugel (**Germany**), Correia (**Portugal**), Rodriguez (**Spain**), Coindreau (**France**), Thörnqvist (**Sweden**), Gumiero (**Italy**), Bindt (**Netherlands**), Caramé (**Spain**), Papaioannou (**Greece**), Dupuis (**France**), Credendino (**Italy**), Paredes (**Spain**), Palma (**Portugal**), Bléjean (**France**)	Elul (**Spain**), Beary (**Ireland**), Aherne (**Ireland**)	Lecointre (**France**), Guibert (**France**)

(Continued)

Table 8.1 (Continued)

Operation	EUFOR Operation Concordia	EUFOR Operation Artemis	EUFOR Operation Althea	EUFOR DRC	EUFOR Chad/CAR	EUNAVFOR Operation Atalanta	EUTM Somalia	EUTM Mali
Contributing Member States[9]	Austria, Belgium, Bulgaria, Czech Republic, Estonia, Finland, France, Germany, Greece, Hungary, Italy, Latvia, Lithuania, Luxembourg, Netherlands, Poland, Portugal, Spain, Romania, Slovakia, Slovenia, Sweden, United Kingdom	Austria, Belgium, Cyprus, France, Germany, Greece, Hungary, Ireland, Italy, Netherlands, Portugal, Spain, Sweden, United Kingdom	Austria, Bulgaria, Czech Republic, Finland, France, Germany, Greece, Hungary, Ireland, Italy, Luxembourg, Netherlands, Poland, Romania, Slovakia, Slovenia, Spain, Sweden, United Kingdom	Austria, Belgium, Cyprus, Czech Republic, Finland, France, Germany, Greece, Hungary, Ireland, Italy, Lithuania, Luxembourg, Netherlands, Poland, Portugal, Slovakia, Slovenia, Spain, Sweden, United Kingdom	Austria, Belgium, Bulgaria, Croatia, Cyprus, Czech Republic, Finland, France, Germany, Greece, Hungary, Ireland, Italy, Lithuania, Luxembourg, Netherlands, Poland, Portugal, Romania, Slovakia, Slovenia, Spain, Sweden, United Kingdom	Belgium, Croatia, France, Germany, Greece, Italy, Luxembourg, Netherlands, Portugal, Spain, Sweden, United Kingdom	Belgium, Cyprus, Estonia, Finland, France, Germany, Greece, Hungary, Ireland, Italy, Luxembourg, Malta, Netherlands, Portugal, Spain, Sweden, United Kingdom	Austria, Belgium, Bulgaria, Czech Republic, Estonia, Finland, France, Germany, Greece, Hungary, Ireland, Italy, Latvia, Lithuania, Luxembourg, Netherlands, Poland, Portugal, Romania, Slovenia, Spain, Sweden, United Kingdom
Contributing non-EU countries	Norway, Turkey, Iceland	Brazil, Canada, South Africa	Albania, Chile, Macedonia, Switzerland, Turkey	Turkey	Albania, Russia	Montenegro, Norway, Serbia, Ukraine	Serbia	Switzerland, Ukraine

Operation Artemis (Democratic Republic of Congo)

In June 2003, the EU launched its second military operation – this time in Africa. Operation Artemis was designed as a stopgap measure to fill a pressing security vacuum in Bunia (Eastern DRC), until reinforcements could be deployed to the United Nations mission in the area. The EU mandate was set out in United Nations Security Council Resolution 1484. This time not quite as many EU Member States contributed, although in this operation Ireland did. Cyprus, which had also not partaken in the previous Operation Concordia, joined Hungary as the only candidate countries to contribute. Brazil, Canada and South Africa also took part (Hadden, 2009). The operation officially ended when it handed over responsibilities to a reinforced United Nations mission in September 2003 (Council Joint Action 2003b/423/CFSP, 2003; Howorth, 2007: 231–241).

Artemis was a French initiative. France played a significant role in persuading other Member States that this was indeed an operation that the EU was ready and willing to undertake. Paris drafted the official EU response to the UN request for an international force – a response which had initially been directed at Paris. France also drafted the mandate, acted as framework nation, hosted the Operational Headquarters[11] and seconded both Operation and Force Commanders. At its peak Artemis comprised 2,200 troops – 1,785 of which were French (Council Joint Action 2003b/423/CFSP, 2003; Howorth, 2007: 231–241). Besides France, the most important EU contributors were: Sweden, which provided an infantry unit including eighty Special Forces; the United Kingdom, which supplied engineering units; and Belgium which sent medical teams. Germany also contributed 350 non-combat troops and a medical component but only once a certain number of other Member States had agreed to take part, so the contribution could be justified in the Bundestag (Hadden, 2009). The United Kingdom's participation was crucial in this regard, as it helped convince reluctant Member States such as Germany to support the operation. It also sought to persuade external actors in the international arena that this was not, despite accusations to the contrary, a unilateral French intervention. British participation therefore also helped secure political support for the operation from Rwanda and Uganda – support without which France had declared that it would not intervene due to their prior engagement in the conflict (Hadden, 2009; ICG, 2005; Ulriksen, Gourlay and Mace, 2004). The United Kingdom, alongside France, also prepared and maintained Bunia Airport and made possible the tactical airlifts necessary to deploy both Artemis personnel and equipment. As such, Franco-British cooperation was essential to both the launch and implementation of this operation (Giegerich, 2008).

Operation Althea (Bosnia and Herzegovina)

The idea that the EU might take over NATO's responsibilities in Bosnia-Herzegovina was first aired at the European Council in Copenhagen in 2002. However, the handover did not take place until the Berlin Plus had first been agreed and tested in Macedonia. Hereafter the Council, endorsed by United Nations Security Council Resolution 1551, unanimously decided to take over NATO's responsibilities in Bosnia-Herzegovina from December 2004 (Cascone, 2008; ICG, 2005: 49–51). Althea was the EU's then largest, and now longest running, military deployment to date. As the operation was launched under the Berlin Plus, Operational Headquarters were located at NATO's SHAPE, and DSACEUR once again became Operation Commander. British Major General Leakey was the first EU Force Commander, later followed by Italian (two), Spanish (one) and Austrian (three) successors (Council of the EU, 2009b, 2012; Howorth, 2007). Althea has enjoyed broad participation from EU Member States. Moreover, Albania, Macedonia, Chile, Switzerland and Turkey have contributed to the operation (Council of the EU, 2012). This broad participation as well as the 7,000-strong[12] deployment indicate widespread support for the operation from its very beginning. An International Crisis Group (ICG) report published at the time confirmed this:

> Bosnia was the painful crucible of European foreign policy in the 1990s demonstrating all too clearly its gravest weaknesses. The EU has a strong commitment – moral, financial and political, to do better this time.
>
> (ICG, 2005: 49)

Alongside their shared frustrations over the Union's previous failure to handle the break-up of Yugoslavia, many Member States had been involved bilaterally and/or through other international initiatives and experienced first-hand the devastating failure to stabilize the region in the 1990s. As argued in Chapter 7, their shared experiences in the Balkans were in part what brought France and the United Kingdom together at Saint-Malo – and one might add, what made the United States support (at least to a greater extent than before) this European initiative to play a more active part in security provision beyond its borders. The numerous extensions of Althea's mandate and the fact that ten years on an EU force, albeit much smaller, is still deployed in Bosnia-Herzegovina demonstrate the extensive Member State support for the operation. This is further illustrated by the open-ended nature of the current mandate, although some Member States are increasingly eager to see the force withdrawn.

EUFOR DR Congo

In June 2006, the EU launched its second military operation in the Democratic Republic of Congo. EUFOR DRC, as it came to be known, was deployed to support the United Nations Organization Mission in the Democratic Republic of the Congo during the period encompassing the 2006 elections. Its mandate was set out in United Nations Security Council Resolution 1671. The EU force initially deployed some 400 military personnel in an advance element to the capital, Kinshasa. An additional 1,200 soldiers were set on standby in neighbouring Gabon. At peak strength in mid-August 2006, EUFOR had 2,466 troops in the field, but a maximum of 1,000 were operating in the Democratic Republic of Congo at any one time.

   This is the EU military operation which has enjoyed the least Member State support so far. Both the United Kingdom and Germany were disinclined to take part or even support the operation at first. Most Member States, including these two, eventually participated in the operation, but more than half of these sent only a symbolic contribution (Haine and Giegerich, 2006). The largest contributors were France (1,090), Germany (780), Spain (130), Poland (130), Belgium (60) and Sweden (55). Turkey was the only non-EU contributing country (Hadden, 2009). Germany eventually, albeit un-enthusiastically, agreed to take on the framework responsibilities. Operational Headquarters were located in Potsdam, and a German lieutenant general was appointed Operation Commander, whilst the Force Commander was French. Two-thirds of the troops came from these two countries. Germany reportedly 'felt she was pushed into leading the mission' by the French (Hadden, 2009: 143). German personnel were only deployed to safe areas around Kinshasa and over-the-horizon in Gabon. Likewise, although France and Belgium favoured an extension of the mandate, Berlin insisted on terminating the operation as planned in

November 2006 (Council of the EU, 2006; Council Joint Action 2006/319/CFSP, 2006; Hadden, 2009).

EUFOR Chad/CAR

EUFOR Chad/CAR was another French initiative. The Chad government had refused the planned military component to the United Nations Mission in the Central African Republic and Chad. In response, the French foreign ministry proposed to its European counterparts that an EU operation was deployed instead. The initial reaction from other Member States was mixed. Although the scepticism was not as profound as in the case of EUFOR DRC, there was still no shared sense of purpose or enthusiasm for the operation. Germany voiced concerns that immense efforts, undertaken and paid for by the EU, to renovate the Chadian infrastructure would be necessary to allow for this relatively short deployment. Berlin hinted that the main beneficiary of such an investment might in fact be France due to her national interests and ongoing engagements in the region (Mattelaer, 2008, 2009; Seibert, 2007). The Member States were eventually persuaded to launch the operation on condition that it would be a French-led endeavour but with a clear-cut aim to act neutrally and impartially in the region. The operation was authorized by United Nations Security Council Resolution 1778 and launched in January 2008. At the initial force generation conference, not a single Member State, other than France, agreed to contribute in any significant way to the operation. Another five conferences would be held before twenty-four Member States eventually agreed to participate – at least in headquarters. France had to fill the gaps and provided half the troops in the field. Operational Headquarters were located in Paris, and the operation was headed up by an Irish Operation Commander and a French Force Commander. Albania, Croatia and Russia also contributed to the operation (Council of the EU, 2009a, 2009c, 2012; Council of the European Union 2007; Mattelaer, 2008, 2009).

Operation Atalanta (Horn of Africa/Western Indian Ocean)

An EU Naval Force launched the Union's first maritime operation in response to piracy off the coast of Somalia in 2008. The naval force, which is still deployed, operates in an area that is one-and-a-half times the size of the European mainland. Operation Atalanta, which is based on a series of UN resolutions, was the first EU operation to have its Operational Headquarters located in the United Kingdom and to be headed up by British Operation Commanders outside the NATO framework. By January 2014, twelve Member States have contributed personnel, and eight of these have seconded Force Commanders to Operation Atalanta. Spain, Portugal, Italy and France have once again proved themselves steady supporters to the defence dimension of the European Union by each seconding several Force Commanders to this operation. Germany too has provided one, and Sweden, Greece and the Netherlands have each appointed their first-ever EU Force Commanders to this operation. Croatia, Belgium and Luxembourg have also taken part, as have Montenegro, Norway, Serbia and Ukraine (Council of the European Union, 2012).

EUTM Somalia

In support of Operation Atalanta and hoping to strengthen the 'comprehensive approach' towards the Horn of Africa, an EU Training Mission (EUTM) was launched in Somalia in

April 2010. EUTM, a new kind of EU operation, was intended to build up and strengthen Somali institutions and armed forces to assist them in their fight against Al Shaabab. By December 2013, EUTM, numbering only 126 staff, had trained more than 3,600 officers. Seventeen Member States had participated. Serbia had been the only non-EU contributor so far. Due to the political and security situation in Somalia, mission headquarters and training facilities were initially located in Uganda. When the Council extended EUTM's mandate in December 2013 the Member States also decided that from 2014 onwards all its activities would be conducted in Somalia. First Spain and now Ireland (twice) have provided EUTM's Mission Commanders in the field, in accordance with United Nations Security Council Resolution 1872 (Council of the European Union, 2012; Rye Olsen, 2012).

EUTM Mali

Inspired by the training mission in Somalia, another EU training mission was launched in Mali in February 2013. United Nations Security Council Resolution 2085 mandated the operation to support Mali's government in its attempt to restore its authority and neutralize the challenge hereto in the North of the country. So far, twenty-three Member States have contributed to this operation, as have Switzerland and Ukraine. France has taken the lead also in this endeavour, parallel to its bilateral engagement in the country, launched whilst awaiting the EU deployment. Once the EU training mission was eventually launched, France also provided two Mission Commanders heading up the headquarters in Mali (Council of the European Union, 2012; Rye Olsen, 2012).

Member States and policy performance: action and change

Eight of the thirty-some Common Security and Defence Policy missions to date were military. These have been some of the most challenging, far-reaching, longest running and extensively resourced deployments that the EU has undertaken in this realm. This reflects a politico-strategic shift towards sustained (albeit not automatic) Member State support for the Union's new role in the military realm of Common Security and Defence Policy in the period appraised. The decision to launch each and every one of these operations was taken unanimously by the Member States. Although some of their practical contributions have been symbolic, this symbolism is important in signalling their official support for the specific operation as well as EU military deployment more generally. The majority of Member States have participated in all eight EU military operations. With the exception only of Denmark and Malta, all Member States have taken part in at least 25 per cent of them. Although the level of enthusiasm for this venture as a whole and participation in specific operations have varied significantly, it still seems the political, diplomatic and institutional changes detected in Chapters 6 and 7 can be confirmed and observed also at the operational level. As a difference does seem to exist between various Member State positions, these will be examined in further detail later in this chapter. This final section investigates whether particular patterns of role-play have started to emerge. In other words, can lead, support, swing, laggard and/or veto states, as characterized in the introductory chapter to this volume, be identified in relation to EU military operations? And, if so, does Member State behaviour in these roles tell us anything about the *modes of change* in this policy domain? To illustrate broader trends and dynamics in this policy field, the following will undertake a thematically structured analysis of these roles rather than a general description of each Member State's position and participation in every operation.

Lead states

France has been and arguably still is the single most important Member State in pushing for an EU able and willing to deploy militarily beyond its borders. Although other Member States have supported and at times led specific initiatives, Paris has been unparalleled in its promotion of European integration in security and defence, although at times France too has had her reservations.[13] It has often been suggested that the French support for EU military operations is an attempt to nationalize European policy according to French interests rather than the result of a Europeanised French policy (Rye Olsen, 2012). This may well be the case, but in the process, the French approach seems to Europeanise according to the preferences of other EU Member States and institutions, illustrating a dynamic inter-relationship between nationalization and Europeanisation processes.

Despite the traditional French preference for European (rather than Atlantic) integration, it was not until the United Kingdom came on board at Saint-Malo that real change occurred. Here, Paris and London finally came together to initiate what became a series of changes, culminating in the Common Security and Defence Policy and the first EU military operations launched in Macedonia and the Democratic Republic of Congo. In the 2003 European Security Strategy and the 2008 Report on its implementation, the full cohort of Member States supported the Franco-British initiative by confirming that the Union's military dimension was there to stay. This fundamental change towards more European cooperation in security and defence thus began by the United Kingdom adopting a more pro-EU stance. Since then the United Kingdom and France have – albeit with different priorities and interests at stake – decided the speed and direction of the Union's venture into this new policy domain.

The Saint-Malo summit itself was a Franco-British initiative, and since then, both countries have repeatedly taken a proactive stance in convincing peers and partners within the EU, in the international community and on the ground in target and neighbouring countries that the Union was ready to undertake military operations – first in Europe and later also in Africa. The United Kingdom was especially important in generating internal as well as external support for the project, in particular with regards to the EU takeovers from and cooperation with NATO (and within it the United States) in Macedonia and Bosnia-Herzegovina. Meanwhile, France volunteered to lead the Union's first military action outside NATO structures, which was also the first time EU forces were deployed in active conflict and beyond the European continent. Since then, France has time and again initiated, supported and led EU military operations, filling gaps in personnel, equipment, political support and leadership when other Member States have been less keen to contribute. In instances when other states, inside and outside the EU, have been sceptical towards the French lead, the United Kingdom's support has proved essential. When British support has wavered, it has therefore been difficult for the EU to conduct these kinds of operations unless another Member State – often but not always France – was willing to take the lead. As such, both France and the United Kingdom, each in their own way, have played the role of lead states in this arena.

Swing states

Due to the significant shift at Saint-Malo and the subsequent pendulum policy of the United Kingdom never fully supporting nor always opposing the Common Security and Defence Policy, that country may indeed also be called a swing state. The United Kingdom has arguably swung back and forth between more and less pro-EU positions. In relation to the

Union's military deployments, the United Kingdom has often been reluctant to take part and at times even to support proposed operations. This has arguably at least in part been due to the country's Atlanticist tradition and its military overstretch in Iraq and Afghanistan in this same time period. Nevertheless, that has not hindered British participation in and support for EU operations. This was most notably the case in Operation Atalanta, where the United Kingdom has proved a committed and decisive leader – perhaps not surprisingly as it is and wishes to remain the Union's strongest maritime power. Whether the United Kingdom will eventually settle in one role – and if so, which one – remains unclear, not least in light of the recent re-emergence of Euroscepticsm within the political elites and general public in that country. What is certain however is that it will be difficult for the Union to do without the United Kingdom – albeit with varying degrees of enthusiasm – in the defence realm.

Laggard states

Although Germany has and still does support the Common Security and Defence Policy in principle, it has often proved reluctant to deploy boots on the ground, especially when and where battle has been expected. Likewise, German participation has seemed dependent on other Member States committing themselves first and firmly, so as to justify her own contribution in the Bundestag, which has often opposed EU military operations – particularly in Africa. This is in no small part explained by the historic legacy of that country and the effect this has had on the German armed forces and the (lack of) political support for their use. An example of Germany's reluctance is its deployment of only medical personnel and non-combat troops to Operation Artemis. EUFOR DRC and EUFOR Chad/CAR confirmed Germany's role as a laggard state in this domain. Berlin only eventually and rather reluctantly agreed to take on the framework responsibilities for EUFOR DRC after considerable pressure from Paris and on the condition that German soldiers would only be deployed to safe areas (Hadden, 2009). The fact that Germany stuck to the original mandate and terminated this operation, despite French and Belgian wishes to extend its mandate, serves as further evidence of its reluctant role in this realm, as did Germany's rejection of the United Nations' 2008 request for another EU operation in the Democratic Republic of Congo. Nevertheless, Chancellor Merkel's recent remarks on European security and defence demonstrate that her government is still in favour of continued cooperation in this domain, as does the German participation in all EU military operations to date.

Much further behind Germany lags her northern neighbour. According to Article 5 of the protocol on the position of Denmark annexed to the Treaty on European Union and to the Treaty on the Functioning of the European Union, this country cannot participate in the elaboration or implementation of EU decisions or actions with defence implications. Denmark has therefore not participated in any decisions made regarding specific operations or indeed the general direction of the Union's defence cooperation. In cases when the EU takes over operations (e.g. from NATO), where Denmark has previously been deployed, Danish personnel must withdraw, illustrating how EU membership does not automatically bring defence cooperation (Europabevaegelsen, 2012). During the past decade and a half, Denmark has adopted an increasingly proactive and some argue militaristic foreign policy agenda, which has resulted in her participation in international interventions in Afghanistan, Iraq, Libya and Mali. Despite this activism in the global security arena, Denmark has retained its defence opt-out and remained disengaged from military engagements under the auspices of the EU (Rasmussen et al., 2014). There has been some debate as to whether Denmark should abandon the defence opt-out, and both sides of the national political spectrum have promised a referendum on the issue, but so far this has not materialized. Danish participation in civilian EU missions suggests that the country is not opposed to the Common Security and Defence Policy as such, although she is not (yet) participating in its military dimension (Rye Olsen, 2012). Denmark may in time change her position and if so become a swing state, but for the time being, she remains a laggard in this realm.

Veto states

Although Germany, and at times the United Kingdom, has been less than enthusiastic about particular deployments, the so-called Big Three have officially supported and taken part in all EU military operations to date. They have each covered important posts as both Operation and Force Commanders and all hosted operational headquarters for operations not housed under the Berlin Plus umbrella at SHAPE. As necessary participants, they have been and still are potential veto players with regard to this type of EU activity. Without their shared consent and at least one of them in the lead, it seems an EU military operation will not take place. This became evident for example in the rejection of the United Nations' request for another EU military operation in the Democratic Republic of Congo in 2008, where none of the Big Three was willing to take the lead. The fact that these are the only three Member States which have hosted temporary operational headquarters for EU military operations supports this point. However, these countries are by no means always staunch supporters of the same initiatives, and at times, the support from other Member State seems more steadfast. As all Member States must agree on the launch (or renewed mandate) of an EU military operation, they are all potential veto players in this sense.

Support states

All the EU's military operations to date have received broad support across the cohort of Member States. A significant part of these Member States have taken part in each and every one of the operations so far – and although their contributions are small at times, they are still significant as they demonstrate political support for the specific endeavours as well as EU military engagements more generally. Belgium, Greece, Italy, the Netherlands, Spain and Sweden have participated in all the operations to date, and of these all but Belgium have seconded EU Force Commanders. So too have Portugal, Austria and Ireland, although they have participated in many, but not all, the military operations so far. Furthermore, Ireland and Spain have seconded Operations Commanders as the only Member States to do so alongside the Big Three.

A particularly interesting group of supporters is made up of former neutral countries Austria, Sweden and Ireland, which have been unusually active in the EU's military endeavours given their former foreign policy tradition as neutrals. Austria has taken part in all but the two operations in and off the coast of Somalia, and Vienna has seconded the last three Force Commanders in Bosnia-Herzegovina, perhaps not so surprising after all as stability in the Balkans is in her national security interest. Sweden too seems to have embarked on a new and now active approach towards military engagement abroad. Sweden has participated in all the EU military operations to date, and provided a Force Commander for Operation Atalanta. The Swedish contributions have been explained as a national recognition of the 'obvious need' for her to play a role in security provision abroad. Although the Swedes have reportedly been aware of other Member States motivated by national interest, Sweden has identified 'common goals' if not necessarily shared motivations in launching these operations. The Swedish lead in the

Nordic battle group was justified along similar lines (Rye Olsen, 2012). Ireland too has left its traditionally neutral position in favour of active engagement in EU military endeavours, most recently in Somalia, where it is currently heading up the EU training mission.

Switzerland is another traditionally neutral state, which has nonetheless participated in a couple of EU operations, this despite the fact that it does not have or seek membership of the Union. This brings us to another interesting group of steady supporters for EU military operations, consisting of non-Member States seeking approximation, integration or membership of the Union. It is clear from the investigation in the first half of this chapter that those countries, which were/are not (yet) members of the EU but who want(ed) membership have often participated in these operations, perhaps to facilitate their own further European integration. There is evidence of this in the case of the Central and Eastern European countries, which joined the EU in 2004 and 2007, respectively, as well as for Turkey, who has sought membership of the Union since the early 1960s. Croatia, which recently joined, and Macedonia, Serbia, Montenegro and Albania, which are hoping to follow, have all adopted the same policy, as has Ukraine, although her European integration is disputed at home as well as in EU Member States. Iceland and Norway, which do not currently seek membership but close cooperation with the EU, have also participated actively in EU military operations, which they, like Sweden, have expressed were necessary for international peace and security, a traditional priority in Nordic foreign policy-making (Howorth, 2007; Rye Olsen, 2012).

Active participation in and support for the Common Security and Defence Policy is perceived as a way for countries seeking a close(r) relationship with the Union to achieve this, whilst also seeming to support a worthy cause and a European policy with potential to expand (Žabec, 2009). An interesting twist to this story is the case of Macedonia, the first target country of an EU military operation. As the EU was preparing to launch Concordia, Macedonian President Boris Trajkovski explained his government's invitation and support for the EU operation in the following way:

> This mission offers us a chance to develop a particularly close collaboration with the EU forces from the moment of their establishment, a chance that we do not intend to miss. . . . Our ambition is full membership in the Union, and I would like to see this mission and our joint efforts in promoting stability as a step in that direction. The more of EU we have in Macedonia; the more of Macedonia there is in the EU.
>
> (Trajkovski, 2003)

Today, Macedonia is recognized as a candidate for EU membership, although whether and, if so, how Trajkovski's plan will materialize is difficult to predict. What is certain however is that the EU enlargements that have taken place since the launch of the Common Security and Defence Policy have included many of its steady supporters in central, south and eastern Europe but also a few whose support has been less consistent, like Malta, which has only participated in one EU military operation.

Conclusion

This contribution has examined Member State policy, positioning and performance related to EU military operations in third countries. Its main focus has been on whether Member States have initiated or changed activities in this realm from 2000 to 2013. The purpose of this undertaking was to identify broad trends and directions in Member State foreign policy as well as specific actions and roles adopted by different Member States in this regard. Following on from Chapters 6 and 7, which examined the EU foreign, security and defence policy context in which Member State decision-making on these issues takes place, the analysis in this chapter supports both their conclusions that there has indeed been a significant *change* towards further intra-EU cooperation in this realm in the period examined. The European Security Strategy and the follow-on report on its implementation explicitly stated the Member States' shared ambition to further align – although not fully integrate – in this policy area. Some thirty Joint Actions have launched Common Security and Defence Policy missions since 2003. These illustrate continued Member State support for the implementation of the change towards further intra-EU cooperation. The fact that eight of these missions were military operations signals a particularly significant aspect of that change, as they mark the entry of the Union and its Member States into a new area of cooperation. There has thus been an overall change in the Europeanisation of some military operations, albeit with different contributions and backing, always determined by national decision-making. This corresponds with Mode II, as outlined in the introductory chapter.

The next part of the analysis went on to examine Member State actions in relation to specific EU military operations. In the time period examined, the EU conducted eight such operations in Macedonia, Bosnia-Herzegovina, the Democratic Republic of Congo, Chad/CAR, Somalia and Mali. This contribution examined Member State policy, positioning and participation in relation to each of these operations in order to identify whether Member State roles and relationships have emerged in particular patterns. It became clear that states have indeed played different roles of lead, laggard, swing, support and (potential) veto states and that, at times, various Member States have played different roles in relation to different operations.

The chapter went on to further examine the specific patterns of role-playing in the foreign policies of particular Member States towards EU-led military operations. France and to a lesser extent the United Kingdom were identified as lead states in the process of change towards further intra-EU cooperation in this policy area. A number of countries consistently supporting these lead states (and thus the change they instigated) were identified in particular among newer members, applicants and close partners of the EU. Germany and Denmark have each in their own way played the role of laggards, although only Germany, as one of the Big Three was able to act as veto player.

The final quest of this chapter was to identify what – if any – mode of change has taken place in Member State foreign policy towards EU military operations in third countries since 2000. It is clear that a change has occurred; it is motivated and driven by EU Member States, who have increasingly engaged in this new realm of intra-EU cooperation. Most Member States have been motivated by national interests, and some have sought to upload these to the European level, but in this process, the Member States have also downloaded priorities, principles and practices from the EU – the greatest evidence of which is the fact that military CSDP operations have regularly been considered and deemed appropriate by the whole cohort of Member States on eight separate occasions over the last decade. This illustrates a mode (II) of change focused on intra-EU cooperation although Member States still can and arguably will continue to cooperate outside the EU framework and with non-EU actors in security and defence matters as well.

Notes

1 The empirical enquiry is based on the most up-to-date information available at the time of writing (January 2014). Discussions in Brussels at the time suggested that another operation may be underway in the Central African Republic. In January 2014, the Political and Security Committee ambassadors unanimously endorsed a proposal to deploy a battalion-sized force (700–1,000 personnel) to protect civilians and help distribute aid in the Central African Republic. This operation is a proposal from France, the former colonial power in the country. France already has troops on the ground, under a United Nations Security Council mandate. The proposed EU force is expected to relieve the current French deployment at Bangui Airport (Rettman, 2014a, 2014b). Alongside the French, Poland has pledged that it will send a handful of soldiers, and Belgium, Germany, Spain and the United Kingdom have promised support such as transport planes (Rettman, 2014a). These are only initial plans for a possible forthcoming EU military operation – a final decision by the Member State foreign ministers has yet to be made. Readers are reminded that such plans do not always materialize, as became apparent with the planned but never deployed EU force to Libya. Nevertheless, it is interesting to note (1) that another operation seems underway, (2) that France is taking the lead and (3) that the 'usual suspects' are supporting it in this endeavour.
2 Until the adoption of the Lisbon Treaty, this policy was known as the European Security and Defence Policy. Hereafter, its official name is the Common Security and Defence Policy, which is why this term is used.
3 In March 2003, an exchange of letters between EU High Representative for the Common Foreign and Security Policy Javier Solana and NATO Secretary-General George Robertson concluded the Berlin Plus agreement, which constitutes a strategic partnership between the two organizations specifically with regard to management of conflicts and crises (NATO, 2006).
4 The information included is the most up-to-date information available at the time of writing (January 2014).
5 NAVFOR ATALANTA operates in a mission area from the south of the Red Sea, the Gulf of Aden and the Western part of the Indian Ocean including the Seychelles. The Area of Operation also includes Somali coastal territory as well as its territorial and internal waters. This area is 1.5 times the size of the European mainland.
6 Until the time of writing (January 2014), EUTM Somalia's Mission Headquarters had been located in the Ugandan capital, Kampala, with training being conducted in a Training Camp in Bihanga, Western Uganda. The mission also included a Liaison Office in Nairobi, a Support Cell in Brussels and a Mentoring, Advisory and Training Element in Mogadishu, Somalia. From 2014 onwards, all of EUTM Somalia's advisory, monitoring and training activities are planned to take place in Mogadishu, Somalia.
7 A maximum of 1,000 troops were in the DRC at any one time.
8 The European Rapid Operational Force (EUROFOR), a multinational rapid reaction force composed of forces from France, Italy, Portugal and Spain, took over Concordia's framework responsibilities on 1 October 2003. Major General Luis Nelson Ferreira dos Santos (**Portugal**) also took over as Force Commander then. Both stayed in command until the operation was terminated on 15 December 2003.
9 The list of 'contributing EU member states' includes all contributing countries that were members of the Union at the time of writing (January 2014). Lists of contributors sometimes vary between sources. To ensure that no contributions however small are left out, all named contributors have been included.
10 The operation was initially mandated for six months, but upon request from the Macedonian president, it was extended until 15 December 2003. When the Council agreed to extend the operation, it was also decided that Eurofor would take over the framework responsibilities from France on 1 October 2003 (Council of the EU, 2012; Council Joint Action 2003/92/CFSP, 2003).
11 The EU Framework Nation Concept, adopted on 24 July 2002, allows for the national headquarters of a Member State to be multinationalized for the purpose and duration of an EU military operation (Ulriksen, Gourlay and Mace, 2004).
12 EUFOR was downsized to 2,200 troops (backed by over-the-horizon reserves) in 2007 and had been reduced to 800 personnel by January 2014.
13 See Chapter 7 in this volume.

Bibliography

Augustin, P. (2005) *Operation Concordia/Altair: Lessons Learnt* [online], http://www.cdef.terre. defense.gouv.fr/publications/doctrine/doctrine06/version_us/retex/art_22.pdf, date accessed 1 June 2009.

Cascone, G. (2008) 'ESDP Operations and NATO: Co-Operation, Rivalry or Muddling-through?', in Merlingen, Michael and Ostrauskaite, Rasa (eds.) *European Security and Defence Policy: An Implementation Perspective*. Oxon: Routledge: 143–158.

Council Decision (2003) '2003/563/CFSP of 29/07/2003 on the Extension of the European Union Military Operation in the Former Yugoslav Republic of Macedonia', *Official Journal of the European Union*, L 190/20–21.

Council of the European Union (2003) *A Secure Europe in a Better World* [online], http://www.consilium.europa.eu/uedocs/cmsUpload/78367.pdf, date accessed 10 June 2012.

Council of the European Union (2006) *Press Statement on EU Military Operation in Support of the MONUC during the Election Process in DR Congo: Council Adopts Joint Action, Appoints Operation and Force Commanders* [online], 27 April, http://www.consilium.europa.eu/ueDocs/cms_Data/docs/pressData/en/misc/89347.pdf, date accessed 26 January 2009.

Council of the European Union (2007) 'Council Joint Action 2007/677/CFSP of 15 October 2007 on the European Union Military Operation in the Republic of Chad and in the Central African Republic', L 279/21–24, http://eur-lex.europa.eu/legal-content/EN/TXT/?uri=CELEX%3A32007E0677, date accessed 24 October 2016.

Council of the European Union (2008) *Report on the Implementation of the European Security Strategy* [online], http://www.eu-un.europa.eu/documents/en/081211_EU%20Security%20Strategy.pdf, date accessed 10 June 2012.

Council of the European Union Secretariat (2009a) *EU Military Operation in Eastern Chad and North Eastern Central African Republic (EUFOR Tchad/RCA)* [online], http://www.consilium.europa.eu/uedocs/cmsUpload/Final%20FACTSHEET%20EUFOR%20TCHAD-RCA%20version%209_EN.pdf, date accessed 4 June 2012.

Council of the European Union (2009b) *EU Military Operation in Bosnia and Herzegovina (EUFOR-Althea)* [online], http://consilium.europa.eu/cms3_fo/showPage.asp?id=745&lang=en, date accessed 26 January 2009.

Council of the European Union (2009c) *EUFOR Chad/CAR* [online], http://consilium.europa.eu/cms3_fo/showPage.asp?id=1366&lang=en&mode=g, date accessed 26 January 2009.

Council of the European Union (2012) *EU Operations* [online], Brussels, http://www.consilium.europa.eu/eeas/security-defence/eu-operations, date accessed 10 June 2012.

Council Joint Action (2003a) '2003/92/CFSP of 29/01/2003 on the European Union Military Operation in the Former Yugoslav Republic of Macedonia', *Official Journal of the European Union*, L 34/26–29.

Council Joint Action (2003b) '2003/423/CFSP of 5/6/2003 on the European Union Military Operation in the Democratic Republic of Congo', *Official Journal of the European Union*, L 143/50–52.

Council Joint Action (2006) '2006/319/CFSP of 27/04/2006 on the European Union Military Operation in Support of the United Nations Organisation Mission in the Democratic Republic of Congo (MONUC) during the Election Process', *Official Journal of the European Union*, L 116/98–101.

Europa (2012) *Common Security and Defence Policy (CSDP)* [online], http://europa.eu/legislation_summaries/glossary/european_security_defence_policy_en.htm, date accessed 10 June 2012.

Europabevaegelsen (2012) *Undtagelsen mht. Forsvarssamarbejdet* [online], http://www.euforbehold.dk/optouts/defence?lang=da, date accessed 9 June 2012.

Folketinget EU-oplysningen (2012) *Danish Opt-Outs* [online], http://www.euo.dk/emner_en/forbehold/, date accessed 9 June 2012.

Franco-British Summit Declaration (1998) *Joint Declaration on European Defence* [online], http://www.atlanticcommunity.org/Saint-Malo%20Declaration%20Text.html, date accessed 10 June 2012.

Giegerich, B. (2008) *European Military Crisis Management: Connecting Ambition and Reality*. International Institute for Strategic Studies, Adelphi Paper No. 397. London: Routledge.

Greens Analyse Institut (2009) *Meningsmaalinger: Undtagelsen mht. Forsvarssamarbejdet* [online], http://www.euforbehold.dk/optouts/defence/opinionpolls, date accessed 9 June 2012.

Hadden, T. (ed.) (2009) *A Responsibility to Assist: Human Rights Policy and Practice in European Union Crisis Management Operations*. Oxford: Hart.

Haine, J. and Giegerich, B. (2006) *In Congo, a Cosmetic EU Operation* [online], International Herald Tribune, 12 June, http://www.iiss.org/whats-new/iiss-in-the-press/press-coverage-2006/june-2006/in-congo-a-cosmetic-eu-operation/, date accessed 26 May 2009.

Hill, C. (2003) *The Changing Politics of Foreign Policy*. Basingstoke: Palgrave Macmillan.

Howorth, J. (2005) 'The Euro-Atlantic Security Dilemma: France, Britain and the ESDP', *Journal of Transatlantic Studies*, Vol. 3, No. 1, 39–54.

Howorth, J. (2007) *Security and Defence Policy in the European Union*. Basingstoke: Palgrave Macmillan.

International Crisis Group (2005) *EU Crisis Response Revisited* [online], Europe Report, 160, http://www.crisisgroup.org/home/index.cfm?id=3220, date accessed 1 June 2009.

Manners, I. (2005) *Europe and the World*. Basingstoke: Palgrave Macmillan.

Mattelaer, A. (2008) *The Strategic Planning of EU Military Operations: The Case of EUFOR Chad/CAR* [online], IES Working Paper, 5/2008, Brussels, http://www.ies.be/files/repo/IES%20working%20paper%205_Alexander%20Mattelaer.pdf, date accessed 1 June 2009.

Mattelaer, A. (2009) 'ESDP Planning Machinery and the Lessons from EUFOR Chad', *CFSP Forum*, Vol. 7, No. 3, 1–6.

Merlingen, M. and Ostrauskaite, R. (2008) *European Security and Defence Policy: An Implementation Perspective*. Oxon: Routledge.

NATO (2006) *NATO Handbook*. Brussels: NATO Public Diplomacy Division.

Nissen, C. (2014) *Det Europaeiske Raad 19–20. December: Nyt Momentum for Oeget Forsvarssamarbejde i Europa* [online], Danish Institute for International Studies. Copenhagen, 14 January, http://www.diis.dk/hjem/diis+comments/diis+comments/diis+comments+-+dansk/diis+comments+2013/det+europæiske+råd+19+20+december-c3-+nyt+momentum+for+øget+forsvarssamarbejde+i+eur opa, date accessed 13 January 2014.

Peen Rodt, A. (2014) *The European Union and Military Conflict Management*. London: Routledge.

Peen Rodt, A. and Wolff, S. (2012) 'EU Conflict Management in Bosnia and Herzegovina and Macedonia', in Whitman, Richard G. and Wolff, Stefan (eds.) *The European Union as a Global Conflict Manager*. London: Routledge, 169–188.

Rasmussen, M.V., Kristensen, K.S., Breitenbauch, H. and Struwe, L.B. (2014) *Sikkerhedspolitisk Barometer: CMS Survey 2014*. Copenhagen: Center for Military Studies – Copenhagen University.

Rettman, A. (2014a) 'EU States Consider Sending Soldiers to Central Africa' [online], *EUobserver.com*, Brussels, 9 January, http://euobserver.com/defence/122669, date accessed 14 January 2014.

Rettman, A. (2014b) 'EU Countries Provisionally Agree African Mission' [online], *EUobserver.com*, Brussels, 10 January, http://euobserver.com/foreign/122690#!, date accessed 14 January 2014.

Rye Olsen, G., (2012) 'The European Union's Africa Policy: The Result of "Nordicization" or Europeanization?', *European Union in International Affairs III*. 3–5 May, Brussels.

Seibert, B.H. (2007) *African Adventure? Assessing the European Union's Military Intervention in Chad and the Central African Republic* [online], MIT Security Studies Programme Working Papers, November, http://web.mit.edu/ssp/Publications/working_papers/WP_07–1.pdf, date accessed 21 May 2009.

Trajkovski, B. (2003) Speech at the European Union Welcoming Ceremony [online], Skopje, 31 March, http://www.nato.int/docu/speech/2003/s030331d.htm, date accessed 1 June 2009.

Ulriksen, S., Gourlay, C. and Mace, C. (2004) 'Operation Artemis: The Shape of Things to Come?', *International Peacekeeping*, Vol. 11, No. 3, 508–525.

Waterfield, B. (2013) 'David Cameron Fights off EU Army Plan', *The Telegraph*, 19 December, http://www.telegraph.co.uk/news/worldnews/europe/eu/10528852/David-Cameron-flies-to-Brussels-determined-to-fight-EU-drones-programme.html#, date accessed 14 January 2014.

Whitman, R. (1998) *From Civilian Power to Superpower: The International Identity of the European Union*. London: Palgrave Macmillan.

Whitman, R. and Wolff, S. (2012) *The European Union as a Global Conflict Manager*. London: Routledge.

Žabec, K. (2009) 'Croatian Troops in Africa Fighting for Accession to the EU', *Jutarnji List*, 15 February.

9 Enlarging the European Union

Member State preferences and institutional dynamics

Meltem Müftüler-Baç[1]

Introduction

One of the most important developments in the European Union in the last decade has been its enlargement process. The uniting of the European continent under its umbrella turned out to be the main instrument for stability, prosperity and cohesion in Europe. Specifically, from 1991 onwards, the Central and Eastern European countries aimed at EU accession in order to stabilize their political and economic transformation. The EU, on the other hand, relied on its enlargement policy as its most effective foreign policy tool (Smith, 2004; Sjursen, 2006; Bickerton, 2011). As a consequence from 1998 to 2012, the EU found itself facing its largest expansion (Schimmelfennig, 2001; Moravscik and Vachudova, 2008), and in 2004, ten new members from the Central and Eastern Europe, Cyprus and Malta joined the European Union. In 2007, this round of enlargement was completed with the Bulgaria and Romanian accessions, and in 2013, Croatia joined the EU as a full member. As of 2016, there are seven countries which are at different stages of their accession to the EU with key differences that set the current process apart from the previous round of enlargement. First, it seems to be that there is declining support amongst EU Member States to continue with the enlargement policy. Second, the Member States have visible diverging preferences over certain candidates' accession, exemplified in the Greek veto of Macedonia and Cyprus' veto of Turkey. As foreseen in the Introduction of this volume, the Member States' increased role in the enlargement policy serves as an empirical illustration of a change in the EU's mode of policy-making over time. The diverging Member State preferences decrease the EU's ability to speak with one unified voice over enlargement and indicate an increasingly nationalized mode for enlargement, rather than a Europeanised mode.

According to the European Commission, the EU has, since its inception, responded to the legitimate aspiration of the peoples of our continent to be united in a common European endeavour. It has brought nations and cultures together, enriching and injecting the EU with diversity and dynamism. More than three-quarters of the EU Member States are former "enlargement" countries' (European Commission, 2012: 2). The EU institutions' role in this process of enlarging the Union is critical. An important concern here, as argued in the Introduction, is whether enlargement policy is part and parcel of European foreign policy, whether Member States contribute to enlargement in line with their own foreign policy preferences or whether it results from a combination of EU-level and MS foreign policy dynamics. Since enlarging the Union turned out to be one of the most visible aspects of the European foreign policy in the period from 2000 to 2013, this chapter analyzes the EU enlargement process, in terms of its past accomplishments and the future prospects. Specifically, the chapter seeks answers to the extent to which enlargement policy has become unfolded in a 'Europeanised' mode or in a nationalized mode in which the Member States impact enlargement. Since EU policies result from the shared competencies (Whitman, 1998; Manners, 2002) between the EU institutions and its Member States, the final outcome of enlargement needs to be seen as a combination of EU and Member State preferences, in line with the key premises of this volume. Consequently, this chapter looks at the interplay of the Member States' preferences and the EU dynamics in the EU's enlargement process in order to assess the merits of the policy as a foreign policy tool.

Context

It is without doubt that the European Union traditionally used enlargement effectively as a foreign policy tool, illustrating the Europeanised mode of the process. The main rationale behind enlargement is summarized in December 2011 by Cyprus' Foreign Affairs minister, Erato Marcouillis: 'We reaffirmed our commitment to the enlargement process, which is one of the most efficient means for reinforcing peace, democracy and stability in Europe'.[2] Ever since the 2001 Gothenburg European Council, all EU Member States committed themselves to EU enlargement 'as an irreversible process'. The recommendations from the European Commission and the European Council decisions turned out to be critical in carrying out enlargement. In the December 2006 summit of the European Council, a renewed consensus on enlargement was adopted as the main basis for enlargement where each applicant country is evaluated based on its own merits.

Yet, even though all EU members are committed to enlargement in principle as reiterated in various European Council conclusions, Member State dynamics become important in enlargement in general and towards specific candidates in particular. As a result, the negotiations process unfolds for the applicant countries subject to the Member States' diverging positions on these applicant countries (Moravcsik, 1993; Sjursen, 2002, 2006; Müftüler-Baç and McLaren, 2003; Müftüler-Baç and Kibris, 2011). This could be explained from an intergovernmental perspective as even though the European institutions' role in enlarging the Union is paramount, enlargement is still subject to Member States' unanimous approval. Enlargement then ultimately depends on the convergence of interests among the EU Member States who would support the process only if 'they consider enlargement to be in their long-term economic and geopolitical interest' (Moravcsik and Vachudova, 2008: 43). This is why; this chapter investigates whether EU enlargement has been guided solely by the EU institutions or whether Member States acted as the main mechanism, either as drivers or brakemen in the process.

The Europeanised and nationalized modes of policy-making for EU enlargement is particularly evident in the current round of enlargement, specifically the possible costs the EU and its Member States would be willing to undertake for their absorption and the expected benefits they would reap as a consequence. It needs to be noted here that economic interests motivate the EU towards certain countries' accession, which could thus be seen as part and parcel of the Europeanised mode of policy-making. Bosnia, Macedonia and Kosovo emerge as prime examples here: in Bosnia, the prospect of EU accession has not been particularly strong or credible, and internal divisions run deep preventing any progress in the enlargement process. Kosovo suffers from internal divisions and the lack of a credible position among the EU Member States, but it was still able to negotiate a Stabilisation and Association Agreement (SAA). In the Macedonian case, the decision to open negotiations has been conditioned for years now by the Council following a resolution on the name dispute with Greece.[3] In absence of clear certainty and stronger appeal of membership, the cost of compliance to the EU conditions is regarded as too high. Even in the cases where some success and upgrading of candidates' relations with the EU are evident – for example in Serbia, Montenegro and Albania – the enlargement policy toolbox has only limited success in helping candidates undertake far-reaching political, economic and societal reforms. This inability in return shape the Member State preferences towards particular candidates as well as enlargement as a whole. However, the increased role of the Member States and the nation-alized mode of policy-making have been more evident in the recent round, rather than the 2004 enlargement. It is, therefore, possible to see a change in the Member State preferences within the enlargement policy and action resulting in the nature of the policy itself as a result of this transition.

Member States and enlarging the EU

The European Union has long been engaged in an extensive process of enlargement. Enlargement is seen as a tool to expand the liberal democratic community that the EU sym-bolizes (Schimmelfennig, 2001; Sjursen, 2002), or alternatively, it is conceptualized as a policy that would be possible only when the material interests of the EU members converge (Moravscik and Vachudova, 2008). The enlargement process could be seen as a three-level process which initially begins as an EU initiative (Schimmelfennig, 2001), administered by the EU institutions, specifically the Commission, subject to unanimous approval in the Council by the Member States, which brings in the Member States' individual interests that affect the pace and nature of the negotiations. The final outcome of enlargement is mutually shaped by the EU's internal dynamics (Smith, 2004; Müftüler-Baç, 2008) and Member State preferences (Preston, 1995; Moravscik and Vachudova, 2008). Even though the EU's initial trigger and continued commitment is absolutely necessary, it is not sufficient on its own to bring about EU expansion; Member States have to unanimously agree.

This brings us to the question as to what kind of Member State considerations come into play in the enlargement process as well as the tools with which they could dominate the process. The large Member States, Germany, France and United Kingdom, emerge as key players in enlargement (Schimmelfennig, 2001; Tonra, 2011), but it is also possible to see coalitions between the smaller states who have common material interests acting as blocs in the decision-making process. Since foreign policy and enlargement are both largely inter-governmental (Hill, 2003; Forsberg, 2011) – i.e. they depend on unanimous approval by all EU members – the bargains between the Member States where any Member State could act as a veto player (Moravcsik, 1993, 1998; Koenig and Junge, 2009; Müftüler-Baç and Kibris, 2011) become critical. In that respect, Member State preferences act as the key in shaping the policy choices (Moravcsik, 1998). Yet, once the enlargement policy is launched at the EU level, the Member States cannot completely stall the process. That is particularly impor-tant as Member States differ with regards to their capacity to download their preferences from the EU level. For example, Member States such as Finland that support the European ideal (Forsberg, 2011), that is the Europeanised mode, also support enlargement in a consis-tent manner whereas France with its own nationalist concerns turns out to be more sceptical on enlargement. This means then the enlargement process combines Europeanised as well as national modes of policy-making.

Policy change

The key issues, of course, are whether a collective European interest in enlargement exists which transcends the national material interests of the EU members and whether the EU as a whole benefits from enlargement. The EU's enlargement policy could be seen as a key instrument for advancing EU's foreign policy goals such as uniting the European continent, securing the EU's borders, expanding the EU's global reach and enhancing security in Europe (Schimmelfennig, 2001; Sjursen, 2002; Smith, 2004). The EU was able to export stability to its periphery and support democratic transformation with its enlargement policy (Schimmelfennig and Sedelmeier, 2002). On the other hand, opponents of enlargement stress its impact on diluting the Union and argue that widening Europe turned out to be an obstacle in deepening Europe and led to institutional gridlock (Hertz and Leuffen, 2011). An important concern here is with regards to the natural limits of enlargement in terms of EU cohesion, sustainability, prosperity, institutional capacity and democratic representation.

In other words, to what extent can the EU continue enlarging without jeopardizing the integration process? This is also partly the reason why some EU Member States are more hesitant both towards enlargement and towards specific countries' accession even though the European Commission favours enlargement in order to advance security and cohesion in Europe. In order to assess this, one needs to take a look at the 2004 enlargement.

In the 1992 Lisbon summit of the European Council, based on the European Commission's recommendation, the EU members agreed on the idea of enlarging the Union towards the East. In 1993, at the Copenhagen summit of the European Council, the EU adopted the main criteria to evaluate the applicant countries and their fit into full membership. Towards that end, the Council adopted the Copenhagen criteria that the applicant countries need to satisfy both to become candidates and for accession negotiations to begin. The Copenhagen criteria include stable institutions guaranteeing democracy, rule of law, human rights and protection of minorities; a functioning market economy able to withstand competitive pressures that will emanate from the Union; and ability to take on membership responsibilities including the adoption and implementation of the *acquis*. In addition, the 1993 Copenhagen conclusions stressed the EU's absorption capacity as a determining factor in accession: the Union's capacity to absorb new members, while maintaining the momentum of European integration, is an important consideration in the general interest of both the Union and the candidate countries[4] This leadership role exercised by the European Commission on enlargement shows that, in this policy area, there is an important element of 'Europeanised' policy-making, and Member States operate within the EU framework as shaped by the Commission. At the same time, from the very beginning of the process, some EU members such as Germany and the UK supported enlargement towards the East wholeheartedly because enlargement also served their material interests of bringing stability to Europe. This is clearly summarized by Joschka Fischer, then German foreign minister, as '[i]f EU did not enlarge to include the Central Eastern European countries, Europe would become a continent of uncertainty . . . if that happened Germany in particular would be the big loser',[5] clearly demonstrating the fit between the European and German foreign policy preferences at the time. This convergence of interests between the EU institutions and key Member States acted as key to launch enlargement in the 1990s. To turn to the main procedures of enlargement, it needs to be pointed out that the enlargement process operates within the institutionalized, supranational European framework with the European Commission and the Council as the key players. When a country applies to the EU for accession, it presents its application to the European Commission, which in turn prepares an Opinion on the country's readiness to meet the EU accession criteria as formulated in the Copenhagen Council and recommends elevating the applicant to a candidate status and/or open accession negotiations. The Commission's Opinion is a recommendation to the Council which unanimously has to agree. Accession negotiations could commence only when the candidate fully satisfies the political aspects of the Copenhagen criteria and the Council unanimously adopts the Negotiations Framework prepared by the Commission. The actual negotiations process begins with an intergovernmental conference. The next step is the screening process where the candidate and the Commission engage in an analytical examination of the candidate's laws in the light of the EU *acquis*, which is divided into multiple chapters. In the negotiations phase, the Commission acts as the facilitator between the candidate and the Council through the drafting of common positions, and the candidate or Member States could ask for transitional periods, financial compensation, safeguard clauses or, in very few cases, permanent derogations from the *acquis*. Since, every chapter opening and provisional closure is subject to unanimous approval by all the EU members, this is how and where individual material preferences of the EU members become visible. Once all the chapters are closed, an Accession Treaty is signed by the candidate and the EU Member States. After the Treaty is ratified in each and every Member State, approved by the European Parliament and ratified in the candidate country, it comes into force and the candidate becomes a full member of the EU. The process itself shows that enlargement is a top-down exercise and an EU-level policy, and the Member States download at least some of their positions from EU level; yet since all chapter openings and closures need to be voted upon unanimously, it also includes elements of a bottom-up exercise, where members upload their national interests to the EU framework. This is particularly important in some candidates, for example for Turkey's accession; both France and Austria declared they would hold a referendum.

To turn to the 2004 and 2007 enlargement, in July 1997, the European Commission adopted its *Agenda 2000* evaluating the fourteen standing applications for EU accession. One of the applicant countries at the time was Morocco, which the Commission declared to be ineligible for EU accession; as for the rest, the Commission recommended candidacy status for some of them as well as opening of accession negotiations. Accordingly, in December 1997, the European Council decided in its Luxembourg summit to open accession negotiations with six of the applicant countries, Poland, Hungary, Estonia, Slovenia, Cyprus and the Czech Republic, and elevated five other applicants, Slovakia, Latvia, Lithuania, Bulgaria and Romania, into candidate status. The accession negotiations with the Luxembourg Six began in March 1998. In December 1999, in its Helsinki summit, the European Council decided to open accession negotiations with the remaining five in addition to Malta and also elevated Turkey into candidate status. In December 2002, ten of these candidates concluded their accession negotiations and signed their Accession Treaties on April 16, 2003, and finally became members of the EU on May 1, 2004. Bulgaria and Romania acceded to the EU in 2007. As a result, from 1997 to 2007, the EU expanded from fifteen to twenty-seven Member States, increasing its population, territorial size and GDP considerably. In 2009, the European Commission reported that the 2004 enlargement benefitted the old and new members in both economic and security terms. The new members increased their GDP by 15 per cent in five years, and the older members received a trade boost, access to a larger market and increased global efficiency as well as a new qualified labour force (European Commission, 2009). The economic interests of the Member States also played an important role in paving the way of enlargement with the European Commission emphasizing the economic impact of the candidates on the European growth. Table 9.1 summarizes the former candidates' economic capabilities.

With the 2004/2007 enlargement, it seems as if, in terms of enhancing the economic capabilities on the continent, enlargement fulfilled the EU's material foreign policy objectives. Equally important, the unification of the European continent was deemed almost complete

Table 9.1 Economic indicators for the new Member States in their year of accession

	GDP (US$)[6]	Population[7]	Contribution of imports to intra-EU trade in %[8]	Contributions of exports to intra-EU trade in %[9]	GDP growth rate (annual %)[10]	Price level ratio of Purchasing Power Parity (PPP) conversion factor (GDP) to market exchange rate[11]
2004						
Poland	253,525,770	38,182,222	2.7	2.3	5.1	0.3
Hungary	103,156,817	10,107,146	1.7	1.8	4.8	0.6
Czech Rep	118,976,023	10,197,101	2.3	2.3	4.9	0.6
Slovakia	57,329,401	5,372,280	0.9	0.9	5.2	0.7
Slovenia	34,470,229	1,997,012	0.6	0.4	4.4	0.8
Estonia	12,057,639	1,362,550	0.2	0.2	6.5	0.6
Latvia	15,267,165	2,263,122	0.2	0.1	8.9	0.5
Lithuania	22,649,483	3,377,075	0.3	0.2	N/A	0.5
Cyprus	17,164,625	1,015,827	0.2	0.0	4.4	0.9
Malta	5,643,525	401,268	0.1	0.0	−0.5	0.7
2007						
Bulgaria	43,637,701	7,545,338	0.5	0.3	6.9	0.4
Romania	170,613,460	20,882,982	1.4	0.8	6.3	0.6
2013						
Croatia	57,868,674	4,255,700	5,588,307	12,123,42	−0.9	0.6

with a recasting of Europe and a defining once and for all who belongs in Europe (Sjursen, 2002). This is why the enlargement process from 1998 to 2007 is seen as a great success for the EU. Beyond the economic implications, enlargement has become the most important tool that the EU relied upon to solve bilateral conflicts in its periphery and to advance the visibility of the EU both in the European continent and globally. Stefan Fule, the Commissioner for Enlargement and Neighbourhood Policy, summarized this point in 2010 as: 'When you look at the challenges facing the EU in the twenty-first century, it is extremely important to look outwards, not inwards. Enlargement is an important element of this process',[12] reflecting both the European foreign policy objectives and the dominant mode of operations in enlargement.

Yet, one could ask whether enlargement has costs for both the EU and the Member States. In that aspect, the possible impact it would have on deepening the Union and the financial burdens it might bring emerge as potential obstacles to enlargement. This might be the reason why Fule's sentiments are not readily shared by all the Member States, either based on concerns on integration or on European cohesion. For example, in 2011, then French President Nicholas Sarkozy reflected on this as 'one cannot plead for federalism and at the same time for the enlargement of Europe. It's impossible. There's a contradiction'.[13] If France is not that enthusiastic about enlargement for integrationist purposes, there are other Member States who stress the financial costs of enlargement. Most notably, prior to the 2004 enlargement, Spain, Portugal, Greece and Ireland formed a blocking minority in the budgetary negotiations to guarantee their share of the structural funds to continue even after the relatively poorer countries from the Central and Eastern Europe join the EU. However, there was a significant amount of convergence of material interests among the EU Member States with few of them acting as the main drivers of enlargement. Specifically, Germany, the UK, Sweden, Denmark and Finland were consistently in favour of enlargement supporting the Commission's position that the EU would become a global power with sustainable economic growth with enlargement. As a result, the brakemen such as France could not stall the process, at least not then.

This meant that enlargement proceeded with supranational leadership supported by Member States that download their preferences from the EU level. In the last round of enlargement, the accession of twelve new members into the EU was an outcome of the EU's institutional commitment to enlargement and the convergence of material interests at the time among the EU members. All the powerful members of the EU, Germany, France and UK, in 2004 agreed on enlarging the Union; however, it seems that since 2008 enlargement as a process slowed down. A key concern in the enlargement process is that it should be conducted in such a way that it would not harm the future prospects of integration. This concern has led the Union to apply an ever-increasing set of membership conditionality to applicant states at each round of enlargement. Equally important, some of the mistakes that were committed in the previous round have now become important lessons for the EU; for example Bulgarian and Romanian accessions showed that, unless the EU has full proof that the candidate is actually enforcing the legislation, it must not become a member. As a result, each enlargement for the EU is a learning experience, and in this learning curve, with every new round of negotiations, the EU toughened up its criteria so as not to repeat the mistakes of the previous rounds or in the European Commission's terminology 'lessons learned'. This is compounded by the 'enlargement fatigue' in some EU members such as France, Austria and the Netherlands where a clear resistance to continuing enlargement is seen.

The leftovers, the newcomers and the next wave of EU enlargement

The enlargement process no longer seems to occupy an important place in the EU's agenda or among the Member State priorities. That being said, the countries that are currently negotiating for accession, such as Turkey as well as the candidates in the Western Balkans, are still a long way away from the EU accession. In 2005, the EU began accession negotiations with both Turkey and Croatia (which joined the EU in 2013). The remaining Western Balkan countries – Montenegro, Albania, Kosovo, Bosnia and Herzegovina, Serbia, Macedonia – are at different stages of their association with the EU, though all of them have the accession perspective. Montenegro began its accession negotiations in 2012 and Serbia in 2014. Moldova, Belorussia and Ukraine do not have the accession perspective yet, but the EU is trying to establish relatively close relations with them without necessarily closing the door completely for eventual accession.

With the current round of enlargement, most of the Western Balkan countries lag behind the CEE candidates at the time of their accession negotiations in terms of their economic preparedness. Among the current candidates, Turkey presents a different picture due to its economic capabilities and as part of the G20. It is the sixth-largest economy in Europe and acts as a power on its own right in the Western Balkans. Furthermore, it is the only one of the current candidates that is characterized by the Commission's progress reports as a 'functioning market economy'. For example, this sits in contrast to Kosovo, a small state that is not even fully recognized, or Bosnia, where the economy is significantly weaker than other

Table 9.2 The economic indicators for the current candidates

	GDP (US$)[14]	Population[15]	Total import value (US$)[16]	Total export value (US$)[15]	GDP growth rate (annual %)[17]	Price level ratio of PPP conversion factor (GDP) to market exchange rate[18]
Current candidates – 2014						
Bosnia	18,344,278	3,817,554	3,329,647	5,025,384	1.2	0.5
Macedonia	11,323,761	2,075,625	3,025,055	3,820,769	3.8	0.4
Montenegro	4,583,198	621,800	249,201	973,307	1.5	0.5
Serbia	43,866,423	7,129,428	7,111,687	10,373,838	−1.8	0.5
Albania	13,370,191	2,894,475	1,248,250	2,471,046	1.9	0.4
Kosovo	N/A	N/A	95,602	728,665	N/A	N/A
Turkey	799,534,963	75,932,348	54,231,644	74,633,155	2.9	0.5

applicants. This is why there is also a key difference between the previous round of enlargement and the new round in terms of their economic capabilities as summarized in Table 9.2.

The Western Balkans' economic levels of development present a key difference from the previous round of enlargement, shaping both the Member State preferences and the EU's position on these candidates. The current candidates also have multiple bilateral conflicts with the Member States. As a result, there is a significant change in the EU enlargement policy with the new round as well as the main mode of policy-making becoming more nationalized.

Policy performance: action and change

It needs to be noted that the enlargement process also has become, for the first time in the EU's history, a process where EU Member States depend upon for the solving their bilateral problems with the acceding states in a multilateral setting (Müftüler-Baç and Kibris, 2011). This, of course, was not the goal in the enlargement process. However, specifically in Croatian and Turkish negotiations, some Member States such as Slovenia and Cyprus used the enlargement process to advance their own material interests through their veto power. Even though Croatia was meeting the EU criteria, Slovenia blocked several chapters in order to force Croatia to concede on their border issue. Cyprus vetoed the opening of six chapters for Turkish accession negotiations and eight more chapters remain frozen due to Turkey's non-implementation of the Additional Protocol on its 1995 Customs Union agreement. Similarly, France vetoed five chapters for Turkish negotiations since 2007. In this fashion, Cyprus, France and Slovenia acted as veto players clearly engaged in a process of uploading their own preferences to the EU level through the accession process. On the other hand, there is also a change in the Europeanised mode of policy-making. In 2011, the Commission adopted a 'new approach' in the enlargement policy by adopting a new tool-prioritizing rule of law and fundamental freedoms in the process. Accordingly, for all candidates beginning their negotiations after 2012, the negotiations would commence with Chapters 23 and 24 – on judiciary, justice, freedom and fundamental rights. This strategy change signals the Europeanised mode's continued relevance in using the enlargement process to ensure the expansion of the European community and values. However, despite this policy change, the Commission's new approach could not be implemented in the case of Turkey, where the Greek Cypriotic government vetoed the opening of Chapters 23 and 24, indicating the increased role of the nationalized mode in the EU enlargament policy.

This increased political nature of the negotiations constitutes further empirical verification of the low degree of solidarity inside the EU as well as the narrow materialistic position of its members (Moravscik and Vachudova, 2008; Koenig and Junge, 2009; Bickerton, 2011). The nationalized mode of policy-making has become more prevalent almost in all the new candidates' experience with the EU impacting their accession processes.

To give an example from a candidate that has now suspended its negotiations, Iceland, an important motivation for Iceland's accession negotiations was its 2008 economic and financial crisis. Even though per capita income in Iceland is very high, and it fulfils the EU's political criteria and has already adopted the EU *acquis* on the single market due to its European Economic Area membership, its accession, at the time, was not certain. Specifically, the fisheries policy of the EU caused a rift in the negotiations shaping the Icelanders' opposition to the EU, making it likely that they would reject membership once accession negotiations are complete. This would be similar to the EU's experience with Norway both in 1973 and 1994 when the Norwegians voted 'No' in the referendum for EU accession after the Norwegian government concluded its Accession Treaty. Iceland, of course, needed an economic anchor that Norway did not need then. However, it is also that the economic problems that made Iceland withdrew, as the banking crisis left Iceland with ongoing contentions with the UK and the Netherlands whose citizens lost a lot of money in Iceland's financial sector meltdown. It is partly due to these two Member States' own material concerns that Iceland suspended its negotiations in 2013 and remained outside of the current enlargement process. Both the UK and the Netherlands played a veto player role in the negotiations with Iceland, enhancing the role of the nationalized mode as opposed to the Europeanised mode.

This issue – nationalized mode over the Europeanised mode – arises as a critical factor in the enlargement negotiations, similar to Croatia–Slovenia, Greece–Macedonia, and Turkey–Cyprus bilateral relations impacting the negotiations, with individual Member States uploading their own preferences to the EU level. However, both Croatia and Iceland are relatively small countries whose accession would not drastically change the EU's institutionally or economically. Their ability to impact the EU's integration and to boost economic growth in the EU is relatively limited. Since their relative impact on European integration – a key concern for laggard states such as France – is low, the EU framework still remains the main mode of operations in their negotiations. Yet, in both these cases, we see individual Member States such as UK and the Netherlands for Iceland and Slovenia for Croatia playing the veto player role in an attempt to have their national preferences uploaded to the EU level whereas previous drivers such as Finland still playing the most supporting role. On the other hand, increased scepticism even in the Member States traditionally supportive of enlargement is a key concern. A case in point illustrating the diverging positions of the EU and individual Member States on enlargement is provided by Norbert Lammert, the president of the German Bundestag in 2012, 'Croatia is clearly not yet ready for membership',[19] questioning the Commission's judgement. The German reluctance signals a divergence between the European and German foreign policy preferences over enlargement in 2013 that did not exist in 2004. However, the Europeanised mode in the Croatian case turned out to be more effective in paving its accession in 2013.

To turn to the Western Balkans, the EU accession perspective in the Western Balkans is a critical anchor in their state-building process as well as integration into the European markets. The 2003 Thessaloniki summit of the European Council granted the accession perspective to the Western Balkan countries; consequently, they are all perceived as potential candidates for membership. Although these six countries are at different stages of political and economic development, their relations with the EU are critical in shaping their development processes. The EU's vast *acquis communautaire* as well as its support to democratic institutionalization is attractive for the Western Balkan countries which are in need of an anchor. The Western Balkan countries are radically different than the Central and Eastern European countries which the EU successfully transformed through its accession criteria (Sedelmeier, 2000; Dimitrova, 2010). The Western Balkan countries still live the aftershocks of the ethnic wars of the 1990s, and the violent disintegration of Yugoslavia is a catastrophic event for all the peoples there, providing also the security rationale for the EU's stabilization efforts in the region (Hill, 2003). In addition, transition to market economy, state-building and democratic transition are still in their infant stages. The Stabilization and Association Process (SAP) adopted for each of these countries comes with a unique set of tools for each country fit to deal with its specific problems. This is because let's say while Kosovo is trying to exert its separation and independence from Serbia, Bosnia and Herzegovina is in need of state structures with administrative reform capacity. They also face different levels of support from the EU members; Macedonia, for example, is blocked by Greece due to a disagreement over its name; Kosovo faces a cold shoulder in EU members such as Spain, Greece, Cyprus, Romania and Slovakia, which are faced with their own separatist movements and as a result do not recognize Kosovo. Both for Western Balkans and the Turkish case, the EU members seem to have a stronger upper hand compared to the 2004 enlargement, and that might be because the EU institutions' commitment is lower for these leftovers. The lack of a clear perspective from the EU, despite its initial commitment and the SAP, lessens the EU's impact on the Western Balkans. However, in the Western Balkan cases, there is a clear evidence of the EU Member States uploading their own preferences to the EU level. This is also a sharp contrast to the previous enlargement as once the EU position was clear, the EU members were less likely to block the process.

In addition, the divergence among the EU members such as the Greek refusal to recognize Macedonia's name, harms the EU's image as a coherent actor that could essentially speak with one voice, and provides empirical proof that it is the Member State preferences that increasingly guide the EU enlargement. Eduard Kukan, a Member of European Parliament from Slovakia, illustrated the difficulty in reconciling the Greek and the European interest on this issue as 'The EU should be more supportive in the process of finding a solution to the outstanding issue between Greece and Macedonia. It is in the EU's interest'.[20] The economic crisis in the EU adds on top of that (Hallerberg, 2011), with the inability of the EU to further invest in the region which requires financial compensation to adopt and implement necessary reforms. Thus, despite the EU's intentions to increase its presence in the Western Balkans through the accession process, the difficulties of stabilization in the region, the diverging Member State preferences over enlargement, the decreased financial capacity of the EU act as the main constraints in achieving these objectives. Yet, if the EU succeeds in stabilizing Western Balkans, enable them to transform their economic and political structures; it would not only reap significant economic benefits – a new market but also a foreign policy victory.

However, Member States are not uniform in terms of their views on the Western Balkans. Traditional supporters of enlargement still are in favour and download from the EU level their positions on enlargement. For example, the UK among the Big Three is the most supportive, along with other EU members such as Sweden, Finland and the Central Eastern

European countries. Despite the UK's own misgivings about its continued role in the EU, the UK still supports the enlargement policy. The British position on enlargement was illustrated by its Minister of European Affairs David Lidington as follows:

> The European Union will remain strong only if it is outward-looking and continues to grow. That is why we in Britain are strong supporters of the EU neighbourhood policy and believe that membership of the EU should be open for any European country that wants to join, and can meet the rigorous accession criteria.[21]

This is, of course, a very different position than France under Sarkozy, the Austrian vision or the German position as illustrated by Chancellor Angela Merkel's statement that Germany is 'advocating a phase of consolidation, during which the strengthening of the EU's identity and institutions take precedence over further EU enlargement.'[22] This view becomes strongest for one of the current candidates, Turkey, as reflected by the Austrian Minister of Foreign Affairs, Michael Spindelegger: 'We will wait and see what happens, be constructive, but remain true to our basic position that we will strive for a special partnership with Turkey'.[23] It seems like the Turkish case emerges as an interesting illustration of the Member State brakes on enlargement.

This in turn was perplexing given the EU's preferences towards Turkish accession along the long-term economic and geopolitical benefits. However, there is a significant divergence among the EU members over Turkey: Austria, Germany and France oppose its accession along identity concerns; Belgium and Luxembourg have doubts due to the Turkish size whereas the UK, Finland, Sweden are highly supportive. Turkey, increasingly since 2007, has become a regional great power, actively engaging in the Middle East and the Balkans. An important factor in making this transformation possible has been the growing Turkish economy. However, despite the positive economic outlook in Turkey, its EU accession is becoming more distant. Given the Turkish ability to meet the EU's economic criteria, even on chapters where there are no technical problems such as energy, financial and monetary matters, education and culture, the EU fails to progress with the Turkish negotiations. This is particularly important as some EU Member States –France and Cyprus specifically – veto the opening of chapters where Turkey meets the *acquis* for political reasons. Especially to the non-EU members such as Turkey which are fulfilling the economic aspects of both the Copenhagen criteria as well as the Maastricht convergence criteria and yet still cannot open these chapters for negotiations, the fact that some EU members themselves do not fulfil the convergence criteria even remotely, decreases both the credibility of the EU and its own attractiveness as an economic magnet (Rauch et al., 2011). The following incident illustrates this point even further.

In June 2007, the European Commission had prepared the chapter on Economic and Financial matters for negotiations with Turkey and declared that Turkey is fulfilling the *acquis* in that chapter, but then newly elected French President Nicholas Sarkozy vetoed its opening based on the argument that it would mean Turkey could adopt the euro. Sarkozy's stated reason was that, since Turkey already meets the EU's Maastricht convergence criteria, this would mean Turkey would be able to ready to adopt the euro prior to its accession. The most important problem in that according to Sarkozy was that it would signal a commitment on the EU's part for Turkish accession; this is of course surprising as the accession negotiations were opened precisely for this ultimate objective. If one considers the fact that Turkey's public debt is 43 per cent of its GDP, much less than the Maastricht criteria's requirement of 60 per cent and much less than the Greek, Italian and Spanish public debts, the significance of this decision becomes even clearer. According to the German officials, the EU's inability to open this chapter with Turkey for negotiations was due to the French veto, and 'This was a political decision emanating from Paris.'[24] In addition, this meant that, even though some members of the EU do not conform to its economic criteria (Hallerberg, 2011; Rauch et al., 2011), and yet when an acceding country such as Turkey does, the EU still cannot open the chapter related to that criteria based on a member's veto which is motivated by political and cultural reasons (Hobolt et al., 2011), illustrating the role of the Member State preferences, both in EU's foreign policy and enlargement process. The French veto on Chapter 17 – Economic and Financial – matters lasted from 2007 to 2015, and the Chapter was finally opened for negotiations in December 2015. One must also consider that, with Turkey's accession process, the EU confronts for the first time since the British accession in 1973 a symmetrical power. This comes together with its own set of complexities, both in terms of foreign policy and economic implications.

In short, it seems that the enlargement process has run out of steam. The slowing down of the enlargement process goes hand in hand with the current challenges in the integration process. Specifically, an unforeseen challenge in the EU's enlargement process lies in the European crisis (Longo and Murray, 2011). Since 2008, the EU confronts one of its worst economic and political crises with severe debt problems in some of its members. A critical question is whether the limits of integration have been reached with the Member States' reactions to the multiple crises erupting in the EU since 2005 (Jones, 2005), specifically to the financial crisis and the Greek debt crisis. In the previous rounds of enlargements, the ability of the candidate country to fulfil the accession criteria, specifically the *acquis communautaire* was sufficient for its accession (Preston, 1995; Sedelmeier, 2000). This no longer holds true. The EU's readiness, at the political, economic and institutional levels plays a critical role in the accession process. This is precisely why the European crisis becomes a determining factor for EU's enlargement. Both the Turkish case and the Western Balkans' experiences demonstrate that the EU's ability to push ahead with enlargement is much less compared to the 2004 enlargement.

Conclusion

This chapter investigated the EU enlargement process as part and parcel of European foreign policy from 2000 to 2012. The chapter illustrated that the EU enlargement began as an EU-level policy with recommendations from the Commission from 1992 onwards, and there was a significant downloading of preferences from the EU level to the Member State level with regards to the incorporation of new Member States, specifically in the 2004 enlargement. Member States began downloading from the EU level their own foreign policy preferences with regards to enlarging the Union. Yet, the diverging preferences of the individual members enabled them to act as veto players in certain instances. The dominant mode of operation in enlargement up until 2007 seems to be a combination of the EU-level and MS foreign policy dynamics. The enlargement policy, as a result, has become Europeanised. However, increasingly after 2008, the EU enlargement policy became subject to individual Member States' vetoes, and it is possible to see the EU members uploading their own preferences to the EU level. The Greek veto on Macedonia, multiple EU members' vetoes on Kosovo and the ongoing debates and vetoes on the Turkish accession process illustrate the increased nationalized mode of policy-making in the enlargement process in contrast to the Europeanised mode. This also fits with the key conclusions of this volume's main theoretical framework.

Consequently, the EU's next round of enlargement is affected from the changing priorities of the EU members towards enlargement as well as the decreased attractiveness of the EU as an economic magnet. The question that remains to be seen is whether the enlargement process could be a new opportunity for revitalizing the EU's integration and renew confidences among the EU publics towards a common future. This is a critical question as the European Union's foreign policy had its most important successes with its enlargement policy. Thus, if enlargement no longer serves as a tool of foreign policy, it remains to be seen what other foreign policy tools the EU would need to develop.

Notes

1 This chapter partly results from research conducted under the Maxcap project, which has received funding from the European Union's Seventh Framework Programme for research, technological development and demonstration under grant agreement no 320115.
2 Press Release, Cyprus Presidency, December 12, 2012. http://www.cy2012.eu/index.php/en/news-categories/areas/general-affairs/press-release-dr-marcoullis-chaired-the-general-affairs-council-on-issues-of-enlargement
3 Greece opposes the use of the name "Macedonia" for the area of the Former Yugoslav Republic of Macedonia, which, it is argued by Greece, does not belong to the historical region of Makedonía with which many Greeks in the Northern part of the country still identify until this very day.
4 European Council Presidency Conclusions, Copenhagen, 21–22 June 1993, SN 180/1/93/, p. 14.
5 "A Survey of European Union Enlargement", *The Economist*, May 19, 2001. http://www.economist.com/node/622780
6 GDP per capita (current $). World Bank, Retrieved October 10, 2015, http://data.worldbank.org/indicator/NY.GDP.MKTP.CD
7 Population (total). World Bank. Retrieved October 10, 2015, http://data.worldbank.org/indicator/SP.POP.TOTL
8 Intra-EU Trade by Member State, Total Product. EUROSTAT. Retrieved October 10, 2015, http://ec.europa.eu/eurostat/tgm/table.do?tab=table&init=1&language=en&pcode=tet00039&plugin=1
9 Intra-EU Trade by Member State, Total Product. EUROSTAT. Retrieved October 10, 2015, http://ec.europa.eu/eurostat/tgm/refreshTableAction.do?tab=table&plugin=1&pcode=tet00039&language=en
10 GDP Growth Rate (annual %), World Bank. Retrieved October 10, 2015, http://data.worldbank.org/indicator/NY.GDP.MKTP.KD.ZG
11 Price Level Ratio of PPP Conversion Factor GDP to Market Exchange Rate. World Bank. Retrieved October 10, 2015, http://data.worldbank.org/indicator/PA.NUS.PPPC.RF
12 Fule: "I am enjoying every minute of my work", *EuActiv*, March 2010. http://www.euractiv.com/enlargement/fuele-im-enjoying-minute-work-co-interview-394972
13 "Two Speed Europe or Two Europes", *The Economist*, November 10, 2011, http://www.economist.com/blogs/charlemagne/2011/11/future-eu
14 GDP per capita (current S $). World Bank, Retrieved October 10, 2015, http://data.worldbank.org/indicator/NY.GDP.MKTP.CD
15 Population (total). World Bank. Retrieved October 10, 2015, http://data.worldbank.org/indicator/SP.POP.TOTL
16 Data for import value and export value have been collected from http://exporthelp.europa.eu/thdapp/comext/ComextServlet?action=output&viewName=eur_partners&simDate=20140101&languageId=en&ahscode1=00&cb_reporters=000&cb_partners=all&list_years=2014&measureList=iv&measureList=ev
17 GDP Growth Rate (annual %), World Bank. Retrieved October 10, 2015, http://data.worldbank.org/indicator/NY.GDP.MKTP.KD.ZG
18 Price Level Ratio of PPP Conversion Factor GDP to Market Exchange Rate. World Bank. Retrieved October 10, 2015, http://data.worldbank.org/indicator/PA.NUS.PPPC.RF
19 "German Skepticism on EU Enlargement Hits Croatia", *EUACTIV*, October 15, 2012, http://www.euractiv.com/enlargement/german-enlargement-skepticism-hi-news-515410
20 "MEPs Scrutinize the EU Hopefuls", *EURACTIV*, March 15, 2011, http://www.euractiv.com/enlargement/meps-scrutinise-eu-hopefuls-case-news-511529

21 "Minister for Europe David Lidington Speaks on the Merits of EU Enlargement During His Visit to Vienna", February 15, 2011, http://www.fco.gov.uk/en/news/latest-news/?view=Speech&id=551925482
22 Ulrich Speck, "Is Germany Closing the Door on Further EU Enlargement?", *Radio Free Europe*, May 28, 2009, http://www.rferl.org/content/Is_Germany_Closing_The_Door_On_Further_EU_Enlargement__/1563457.html
23 "Austria Says It Does Not Want Turkey as a EU Member", *EURACTIVE*, May 3, 2011, http://www.euractiv.com/enlargement/austria-want-turkey-eu-member-news-504493/
24 Dan Bilefsky, "Sarkozy blocks key part of EU entry talks with Turkey, *New York Times*, June 25, 2007, http://www.nytimes.com/2007/06/25/world/europe/25iht-union.5.6325879.html

Bibliography

Bickerton, C. J. (2011) *European Union Foreign Policy: From Effectiveness to Functionality*. London: Palgrave Macmillan.
Dimitrova, A. L. (2010) 'The New Member States of the EU in the Aftermath of Enlargement: Do New European Rules Remain Empty Shells?', *Journal of European Public Policy*, Vol. 17, No. 1, 137–148.
The European Commission (2009) *Five Years of an Enlarged EU: Economic Achievements and Challenges*, http://ec.europa.eu/economy_finance/publications/publication_summary14081_en.htm, date accessed 1 December 2013.
The European Commission (2012) *Strategy Paper for EU Enlargement*. COM (2012) 600 final Brussels, 10 October.
Forsberg, T. (2011) 'Normative Power Once Again: A Conceptual Analysis of an Ideal Type', *Journal of Common Market Studies*, Vol. 49, No. 6, 1183–1204.
Hallerberg, Mark (2011) 'Fiscal Federalism Reforms in the European Union and the Greek Crisis', *European Union Politics*, Vol. 12, No. 1, 127–142.
Hertz, R. and Leuffen, D. (2011) 'Too Big to Run? Analysing the Impact of Enlargement on the Speed of EU Decision-Making', *European Union Politics*, Vol. 12, No. 2, 193–215.
Hill, C. (2003) *The Changing Politics of Foreign Policy*. New York, NY: Palgrave Macmillan.
Hobolt, B. S., Van der Brug, W. and De Vreese Claes, H. (2011) 'Religious Intolerance and Euroscepticism', *European Union Politics*, Vol. 12, No. 3, 359–379.
Jones, E. (2005) 'The Politics of Europe 2004: Solidarity and Integration', *Industrial Relations Journal*, Vol. 36, No. 6, 436–455.
Koenig, T. and Junge, D. (2009) 'Why Don't Veto Players Use Their Power?', *European Union Politics*, Vol. 10, No. 4, 507–534.
Longo, M. and Murray, P. (2011) 'No Ode to Joy? Reflections on the European Union's Legitimacy', *International Politics*, Vol. 48, No. 6, 667–690.
Manners, I. (2002) 'Normative Power Europe: A Contradiction in Terms?', *Journal of Common Market Studies*, Vol. 20, No. 2, 235–258.
Moravcsik, A. (1993) 'Preferences and Power in the European Community: A Liberal Intergovernmentalist Approach', *Journal of Common Market Studies*, Vol. 31, No. 4, 473–524.
Moravcsik, A. (1998) *The Choice for Europe: Social Purpose and State Power from Messina to Maastricht*. Ithaca, NY: Cornell University Press.
Moravcsik, A. and Vachudova, M. (2008) 'National Interest, State Power and the EU Enlargement', *East European Politics and Society*, Vol. 17, No. 1, 42–57.
Müftüler-Baç, M. (2008) 'Turkey's Accession to the European Union: The EU's Internal Dynamics', *International Studies Perspectives*, Vol. 9, No. 2, 208–226.
Müftüler-Baç, M. and Kibris, A. (2011) 'The Accession Games: A Comparison of Three Limited-Information Negotiation Designs', *International Studies Perspectives*, Vol. 12, No. 4, 405–433.
Müftüler-Baç, M. and McLaren, L. (2003) 'Enlargement Preferences and Policy Making in the EU: Impacts on Turkey', *Journal of European Integration*, Vol. 25, No. 1, 17–30.
Preston, C. (1995) 'Obstacles to EU Enlargement: The Classical Community Method and Prospects for a Wider Europe', *Journal of Common Market Studies*, Vol. 33, No. 3, 451–463.

Rauch, B., Goettsche, M. and Braehler, G. (2011) 'Fact and Fiction in EU-Governmental Economic Data', *German Economic Review*, Vol. 12, No. 3, 243–255.

Schimmelfennig, F. (2001) 'The Community Trap: Liberal Norms, Rhetorical Action, and the Eastern Enlargement of the European Union', *International Organization*, Vol. 55, No. 1, 47–80.

Schimmelfennig, F. and Sedelmeier, U. (2002) 'Theorizing EU Enlargement: Research Focus, Hypotheses and the State of Research', *Journal of European Public Policy*, Vol. 9, No. 4, 500–528.

Sedelmeier, U. (2000) 'Eastern Enlargement: Risk, Rationality and Role Compliance', in M. G. Gowles and M. Smith (eds.) *The State of the European Union: Rules, Reforms, Resistance and Revival.* Oxford: Oxford University Press, 164–185.

Sjursen, H. (2002) 'Why Enlarge', *Journal of Common Market Studies*, Vol. 40, No. 3, 491–515.

Sjursen, H. (2006) *Questioning EU Enlargement: Europe in Search of Identity.* London: Routledge.

Smith, K. (2004) *The Making of EU Foreign Policy: The Case of Eastern Europe.* London: Palgrave Macmillan.

Tonra, B. (2011) 'Democratic Foundations of EU Foreign Policy: Narratives and Myths of EU Exceptionalism', *Journal of European Public Policy*, Vol. 18, No. 8, 1190–1207.

Whitman, R. (1998) *From Civilian Power to Superpower? The International Identity of the European Union.* Basingstoke: Palgrave Macmillan.

10 European energy policy

Amelia Hadfield

Introduction

EU energy policy is something of a paradox. Tying together three facets of competition, sustainability and energy security, EU energy policy is host to both innovative and reactive dynamics. The policy thus emerges from regionally integrative ambitions based on a growing body of law comprised in the energy *acquis*, while being deeply constrained by Member State ambitions. Its sustainability dimension has catalysed the EU's arguably pioneering global stance on climate change, while the energy security aspect has struggled to construct and maintain a set of Union-level norms around which the majority of Member States' policies can feasibly converge. European energy security is split between the host of exogenous supply shocks from which the policy first emerged in 2006 as well as the tremendous variability of endogenous reactions from twenty-eight Member States who are unevenly dependent on various sources, suppliers, and routes and present a varied picture in both the market-based and foreign policy responses that underwrite energy security. Alongside other chapters within Part II of this text, this chapter focuses on *changes to policies* and *actions impacting on policies* which Member State preferences have undergone in the area of energy security in the past decade. In some cases, this has increased the overall capacity for energy security to become genuinely Europeanised. In others, key facets of energy security remain defiantly national. Using the Four Modes set out in the Introduction, this chapter illustrates how *change* by Member States – in both national attitude and national policy-making – and ensuing *actions* pursuant to those changes, explain the fixity of energy security in its national orientation and key facets of an emergent European foreign energy policy.

Internally, a number of considerations have impacted upon energy security: attempts by the European Commission since the 2009 gas spat with Russia to comprehensively Europeanise all aspects of energy policy; the Lisbon Treaty (Article 194 in particular); and, most recently, efforts to define a European Energy Union. Externally, geopolitical volatilities have highlighted energy vulnerabilities, from post-Arab Spring supplier transitions, ongoing collisions involving both the reliability and appropriateness of Russian natural gas supplies (and to lesser extent oil) to the EU wreaked by the diplomatic fallout over Ukraine from 2014 onwards, the collapse of oil prices, and an upswing in violence across the Levant. Internally, the harmonising ambitions of the European Commission appear to have moderated competitive unevenness in some respects, but neither it nor the European Council have provided a foreign policy formula robust enough to satisfy the Member States vis-à-vis a suitable strategic attitude to third-party suppliers. Equally, large swathes of energy policy, including energy security, have become Europeanised over time. However, the way in which this has occurred runs counter to traditional understandings of Europeanisation. As explored later in this chapter, top-down multilateral-induced cooperation offers a poor explanation for much of the policy convergence observed within European energy policy. Instead, a combination of uploaded Member State counter-offensives at the perceived coercion of the Commission's Europeanising demands, in the shape of 'policy diffusion' comprising 'cross-national policy coordination' based on growing similarity of perceptions of both internal needs and external threats best explains the types of Europeanisation at work in recent energy policy (Busch and Jorgens in Morata and Sandoval, 2012: 67). Following the formula established throughout Part II of this text, this chapter deconstructs aspects of European energy security to discern Europeanising or nationalising dynamics of its internal and external dimensions. The contributions of Germany, France and Britain are central: each comprise climate-change, market-based and foreign policy value-sets impacting differently upon the construction of a Europeanised energy policy.

The ambiguous nature of what constitutes a *Europeanised* energy security complicates clear analyses. Typologies help remedy this to some extent, providing a rationale for classification by which Europeanised Member State foreign policy behaviour can be seen to represent the supranational dynamics of Mode I (German commitment to leading on the EU 2050 agenda). Intra-EU cooperation is associated with Mode II, in which Member State cooperation operates at an intergovernmental level within the EU mainframe (Visegrad Four cooperation in identifying common energy security needs) or via bilateral agreements (the construction of cross-national infrastructure developments in line with EU legislation). Specifically *nationalised* foreign policy behaviour stems from Mode III in which the dominant mode is Member State to Member State but undertaken outside any formal EU framework (cooperation on various treaties, like the Energy Charter Treaty or other conventions outside of EU legislative requirements). The EU to non-EU relations represented in Mode IV are found in the preponderance of external agreements between Member State and non-EU suppliers and transmitters in the European energy chain. Many Member States, whose foreign energy policy is dominated by bilateral agreements with Russia or other energy producing states, fall into this category. It is equally likely that one country may exemplify one or more typologies, particularly due to the complexity of interests of a Member State when it comes to energy security policy (e.g. Germany's agreement with Russia permitting the completion of the Nord Stream pipeline and its pro-renewables stance in line with EU legislation).

Context: EU energy security

The overview of the EU is one of variety and dependence, but with some surprising outliers. Its energy mix is spread unevenly between consumption of five main types of energy: oil (34 per cent), natural gas (23 per cent), solid fuels (17 per cent), nuclear (14 per cent) and renewables (11 per cent) (European Commission, 2014a: 44). While fossil fuel reliance remains a material reality for the majority of states, some like France and Germany, favour specific sources, in terms of the gross consumption of their national energy mix. The EU's overall energy import dependency is what captures the headlines and has been a prime catalyst in the argument for a progressively Europeanised energy policy (specifically where security of supply is concerned). European fuel import dependency has grown steadily over the past fifteen years. Total dependency has grown on average by roughly

25 per cent, but it is the increase in solid fuel dependence to 42.2 per cent, petroleum to 86.4 per cent and gas to 54.02 per cent that is most significant, coupled with the nature of its transit (European Commission, 2014a: 24). With a quarter of Europe's gas arriving from Russian sources, originally via Ukraine and now via the Nord Stream and other transit routes, political strife over Ukraine has focused the EU upon its eastern security of energy supply, in a desperate effort to avoid the prospect of cut-offs and price spikes but also to transform a situation in which the EU 'remains highly vulnerable to Russian control over gas supplies' (*The Economist*, 5 April, 2014). The economic cost of dependence is equally critical: the EU pays roughly €400 billion per year for imported fossil fuels (EurActiv, 18 November, 2014).

Dependence upon energy mixes tends to inhibit competition dynamics for predictable prices (enhancing the continued use of long-term contracts), and a tendency to retain current traditional suppliers rather than cultivate new energy sources, routes or suppliers (Kuzemko, 2014). In terms of national preferences, this form of path dependency can become worry-ingly entrenched. Against Europe's rigid national preferences is the irony that the distinctly national approach underwriting Russian energy security is principally what has 'run rings around the EU', enabling the Russian state to act singularly to underwrite – via Gazprom – 'nationalized reserves, monopolized pipelines . . . a bilateral special relationship with Germany, and undermine the development of competitive pipeline proposals from the Caspian' (2007: 1–2). EU policies to promote genuine structural changes, whether they be active or reactive, are impressive in ambition but also unhelpfully slow in practice. In consequence, this has forced the EU to accommodate itself to uncompetitive or poorly regulated market practices, including artificially increased prices, modes of payment and inefficient uses of energy in all sectors, as well as being functionally unable to extract itself from its depen-dence upon Russia for a decade at least. Worse still is a negligent attitude to the 'interna-tional externalities like geopolitical insecurity and its social costs' which impact negatively on the EU as a whole, with Member States unable to significantly alter their dependence upon a given energy type, route, supplier, and even price (Francés, 2011: 40). Aside from Denmark and Britain, currently able to sidestep import dependency, the majority of Mem-ber States who acceded in 2004 and 2007 represent upwards of 90 per cent dependence on Russian-sourced and Ukraine-transited natural gas. However, numbers tell only part of the story. As illustrated later in this chapter, major shifts in what constitutes a reasonable bal-ance between imports and exports, between hydrocarbon and carbon-free options, between tightly regulated and loosely managed national markets are cardinal dualities in an emerging European energy policy.

Constructing European energy definitions

Contemporary energy structures and policies have underwritten key facets of European inte-gration, having driven the construction of the early EEC in terms of its initial coal and steel cooperation (ECSC), with the Euratom Treaty (1957) operating as the earliest example of Europeanised energy policy. Commonality enjoyed between Member States and the EU in the firm of a nascent common energy policy, however, had to wait more than sixty years. Despite external events like the 1970s oil embargoes and the creation of the International Energy Agency, the construction of a trans-national European energy market simply failed to materialise. The majority of energy agreements from the IEA in the 1970s, to the post-Cold War Energy Charter Treaty arose intergovernmentally and (usually subsequently) in an extra-EU forum (Mode III). Only growing unease at global price uncertainties as well as the sense that revanchism in a variety of key strategic exporters prompted the European Commission to move from commissioned reports (e.g. Clingendael, 2000) to overseeing its own investigations on the strategic aspects of energy policy. Accelerated by major gas spats and east-west divisions externally, and increased calls for market the completion and political coordination internally, a European energy policy slowly emerged. The subsequent shift of energy policy into a vehicle both of, and for, Europeanisation is the most recent incarnation of these various efforts.

The irony is that the component of energy security has itself produced such spectacular examples of national backlash, squashing any real potential for Europeanisation-led policy convergence in this (and many other) areas. The Clingendael paper and others (Cameron, 2003) early on argued what the Commission would take a decade to learn, in other words 'energy security and – insofar as it might be possible – self-sufficiency have always lain at the heart of the Member States' energy policies', and as such, post-Cold War energy policy was bound to be different from the 'cornerstone of European harmony as conceived by the Union's founding fathers' (Gotev, 2016). Between the 2006 and 2009 gas spats, the tension between national and Europeanising forces, as well as the variety of internal macro-economic and neighbourhood tremors kept *energy security* as the most prominent of the three components of European energy policy (competition, security and sustainability). Unable to surmount the sovereign hold on national energy mixes and purchasing power, the 2009 Lisbon Treaty highlighted the need to understand energy policy as increasingly strategic, and the Member States' actions as consequently based on solidarity. EU-level policy areas (if not actual competences) expanded to include a raft of internal market-based responsibilities including market functioning, aspects of security of supply, energy efficiency and promoting the regional interconnection of networks (Mellár and Nenova, 2012). The post-Lisbon transitions in all three areas of competition, security and sustainability have been paradoxically both impressive and inadequate, chiefly because decent material progress is still beset by a lack of clear vision and definitions, causing confusing between EU-level and Member State objectives.

Until the gas spat of 2006, the foreign policy dimension of European energy policy had been largely eclipsed by the focus on **climate change**. Here, the strongest sense of broad-based Europeanisation remains, though not without some key dissenters. The recently rene-gotiated UNFCCC Paris 2015 climate package illustrates the EU's ongoing commitment to reform internally, and represent externally, upon a benchmark of the most globally stringent GHG-reducing strategies. Bureaucratic blunders over the emissions trading system, the uneven application of state aid for renewables and unclear strategies as to how energy efficiency translates practically into diminishing demand have periodically blighted the EU's internal 'green' credibility, but not usually the momentum of the EU's overall climate discourse nor the integrity of its international credentials. **Competition**, as the second of the three energy policy components possesses innately third-party dynamics key to foreign policy relations; yet energy competition in Europe is largely preoccupied with internal market legislation aimed at liberalising the types of and access to energy, encouraging greater competition amongst gas and electricity providers to guarantee consumer choice and drive down prices. Much depends on the physical practicalities of sizeable, cross-border grids. While 'national gas [and electricity] companies have long disliked cross-border interconnectors, a free flow . . . means more choice consumers and thus lower prices' (*The Economist*, 5 April, 2014). Despite the neoliberal tenets of various Energy Packages (themselves representing a Europeanising dynamic with generally positive (if sluggish) outcomes), the temptation for Member States has been to preserve the structure and clout of their national energy champions, retaining a toehold in terms of ownership and national market regulation. This, combined with competence over energy mix purchases in which Member States as 'consumer governments' deal directly with 'producer governments' for required production capacity, keeps Member States largely in the driver seat in those areas where competition overlaps uneasy with security of supply.

Energy security comprises both security of supply for importers like the EU, and security of demand for exporters like Norway, Algeria, Qatar and Russia. Despite swathes of legislation surrounding increasing areas of energy policy, and the visibly Europeanising effect of a common *acquis*, emergent electricity and gas markets, regulatory structure and climate change targeting, European energy policy has progressed least in the area of energy security, and as such, Europeanising dynamics of the traditional variety have not yet taken root beyond episodic intergovernmental cooperation. This diminishes both the internal and external ability of the EU to cultivate (and export) a degree of 'European energy actorness' with any real efficacy. Ironically, regular political fallout with key suppliers like Gazprom (whether over pricing, transit tariffs or political norms of the 'exporter regime') have forced a clearer understanding of the dual nature of energy security. For both the EU and EU Member States, energy security represents both 'a certain quantity of hydrocarbons supplied at a price considered to be compatible with maintaining the well-being of the population; and the psychological concept of security', influenced by the perception and context 'of [the] political relations between the consumer and exporting countries' (Francés, 2011: 40–41). Energy security is also directly keyed into the external affairs of the EU, including – inter alia – Development Policy, European Neighbourhood Policy (ENP), and the Common Foreign and Security Policy (CFSP), various EU's Strategic Partnerships, and the 2016 EU Global Strategy. EU energy security thus plays an undeniably central though not yet unifying role in European foreign affairs. Equally, however, the very buying and selling, the choice and direction, the procuring and use of energy supplies continues to be directed, not by EU actors, but by private national energy companies under the watchful eye of Member States (themselves, a major shareholder), who thus bear the brunt of the 'foreign' aspect of energy security, as they deal daily with third parties in trans-border fashion and subsequently complicate vital components of a 'Europeanised' energy security from the EU itself.

DG Energy: shifting gears

Knowing full well the dangers of an energy security policy at the mercy of twenty-eight Member States' national visions and despite 'the Commission's relatively weak mandate in energy matters' (Francés, 2011: 48), DG Energy in particular has hit back with some impressively revanchist rejoinders. Energy Commissioners Gunther Oettinger (under President Barroso) and Maros Šefčovič (within the 2014 Juncker Commission) grew increasingly discontent with the fragmentation by which separate national energy policies across the EU operate only in rudimentary parallelism with Council strategies and even EU legislation. After the second gas spat of 2009 (hard on the heels of the invasion of Georgia by Russia), Oettinger argued in 2010, with no little impatience that:

> National sovereignty in energy is no longer an option when we have a single internal energy market, stretching from the Balkans to Scandinavia, from the Baltic to the

Mediterranean. Energy independence is an illusion when gas can move around Europe from Greece to Ireland. Member States are not rivals vis-à-vis third countries. We are in the same team. The energy security of every Member State will be stronger and cheaper when the EU learns to speak with a single voice and leverage its real power.

(Oettinger, 2010: 5)

From 2010 onwards, Oettinger, Barroso and many others in the Commission began to speak increasingly stridently of the Europeanisation of energy policy. Oettinger's (2010) speeches to the European Parliament and the European Energy Forum made clear that Europeanisation, constituted a trinity of *external forces*: 'challenges which bring Member States together' including energy security (on the basis of rising imports and declining indigenous production); economies of scale brought about by global shifts (requiring a collective response to ensure continued investment in the energy and technology sectors); and *internal requirements* (commonality, solidarity, harmonisation) (Oettinger, 2010: 2). Accordingly, a viably Europeanised energy policy flowed from the intrinsic weaknesses of rising dependence, vulnerability and poor connectivity, towards diversification-driven scenarios that capitalised on the few goals which had already been achieved but rendered the remaining priorities, and the overall policy itself, as categorically 'Europeanised'. Citing the European Parliament as 'a strong supporter of the Commission's initiatives' in this area (Oettinger, 2010: 3), the building blocks of a Europeanised energy policy comprised the following components:

- Article 194 of the Lisbon Treaty: laying down clear energy policy goals in terms of competitiveness, security of supply and sustainability;
- a basic energy *acquis* comprising legislation to create and complete a competitive European energy market, with the Third Energy Package as centrepiece;
- the 2020 and 2030 Packages of Renewables and Emissions Trading Directives creating 'a push to renewable and low-carbon energy in all Member States'; and
- EU investments in energy research and infrastructure, of which major regional interconnector projects remain key.

Subsequent policies from the DG Energy have indeed focused on the challenges of completing these goals through further policy convergence across Member States in the areas of completing the internal energy market, and a rigorous oversight of 2030 carbon-free targets.

Energy security, however, reflects the most critical goal to be attained. In 2014, Energy Commissioner Šefčovič took up the challenge of constructing a broader framework, targeting the lack of a common external approach towards suppliers and transit states among a broad range of goals. The most ambitious of these was seen first in the form of the 2014 European Energy Security Strategy, followed by the announcement of a fully fledged European Energy Union (EEU). Launched in 2015, and appraised in 2016 as 'deep long-term transition' impacting virtually every area of energy policy, the European Energy Union attempts to combine energy software (legislation) with market hardware (interconnectors and technology) that overlay the persistently different market and political attitudes of the Member States in order to improve the shared European qualities of an increasingly interdependent market (Šefčovič, 2016). The EEU encompasses five dimensions: energy security, a completed and integrated internal energy market, improved energy efficiency, decarbonisation targets, and research, innovation and competitiveness (European Commission, 2015). For the Member States however, the EEU constitutes potential curtailing – or collectivising – depending on their outlook – of previous freedoms. Chief among the new rules is the Commission's insistence on examining energy contracts prior to their completion by Member States with non-EU suppliers, in order to ensure they conform to the strategic requirements of the EU's overall energy security: in effect, a Mode IV form of scrutiny in pursuance of Mode II and even Mode I energy policy. In addition, competition investigations into unfair pricing, monopolistic actions and structures and greater transparency on commercial contracts particularly where a firm possess 40 per cent or more of the market. Gazprom itself is a natural target for such investigations but so too is the lopsided competition in most central and eastern European gas markets (Lithuania, Latvia, Estonia, Bulgaria, the Czech Republic, Hungary, Slovakia and Poland).

EU-wide soundings taken by Šefčovič in the wake of this unveiling suggest that, while the EEU 'was generally well received', the project itself 'could not be built in Brussels' alone. In other words, while Europeanised projects boosting renewable and sustainable mechanics were deemed worthy and indeed European in nature, 'giving political guidance' (Šefčovič, 2015) to Member States on the internal logic of the EEU – not least its ambiguous governance structure – 'remains a vital part of communicating not only the message, but the modus operandi of the European Commission' (Froggatt and Hadfield, 2015: 11). Put more bluntly by outside observers, 'efforts to centralize energy policy in Brussels are potentially divisive as EU Member States jealously guard the right to decide their own energy mix' (Hurriyet, 10 February, 2016). Constructing a common energy security policy therefore requires identifying commonalities amongst Member States that effectively outweigh their individual ability to identify with energy security purely as a national policy area, and respond individually to spikes and stoppages. Member States are clearly consumers in common, with the majority on the receiving end of the same type of import (natural gas and oil) from the same source (Russia, transited through Ukraine, Nord Stream II or southern hubs). However, specific Member State dependence upon Russia as well as their geopolitical attitude to it varies considerably, with predictable consequences for constructing the external facets of a European energy policy. As established in Part I of this text, *national value-sets* have much to tell us about both regional groupings and individual preferences.

EU Member States: policy change

Germany

The energy landscape in Germany has shifted dramatically as a result of the policy of *energiewende*, or energy turn-around. This refers to the dramatic transition of consumption from nuclear to renewable energy, legislating the phasing out of all operating nuclear plants by 2021. In addition to the fears prompted by the Fukushima nuclear plant in Japan, the German Federal Government cited European and global trends, including the lessening of Europe's fossil fuel reserves, and its growing dependency as a whole on energy imports and attendance vulnerability, as driving factors for the new approach (Federal Ministry, 2012). The task appears daunting; as of 2012, Germany was the world's second-largest net importer of natural gas, sixth-largest net importer of coal, and the sixth-largest net importer of oil, as well as representing at 37 per cent an above-Union dependence (the average being 24 per cent) on energy imports (Noronha, 2012: 46; International Energy Agency, 2014: 11–16).

Germany remains undeterred for the most part. Foreign Minister Guido Westerwalle asserted that the change of orientation will be supplemented by a drastically improved national grid, and radically increased ratio of renewables alongside increased energy efficiency. Using EU 2020 and 2030 targets as its national template, Germany plans to increase the share of renewable energy of its energy consumption to 30 per cent by 2020, increasing the share to 50 per cent by 2030 (Noronha, 2012).

As argued by Westphal, 'Germany stands out not only for its economic weight and industrial structures, but also for pursuing the double goal of phasing out nuclear power and decarbonizing its energy system' (2012: 2). As the leading national economy in Europe, the German transition represents a watershed in both the mainstreaming of European renewable energy sources (RES) and the dedicated use of climate change targets to orient market reforms and a comprehensive energy 're-mix' (Westphal, 2012).

Germany's *energiewende* policy is motivated largely by the national *zeitgeist* which remains supportive of mainstreaming renewables, reducing demand and boosting energy efficiency, underwritten by a host of market modalities to keep such options affordable and available. Germany is not, however, wholly committed to a fully carbon-free future, preferring to retain the use of natural gas (and possible developments in carbon capture and sequestration), producing 'an energy policy that aims at close cooperation with Russia nested in a "strategic relationship" as the most effective instrument in the interest of both sides' (Baumann and Simmerl, 2011). As such, the Nord Stream Pipeline (the second-largest conduit of Russian natural gas after the Ukrainian transit system) simultaneously strengthens the German and Russian partnership by ensuring long-term flows of natural gas for Germany and a host of other Member States via interconnectors to Italy, Poland and the Czech Republic, sending politically ambiguous signs about ongoing German–Russian policy whilst upholding the need to carve out an enhanced solidarity-based European energy security.

For optimists, this strategy, alongside recent decisions to increase diversification of energy imports should transform German energy policy into a microcosm of the Europeanised energy policy expounded by Commissioner Oettinger. A more pragamatic reading cannot escape the irony that Germany has not only retained a decidedly national dimension to the foreign aspect of its energy policy but, since the fracas with Russia beginning in 2013, has simultaneously deployed Europeanisation as the sole response to both the EU's foreign policy and energy security responses. Despite material and diplomatic links with Russia, the 2009 Russia–Ukraine gas dispute affected Germany as much as other EU Member States; equally, President Putin appeared no more swayed by Chancellor Merkel than any other EU decision-maker since the political stalemate of 2014. The point made by the Federal Ministry in 2012 is clear: national prerogatives over energy security permitting diplomatic latitude work well for Germany when relations with Russia were stable but prove impossible to sustain in foreign policy terms in the face of serious eastern provocation:

> [T]he Commission should play an important role in the early coordination of Member States. At the same time, however, the Federal Government must pursue its own foreign energy policy agenda to accommodate Germany's specific interests and circumstances at the national level.
>
> (Federal Ministry, 2012)

Germany is currently in the midst of an energy security *volte face*: torn between accepting the principle that the EU can only confront geopolitical impunity and regional energy needs by operating with solidarity on the basis of steadily Europeanised mores, while attempting to reserve the right to orient its own foreign energy policy choices. Germany thus represents both the deepest degree of Europeanised energy policy in the dimensions of market liberali-sation and market-led climate change policies (Mode I), while retaining intergovernmental preferences regarding energy security choice, and engaging with non-EU states like Russia in the most abiding form of energy security (Mode IV). Germany operates as an icon of climate change and yet it joined France and the UK in opposing Oettinger's 2011 Com-munication on improving the EU's approach to energy security issues, entailing enhanced authority to scrutinise bilateral agreements with third party exporters and the power to negotiate EU energy deals independently. Equally complicated signals include German support for the EEU which has been generally positive, whilst in the throes of sanction-ridden relations with Russia, news emerged that Germany intended to move ahead with a second Russian-routed pipeline. Nord Stream II is designed to double gas flows to Germany and consequently has inflamed key transit Member States (including the Visegrad Four) while creating complications for Commissioner Šefčovič who subsequently deemed the project 'not in conformity with the Energy Union's goals' and implicitly un-, or even anti-Europeanising in its overall impact. Germany will consequently require a swift untangling of its Modes in order to restore its various energy and foreign policy roles (EurActiv, 25 February, 2016).

France

France is less dependent on energy imports than other EU Member States, due largely to its nuclear-dominated energy sector. France is unsurprisingly the strongest advocate in the EU for nuclear energy with 80 per cent of its electricity and 40 per cent of the overall energy supply being nuclear-generated (International Energy Agency, 2009). Like Germany's reac-tion to Fukushima, France used a major global energy event as the rationale for its current setup; French nuclear energy arose from oil embargoes in the 1970s, in a concerted effort to increase the country's energy independence (Meritet, 2011). The decision produced not only a healthy non-carbon production of electricity well ahead of carbon-free market demands (France is the largest exporter in the world of electricity), but reinforced a successful export market of nuclear reactors and related products, sold to Switzerland, Belgium, Spain and the UK, while historically low electricity costs also sets it up as something of a beacon of well-managed nuclear-driven market practices.

France makes for an interesting comparison to its neighbour Germany. As explored in the previous section, German national energy policy has seen a determination not only to wean itself off fossil fuels but to radically reduce its nuclear profile, the shortfall of both being a rigorous dedication to enhancing the productivity of renewables. France has no such ambitions and yet enjoys a pragmatic, if not entirely balanced energy mix. Its energy supply is better than most other EU countries in balancing nuclear energy with a wide portfolio of multiple oil and gas suppliers. With the exception of Norway, France uses no more than 20 per cent of its natu-ral gas consumption from any given importer, which includes Norway, the Netherlands, Rus-sia, Algeria and Egypt. While its reliance upon oil is almost total and represents the only major weakness in its energy makeup, France attempts to ensure a diverse supply. Diversity amongst suppliers in the Maghreb initially proved trouble-free. Under former President Sarkozy, the Mediterranean region was considered of prime strategic importance for French energy secu-rity (Youngs, 2009), an indication being the 2006 treaty signed between France and Algeria to ensure greater security of Algeria's gas supplies to France, in return for long-term nuclear energy cooperation. Healthy extra-EU relations (Mode III) were deemed necessary not only to underwrite domestic diversification but to ensure the continued projection of French foreign policy. Recently, however, Mediterranean security of supply and indeed French-African relations have proved politically difficult. The Arab Spring upended much traditional gas and oil output from Libya and to a lesser extent Algeria, while the fallout of Sahel security and related shocks to energy outputs in the Gulf of Guinea have undermined chances of French energy security reliant on African outputs to any significant extent beyond Algeria.

Apart from the political volatility entailed in extra-EU fossil fuel diversity, two other shifts in the French energy makeup indicate a diminishing of foreign policy-driven energy options in favour of Europeanised ones. First, the potentially dramatic row back in French nuclear policy under President Francois Hollande, who had pledged to close France's oldest operational nuclear plant. Hollande's party, the *Parti Socialiste* (PS) further asserted that they would reduce French dependence on nuclear energy from 75 to 50 per cent by shutting down twenty-four reactors across the country by 2025 (Boselli, 17 November, 2011), signifying a major change to its nuclear-powered energy policy. Second, the rejection of a number of government proposals on shale gas exploration in France, as a result of environmental concerns. Against the backdrop of unbundling requirements arising from the Third Energy Package, which necessitates the gradual unpicking of its two state-owned national energy champions Electricité de France (EDF) and Gaz de France Suez (GDF Suez) (Meritet, 2011), French energy policy faces an uncertain future. The fall-off in nuclear-generated electricity could be met by an emphatic commitment to renewables or by a combination of clean-coal and bridging technologies. However, absent a dramatic about face regarding nuclear or fossil fuel reliance, calls for an increasingly Europeanised energy policy in which fossil fuel scale-back alongside a robust commitment to a carbon-free energy market have now taken on added salience for France.

In 2012, a cross-ministerial publication emerged bringing together Foreign Affairs with Ecology, Sustainable Development and Energy ministries, entitled *Europe Needs a Foreign Policy for Energy*. Asserting a European approach on everything from the environment and energy efficiency to price controls, from the development of renewable and decarbonised industries to ensuring a beneficial social impact to consumers and citizens alike, the strategy represented an initial challenge by France to the EU, attempting to secure for itself an unrivalled position as the top producer of renewable energy, ensuring both indigenous security of supply and a climate-friendly output capable of constructing a carbon-free market. The dual requirements for such a shift were to secure the massive investment required for this transformation and, in parallel, to develop a common foreign energy policy could revitalise Europe entirely (Fabius and Batho, 2012).

The 2012 publication, echoed by calls from other ministries to develop a more comprehensive European approach, suggests that French energy policy is at a crossroads. Shifting from an energy policy that favoured extra-EU options (Mode III) to one that identifies either with other Member States in promoting increased cooperation (Mode II) or regards EU-level options (Mode I) as necessary to coordinate at a deeper level suggests that its independent stance may see it participate more positive in the framing of an EU energy strategy. However, shifting the makeup of its domestic energy mix is one thing; engaging cooperatively and sustainably on areas that have traditionally proved fractious, including key internal market rules, modalities of investment, and choice of supplier in a way that produces a genuinely European energy policy capable of commanding the heights of renewable European energy production, is quite another.

United Kingdom

Historically, the UK has enjoyed high levels of self-sufficiency when it comes to energy security. Resources from the North Sea currently permit the UK no dependence upon Russian-sourced gas. In addition, a strong if uneven market-based economy comprising numerous large energy suppliers have granted Britain relative, if temporary security of energy supply. Threats to UK energy security are thus rather broadly drawn, comprising 'severe weather, terrorist attacks, technical failure and industrial action' (Department of Energy, 2013), as well as 'changes to market structure, geopolitical patterns and climate change' (Department of Energy, 2012). Consequently, responses range from a combination of preventative measures mitigating weather impacts (e.g. anti-flooding improvements to the Thames Estuary and other vulnerable regions), emergency gas storage and enhanced National Grid responsiveness, and enhanced transparency regarding the sharing of its emergency plans with other Member States, outlined in the EU Security of Gas Supply Regulation (Department of Energy, 2012). The UK thus favours a fully liberalised, highly competitive energy market. While it has some way to go to achieving this goal, its consumer-oriented economy favours private rather than government energy actors, many of them foreign-owned, and with unburdensome regulation apart from scrutiny of market prices provided by Ofcom. With a relatively well-balanced relationship between suppliers and purchasers, and a relationship regulated by market forces rather than significant government intervention, and buoyed by indigenous oil and gas resources, the UK's energy strategy is not regarded as overtly geopolitical in nature and appears decidedly 'domestic', even insular, in nature. (Baumann and Simmerl, 2011). The emphasis is primarily upon increasing the competitiveness of Britain's energy market rather than fostering the growth of linkages with EU or non-EU energy partners. Having supported climate change as assertively as the EU itself (best demonstrated in the Stern report), the UK's carbon-free commitments replicate rather than reinforce those of the EU in terms of reducing demand-side requirements, improving transparency of information and working to diversify the country's energy mix (Department of Energy, 2012). A careful reading of key documents suggests that, while the UK supports the 'green growth' that EU leadership can help promote and is itself a strong supporter of the completion of the single energy market, British policy-makers make sporadic rather than strategic use of the EU's emergent energy security goals (or its collaborative potential), beyond those invoked in competition and climate change legislation (Davey, 2012).

However, the UK is not immune from the need to pursue energy diplomacy to secure oil and gas imports in the medium and long term. Depleting resources in the North Sea, domestic discontent over cartel-like market practices from the major half dozen energy suppliers, and the broader liberalisation requirements entailed in the EU's Third Package to help complete a single European energy market as well (Department of Energy, 2013) are together transforming key aspects of the UK's energy terrain. Such changes are acknowledged in the House of Lords' European Union Committee, ironically entitled *No Country Is an Energy Island: Securing Investment for the EU's Future.* The report balances criticism of the EU whilst acknowledging the need to work collectively to mitigate various trans-border problems, specifically via enhanced cooperation on the *Energy Roadmap to 2050* (European Commission (2011), COM 885). Criticism is levelled at the EU 'at the degree of uncertainty, complacency and inertia about how an affordable supply of secure and low carbon energy will be provided in the European Union' (House of Lords, 2013: 3). From this perspective, energy security is intimately bound up with Europe's incomplete energy market, 'price volatility', lacklustre investment climate (worsened by) stringent EU environmental rules forcing 'the imminent closure of large numbers of coal plants' and the 'continued reliance on imports for the supply of over 50% of the EU's energy' (House of Lords, 2013: 3). Charting a path between inter-EU and extra-EU policy typologies, the British response determinedly acknowledges that 'no country is an energy island', and as such there are 'clear benefits to be derived from working within the EU on the energy challenge'. The dilemma, however, is that, despite the economies of scale on offer from an increasingly integrated energy market, the Lords themselves assert that 'it is for each Member State to decide what mix of energy is the most appropriate for them' (House of Lords, 2013: 3).

In relation to EU energy policy, the UK has largely supported the Third Energy Package, viewing a common European energy policy as beneficial to the promotion of a common energy market, and remaining largely supportive of climate change requirements and modalities expounded by the Commission. Harmonising the externalities of energy however is a tougher task. The European Union Committee appointed by the House of Lords articulated precisely this point, arguing that unless the Commission articulates more systematically precisely where a more coordinated (European) approach to energy policy would generate more favourable outcomes for individual Member States, they would be unlikely to abandon the principle of subsidiarity, entrenched in Article 194 of the Lisbon Treaty, and to support the transfer of national power towards the EU (House of Lords, 2006: 6). As brought radically into focus by the June 2016 Referendum, Britain (and a variety of other Member States) remain keenly sensitive to overt forms of Europeanisation in areas that touch upon the national prerogative. Indeed, Brexit has prompted the revision of many UK-EU energy verities, including the prospect of a 'hard Brexit' entailing UK withdrawal from the Single Market. However, there may be benefits to the UK supporting the European Energy Union, given the degree of its material and market interconnectivity with continental Europe, and its policy of promoting cross-border energy markets. However, unless the UK negotiates a method of retaining a toehold within the institutions governing EU energy regulation, it will have no say in the construction of the rules which govern the EEU. More positively, the UK's own liberalised energy policy makes it more likely to 'continue to implement and be supportive of many aspects of the EU's Third Energy Package' in terms of unbundling, transparency and energy market-based interventions, as well as supporting broadly its domestic climate change goals (established under the 2008 UK Climate Change Act), despite being able to recalibrate its renewable energy targets (currently mandated by the EU Renewable Energy Directive) (Norton Rose Fulbright, 2016: 1).

Policy performance: action, change and roles

This final section examines the challenge of balancing abiding desires for nationalised energy security with an upsurge in distinctly Europeanised modes of constructing a European Energy Union. It focuses on identifiable *Member State preferences* regarding energy security policy in the shape of *change* towards, and the subsequent *actions* that such changes prompt, and the given roles that key states adopt in consequence. The key problem of course is in identifying common ground for the internal modalities of implementing market-based reforms aimed at enhanced competition (most notably the requirement of the Third Energy Package to unbundle vertically integrated, usually national energy companies) and, more challengingly, determining a common external vision regarding choice of, and attitude toward, suitable suppliers. It is one thing to 'develop a European reference framework' for Member States to 'accelerate market uptake and technologies' (Oettinger, 2010: 4); it is quite another to either manufacture a common external vision like the European Energy Union.

DG Energy may thus have gained substantial, if unintentional, support from the seriousness of a stoppage in Russian gas and oil supplies to key parts of the EU's supply chain attendant on the post-2013 Vilnius fallout and the ensuing hostilities in the Crimea and Ukraine. As events in Eastern Europe have demonstrated since 2014, there is nothing as valuable as a foreign policy threat to instigate commonalities across the Union (even temporarily).

The high vaunting requirement in the Lisbon Treaty of 'solidarity' amongst EU Member States regarding supplier and access choice took on dramatic salience throughout 2014, not because energy disruptions occurred in dramatic style (although Germany and Poland received warning shots in September), but rather because the economic fallout and political impasse between the entire EU and Russia as its prime energy supplier became swiftly and seriously entrenched; and because any and all resolutions reached regarding both Ukraine, and the stability of political relations necessary to guarantee security of supply remain as yet precarious.

As suggested, there is an existing foundation in which key aspects of the energy market, structure and *acquis*, as well as associated climate change goals, have been progressively Europeanised and that all the remains is to ensure that security of supply, as the third dimension of this triptych falls into place, with revanchist Russian attitudes providing an ideal catalyst by which to subsume fractious Member State attitudes. To some extent, this may be the case. Equally, however, there are a few points that suggest that these areas do not actually represent typically Europeanised outcomes. This is the case for two reasons. First, there is enough Member State resistance on every one of these areas (including climate change) to prevent them from representing genuinely integrated areas. Second, whether in the form of active support, neutral consensus or vehement opposition, Member State attitudes on energy security are every bit as defensively drawn and sovereignty-oriented as traditional areas of foreign and security policy. As such, agreements reached, and broken, are generally on the basis of national attitudes *found in common* across Member States at a given time, not as a result of *policies made in common*, to instil communality by the Member States across the Union. This is truest of foreign policy components underwriting security of supply, but an equally good indicator of standoffs encountered in the past five years over the modalities of securing a competitive energy market (explaining the intense unpopularity of unbundling), opinions regarding regulation versus deregulation, attitudes at the requirements of implementing carbon-free economies and even the methods of undertaking refurbishments to trans-European energy networks.

This pattern of policies emerging from attitudes *found in common* across Member States is best explained as a form of 'Europeanisation through diffusion', rather than concentration, and as argued by Busch and Jorgens (2012), is a particularly apt description of the tug-of-war encountered in European energy security. Arguing that far more national elements comprise the apparent Europeanisation of renewable energy sources (RES) than is generally accounted for (a good example being opposition from Poland, Hungary, Romania and Bulgaria to the October 2014 climate change deal (Oliver and Foy, 2014)), Busch and Jorgens suggested that agreements which have been reached arise via diffusion: 'processes of voluntary imitation and learning among governments [which] has played a major role in the Europeanisation of domestic RES policies (that is 'green Europeanisation' of energy policy) (in Morata and Sandoval, 2012: 66–67). Whereas traditional modes of Europeanisation operate in top-down fashion, under the pressure of multilateralism, a common body of law or supranational decision-making entailing a 'conscious modification of internal policies by governments committed to multilateral standards which they have had a hand in drafting', reactionary and mid-range responses are represented by coercion (which has both top-down and bottom-up dynamics) and diffusion respectively. Diffusion has a less precise causal configuration; it can occur 'voluntarily and unilaterally by an increasing number of countries' or, as in the case of energy security, via a combination of internal and external factors, that is 'an international spread of policy innovations [or developments] driven by information flow rather than [or in the absence of] hierarchical pressure or collective decision-making within international institutions'; here, decision-making is fundamentally 'decentralized and remain[s] at the national level' (Busch and Jorgens, 2012: 70). A critical mass of collective experience internally, or a significant external change or threat, constitutes a 'system-level effect' in which diffusion arises 'through the accumulation of individual cases of imitation or learning with respect to one and the same policy item', in this case the relatively uniform threat of Russian stoppage of gas supplies to the EU, coupled with the more uniform geopolitical fallout between the EU and Russia (Busch and Jorgens, 2012: 70). Energy security currently operates largely at the national level, and in the absence of a 'centralized regulatory system' compelling Member State solidarity, national policy-clusters that emerge to support a subsequently European approach may and likely will arise. They may over time represent a first step in consolidating Europeanised energy security; the point is that the process is rather unlike traditional forms of Europeanisation.

As illustrated earlier this chapter, a simple national versus Europeanised dyad does not fit easily within the dynamics of European energy security. First, Germany and France, as two of the largest EU Member States have of late begun to reassert the very real need for a European dimension in energy security. Second, the fallout of the Eurozone crisis, as well as the Russia-Ukraine farrago, has increasingly brought market imperatives to the forefront of policy-makers' minds as the correct modality by which to ensure the solidarity needed to pursue a collective response with volatile suppliers like Russia. Third, the implicit foreign policy component of energy security, and the deeply interconnected nature of neighbourhood suppliers – from Russia to Norway, from Algeria to LNG – implies that internal market stability via cheap and reliable sources of energy must have a natural counterpart in strong external relations with strategic energy partners.

While climate change remains a catalyst driving R&D and stimulating investment (and presents a carbon-free market obtainable over the *longue durée*), the overlap between competition and energy security as synergetic, if not yet wholly symbiotic, dimensions of Europe's tripartite energy policy is becoming steadily clearer. The EU will need to invest its way out of its internal energy market maladies as much as it will have to stimulate new and reformed relations with external suppliers. In the absence of any shift of competence, this twofold demand will almost certainly require a modicum of Europeanisation in terms of what market-induced fail-safes can be agreed to and rolled out across the Union, not least to keep prices of gas and electricity steady. Following some of the Commission's suggestions made in its June 2014 plan to reduce energy dependence, these could likely include enhanced storage capacity, larger and more numerous gas and electricity interconnectors, strategic gas reserves, sector-specific energy efficiency plans, enhanced LNG terminals and a commitment to support extant or future pipeline consortia in which EU stakeholders hold the majority share (European Commission, 2014c).

Two final observations are necessary. First, such policies – once they emerge – will not be testament to any form of Europeanisation while they operate as instrumental or technical outputs; they will represent a genuinely Europeanised rationale because they are ordained by, and flow from, a majoritarian rationale that sees them as the best, possibly only method of endowing European energy policy with a third and final dimension. Second, such policies may reflect an emergent Europeanised credo that defines the contours of energy security for the Union, while simultaneously not reducing instances of national policy-making at odds with an envisaged Union approach. Until the modalities of the competence itself shift and while bilateral contracts operate, and indeed while inconsistencies operate in the 'stated goals [of energy security], such as the spreading of democracy and securing access to hydrocarbon supplies' (Youngs, 2009; Francés, 2011: 48), Member State particularisms will both boost and beset the need to 'promote EU policies beyond its borders' (European Commission, 2011: 4).

Conclusion

Energy security remains the most potent area of unresolved tensions between Europeanising goals and national ambitions. There is much evidence to suggest that Modes III and IV will continue to predominate, with security of supply conceived of, and responded to, via national rather than collective interests. Member State responses beyond the specific purchase of energy supplies are hard to categorise, particularly between Modes II and III. EU Third Energy Package legislation impels cooperation on infrastructure in terms of enhanced pipeline, grid and interconnector construction, as well as cooperation on storage capacity (e.g. the Poland-Czech Republic Stork pipeline or Slovakia–Hungary pipelines; German gas connections to Italy, Poland and the Czech Republic); yet these are frequently undertaken by national energy actors and justified as national solutions concomitant with the sovereign dynamics inherent in Mode III. At best, this suggests the increase of mutual responses to cross-border problems, rather than wholesale collective responses within a newly established European energy union.

Attempts to cultivate a deeper, Europeanised energy security are critical, whether they emerge from the Commission or the Council. A variety of internal and external factors, from EU–Russia brinkmanship,[1] to the material realities of short-term stoppage and long-term finite supply to the iterative demands of EU climate change policy have seen the rise of various 'scenarios' drafted by the Commission, from gas stoppage induced stress-tests to common gas purchase, to efforts to create a full-blown energy 'union', as proposed by European Council President Tusk and masterminded by Energy Commissioner Maroš Šefčovič. If Europeanised demands and Member States' needs in energy security are to operate symbiotically rather than in suspicion of each other, Member States will need to be assured of the political gains to be had in committing to collective bargaining in both market-led and supply terms. Equally, EU-level energy security will need to accept that fossil fuel reliance (particularly regarding LNG, potential shale uplift), and the traditional pipeline infrastructure that accompanies it, will form as large a part of an energy union as innovative unbundling and regenerative clean coal renewable innovations. If the point of generating scenarios is to reconcile 'alternative narratives . . . with the aim of generating consistent 'global visions'' (Francés, 2011: 42), the Commission's 'European Energy Security Strategy' (European Commission (2014b), COM 330 Final) released in May 2014 represents a small step in the right direction, balancing across eight key areas' short-term needs to address storage capacity, the strengthening of solidarity mechanisms and protection of strategic infrastructure with long-term goals of internal market construction based on moderated demand, infrastructure uplift (European Commission, 2014b: 19–20). In terms of viable visions, the final point acknowledging the need for 'improving coordination of national energy policies and speaking with one voice in external policy' (European Commission, 2014b: 17) is by far the most salient. Whether – qua Marshall McLuhan – the *message* of a common Union voice balancing national and Europeanised narratives can produce a *medium* whereby a systematic use of foreign policy instruments can produce security of supply policies remains to be seen.

Note

1   As pithily argued by *The Economist* (2004),

> [t]he shock of Crimean annexation should speed up sluggish European decision-making on storage, interconnection, diversification, liberalization, shale gas and efficiency. And though the decision-makers may detest Mr Putin, in private they will admit that he may thus have done them a favour. They already know what they have to do. They just didn't want to do it.

Bibliography

Baumann, F. and Simmerl, G. (2011) 'Between Conflict and Convergence: The EU Member States and the Quest for a Common External Energy Policy', *Center for Applied Policy Research at the University of Munich*. Discussion Paper, http://www.cap-lmu.de/publikationen/2011/baumann-simmerl.php, date accessed 6 March 2014.

Boselli, M. (2011) 'France Needs to Upgrade All Nuclear Reactors', *Reuters*, 17 November, http://www.reuters.com/article/2011/11/17/us-france-nuclear-tests-idUSTRE7AG0HQ20111117.

Busch, P. and Jorgens, H. (2012) 'Europeanization through diffusion? Renewable energy policies and alternative sources for European convergence', in F. Morata and I. S. Sandoval (eds.) *European Energy Policy: An Environmental Approach*. Cheltenham: Edward Elgar Publishing, 66–84.

Cameron, F. (2003) 'An EU Strategic Concept', *European Policy Centre Publication*, http://www.epc.eu/pub_details.php?pub_id=1&cat_id=2, date accesses 10 April 2014.

Clingendael (2000) *Clingendael Jaarverslag 2000*, https://www.clingendael.nl/publication/clingendael-jaarverslag-2000, date accessed 18 August 2016.

Davey, E. (2012) 'The UK's Vision for Tackling Climate Change', *Chatham House*, http://www.chathamhouse.org/sites/default/files/public/Meetings/Meeting%20Transcripts/110712davey.pdf, date accessed 17 February 2013.

Department of Energy and Climate Change (2012) *Energy Security Strategy*, https://www.gov.uk/government/publications/energy-security-strategy, date accessed 22 March 2013.

Department of Energy and Climate Change (2013) *Maintaining UK Energy Security*, https://www.gov.uk/government/policies/maintaining-uk-energy-security–2, date accessed 22 March 2013.

The Economist (2014) 'Conscious Uncoupling', *The Economist*, 5 April, http://www.economist.com/news/briefing/21600111-reducing-europes-dependence-russian-gas-possiblebut-it-will-take-time-money-and-sustained, date accessed 5 August 2016.

EurActiv (2016) 'Šefčovič: "We Should Explore Common Purchasing of Gas"', *EurActiv*, 18 November, http://www.euractiv.com/sections/energy/sefcovic-we-should-explore-common-purchasing-gas-310091.

European Commission (2011) 'Security of Energy Supply in Europe', *European Commission*, http://ec.europa.eu/energy/publications/doc/20110601_the_european_files_en.pdf, date accessed 31 March 2013.

European Commission (2014a) *EU Energy in Figures: Statistical Pocketbook 2014*. Luxembourg: Publications Office of the European Union.

European Commission (2014b) 'European Energy Security Strategy: Communication from the Commission to the European Parliament and the Council', COM (2014) 330 final, 28 May, Brussels.

European Commission (2014c) 'In-Depth Study of European Energy Security', SWD (2014) 330 final/3, 2 July 2014, Brussels.

European Commission (2015) 'Energy Union Factsheet', MEMO-15-4485, Brussels, 25 February 2015, http://europa.eu/rapid/press-release_MEMO-15-4485_en.htm, date accessed 10 August 2016.

Fabius, L. and Batho, D. (2012) 'Europe Needs a Foreign Policy for Energy', *Embassy of France in London*, http://ambafrance-uk.org/Europe-needs-a-foreign-policy-for, date accessed 21 March 2013. Originally published in Les Echos 16 November.

Federal Ministry of Economics and Technology (2012) 'Germany's New Energy Policy', *Federal Ministry of Economics and Technology*, http://www.bmwi.de/English/Redaktion/Pdf/germanys-new-energy-policy,property=pdf,bereich=bmwi,sprache=en,rwb=true.pdf, date accessed 20 March 2013.

Foy, H. (2014) 'EU's Eastern Members Plot Joint Raid on €315bn Juncker Fund', *The Financial Times*, 8 December, http://www.ft.com/cms/s/0/70e1089a-7ba9-11e4-b6ab-00144feabdc0.html#axzz3MTLohWtr.

Francés, G. E. (2011) 'Market or Geopolitics? The Europeanization of EU's Energy Corridors', *International Journal of Energy Sector Management*, Vol. 5, No. 1, pp. 39–59.

Froggatt, A. and Hadfield, A. (2015) 'Deconstructing the European Energy Union: Governance and 2030 Goals', EPG Working Paper: EPG 1507, UKERC, CCCU and University of Exeter, December, www.ukerc.ac.uk/asset/2E1B4168-66C7-4DD9-93E72E5137AC91C5/, date accessed 25 October 2016.

Fulbright, N. R. (2016) 'Impact of Brexit on the energy sector', P NRF25674_B 07/16, June, available at: http://www.nortonrosefulbright.com/files/impact-of-a-brexit-on-the-energy-industry-137260.pdf

Germany Federal Foreign Office (2012) 'Russia Economic and Energy Cooperation', *Germany Federal Foreign Office*, http://www.auswaertiges-amt.de/EN/Aussenpolitik/RegionaleSchwerpunkte/Russland/Russland-Wirtschaft-Energie_node.html, date accessed 21 March 2013.

Gotev, G. (2016) 'Green MEP Denounces Gazprom's Bullying Tactics over Nord Stream 2', *EurActiv* 25 February, http://www.euractiv.com/section/energy/news/green-mep-denounces-gazproms-bullying-tactics-over-nord-stream-2/, date accessed 5 August 2016.

Helm, D. (2007) 'The Russian Dimension and Europe's External Energy Policy', 3 September. University of Oxford: Professor of Energy Policy, http://www.dieterhelm.co.uk/node/655.

House of Lords (2006) 'The Commission's Green Paper, "A European Strategy for Sustainable, Competitive and Secure Energy: Report with Evidence"', *European Union Committee*, 41st Report of Session 2005–06, HL Paper 224. London: The Stationery Office.

House of Lords (2013) 'No Country Is an Energy Island: Securing Investment for the EU's Future', *European Union Committee*, 14th Report of Session 2012–13, HL Paper 161. London: The Stationery Office.

Hurriyet Daily News (2016) 'EU to Unveil New Energy Plan to Curb Reliance on Russia', *Hurriyet Daily News*, 10 February, available at: http://www.hurriyetdailynews.com/eu-to-unveil-new-energy-plan-to-curb-reliance-on-russia-.aspx?pageID=238&nID=94927&NewsCatID=348, date accessed 15 February, 2016.

International Energy Agency (2009) 'France: 2009 Review', *International Energy Agency*, http://www.iea.org/publications/freepublications/publication/france2009.pdf, date accessed 27 February 2013.

International Energy Agency (2014) 'Key World Energy Statistics', *International Energy Agency*, http://www.iea.org/publications/freepublications/publication/KeyWorld2014.pdf, date accessed 10 December 2014.

Kroes, N. (2007) 'More Competitive Energy Markets: Building on the Findings of the Sector Inquiry to Shape the Right Policy Solutions', *European Energy Institute*, Speech, 19 September, Brussels.

Kuzemko, C. (2014) 'Ideas, Power and Change: Explaining EU-Russia Energy Relations', *Journal of European Public Policy*, Vol. 21, No. 1, pp. 58–75.

Mellár, B. and Nenova, S. (2012) 'Energy Policy: General Principles, Fact Sheets on the European Union-2013', *European Parliament*, http://www.europarl.europa.eu/ftu/pdf/en/FTU_4.13.1.pdf, date accessed 5 July 2013.

Meritet, S. (2011) 'French Energy Policy within the European Union Framework: From Black Sheep to Model?', *Université Paris Dauphine*, http://basepub.dauphine.fr/xmlui/bitstream/handle/123456789/5533/Meritet-June2010.pdf;jsessionid=C98A308B4B09768CDB87577CCD9 C7F27?sequence=1, date accessed 28 February 2013.

Morata, F. and Sandoval, I.S. (eds.) *European Energy Policy: An Environmental Approach*. Cheltenham: Edward Elgar Publishing.

Noronha, L. (2012) 'Energy and Resource Security: Towards an Inclusive Agenda', *Konrad Adenauer Stiftung*, http://www.kas.de/wf/doc/kas_33377–1522–2–30.pdf?130129094519, date accessed 18 February 2013.

Oettinger, G. (2010) 'Europeanisation of Energy Policy', *European Commission*. Speech of Commissioner Oettinger at the Dinner Debate with the European Energy Forum, Speech/10/573, 19 October, Strasbourg.

Oliver, C. and Foy, H. (2014) 'Can Europe Wean Itself Off Russian Gas?', *The Financial Times*, 14–15 October, http://www.ft.com/intl/cms/s/0/0078c61c-52d5–11e4-a236–00144feab7de. html#axzz3MTLohWtr, date accessed 20 November 2014.

Šefčovič, M. (2015) 'Speech by Vice-President for Energy Union Maroš Šefčovič at the Stakeholders Forum on Energy Union', SPEECH-15-6124, Brussels, 18 November 2015, http://europa.eu/rapid/ press-release_SPEECH-15-6124_en.htm, date accessed 8 November 2016.

Šefčovič, M. (2016) 'Energy Union – 1 Year On'. Speech at the Conference Organized by Jacques Delors Institute, 25 February, Brussels.

Westphal, K. (2012) 'Globalising the German Energy Transition', *German Institute for International and Security Affairs*, http://www.swp-berlin.org/fileadmin/contents/products/comments/2012C40_ wep.pdf, date accessed 18 February 2013.

Youngs, R. (2007) 'Europe's External Energy Policy: Between Geopolitics and the Market', *Centre for European Policy Studies*. Working Document No. 278, http://www.ceps.be/book/europes-external-energy-policy-between-geopolitics-and-market, date accessed 29 May 2013.

Youngs, R. (2009) *Energy Security: Europe's New Foreign Policy Challenge*. London: Routledge.

11 European Neighbourhood Policy and the migration crisis

Amelia Hadfield

Poor naked wretches, whereso'er you are,
That bide the pelting of this pitiless storm,
How shall your houseless heads and unfed sides,
Your looped and windowed raggedness, defend you
From seasons such as these? Oh, I have ta'en
Too little care of this! Take physic, pomp.
Expose thyself to feel what wretches feel,
That thou mayst shake the superflux to them
And show the heavens more just.

(Shakespeare, *King Lear*, III (iii) 28–36)

This chapter explores the role played by the European Neighbourhood Policy (ENP) within the foreign policy objectives of key Member States and the ensuing challenges posed in the wake of the 2015–16 migration and refugee crisis. As an ambitious regional policy, the ENP has undergone a number of significant shifts since its 2003 launch, driven largely by the turbulence of its key areas. Operating within the foreign policy architecture of both the EU and its Member States, the ENP's role as a geopolitical opportunity or a security risk remains in question. Given the enormous challenges to the EU, the Member States and the wider neighbourhood posed by recent migratory pressures, the role of migration and asylum in shaping the ENP and Member States' foreign policy responses to the crisis also requires investigation.

Established when its proximate regions were relatively stable, the ENP was launched by the EU on economically strong grounds. Unveiled to underwrite the geopolitical shifts accompanying enlargement, the ENP was designed to 'prevent the emergence of dividing lines between the enlarged EU and its new neighbours' by offering visible political dialogue and viable economic benefits, rather than formal membership (European Commission, 2003a, p. 3). By transforming the concept of membership from that of an absolute, accession-based status into a relativised role that relied heavily on programmatic conditionality, the EU hoped initially to improve the norms of its neighbours (chiefly rule of law, democracy and human rights), while simultaneously reinvigorating north-south relations with North Africa and Middle East neighbours, and initiating east-west engagement with Black and Caspian Sea states. The designation of 'neighbour' however was contentious. States with prospects (however distant) of membership including Turkey and the Balkans were not included in the ENP despite their geographic proximity. Nor was Russia, which declined the invitation extended by the European Commission prior to the ENP's official launch, arguing that the logics of divisiveness within the ENP would create east-west regional fractures. Russia also bridled at a regional programme intended to assist states to overcome troublesome autocratic histories and structures and the bestowal of a position which – in its eyes – ranked far below that of an EU Strategic Partner (Maass, 2016, pp. 65–66).

The remaining sixteen ENP partners have since assumed distinct geopolitical dimensions. The Mediterranean group encompasses Algeria, Egypt, Israel, Jordan, Lebanon, Libya, Morocco, Palestine, Syria and Tunisia, while the Eastern group is made up of Armenia, Azerbaijan, Belarus, Georgia, Moldova and Ukraine. Individually, these states represent a strikingly wide range of attitudes towards the EU. Some, like the Republic of Moldova, the Ukraine and Georgia early on equated the ENP with viable accession prospects, while Middle East and North African (MENA) states remained deeply pragmatic regarding ENP advantages. Others, including Belarus, Syria and Algeria, found the programme either diplomatically untenable or uninspiring.

In terms of composition, ENP incentives include market access and economic agreements, including aid, assistance and co-operation, as well as enhanced political dialogue and visa facilitation. ENP tools entail the range of provisions built into ENP Action Plans, or Association Agreements. Initial ENP logic regarding the use of these tools was twofold: first, that the prospect of drawing closer to the EU would incentivise a range of national transformations; second, that a single geopolitical approach would apply consistently to all neighbourhood states despite their political, economic and socio-cultural differences. Neither of these logics ultimately worked. As an outcome, these dual objectives have never been fulfilled. As Blockmans argues, 'the absence of a clear membership prospect for ENP countries, the EU's demands and prescriptive methods of harmonising legal frameworks and reforming institutions and economies have largely failed to inspire the neighbours, especially those who do not share the Union's values' (Blockmans, 2015, p. 2).

The European Commission has however argued that some ENP benefits are in evidence and that, after a decade of involvement,

> partnerships with the neighbours have a higher profile in EU affairs; the EU is the main trading partner for most partner countries . . . the EU has used the ENP to foster and evaluate, on an annual basis, reform efforts in each country, in particular on governance issues, on the basis of action plans agreed with the individual partners.
>
> (European Commission, 2015a, p. 4)

Regardless, the outcomes at the national level remain uneven. In merely identifying surface transitions, rather than targeting structural problems, the ENP failed in the MENA region to anticipate 'the root causes of the protracted conflict in the region: poverty, lack of education and employment', nor possessed the required conflict prevention or crisis management and instruments to respond to political volatility in the east (Blockmans, 2015, p. 2). Equally uneven are the geopolitical outcomes. While the ENP laboured to instil any genuine transformation with southern partners, the policy was ironically viewed as far greater than the sum of its parts in the east. Ukraine for instance interpreted its partnership status as indicative of future EU membership, whilst Russia viewed the bestowing of Association Agreements and Deep and Comprehensive Free Trade Agreements (DCFTAs), as well as the ENP (alongside EU and NATO enlargement) as cumulatively threatening to its post-Soviet provenances.

It is challenging to make identifiable connections between broad EU (and NATO) policies premised on neighbourhood stability and integration, and the aggressive responses by Russia to these same projects. The calendar of events, however, suggests a pattern of geopolitical intent. The invasion of Georgia in 2008, the increase in embargos against the food exports of Baltic states, ongoing repression of civil society in Belarus, interference in the political and economic preferences of Ukraine and Armenia at the 2013 Vilnius Eastern Partnership

Summit, the subsequent violence in Kiev's Maidan Square (itself a repeat of the Orange Revolution of 2004), and the invasion and annexation of the Crimea in 2014, followed by ongoing aggression in eastern Ukraine, are all arguably illustrative of Russian attempts at rearranging the east-west power distribution of 'its' neighbourhood and the preferences of the nation-states within it (Aslund and McFaul, 2006). Despite a degree of pro- and anti-Putin polarisation, Russian attitudes to these events are based on the 'intra-systemic ultra-nationalism of Putin's regime' and a combination of hard-power aggression and soft-power and increasingly heavy-handed propaganda aimed at neighbourhood states (Umland, 2013, p. 2). After a decade and more of lacklustre projects internally, and significant opposition externally, the ENP today has little to show, even in the area of Europe most conducive to its objectives. The EU now confronts a divided Ukraine, a diplomatic impasse with Russia, improved but inconclusive relations with both Georgia and the Republic of Moldova (Armenia retreating to the Russian fold having refused to sign the negotiated AA/DCFTA with the EU in 2013) and little viable influence with the authoritarian regimes in Azerbaijan and Belarus. Rather than a revived vanguard, the 2015 Riga Eastern Partnership Summit represented the inconclusive attributes of the EU's flagship regional programme. Rather than creating a viable ring of friends for the EU, EaP states remain torn between an unrewarded allegiance to Brussels, Kremlin inducements to recalibrate their political preferences to Moscow, or in some cases, join a new, rival region: the Eurasian Economic Union.

Neighbourhood and Member State preferences

With a few exceptions, EU Member States have remained largely ambivalent to the ENP. To be sure, the ENP has provided key opportunities for regional patronage with the Union for the Mediterranean (France, after Spanish leadership of the preceding Euro-Med Partnership) and the Eastern Partnership (Poland, Sweden and Germany). Within the ENP, Member States demands represent an overlap of intergovernmental cooperation of an EU-design (Mode II), fostering Member States' extra-EU cooperation (Mode III), while prioritising their own foreign policy preferences with non-EU others (Mode IV). Yet the damning 2015 ENP Review by the European Commission and the European External Action Service (EEAS) indicated that the project had benefitted neither the security of the EU, nor that of its Member States, nor afforded its recipients much in the way of improved stability.[1] Seen as 'idealistic in its conception as it was timid and insufficient in its implementation', the ENP was judged a lacklustre EU foreign policy, and the EU itself an ineffective regional actor, having 'greatly overestimated its own influence and underestimated the structural problems and risks in its neighbourhood' (Lehne, 2015). From a material perspective,

> the EU suffered a radical insufficiency of foreign policy instruments in terms of allocated resources, clear implementation and robust evaluation, whether competing with the hard power tools of Russia or terrorist organisations, or attempting to eradicate sources of chronic poverty in MENA and ex-Soviet areas.
>
> (DG NEAR, 2016)

Part of the reason that the ENP suffered from inadequate foreign policy power was that the program failed to *align* the different national interests of those EU Member States with major stakes in the neighbourhood to enable a coherent EU message, and a further failure to subsequently *catalyse* that same message to promote genuine progress in ENP partners. As such, the principle of neighbourhood itself was artificially 'upheld only at the EU level' because Member States simply 'did not align their bilateral policies with those of the EU' (Kostanyan,

2015, p. 2). While managed operationally by the European Commission and more recently, the European External Action Service, the attitudes of EU Member States ultimately remain key to the success or failure of EU policy. Yet across the neighbourhood 'the management of these complex policy crises has been hampered by divisions between Member States', producing in turn a 'decreasing influence' of EU-level foreign policy initiatives 'on how Member States in practice conduct their foreign policies' (Witney et al., 2014, pp. 1–2).

A key change occurred in 2008, when the ENP divided into two regional subgroups reflecting the geopolitical preferences of patron Member States. First, the Union for the Mediterranean (UfM), constituting twenty-eight EU Member States, the European Commission, and fifteen Mediterranean countries emerged, designed to boost political cooperation, and regional and sub-regional projects tailored to the needs of Mediterranean citizens. Whether regarded as a French project to rework an unhappy heritage or an attempt to provide the EU with an improved regional toehold, the UfM illustrated the ENP's ability to support the foreign policy preferences of a single Member State rather than operating as an EU-level magnifying force for all. Other Member States recognised the advantage, and the Mediterranean coalition led by France widened to include Italy, Spain, Portugal and laterally Greece and the Benelux countries. With the 2008 invasion of Georgia by Russia, Swedish and Polish (as well as Lithuanian, Romanian and German) preferences supported an Eastern counterpart that could reconcile requirements for an anti-Russia buffer zone with normative projects encouraging long-term transformation. Unfortunately, Member State preferences for the ENP remained more security-driven than the original 'reform-transform' ethos first outlined by the European Commission in its 'Wider Neighbourhood' policy (European Commission, 2003b). Where the latter had envisaged the collective take-up of a value-based nexus by which to influence neighbouring states, Member State demands instead revolved around more immediate security-led challenges, paralleling their short-term national preferences (a trend echoed in national responses to the current migration crisis). Consequently, the ENP itself remained critically unfit to provide any real response to the range of increasingly severe regional crises in the Mediterranean, from the Arab Spring and ensuing socio-political upheavals in key MENA states, to the 2015 migration crisis. The Eastern Partnership meanwhile witnessed geopolitical turbulence break into open aggression with Russian annexation of the Crimea in 2014, in which the ENP was at best a bystander, and at worst a naïvely managed catalyst.

The challenge has always been to balance EU actorness in its own neighbourhood between the nationally oriented foreign and security *prerequisites* of its own Member States, the *Europeanised* nature of those prerequisites when operating collectively as an EU policy, and the specific necessities and regional demands of North African (Maghreb), Middle Eastern (Mashreq), Black Sea and Caspian Sea states. The peculiar irony here is that, because of the ENP's potential to operate as a significant vehicle of the EU's emerging strategic and normative dynamics, its Member States each desire to upload precise national requirements which they then want translated on behalf of the EU as a whole. This process lies at the heart of EU integration. Within the ENP unfortunately, the end result has been negative, due to the incommensurate rather than complementary range of national preferences and EU demands. Taken together, these uneven objectives constituted the ENP's inputs, while the basic failure to address the real needs of ENP recipients (as well as feeble implementation and evaluation) blighted its outputs. The ENP's specific failure is therefore found in overblown EU *value-based* demands, rival security demands uploaded from Member States, and the increasingly *interest-based* attitude of ENP partners themselves, ranging from membership and trade deals to crisis resolution tools (DG NEAR Interview, Brussels, March 2016).

ENP update: pre-empting or ignoring migration?

After a slew of criticism from the European Parliament, the Court of Auditors, stinging Member States rebukes, and the 2015 ENP Review (European Commission, 2015b) the ENP itself clearly demanded a serious overhaul. Changes to ENP *inputs* included upgraded stabilisation tools; Generic Action Plans were scrapped in favour of permitting 'a more tailor-made and flexible policy framework adaptable to the diversity of partner countries, and a more consistent implementation of the 'differentiated approach' (European Parliament, 2015, p. 6).

ENP outputs meanwhile directly reflected Member State desires both to improve the strategic carrying capacity of the ENP and to enhance its ability to underwrite national requirements, particularly in the wake of serious volatilities along Europe's southern and eastern flanks. The multilateral, macro-ENP structures of the Eastern Partnership and the Union of the Mediterranean were retained for this reason, while micro-level improvements reflecting *interest-based* rather than *value-led* goals included security sector reform (including conflict prevention, border management, counter-terrorism etc.); enhanced socio-economic development (improved job creation); healthier crisis-response capacities; attention to energy security commonalities; and crucially, a strategy to balance legal mobility with irregular migration, including asylum seeking, human trafficking and smuggling.

Were such changes in line or at odds with Member State requirements? The 2015 German Marshall Fund policy paper is instructive here, highlighting the ENP's historically problematic dualities while insisting that such oppositions could become strategic complementarities with better management. These include – inter alia – 'an approach that is tailored to an *individual* country but utilises stronger *regional* cooperation formats'; a structure 'unambiguous and adamant in projecting its own *normative* model' but which but must improve on 'its omission of the *security* needs of individual countries and the region'; and lastly, full membership for some states based on an 'approximation with EU legislation and norms', alongside looser partnerships for states unwilling or unable to pursue such standards of approximation (Inayeh and Forbrig, 2015, pp. 3–4, emphasis added). A critical reading suggests that a revamped ENP maintaining such logical incoherence is doomed to be as ineffectual as its predecessor. A more charitable analysis could argue that EU Member State preferences regarding border-based security, and regional stability operationalised through area-specific patronage may conceivably balance broader EU goals of normative and legislative approximation, underwritten by country-specific schedules. What remains is the ongoing tension between the *promotion of values*, and the *identification of interests* as the overarching incentivising logic of the ENP, as well as unresolved frictions between EU-driven and Member State-led governance of the neighbourhood as a whole. Critically, neither the uploaded Member State preferences to the ENP nor collective EU goals downloaded on behalf of the ENP have remedied the ENP's critical weak spot: its external borders.

ENP and the migration crisis

As the Title V of the TFEU regarding the Area of Freedom, Security and Justice (AFSJ) and Title XXI (European Union, 2016a) illustrate, the EU has attempted to safeguard itself against a host of globalising dynamics, particularly in the area where internal policies have external dimensions (Keukeleire and Delreux, 2014, p. 222). As Part II of this text illustrates, the extent of EU foreign policy reaches far beyond the CFSP/CSDP framework and yet is frequently a supporting structure to make such policies effective. This problem is exacerbated in areas where internal and external policies overlap, complicating the EU's 'domestic' terrain with foreign policy ambitions that extend from, and beyond, its external borders.

As examined, the ENP was an ambitiously crafted but poorly implemented attempt at a domesticated foreign policy, one that attempted simultaneously to allowed the EU and its Member States to engage with non-EU states, themselves transformed into a 'ring of friends' based on progressive convergence. What is striking is that key facets of the AFSJ, the CFSP, the CSDP and the ENP have never been fully synchronised to support a joined-up policy for the EU's external borders, migration, asylum or neighbourhood requirements. Nor have structures like the Schengen Area (operating initially as an extra-EU Mode III and IV agreement between EU Member States and non-EU states) and EU agencies like FRONTEX (the EU border guard agency) been decisively tasked to work with ENP partners. This is odd given that key anxieties following the end of the Cold War, successive enlargements, and the ENP itself have routinely focused on border security issues (including immigration and migration, trafficking, smuggling etc.) emanating directly from the EU's new neighbourhood.

After the Amsterdam Treaty, the Europeanisation of migration and asylum policies increased rapidly. Directives regarding refugee status, third-country nationals and asylum-seekers (including the Dublin Convention and successor regulations), along with FRONTEX and the 2005 Global Approach to Migration Management (GAMM), together 'created a highly diverse and far-reaching legislative framework', albeit one which in the post-9/11 context 'established migration as a phenomenon that poses risks' (Karamanidou, in Lazaridis and Wadia, 2015, p. 38). Despite the complete integration of the AFSJ within the Community method under the Lisbon Treaty, specifically encompassing border controls, asylum and immigration (as well as judicial and police cooperation), the emphasis was, as per Article 3(2), upon:

> freedom, security and justice without internal frontiers, in which the free movement of persons is ensured *in conjunction with appropriate measures* with respect to external border controls, asylum, immigration and the prevention and combating of crime.
>
> (European Union, 2016a, p. 19)

These external measures, however, have proved both inappropriate and ineffective. Equally problematically, migration has historically been 'constructed as a process that poses threats to the security, identity and wellbeing of European states and societies' (Karamanidou, 2015, p. 37). Further, while policies on migration, borders and neighbourhood 'are often articulated at the national level, the European Union has been the locus of both discourses and practices securitising migration in the European context', with Europeanising dynamics capable of magnifying rather than actually managing national imagery and perceptions of external and internal threat (Costea and Costea, 2015). Thus, despite progress towards the construction of a Common European Asylum System (CEAS), accompanying structures to deal with neighbourhood-derived migration remained weak. The Migration Policy Institute observed in June 2014 that:

> the evolving global context of conflict and displacement, highlighted by the Syria crisis, failures by many States to protect their citizens, and mixed migration more broadly will continue to throw up new challenges in the asylum domain in the years ahead for the European Union and Member States, requiring robust systems and policies that can be adapted to meet them.
>
> (Garlick, 2014, p. 1)

While the June 2014 European Council adopted a range of asylum guidelines, these failed in definitional terms to identify the connection between migration and asylum and subsequently failed to produce common working policies on migration across the Member States and the EU institutions. As the MPI observed a full year before the 2015 crisis, the key recommendation was 'increased engagement by Member States in practical cooperation as a way to strengthen implementation and consolidation of existing EU laws and achieve more consistent, high-quality asylum decision-making' and notably to agree in pragmatic terms to 'concrete measures to put these key principles into practical effect' (Garlick, 2014, p. 1).

In foreign policy terms, this diverse legislative structure, coupled with unsynchronised approaches between AFSJ, CFSP, CSDP and ENP produced a severe disjuncture between those in FRONTEX witnessing the growing influx of illegal migration and asylum-seeking primarily across the Mediterranean, and those overseeing the ENP (at home and abroad) including UfM staff, EU Special Representatives and other EU delegations within the MENA region. Thus, despite its mandate to 'enhance the stability of the circle of states surrounding the EU', the ENP – the very crucible of the migrant crisis – has become the policy least able to foresee or contribute to the crisis (Garlick, 2014, p. 234).

The year 2014 witnessed the beginning of Europe's severest post-war migratory and asylum crisis, in which 280,000 people reached European shores. In 2015, during the height of the crisis, as estimated by the International Organization for Migration (IOM), roughly 1,011,700 migrants arrived by sea and 34,900 by land (BBC, 2016). With each passing week, EU heads of government found themselves under increasing pressure to agree to increasingly large-scale solutions. The *proximate* response agreed in April constituted an emergency mission to prevent migrant deaths in the Mediterranean Sea due to manifestly unsafe modes of crossing and to manage the physical influx of migrants and asylum-seekers at, and between the borders of EU Member States. The *remote* response is necessarily longer-term and preventative in nature, ranging from eradicating people-smuggling networks in North Africa, to tackling the broader causes of volatility in failing neighbourhood states (Libya, Syria) and those beyond (Somalia, Iraq and Afghanistan).

Rebranded the *European Agenda on Migration* (EAM) emergency **EU-level responses** in September 2015 involved immediate and structured policies to improve its management of migration: (1) reducing incentives for irregular migration, (2) a strong asylum policy, (3) saving lives and securing the external borders and (4) a new policy on legal migration (European Commission, 2015c). Extending the initiatives begun at the April summit, 'immediate responses' included tripled capacity for two FRONTEX Joint operations (Triton and Poseidon), an additional €60 million for frontline Member States primarily for the construction of migrant processes hotspot centre (co-managed by the Commission, the European Asylum Support Office (EASO, created in 2011), FRONTEX and Europol), whilst other Member States were given €50 million to underwrite the safe distribution of 20,000 migrants across Europe, alongside an increase in European Migration Officers in transit countries. In terms of joined-up policy, migration itself was at last designated a component of the CSDP, with CSDP Med-based operations given a mandate to capture and destroy boats and with ops in Niger and Mali broadened in terms of border management. Set against the organising principles of the text, the four pillars of the EAM are a combination of Mode II intergovernmental approaches (e.g. border-crossing actions designed to 'align return practices in all Member States' and the improved use of a FRONTEX) alongside Mode I legislative outcomes in improving the common asylum policy and establishing a new policy on legal migration.

The role of Member States in uploading their own preferences, and the ensuing 'leader versus laggard' roles in constructing EU-level responses, is key. National narratives on the migration crisis became increasingly strident throughout 2015, with national preferences driven at the outset by the irreducible minimum of border security: as witnessed by Hungary, Croatia, Slovenia, Austria, Greece and Slovakia who all erected fences across large areas of their borders to prevent migrant entry. The Dublin Regulation No 604/2013 also became deeply symbolic. Succeeding the EU Dublin Regulation (343/2003), the EU Dublin III Regulation establishes both 'the criteria and mechanisms for determining the Member State responsible for examining an application for international protection lodged in one of the Member States by a third-country national or a stateless person' (European Union, 2013, p. 1). The Regulation thus determines migrant and asylum claims on a 'first point of entry' system within the EU. Within Germany, and from the perspective of Chancellor Angela Merkel however, the application of Dublin III to Syrian nationals, specifically the possibility of enforced repatriation, was deemed unworkable (Asylumineuropa, 2015). Taking the lead by registering 44,417 Syrian applications between January–July 2015 and preparing for a further 800,000 such applicants – as well as setting the tone for the broader treatment of Med migrants – Germany suspended the Dublin Regulation's provisions dealing with the transfer of Syrian nationals on 21 August 2015.

The decision proved divisive amongst the Member States, some of whom were swift to point out that Germany had not only violated the Dublin Regulation in point of law but embarked on a major policy shift without prior consultation with other Member States. For others including Greece and Italy (where 850,000 and 200,000 migrants entered respectively during 2015), the pressure was temporarily relieved, and Germany's Dublin decision interpreted as a 'significant statement of solidarity with the countries on the edge of Europe' (Ceallaigh, 2015). Germany was then joined by Sweden and to a lesser degree Austria in favouring a proactive, intergovernmental rather than EU-led approach to tackling the migration routes arising across South-eastern Europe. The Austrian foreign minister for example 'expressed sympathy . . . with the Balkan countries' as hard-hit transit states, observing 'that the Dublin system simply does not work' (Ceallaigh, 2015). Others, including Slovakia, Poland and Hungary argued that the distribution of migrants within the EU, as well as combatting the root causes of their flight, would overwhelm their national carrying capacity and remained largely disobliging in pursuit of collective solutions.

Beyond the treatment of Syrian asylum-seekers, the material question of distributing and accepting migrants, refugees and non-Syrian asylum-seekers across Member States remained. Unable to generate a Member State-led internal policy, the European Commission proposed sweeping reforms to the Dublin Regulation, moving toward a Mode I harmonisation of asylum strategy for the entire Union. Examples of this included bolstering the EASO's mandate to intervene in cases of Member State non-compliance, standardised asylum-granting systems across the Member States themselves, alongside harmonised equal treatment for refugees. Initial attempts by the Commission at a top-down quota system however were roundly rebuffed, with Member States insisting that any systemic relocation operate on a case-to-case basis. This in turn prompted stark warnings from the European Commission that 'the European Union can only function if everybody plays by the rules' (Steinhauser and Norman, 2015).

The current situation remains difficult. The year 2015 saw the first two implementation packages providing emergency responses to the Med region (May and September), followed by a raft of Communication annexes regarding the refugee crisis (immediate operational, budgetary and legal measures), which were subsequently widened to implement Priority Actions under the European Agenda on Migration (European Commission, 2015d). In July 2016, the Commission proposed an EU Resettlement Framework that would 'establish a common European policy on resettlement' by providing 'for a permanent framework with a unified procedure for resettlement across the EU', effectively giving Member States the freedom to decide how many people they can resettle annually (European Commission, 2016a), representing a mixed Mode I and II outcome. The EAM itself now comprises a host of additional communications, reports recommendations and proposals for Regulations and Directives, cumulatively: *Managing the Refugee Crisis, Legal Migration and Integration,* and including specific proposals for improving the Common European Asylum System (via Dublin reforms, Eurodac security data, reworked EASO mandates, the Schengen structure and visa liberalisation) and a 'smart borders' initiative.

In terms of the redefinition of Member State foreign policies, the June 2016 Communication 'establishing a new Partnership Framework with third countries under the European Agenda on Migration' is most pertinent (European Commission, 2016b, p. 1). Arguing from the outset that 'external migratory pressures is the 'new normal' both for the EU and for partner countries', the Partnership Framework (PF) is visibly interest-based in terms of operationalising wide-ranging EU responses to major demographic shifts in and beyond the EU neighbourhood. Combining existing tools of development policy and the reworked ENP to 'reinforce local capacity-building' while assisting groups 'in need [with]in their countries of origin and transit', the PF attempts to balance 'genuine prospects of resettlement to the EU' with the 'return of illegally staying third country nationals' (European Commission, 2016b, p. 2).

Most notable are the strikingly regional structures and use of multilateral tools devolved from the ENP itself, as well as sub-regional projects (e.g. the Rabat and Khartoum processes) and region-specific funding (e.g. EU Regional Trust Fund in Response to the Syrian Crisis). Targeting specific migratory sources are sixteen countries' 'compacts' with states in North Africa, the Sahel and Afghanistan, Bangladesh and Pakistan in order to 'foster cooperation on migration, including on return and readmission' (European Commission, 2016b, p. 8). Delivery of the PF, however, rests strongly upon lessons learned from managing the ENP itself:

> An effective approach vis-à-vis third countries requires not only **a tailored approach but also a common and better coordinated approach between all EU actors and Member States**. The EU can achieve greater results only by speaking with a single voice.
> (European Commission, 2016b, p. 7, original emphasis)

Whether the Member States will be able to simultaneously redefine both their national preferences and EU-level demands for a neighbourhood policy revamped to tackle past failings and current migratory challenges remains to be seen. The enhanced securitisation of external EU borders, however, still appears capable of undermining the regional foreign policy goals of the ENP in working cooperatively with neighbouring states, themselves the source and/or transit points for the 2015 migratory surges. In this respect, the migration crisis has highlighted the most challenging of the ENP's logic: that EU borders may promote the security of the EU, but their increasing securitisation may ultimately prove antithetical to regional stability as a whole. Using national examples of Germany, Greece and Slovakia, the chapter explores the symbiotic relationship between ENP and migratory challenges in terms of the *uploaded* and *downloaded* foreign policy preferences of Member States.

Germany

Germany has maintained its support toward its adopted eastern regions, and worked to galvanise other Member States to support the EaP coalition. German and EU-level foreign policy strategies generally coincide in terms of their integrationist ambitions for proximate states. This makes central the role that Germany plays within the contemporary EaP and retains the ENP as the most extensive instrument of German foreign policy. While under Chancellor Gerhard Schröder, the ENP was viewed largely through instrumental and security-driven lenses, Chancellor Angela Merkel's government prioritised an agenda of Europeanisation based on the transformative capacity of the ENP/EaP at the state level, and its integrative potential regionally. German perspectives tend not to automatically regard former Soviet states as a buffer zone to be secured via stabilisation, but countries to be enhanced through the soft-power arsenal of the ENP included deepened trade and improved convergence in key norms and values, which could be upgraded via incentives including visa-free travel. Visegrad Group views however remain categorically different, preferring that the EaP contain the domestic volatility of EaP states and deter Russian aggression, rather than inadvertently exporting such turbulence to the EU, jeopardising the integration-based objectives of the ENP itself.

The keenest tension flows from attitudes to Russia. While Poland remains adamant in keeping Russia at bay, German preferences have traditionally favoured closer relations, not least because of the significant amount of German manufactured products exported to Russia and the supply of Russian gas to and through Germany via the Nord Stream pipeline. The post-Cold war detente entailed in Russia-German relations, however, has been radically upended with Russia's annexation of the Crimea in 2014 and its subsequent aggression in eastern Ukraine, forcing Germany to calibrate its eastern interests. Germany has transformed (even if temporarily) from east-west diplomatic conduit to EU bulwark, fostering agreement amongst EU Member States on sanctions against Russia, and clear support of the EaP as a priority of both German and EU foreign policy. Medium-term shifts, however, are likely, permitting German foreign policy to improve its regional patronage by advancing the individual interests of EaP states in a renewed ENP while keeping open diplomatic channels with Russia to foreground post-sanction relations.

Germany has since 2015 emerged as symbolic of the struggle to rework Europe's contemporary migration history. Key to much of its current national interests are the series of World War and Cold War identities that have forced painful collective refashionings, including its responsibility for the profound refugee crisis that followed World War II (Traub, 2016). Strategically, this has rendered Germany cautious regarding both military involvement and cross-border activities that hint at interference rather than intervention. As the Preamble to the German Basic Law makes clear, the task of German foreign policy is simply 'to promote world peace as an equal partner in a united Europe' (Federal Foreign Office, 2016). In terms of policy change, and action, the 2015 migration crisis compelled Germany to reconsider the appropriateness of tacit principles versus required action.

The lack of Member State unity and/or EU-level response, as well as the sheer humanitarian needs inherent in the migration crisis, compelled Merkel to suspend the Dublin III Regulation in August 2015, permitting Syrian migrants to apply for asylum in Germany regardless of their entry point in the EU. Merkel's particular policy of 'Wir schaffen das' ('We will manage that'), however, created domestic opprobrium within Germany for the Chancellor at the social and cultural risks associated with importing high numbers of migrants. This policy, as well as the broader implications of individual Member States unilaterally suspending European law, was received with approval from key Member States (notably the Visegrad Group) and equivocation from EU intuitions. Arguing that '[i]f we now have to start apologizing for showing a friendly face in response to emergency situations, then that's not my country', Merkel challenged other Member States to improve their humanitarian response to the crisis in an approach regarded as 'unapologetic, unequivocal' by the German media (Nelles, 2015).

The issue of EU external borders galvanised the majority of Member State attitudes. For Germany, the tension was keenly felt. At the EU level, Germany encouraged neighbourhood-oriented responses that focused on the source of migration, stressing the need to balance protective and preventive responses. However, with the rise of anti-migrant violence, and increasing support for Germany's far-right *Alternative für Deutschland* Party, Germany's open-door policy shifted. German borders to Austria were temporarily closed in September 2015, followed by the Bundestag vote to reduce benefit-based incentives, speed up asylum application processing, and declare Albania and Serbia as countries of safe origin for migrant returns.

The German government in October 2015 pushed hard, along with the European Commission, to produce a mix of legislated and negotiated solutions involving EU and non-EU states to settle migrants stranded in Italy and Greece. Favouring a generous but also equitable quota-based approach, Germany led a 'quota coalition' pulling together like-minded Member States in supporting a redistributive, European solution. However, the Visegrad Group (Czech Republic, Hungary, Poland and Slovakia) as well as others, including Romania, opposed this plan, demanding internal and external border closures and increased border security personnel. In a mix of Modes I and II, intergovernmental approaches to the migration crisis constituted the initial means to solve the crisis, but the ultimate solution has since shifted to EU-level solutions, underwritten by *communautaire* structures.

Germany's rewards for its single-minded pursuit of a solution to the migrant crises have been mixed: combining burnished humanitarian credentials and a dented geopolitical reputation, with Merkel's approach seen as reckless rather than merely relentless. Solidarity amongst frontline Member States over suspending Dublin III was tempered with anger by those who viewed German open-door attitudes as tantamount to an EU-wide policy of unrestrained welcome, placing an unreasonable burden on them at the national level. German attitudes continue to reconcile the demand of Juncker's September 2015 State of the Union address to react in a quintessentially European fashion, with Member States alike sharing a 'common history . . . is marked by millions of Europeans fleeing from religious or political persecution, from war, dictatorship, or oppression' (Juncker, 2015). The subsequent realist-oriented observation by European Council President Tusk argued that:

> [so]lidarity can no longer be equivalent to naivety. . . . We cannot abdicate from our most important duties . . . the primary duty of public authorities has always been to provide security to its own community and protect its own borders.
>
> (Heath, 2015)

Germany foreign policy has changed significantly since 2014. The migration crisis has widened traditional German support for EaP states to the borders of the Mediterranean. Consequently, preferences privileging normative goals over stabilisation prerogatives within the ENP have been tempered by pragmatic assessments of security-focused, border-oriented responses, and an acceptance that long-term resilience projects will be required to de-incentivise widespread migration to the EU from states within and beyond the ENP. Such recalibrations may push German foreign policy into an uneasy paradox: continued support for EU-level approaches to shared foreign and security policies, set against the necessity of implementing them through active, physical involvement in a range of volatile states, with a high likelihood of utilising CSDP operations.

Beyond constitutional issues regarding militarised intervention, and despite the domestic bruising and intergovernmental wrangling that accompanied migratory issues, Germany looks well placed to deepen its leadership in three key areas: the EaP, the European Agenda on Migration, and aspects of an overhauled ENP. In terms of its current 'economic weight and diplomatic influence', its prospective shift to counterbalance the UK's eventual departure from the EU, 'its relative political stability and consensus on key national interests, and the skills and experience of its chancellor' together suggest that 'Germany has become the unrivalled leader in Europe', through a skilled blend of intergovernmental-led Mode II negotiations regarding ENP development and a combined use of Modes I and II in response to the migration crises (Dempsey, 2016).

Greece

Within the southern dimension of the ENP, Greek participation illustrates the intergovernmental agreements found in Mode II. Migration responses have fostered Mode III interactions with Member States beyond established ENP policies, and migration and asylum legislation, and fostered Mode IV interfaces with Balkan states, Turkey and MENA partners. Greek activities in the ENP reflect both national preferences and EU goals to 'avert the emergence of new dividing lines between an enlarged Europe and its southern neighbours, while also strengthening prosperity, stability and security for all' (Ministry of Foreign Affairs of the Hellenic Republic, 2016a). The main changes for Greece encompass the multilateral dimension added in 2008 with the UfM, and the post-Arab Spring ENP revision of a more regionally focused neighbourhood roadmap in May 2012. Within the ENP's transformational logic of rewarding the uptake of value-based reforms, Greek effort is specifically based on 'consolidating democratic reforms and socio-economic development' amongst MENA states; within the UfM, Greek goals include maritime transport, climate and sustainable development, energy security, environment and water and regional tourism (Ministry of Foreign Affairs of the Hellenic Republic, 2016a). Greek participation, rather than overt leadership, has been in evidence in these areas. Other geopolitical dynamics have seen tentative Greek-Russian energy security relations emerging – usually as part of a seasonal balancing act that includes key states on some occasions, while excluding others. Turkey as a host or transit state for Russian pipelines, depending on diplomatic temperament. To this can be added a degree of nascent regional leadership by Greece in charting energy relations with Cyprus and Israel.

As illustrated, regional projects can operate as a vehicle for both national interests and as EU objectives. While a source of leadership for France, Greece has fared less well in projecting its national preferences against the regional contours of the Mediterranean. With the expansion of the UfM to include activities within the Balkans, and the participation of Turkey, Greek activity in the UfM has been somewhat circumscribed by its own historical tensions between Turkey, Cyprus and Macedonia. Despite this, Greek UfM participation has contributed to 'the depoliticization of one of the very few progressive chapters in Euro-Mediterranean relations, namely human rights and good governance' (Bicchi and Gillespie, 2012). Despite viewing itself as 'linked by traditional ties to the countries of North Africa and the Middle East', allowing Greece to lead in 'the role of a communication facilitator and expert on the neighbouring regions', it has struggled to operate as an exemplar of Europeanised approaches to the Mediterranean, due largely to the severe turbulence of its own politics, finance, society and border security, as well as its chaotic responses to migratory and neighbourhood challenges (Ministry of Foreign Affairs of the Hellenic Republic, 2016b).

Greece relies heavily on the solidarity of EU Member States and the broad Europeanisation of pragmatic responses to resolving both Cypriot and Turkish issues. In doing so, however, such preferences are periodically regarded as unbendingly nationalist, with Greece obdurately uploading the content of its particularlist disputes, rather than working consensually on regional goals to support local stability and regional security in the UfM and ENP alike. Tsardanidis and Stavridis (2011, pp. 111–130) for example argue that the Europeanisation of Greek foreign policy is not only erratic but based on selective approaches that correspond exclusively to its foreign and security preferences. Greece's chronically problematic financial situation, and inconsistent method of addressing EU fiscal stability and IMF repayments have since 2010, undermined its role as a dependable Member State, let alone regional leader. Defiant attitudes between Athens, Brussels and Berlin regarding Greek demands and Eurozone rules reached their zenith in 2015 under Prime Minister Tsipras, whose radical left Syriza Party was elected and re-elected in January and September 2015.

Despite the flamboyant rhetoric accompanying Greece's June 2015 Referendum on whether to accept the bailout conditions proposed by the Commission, the IMF and the European Central Bank, and the accompanying risk of expulsion from the Eurozone, Greek voters ultimately opted for a European, rather than a national, solution. Re-establishing working relations between national and EU authorities has since proven difficult. Rescue package conditions have arguably hollowed out the country, triggering 'unprecedented harsh austerity measures which affected society as a whole and increased poverty', as well as pitting Greek society against 'strong central European governments and European elites' (Lazaridis and Konsta, 2015, p. 188).

Against this precarious backdrop, Greece was transformed throughout 2015 into a frontline state in the migration crisis, becoming the key entry point for hundreds of thousands of migrants and asylum-seekers fleeing autocratic regimes, social instability and economic turbulence from across the neighbourhood. It was soon overwhelmed. Despite €146 million in emergency assistance in 2015, and €12.7 million in February 2016 alone from EU funds, the country struggled. Allegations by the European Council then identified 'serious deficiencies . . . of Greece's application of the Schengen *acquis* in the area of external border management' (Consilium Europa, 2016). The Greek government, unable to sufficiently regulate the treatment of the 857,363 migrants and refugees who entered the country throughout 2015, resorted to an assortment of civil servants, aid volunteers and NGO staff to process the swathes of migrants, frequently shifting large numbers of unprocessed migrants to other EU Member States and Balkan countries.

Blamed by neighbouring Member States for chronic mismanagement of a volatile situation, Greece was effectively cut off within the Schengen Area, with Balkan states closing their borders. Greek national interests have since suffered enormous reputational damage, in particular revelations regarding its legacy of 'deliberatively exploitative migration policies' that have historically encouraged the abusive use of illegal migrant labour in menial jobs to maintain a shadow economy, alongside official discourses designating migrants as scapegoats, fuelling the 'harsh and discriminatory treatment of migrants and refugees landing on Greece's shores' from 2015 onwards. Cheliotis for example argued recently that:

> despite repeated official proclamations to the contrary, the Greek state itself has in the past introduced policies and promoted practices that have helped to maintain the size of the irregular migrant population in the country at consistently high levels, not only engaging in piecemeal attempts at blocking irregular migration routes into Greece, but

also failing to facilitate processes of asylum, regularization, deportation, or even voluntary repatriation for migrants without papers.

(Cheliotis, 2016, p. 5)

National interests appear torn between deliberately lax border controls to promote 'the mass import of exploitable migrant labour' to Greece itself to attempt to engage with EU efforts to establish a working migration policy by way of improved external border security and more efficient asylum claim processing (Cheliotis, 2016, p. 5). Prime Minister Tspiras argued defiantly at the UN General Assembly in October 2015 that Greece had demonstrated 'solidarity with migrants and refugees' and that the fault lay rather with individual Member States and ineffective EU-level responses, which were lacking in material support and illustrative of widespread regional bigotry: 'We cannot allow racism and xenophobia to destroy our common principles' (United Nations, 2015). Despite its centrality to European migration challenges, Greece has become isolated from the emerging Europeanisation of asylum and migration policy. It has become a recipient of, rather than watchdog for, the added funding, improved hotspot administration and 4,000 additional EU staff to process individual asylum claims, with Germany instead using a Mode II and Mode I approach to construct the European Agenda on Migration (European Commission, 2015e) and the contentious pact with Turkey in March 2016 to halt illegal migration flows.

Greece has consequently become a microcosm of conflicting European attitudes to migration. Torn between generosity, enforced hospitality and securitised attitudes to migration, Greek and European narratives alike have shifted from 'people-centred or human security approach' grounded in humanitarianism to realist-oriented state-based security (Lazaridis and Konsta, 2015, pp. 189–190). In foreign policy terms, while the ENP and the UfM together offered opportunities to refashion the core problematic aspects of its regional identity, the migrant crisis saw Greece increasingly at odds with extant EU asylum legislation and emerging migration policies in terms of its own responses and adopt a largely securitised attitude to its subsequent engagement with other Member States.

Connections between Greece's penurious economy and its impoverished attitude to the treatment of migrants are evident but complex. German sponsorship of EU austerity policy has arguably proved a poor solution to the socio-economic and political requirements of Greece. In strategic terms, Greece will likely find much in the European Agenda on Migration challenging, remaining diminished in contributing significantly to the revamped ENP and ongoing UfM goals, and disadvantaged in utilising foreign policy options like enhanced or structured cooperation in areas including the CSDP, as outlined in the 2016 EU Global Strategy (European Union, 2016b, p. 11).

Slovakia

Smaller and newer in Member State status, Slovakia has obtained a high-profile role in drawing upon its national value-sets and foreign policy preferences to oppose key EU policies. In foreign policy terms, EU membership has undoubtedly proved beneficial, allowing Slovakia increased visibility internationally and improved diplomatic resources (Denca, 2009). Unlike other Member States from the 2004 and 2007 accession groups, Slovakia initially had little experience in terms of identifying and deploying a distinct national interest within the region, and beyond. Instead, EU frameworks themselves have downloaded a critical mass of national self-actualisation to Slovakia, leading in its first decade of membership to strong harmonisation with, and even mimicry of, EU foreign policy within its own external policy (Bátora and Pulisová, 2013).

In recent years, however, Slovakia has capitalised on the breadth of EU interaction in the region, the lack of specific integration in the field of foreign policy to define areas of niche expertise and a more individuated role among Member States, particularly within the Visegrad group (which includes Poland, Hungary and the Czech Republic). Key Slovak interests include energy security (specifically dependence on Russian gas imports), the democratisation of EaP states, Croatian EU membership and future accession for Serbia and Montenegro. Despite supporting key EU goals, contemporary Slovak preferences operate within the regional-specific process of 'Visegrad-isation', preferring the intergovernmental coalition-building of Mode II, and Mode III extra-EU regional diplomacy, via the Central European Initiative (CEI), the Danube Cooperation Process and the Adriatic-Ionian Initiative, to the intrinsically Europeanised dynamics of Modes I or even II.

With the 2008 launch of the Eastern Partnership, however, an EU-level foreign policy structure emerged that permitted newly acceded EU Member States like Slovakia to reflect their emerging strategic requirement, engage in the conceptual exercise of defining the European neighbourhood and participate in new dialogues with EaP partners. Through the EaP, therefore, Slovakia, was 'provided with an opportunity to actively participate in the conceptualization of EU Eastern policy' (Marusiak, 2010, p. 135). As evidenced by the 2015 Slovak Republic Medium-Term Foreign Policy Strategy, 'the EaP remains present within Slovakia's foreign policy in the long term', with goals including the integration of Ukraine into Euro-Atlantic structures, and ongoing work to democratise Belarus, 'together with support for the integration process of the Balkans' (Policy Documentation Center, 2015).

Taken together, however, Slovakia's preferences for extra-EU group-based diplomacy and wide-ranging EaP goals have produced a rather indistinct set of foreign policy preferences, which are not clearly translatable into consensus-driven EU frameworks. In responding to the 2014 Ukraine conflict, and the security challenges it posed for the EaP as a whole, President Andrej Kiska, Prime Minister Robert Fico and Foreign Minister Miroslav Lajčák for example all advocated widely differing approaches, Fico criticised Russian-oriented sanctions by the EU; Kiska demanded 'strong Atlanticism' supporting a robustly pro-Ukraine stance, while Lajčák attempted his own balance (Nič and Majer, 2015). This renders problematic both a clear understanding of Slovak national preferences and contestable the appropriate space within which to place them.

The 2015 migration crisis revealed the severity of this and other disjunctures. Despite his government's largely pro-European stance, Prime Minister Fico repeatedly used anti-EU rhetoric during 2015 in describing the migrant crisis, making clear his rejection of an EU-wide response, arguing that 'nobody can force us to accept migrants in Slovakia' and more divisively, that he would 'never allow a single Muslim immigrant under a quota system' (Foy, 2016). Slovakia's status transformed from a transit to a frontline state when individual Member State policies themselves shifted and aspects of the European Agenda on Migration gradually began to take effect. Caught between rival attitudes to both border controls and attitudes to the crisis itself, the Slovak government grew notorious its consummate rejection of open-door attitudes, integrationist requirements, and a broader European ethos.

After a variety of vividly negative portrayals of migrants and asylum-seekers and a statement during August 2015 from the Interior Ministry indicating its willingness 'to accept Syrian refugees under the condition that they are not Muslims' which constituted an infringement of EU rules banning discrimination, Slovak responses drew 'widespread criticism' from human rights groups and EU authorities alike (Bacchi, 2015). Subsequent Commission responses however did not convert such discriminatory activities into material infringements of the Common European Asylum System, which by February 2016, had been issued against Germany, Estonia, Slovenia, Greece, France, Italy and Latvia. All had 'two months to respond to the Commission, notifying the measures taken to ensure full transposition or bring national legislation in line with EU law' or face financial sanctions imposed by the European Court of Justice (European Commission, 2016c). Shifting its emphasis from the identity of migrants and refugees to the method of allocation, Bratislava continued to oppose relocation schemes in which the carrying capacity of Member States was used to determine their ability – rather than their national attitude – to receive migrants. Reacting to Mode II Member State-based suggestions for solutions, Fico made clear: 'We won't bow down to Germany and France. Quotas are irrational' (Traynor, 2015).

In failing to install liaison officers designated to resettle refugees from Greece to Slovakia, rejecting designated numbers to be accommodated nationally (accepting 200 rather than the envisaged 802), and ignoring warnings from the EU Representation in Slovakia that 'the Commission expects that every member country including Slovakia will fulfil its duties', Slovakia made clear its rejection of the European Agenda on Migration, regarding it as diametrically opposed to its foreign and security requirements (Cuprik, 2015). In December 2015, Fico then launched a legal challenge against EU migration policy, labelling it 'ritual suicide', a move supported by the Hungarian government (*The Economist*, 2016).

Future rifts are bound to arise in a number of quarters. First, regional splits between the Visegrad group and other Member States regarding the former's ability to anchor reform within the EaP due to rejectionist attitudes to crises within, and from, other parts of neighbourhood. Visegrad states, led primarily by Slovakia, stand accused of securitising the migrant crisis, causing 'deep-seated discrepancies between the Eastern and Western European countries', while portraying the Syrian refugee crisis exclusively as a European security issue. Instrumental dismissals of mandatory refugee quotas via of Mode I proposals by the European Commission were actively accompanied by the official use of xenophobic, anti-immigration rhetoric, creating a discourse 'spread a mood of fear' at best, and at worst 'turn[ed] a human tragedy in to a security threat' (Neweastplatform, 2016).

In addition, Mode II fractures between Member States could worsen. Despite strongly conflicting attitudes towards the migration crisis, the increasingly exclusivist geopolitical ambitions of its Visegrad partners, Bratislava – like the other Visegrad capitals – continues to regard Germany as its most important partner in the EU, despite differing attitudes to Russia, neighbourhood engagement, energy security and migration. In turning from leader to laggard, Slovakia, however, risks a wholesale circumvention by Germany in its future attempts to construct joint solutions on ENP.

Conclusion

Borders, territory and neighbours have proven a tough mix to resolve. As recent events have illustrated, EU decision-makers have consistently underestimated the territorial sensitivity intrinsic to the ENP. Within the EaP for instance, the role of borders and belonging within a European neighbourhood having arguably provoked Russian aggression in both hard- and soft-power terms (Maass, 2016). The EU's response has been to split the diplomatic difference, preferring robust statements and selective economic support but offering little in the way of genuine strategic change. Conversely, the EU significantly overestimated the robustness of its own external borders and those of its Med partners in terms of their ability to withstand or prevent the migratory pressures that began in 2015. In terms of migration, stark differences remain between increasingly entrenched attitudinal differences between the Member States and the flood of EU-level policy and legislation. Germany has propounded the legal and moral obligation to provide emergency and structured humanitarian responses, at pains to stress the innately Europeanised quality of these values and the increasingly pragmatic need of operationalising them. Slovakia, however, buoyed by the platform of its 2016 Presidency has argued that migration requires a far tougher response, beginning 'at the external borders', depends entirely upon 'closer cooperation between Member States in the field of internal security' and ultimately rests on discussions 'about how we want to reshape the European Project' (Gavlak, 2016, p. 3). The axiom of EU foreign affairs remains intact: the effectiveness of the EU's renewed neighbourhood and migration programmes relies heavily upon generating convergence, rather than falling prey to continued divergence, between the individual foreign attitudes of its constituent Member States.

Note

1   The annual ENP Review is published jointly by the European Commission and the High Representative of the European Union for Foreign Affairs and Security Policy. Reports on the implementation of the ENP in 2014 were adopted on 25 March 2015, and are available online in the form of individual country reports, and regional progress reports for the Eastern Partnership, and the Southern Mediterranean, available here: http://eeas.europa.eu/enp/documents/progress-reports/index_en.htm.

Bibliography

Aslund, A. and Mcfaul, M., (2006), *Revolution in Orange: The Origins of Ukraine's Democratic Breakthrough*. Washington: Carnegie Endowment.

Asylumineuropa, (2015), *Germany: Halt on Dublin procedures for Syrians*, Asylum Information Database, Available at: http://www.asylumineurope.org/news/24–08–2015/germany-halt-dublin-procedures-syrians (Accessed 16 August 2016).

Bacchi, U., (2015), *EU migrant crisis: Slovakia criticised for no-Muslim refugee policy and taking only Christians*, Available at: http://www.ibtimes.co.uk/eu-migrant-crisis-slovakia-criticised-no-muslim-refugee-policy-taking-only-christians-1516382# (Accessed 16 August 2016).

Bátora, J. and Pulisová, V., (2013), 'Slovakia: Learning to add value to EU foreign policy', in Baun, Michael and Dan, Marek (eds.), *The New Member States and the European Union: Foreign Policy and Europeanization*, London/New York: Routledge, pp. 68–83.

BBC, (2016), *Migrant crisis: Migration to Europe explained in seven charts*, 4 March, Available at: http://www.bbc.com/news/world-europe-34131911 (Accessed 14 August 2016).

Bicchi, F. and Gillespie, R., (2012), *The Union for the Mediterranean*. London: Routledge.

Blockmans, S., (2015), *The 2015 ENP Review: A policy in suspended animation*, CEPS Commentary, Available at: https://www.ceps.eu/system/files/SB%20ENP%20Review%20CEPS%20Commentary.pdf (Accessed 14 August 2016).

Ceallaigh, G., (2015), *Germany suspends Dublin III transfers for Syrians*, Free Movement Online, Available at: https://www.freemovement.org.uk/germany-suspends-dublin-iii-transfers-for-syrians/ (Accessed 3 April 2016).

Cheliotis, L., (2016), 'Punitive inclusion: The political economy of irregular migration in the margins of Europe', *European Journal of Criminology*, Special issue on crimmigration, pp. 1–22, Available at: http://www.lcheliotis.net/uploads/2/2/0/5/22057848/punitive_inclusion_-_the_political_economy_of_irregular_migration_in_the_margins_of_europe_-_leonidas_cheliotis_-_final_proofs.pdf.

Consilium Europa, (2016), *Schengen evaluation of Greece: Council adopts recommendation to address deficiencies in external borders*, Available at: http://www.consilium.europa.eu/en/press/press-releases/2016/02/12-schengen-evaluation-of-greece/ (Accessed 15 August 2016).

Costea, S. and Costea, M., (2015), 'Challenges of the EU in the migrant/refugee crisis in 2015', in *Discourse as a Form of Multiculturalism in Literature and Communication*, Mureş, Romania: Arhipelag XXI Press, pp. 166–175.

Cuprik, R., (2015), *Slovakia ignores EU rules on refugees*, The Slovak Spectator, Online, Available at: http://spectator.sme.sk/c/20063001/slovakia-ignores-eu-rules-on-refugees.html (Accessed 15 August 2016).

Dempsey, J., (2016), *Judy asks: Is German strength an illusion?*, Carnegie Europe, Available at: http://carnegieeurope.eu/strategiceurope/?fa=64075 (Accessed 7 August 2016).

Denca, S.S., (2009), 'The Europeanization of Foreign policy: Empirical findings from Hungary, Romania and Slovakia', *Journal of Contemporary European Research*. Volume 5, Issue 3, pp. 389–404.

DG NEAR (Directorate General for Neighbourhood Policy and Enlargement Negotiations), (2016), Interview. Brussels, July 2016.

The Economist (2016) 'Illiberal Central Europe: Big, Bad Visegrad', *The Economist*, Available at: http://www.economist.com/news/europe/21689629-migration-crisis-has-given-unsettling-new-direction-old-alliance-big-bad-visegrad (Accessed 15 October 2016).

European Commission, (2003a), *European Neighbourhood Policy: Strategy Paper*, p. 3, Available at: http://trade.ec.europa.eu/doclib/docs/2004/july/tradoc_117717.pdf (Accessed 14 August 2016).

European Commission, (2003b), *Wider Europe – neighbourhood: A new framework for relations with our Eastern and Southern neighbours*, Brussels, 11th March, COM(2003) 104 final, Available at: https://eeas.europa.eu/enp/pdf/pdf/com03_104_en.pdf (Accessed 16 August 2016).

European Commission, (2015a), *Joint consultation paper: Towards a new European neighbourhood policy*, Available at: http://ec.europa.eu/enlargement/neighbourhood/consultation/consultation.pdf (Accessed 14 August 2016).

European Commission, (2015b), *Review of the European neighbourhood policy*, Brussels, 11th November, JOIN(2015) 50 final, Available at: http://eeas.europa.eu/enp/documents/2015/151118_joint-communication_review-of-the-enp_en.pdf (Accessed 15 August 2016).

European Commission, (2015c), *European agenda on migration 2015 – four pillars to better manage migration*, Available at: http://ec.europa.eu/dgs/home-affairs/what-we-do/policies/european-agenda-migration/background-information/docs/summary_european_agenda_on_migration_en.pdf (Accessed 15 July 2016).

European Commission, (2015d), *A European agenda on migration*, Brussels, 13th May, COM(2015) 240 final, Available at: http://ec.europa.eu/dgs/home-affairs/what-we-do/policies/european-agenda-migration/background-information/docs/communication_on_the_european_agenda_on_migration_en.pdf (Accessed 15 August 2016).

European Commission, (2015e), *Managing the refugees crisis: Immediate operational, budgetary and legal measures under the European Agenda on Migration*, Brussels, 23rd September, COM (2015) 490 final, Available at: http://ec.europa.eu/dgs/home-affairs/what-we-do/policies/european-agenda-migration/proposal-implementation-package/docs/communication_on_managing_the_refugee_crisis_annex_1_en.pdf (Accessed 15 August 2016).

European Commission, (2016a), *Establishing an EU resettlement framework: Frequently asked questions*, 13 July, Available at: http://europa.eu/rapid/press-release_MEMO-16–2437_en.htm. http://europa.eu/rapid/press-release_MEMO-16–2437_en.htm (Accessed 15 August 2016).

European Commission, (2016b), *Communication on establishing a new partnership framework with third countries under the European agenda on migration*, Strasbourg, 6th June, COM (2016) 385 final, pp. 1–2, Available at: http://ec.europa.eu/dgs/home-affairs/what-we-do/policies/european-agenda-migration/proposal-implementation-package/docs/20160607/communication_external_aspects_eam_towards_new_migration_ompact_en.pdf (Accessed 15 August 2016).

European Commission, (2016c), *Implementing the common European asylum system: Commission acts on 9 infringement proceedings*, Available at: http://europa.eu/rapid/press-release_IP-16–270_en.htm (Accessed 15 August 2016).

European Parliament, (2015), *Draft report on the review of the European neighbourhood policy*, 22nd April, (2015/2002(INI)), p. 6, Available at: http://www.epgencms.europarl.europa.eu/cmsdata/

upload/d492e0eb-47ed-48eb-aace-99e63d02d978/Draft_report_on_the_review_of_the_European_
Neighbourhood_Policy.pdf (Accessed 4 April 2016).

European Union, (2013), 'Regulation (EU) No 604/2013', *Official Journal of the European Union*, 26 June, p. 1, Available at: http://eur-lex.europa.eu/legal-content/EN/TXT/PDF/?uri=CELEX:32013R0604&from=EN (Accessed 14 August 2016).

European Union, (2016a), 'Consolidated versions of the treaty on European Union and the treaty on the functioning of the European Union', *Official Journal of the European Union*, C 202/01, Available at: http://eur-lex.europa.eu/legal-content/EN/TXT/PDF/?uri=OJ:C:2016:202:FULL&from=EN (Accessed 13 May 2016).

European Union, (2016b), *Shared vision, common action: A stronger Europe: A global strategy for the European Union's Foreign and security policy*, Brussels, June, 2016, Available at: http://europa.eu/globalstrategy/sites/globalstrategy/files/eugs_review_web.pdf.

Eurostat, (2015), *Facts and figures about the Eastern Partners of the European Union*, 20 May, Available at: http://ec.europa.eu/eurostat/documents/2995521/6836772/6-20052015-BP-EN.pdf/1b8e0bd3-a47d-4ef4-bca6-9fbb7ef1c7f9 (Accessed 7 April 2016).

Federal Foreign Office, (2016), *Peace and security*, Available at: http://www.auswaertiges-amt.de/EN/Aussenpolitik/Friedenspolitik/Friedenspolitik_node.html (Accessed 14 August 2016).

Foy, H., (2016), 'Slovakia election: PM uses migrant fears to boost poll support', *Financial Times*, 3 March, Available at: http://www.ft.com/cms/s/0/f3c6a6f8-e11e-11e5-8d9b-e88a2a889797.html#axzz4HLV1wXhn (Accessed 14 August 2016).

Garlick, M., (2014), *Strengthening refugee protection and meeting challenges: The European Union's next steps on Asylum*, Migration Policy Institute, p. 1, Available at: http://www.migrationpolicy.org/research/strengthening-refugee-protection-and-meeting-challenges-european-unions-next-steps-asylum (Accessed 14 August 2016).

Gavlak, J., (2016), 'Slovakia's presidency: "We are facing old problems, new problems"', *New Europe*, Number 1172, 3–9 July, Brussels, Available at: https://www.neweurope.eu/article/issue-1172-slovakias-presidency-print-edition/.

Heath, R., (2015), *We are in deep trouble*, Politico Online, Available at: http://www.politico.eu/article/orban-refugees-hungary-we-are-in-deep-trouble/ (Accessed 4 April 2016).

Inayeh, A. and Forbrig, J., (2015), *Reviewing the European neighbourhood policy: Eastern perspectives*, The German Marshall Fund of United states, Europe Policy Paper 4/2015. Available at: http://www.gmfus.org/publications/reviewing-european-neighbourhood-policy-eastern-perspectives (Accessed 4 April 2016).

Juncker, J.-C., (2015), *State of the Union 2015: Time for honesty, unity and solidarity*, Available at: http://europa.eu/rapid/press-release_SPEECH-15-5614_en.htm (Accessed 14 August 2016).

Karamanidou, L., (2015), 'The securitisation of European migration policies: Perceptions of threat and management of risk', in Lazaridis, G. and Wadia, K. (eds.), *The Securitisation of Migration in the EU*, Basingstoke: Palgrave, pp. 37–61.

Keukeleire, S. and Delreux, T., (2014), *The Foreign Policy of the European Union*. London: Palgrave Macmillan.

Kostanyan, H., (2015), *The European neighbourhood policy reviewed: Will pragmatism trump normative values?*, CEPS-European Neighbourhood Watch, Available at: https://www.ceps.eu/system/files/NWatch201_0.pdf (Accessed 14 August 2016).

Kratochvíl, P., (2007), 'New EU members and the ENP: Different agendas, different strategies', *Intereconomics*, July/August, Online, Available at: http://www.dokumenty-iir.cz/CV/Kratochvil/New_EU_Members.pdf (Accessed 7 April 2016).

Lazaridis, G. and Konsta, A., (2015), 'Identitarian populism: Securitisation of migration and the far right in times of economic crisis in Greece and the UK', in Lazaridis, G. and Wadia, K. (eds.), *The Securitisation of Migration in the EU*, Basingstoke: Palgrave, pp. 184–206.

Lehne, S., (2015), 'Toward a European neighborhood realpolitik?', *Carnegie Europe*, Available at: http://carnegieeurope.eu/strategiceurope/?fa=62029 (Accessed 16 August 2016).

Maass, A., (2016), *EU-Russia Relations, 1995–2015: From Courtship to Confrontation*. London: Routledge.

Marusiak, J., (2010), 'Slovakia and the Eastern Partnership', *Academia.edu*, Online, p. 135, Available at: https://www.academia.edu/7495284/SLOVAKIA_AND_THE_EASTERN_PARTNERSHIP (Accessed 16 August 2016).

Ministry of Foreign Affairs of the Hellenic Republic, (2012), *Deputy FM Kourkoulas meets with the Secretary General of the Union for the Mediterranean*, Hellenic Republic Ministry of Foreign Affairs, Online, Available at: http://www.mfa.gr/en/current-affairs/news-announcements/deputy-fm-kourkoulas-meets-with-the-secretary-general-of-the-union-for-the-mediterranean.html (Accessed 14 August 2016).

Ministry of Foreign Affairs of the Hellenic Republic, (2016a), *External relations – EU enlargement: A successful policy*, Hellenic Republic Ministry of Foreign affairs, Online, Available at: http://www.mfa.gr/en/foreign-policy/greece-in-the-eu/external-relations-enlargement.html (Accessed 15 August 2016).

Ministry of Foreign Affairs of the Hellenic Republic, (2016b), *External relations – European neighbourhood policy*, Hellenic Republic Ministry of Foreign Affairs, Online, Available at: http://www.mfa.gr/en/foreign-policy/greece-in-the-eu/external-relations-european-neighbourhood-policy.html (Accessed 14 August 2016).

Nelles, R., (2015), *Unapologetic, unequivocal: The real Merkel finally stands up*, Spiegel Online, Available at: http://www.spiegel.de/international/germany/merkel-refuses-to-apologize-for-welcoming-refugees-a-1053253.html (Accessed 11 June 2016).

Neweastplatform, (2016), *Securitizing the Syrian refugee influx: How Visegrad group countries use language to turn migrants into threats*, New East Platform Online, Available at: https://neweastplatform.org/2016/04/05/securitizing-the-syrian-refugee-influx-how-visegrad-group-countries-use-language-to-turn-migrants-into-threats/ (Accessed 15 August 2016).

Nič, M. and Majer, M., (2015), 'Letter from Bratislava', *Carnegie Europe*, 6 March, Online, Available at: http://carnegieeurope.eu/strategiceurope/?fa=59269 (Accessed 7 April 2016).

Policy Documentation Center, (2015), *Medium-term Foreign policy strategy of the Slovak Republic until 2015*, Policy Documentation Center Online, Available at: http://pdc.ceu.hu/archive/00002703/01/strategy_fp_sr_until_2015.pdf (Accessed 14 August 2016).

Steinhauser, G. and Norman, L., (2015), 'Clashing national interests Hamstring EU's response to migrant crisis', *The Wall Street Journal*, 1 September, Online, Available at: http://www.wsj.com/articles/clashing-national-interests-hamstring-eus-response-to-migrant-crisis-1441141465 (Accessed 15 August 2016).

Traub, J., (2016), *The death of the most generous nation on earth*, Foreign Policy Online, Available at: http://foreignpolicy.com/2016/02/10/the-death-of-the-most-generous-nation-on-earth-sweden-syria-refugee-europe/ (Accessed 15 August 2016).

Traynor, I., (2015), 'Refugee crisis: Juncker calls for radical overhaul of EU immigration policies', *The Guardian*, Online, Available at: http://www.theguardian.com/world/2015/sep/09/refugee-crisis-eu-executive-plans-overhaul-of-european-asylum-policies (Accessed 15 August 2016).

Tsardanidis, C. and Stavridis, S., (2011), 'Greece: From special case to limited Europeanisation', in Wong, R. and Hill, C.J., (eds.), *National and European Foreign Policies: Towards Europeanization*, London: Routledge, pp. 111–130.

Umland, A., (2013), 'New extreme right-wing intellectual circles in Russia: The anti-orange committee, the Isborsk Club and the Florian Geyer Club', *Russian Analytical Digest*, Number 135, Available at: http://www.css.ethz.ch/content/dam/ethz/special-interest/gess/cis/center-for-securities-studies/pdfs/RAD-135-2-5.pdf (Accessed 15 August 2016).

United Nations, (2015), *Future of Europe cannot be built on 'ever-higher walls'*, *Greek Prime Minister tells UN*, Available at: http://www.un.org/apps/news/story.asp?NewsID=52098#.V7oNrmXpSop (Accessed 15 August 2016).

Witney, N., Leonard, M., Godement, F., Levy, D. Liik, K. and Tcherneva, V., (2014), *Rebooting EE Foreign policy*, European Council on Foreign Relations, Available at: http://www.ecfr.eu/page/-/ECFR114_EU_BRIEF_SinglePages_(1).pdf (Accessed 15 August 2016).

12 Development

Shallow Europeanisation?[1]

Jan Orbie and Simon Lightfoot

Introduction

The oft-heard statement that 'Europe' is the biggest aid provider in the world refers to the collective aid disbursed by the European Union (EU) Member States (MS) and the EU institutions, thereby suggesting that there must be a common 'European' development policy. It remains however unclear whether we see anything more than face-value Europeanisation in the area of development. In this chapter, we argue that, in relation to the 'change and action' framework, we have clearly seen change at the EU level, especially since the 2000s. We have also seen change at the MS level, since the end of the Cold War (see Arts and Dickson, 2004). There has been a greater emphasis on poverty reduction but also security (see Faust and Messner, 2005). The extent to which these changes are as a result of EU action is less clear, as we will show. Whilst the Commission has acted as a supranational actor in this field, the variety of actors in the global development field, such as the OECD DAC, the UN etc. muddy the waters somewhat. The global development architecture is in a state of flux at present, with non-DAC donors such as China and India yet to embrace the existing aid architecture. At the same time, budgetary pressures have led EU MS to reconsider previous aid commitments, and geopolitical evolutions have fuelled calls for a more pragmatic and security-oriented EU approach to developing countries.

This chapter focuses on the post 2000s evolution of international development policy in the EU in terms of change and action. There are two reasons for this time demarcation. First, legally speaking, 'development cooperation' has only been an EU competence since the Maastricht Treaty, and arguably, the European Commission has only become a 'real' development donor since the 2000s. Over the past decade, the Commission has restructured itself in order to better define and organize development aid and as a result become a more effective and full-fledged development donor. This also involves a clearer articulation of the EU's added value (e.g. development policy statement 2000); the elaboration of development strategies (e.g. country strategy papers and national indicative programmes since 2002); an increased focus on implementation (e.g. EuropeAid, decentralization); and a rationalization of financial instruments (from 2006). The EC has become an important '29th donor' besides the 28 MS, and it is considered to be one of the most effective donors[2] (DAC, 2012). While pleas for a renationalization of development policy are still regularly heard, it is more likely that the EU will continue to be a recognized donor on the international aid landscape (Holland and Doidge, 2012: 11).

Second and most importantly, the European Commission has shown an outspoken ambition to Europeanise the MS' development policies since the 2000s (Orbie, 2012; Orbie and Carbone, 2016). Integration of national policies alongside the creation of supranational powers has never been the goal, but rather the Commission has sought to foster a more 'European' policy. As former Development Commissioner Louis Michel (2006) stated: 'Although development is and will remain a competence shared by the Community and the Member States this does not prevent us joining forces, harmonize our procedures and share the job'. While initiatives to coordinate Member States' development policies failed in the 1990s (Carbone, 2008: 330), the early 2000s showed a new momentum for Europeanisation. In terms of streamlining the objectives of EU donors, an obvious illustration is the 'European Consensus on Development' (2005) between the Commission, the Council and the European Parliament. Initiatives such as the annual European Report on Development (since 2009) and the European Development Days (since 2006) are meant to further highlight the EU's distinctive profile in international development. Besides outlining a common vision, the EU also developed procedural initiatives to stimulate coordination between EU donors such as the 'Common Framework for Elaborating Strategy Documents per Country and Common Multi-annual Programming' (2006) and the 'EU Code of Conduct and Division of Labour' (2007). The search for a 'whole-of-the-union' and joint approaches has dominated the thinking within the Commission, although the creation of the EEAS may have muddied the waters somewhat in this area (see Gänzle et al., 2012).

Although the proliferation of European coordination initiatives seems quite remarkable, Europeanisation cannot a priori be assumed from this. Keeping in mind the editors' warning in the introduction to this volume, the 'new season' of EU development policy (Carbone, 2008) may not be much more than face-value Europeanisation (Szent-Iványi and Lightfoot, 2015). As will become clear later in this chapter, development is only a shared parallel competence, and EU MS are reluctant to give up sovereignty in this area. This is not surprising since this development cooperation involves considerable sums of money and tends to be closely linked to foreign policy (Alesina and Dollar, 2000; Younas, 2008). Therefore, to the extent that Europeanisation occurs, it could also be that it involves a more pragmatic and less development-friendly orientation that is primarily informed by economic and security interests. Moreover, this chapter will show that a certain convergence of MS development policies may be related more to the level of the Development Assistance Committee (DAC) than to the EU. Therefore, it may be more accurate to speak of a shallow Europeanisation or even a DAC-ization of EU development policy.

The first section of this chapter looks at the EU competences in development and suggests that only 'shallow' Europeanisation has taken place. MS. The second section focuses more closely on the differences between the MS' development policies, as it is clear that key Member States account for change and action in this policy field over time. The third section explores the challenges of politicization and securitization of aid at the EU and MS levels and the limits of Europeanisation in this area. The conclusions highlight the importance of domestic preferences and international developments in explaining convergence and divergence between EU MS. However, since comparative studies of MS development policies and their interaction with the EU are nearly absent, there is much scope for deeper and more qualitative research in this area.

Limited EU competences and shallow Europeanisation

Since the Maastricht Treaty (1993), development policy has been a 'mixed system' with competences shared by the EU and the MS. Development and cooperation policy in general was set out in Articles 130u-x of the EC Treaty. These articles include the overarching objectives for EU development policy and some key concepts – that policies in other fields must be coherent with the aims of development policy and that MS should aim to coordinate and cooperate in aid policy. The main changes introduced by Lisbon were to provide a specific legal basis for humanitarian aid (TFEU, 212–213), whilst development cooperation is now included in articles TFEU 208–211. Article 4 of the TFEU clarifies that development is a shared competence between the Union and the MS, but in contrast to other shared competences such as internal market, agriculture and consumer protection (TFEU 4.2), it adds explicitly that 'the exercise of that competence shall not result in Member States being prevented from exercising theirs' (TFEU 4.4). EU and MS legislation could develop 'side by side' without affecting each other. There is also an explicit commitment to mutual complementarity between the EU and the MS, implying that neither takes precedence over the other (Broberg, 2011: 545, 554). Therefore, the scope of EU development policy qualifies as a 'shared parallel competence' in the conceptualization of the editors (see the Introduction of this book), and it can be located in the middle of the 'strong-weak competence spectrum'.

Nevertheless, in practice, the difference with the other category of 'coordinated' policies such as economic, employment and social policies are rather small. While the EU does have a (significant) development policy of its own, this does not necessarily have any impact on the MS' development policies. While the ordinary legislative procedure applies to development policy, much of the EU's development policy is being shaped outside the traditional legislative framework. The impact of EU measures falls mainly on the developing countries themselves and it barely affects MS' autonomy. For example, when cooperation programmes are established following the ordinary legislative procedure, these programmes will not preclude the MS to develop their own programmes that may have different aims and procedures. Also, the co-decision procedure only applies to EU budgets (the Development Cooperation Instrument) and not to the intergovernmental European Development Fund (EDF). As with all Treaty articles, there is a tension between EU power and Member States' control over any given policy field. This is evident in Lisbon where 'there is much emphasis on the MS' continuing prerogatives, although there is also a rather vague commitment to coordinate more (Carbone, 2013; Smith, 2013).

Therefore, the differences with a 'coordinated competence' are smaller than it may seem at first sight. Just like in the coordinated policies of Article 5, the EU's impact on MS happens through political pressure rather than legally binding measures. In order to pursue a Europeanisation of MS' development policies, the EU employs a number of soft integration strategies that are similar to the Open Method of Coordination in social and employment policies, relying on benchmarking, peer pressure and blaming and shaming. Noticeable examples are the annual evaluation of MS' Official Development Aid (ODA) figures (since 2002) and the bi-annual reports on Policy Coherence for Development (since 2007). Also, MS participation in initiatives such as Joint Country Strategy Papers, (Joint) Multi-Annual Programming and the Code of Conduct and Division of Labour remains voluntary. There are little or no formal mechanisms to ensure compliance, and in any case, the *acquis* in this field is 'soft', or political rather than legal (Gänzle et al., 2012: 7).

Turning to the zones of diplomatic action according to Larsen's (2009) modes (see the Introduction of this book), this means that the intra-EU policy-making mode will probably not be dominant. To be sure, as mentioned earlier in this chapter, there are political and legal commitments to coordinate more in the EU framework. The Commission and the MS have developed a number of common initiatives. Prominent examples are the European Consensus on Development (2005), the EU Strategy for Africa (2005) and the Joint Africa-EU Strategy (2007), the Agenda for Change (2011), the communication on EU Budget Support (2012) and the EU 'A Decent Life for All' position on the post-2015 framework for Sustainable Development Goals (SDGs) (2013). Also, the EU has usually managed to speak with one voice within international aid forums. The UN Conference on Financing for Development (2002) marked the beginning of a decade of relatively ambitious development commitments by the EU on the international level. At the High Level Forums on Aid Effectiveness in Paris, Accra and Busan, the EU also managed to come up with common positions, although by 2015 (the so-called Year of Development) we see the EU toning down its ambitions (Gunzburg, 2015).

However, these commitments are relatively vague and do not necessarily translate into tangible domestic reforms within the MS. Development Commissioner Poul Nielson (1999–2004) suggests that some MS have accepted these initiatives because they are considered not important, as development is typically a 'soft' policy field (quoted in Olsen, 2013: 421). More than a decade after the initial optimism about a 'new season' in EU aid policy, the limits of soft integration within the EU development framework have clearly come to the surface. In order to illustrate this, we briefly outline two EU initiatives that were supposed to set in motion a gradual process of Europeanisation: the collective commitment to reach the 0.7 per cent target by 2015 and the initiatives for the untying of aid.

In the run up to the UN Monterrey Conference on Financing for Development in 2002, EU MS agreed on a time schedule with concrete intermediate benchmarks. A peer review process was established authorizing the Commission to make annual progress reports of the MS' performances in ODA. What seemed remarkable about this decision was not only the promise of (collective) aid increases but, more importantly, the potentially significant opportunities it provided for the EU level to influence MS' aid budgets through 'naming and shaming' approaches. However, even before the economic crisis, it had become clear that the EU's collective benchmarks would not be reached, and in 2011, the EU's collective aid even decreased for the first time in many years. More important for the purpose of this chapter is to note that the anticipated Europeanisation of MS' aid figures has not materialized (Delputte et al., 2016). We see three distinctly discernible groups of EU MS: those Member States (Sweden, Denmark, Luxembourg, the Netherlands and the UK) that are or have historically committed to the 0.7 per cent target; Greece, Italy, Portugal, Spain (joined by the new MS in 2004/2007) still lag far behind, and in between is still a large middle group of countries with large aid budgets but without a prospect to reach the 0.7 per cent target. Thus, after ten years of benchmarking, monitoring and peer pressure, it is hard to find any evidence of Europeanisation. Although there has been a noticeable convergence of the countries belonging to the middle group, including the France and Germany, it is doubtful that this collective growth of aid figures is related to the EU context. A recent study concluded that 'nothing is like it seems': ostensible compliance with EU targets appears mostly unrelated to the EU, while the EU might have contributed to non-compliance. Existing convergence rather seems to reflect global trends. Meanwhile, the EU's 'beyond aid' discourse, its emphasis on policy coherence for development and austerity politics have eroded the possibilities for ambitious ODA policies within EU Member States (Delputte et al., 2016).

Moreover, despite the ODA rise of the UK, Germany[3] and (to some extent) France since 2002, a smaller proportion of these countries' aid budgets have been channelled through the EU institutions (see Table 12.1). This means that the additional ODA has gone to bilateral activities or to other multilateral donors such as the UN agencies and the World Bank. Overall, the level of MS' aid disbursed by the EU has remained fairly stable, although the recent 'role switch' between the Netherlands and the UK inside/outside the 0.7 per cent camp is noticeable.

When looking at the use of the multilateral system for aid disbursements excluding the EU institutions (i.e. not taking into account the contributions to the EU budget and the EDF), it

Table 12.1 EU-15 aid budgets as % GNI and as % channelled through the EU

ODA EU MS	2002		2011		2014	
	% GNI	*% to EU*	*% GNI*	*% to EU*	*% GNI*	*% to EU*
Sweden	0.74	4	1.02	7	1.09	7
Luxembourg	0.82	10	0.97	9	1.06	8
Denmark	0.96	7	0.86	9	0.86	9
Netherlands	0.80	6	0.75	11	0.64	12
United Kingdom	0.33	19	0.56	14	0.70	10
Belgium	0.42	19	0.53	19	0.46	21
Finland	0.33	14	0.52	15	0.60	12
Ireland	0.41	16	0.51	17	0.38	18
France	0.36	23	0.46	19	0.37	22
Germany	0.27	24	0.40	19	0.42	17
Portugal	0.25	23	0.31	26	0.19	39
Spain	0.25	24	0.29	28	0.13	55
Austria	0.24	19	0.27	28	0.28	25
Italy	0.20	33	0.20	44	0.19	41
Greece	0.17	45	0.15	60	0.11	73

Source: Own calculations based on OECD-DAC aid statistics.

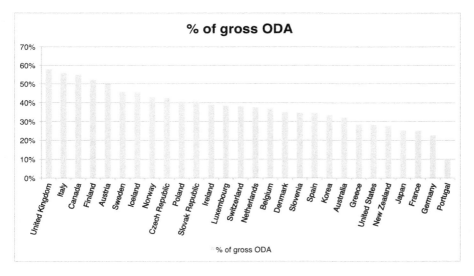

Figure 12.1 Use of the multilateral system as % gross ODA disbursements excluding contributions to the EU (data of 2013)

Source: OECD, 2015: 85; authors' calculations based on OECD/DAC Creditor Reporting System (CRS) data (2015).

becomes clear that no distinctive European preference for multilateralism can be discerned (see Figure 12.1). While some MS make extensive use of multilateral institutions (e.g. UK and Italy) besides the EU, others are more focused on bilateral aid (e.g. Greece and Portugal but also France and Germany). Non-EU DAC members fall in between these two extremes, with Canada's share in multilateral aid coming closer to that of the UK, while the US' and

Japan's share is similar to that of France. Again, no clear distinction between EU and non-EU DAC members can be discerned.

The case of untying aid also illustrates the limits of intra-EU foreign policy. Again, the European Commission pursued a Europeanisation of MS' development policies, *inter alia* by using the 2002 Monterrey conference as a window of opportunity. As explained by Carbone (2007: 101–20), whereas the untying of EC aid in line with the 2001 DAC Recommendation was relatively uncontroversial, the Commission proposal on the bilateral policies of the MS was heavily contested by several EU countries. The debate can roughly be structured around the familiar distinction (see also later in this chapter) between like-minded countries such as the United Kingdom, Sweden and the Netherlands, which supported the Commission, versus Southern donors such as Spain, Portugal and France, which resisted a Europeanisation of untying aid commitments. Although the Commission managed to politicize the issue within the EU and to gather significant support within the Council for the untying of MS' bilateral policies, it failed to reach a binding agreement in 2003 because of resistance by Spain (Carbone, 2007: 117). Subsequently, the Commission continued to push for more ambitious EU commitments on the untying of aid at the DAC, not only because this would be a sign of generosity, but also because this would 'confirm that the EU is a single actor in international development' (Carbone, 2007: 119). However, Europeanisation has not taken place. It is also telling that, from the mid-2000s, the issue of untying aid is scarcely mentioned in the Commission's progress reports.[4] The figures (see Table 12.2) also suggest the

Table 12.2 Share (in %) of untied aid EU-15

	2005	*2007*	*2009*	*2010*	*2012*
Austria	39	38	68	58	37
Belgium	97	86	91	95	95
Czech Republic	–	–	–	–	45
Denmark	94	94	97	97	96
Finland	98	100	87	89	95
France	90	74	87	95	96
Germany	94	99	98	75	79
Greece	–	–	–	48	6
Ireland	100	100	100	100	100
Italy	35	35	48	58	82
Luxembourg	100	100	99	99	94
Netherlands	90	94	100	96	98
Portugal	26	14	10	43	25
Spain	75	61	68	64	83
Sweden	100	100	100	94	93
United Kingdom	100	100	100	100	100
Average EU-14	*81*	*78*	*82*		
United States	*70*	*79*	*80*	*70*	*75*
Canada	*79*	*87*	*100*	*87*	*92*
Japan	*89*	*88*	*98*	*79*	*71*
Average DAC	*83*	*84*	*88*	*77*	*79*

Source: OECD-DAC Survey 2011 and Survey 2014.

absence of Europeanisation. Even if many MS have significantly untied their bilateral aid, a large gap with Southern MS' performances continues to exist. Again, there is no clear difference between EU and non-EU countries.

This brief analysis of EU commitments on the level of aid and the untying of aid suggests that Europeanisation has been limited and that, to the extent that there have been changes to MS' policies, this is more a reflection of DAC-ization than Europeanisation. That said, it should be noticed that EU MS, in particular the Nordics and the European Commission, which has been a full member of the DAC since its establishment in 1961, often attempt to upload their preferences on aid policies onto the level of the DAC (Verschaeve and Orbie, 2015). To what extent we witness a wholesale downloading of DAC policies into the EU or rather an uploading from the EU to the DAC, or more accurately how exactly both dynamics are interacting, remains unclear and worthy of further research. What is important to notice here is that the DAC and the EU are surprisingly similar when it comes to development policy, both in terms of substance and procedures. There is a broad consensus within the EU and the MS that the global aid and development effectiveness agenda (Paris/Accra/Busan) should guide actions in this policy field. Also, both the EU and the DAC largely rely on soft integration/harmonization procedures based on standard setting, peer reviewing and expert knowledge. As such, both institutions also leave ample room for their members to pursue their own bilateral development policies. Since development policy involves considerable redistribution of budgets and closely links with foreign policy priorities, national sovereignty in this so-called 'soft' external policy domain remains quintessential.

This sheds light on why extra-EU foreign policy continues to be the dominant mode. Within the broadly accepted normative frameworks and procedures of the DAC and the EU, Member State governments can still pursue their own development policies. These are often marked by specific preferences as regards sectors and countries. The 2011 DAC peer review highlighted that EU institutions providing aid to about 130 countries in 2009/10, whilst in relation to sectors, the most important sub-sector is 'government and civil society', reflecting strong support to governance and capacity development. Economic infrastructure and services, together with the productive sectors, account for 24 per cent, while humanitarian aid remains stable at 11 per cent. The DAC peer review highlighted that 'there is a risk that aid is spread too thinly across sectors to have a real impact' (DAC, 2012: 58).

As such, a diversity of focuses should not necessarily preclude a Europeanisation of development policy. Indeed, the general thrust of the EU code of conduct and division of labour and joint multiannual programming initiatives is that national aid policies can be complementary by embedding them within a European framework. According to these commitments, EU donors would restrict themselves to focusing on a maximum of three sectors per country, donor leadership arrangements on specific sectors in each country would be created and the number of partner countries per EU donor would be limited. The novelty of these initiatives is that EU MS' bilateral aid policies are informed by a dialogue, not only with developing countries, but also with the European peers. However, the code of conduct and joint multiannual programming initiatives have barely been implemented so far, not only because some developing countries are hesitant, but also because of EU MS fearing a loss of influence and visibility. Some European aid officials speak of a 'coordination fatigue' (Carbone, 2008: 338–9), and for a long time, European coordination did not go beyond information-sharing (Delputte and Orbie, 2014; Klingebiel et al., 2016), although more recently an increase of joint programming may be noticed.

EU Member State roles

The previous section illustrated that significant differences continue to exist between EU MS' development policies. This section will look more closely at political cleavages within the Council by considering not only the familiar North-South division but also the particular position of the 'Nordic-plus' and the 'non-DAC' EU donors which are both engaging in inter-EU and intra-extra EU foreign policy.

Accounts of EU development policy generally make a distinction between Northern and Southern MS. Utilizing a framework from environmental policy, we can identify leaders, laggards and fence-sitters or, refined to EU aid policy, drivers, carers and observers (Szent-Iványi, 2012).[5] The drivers in this area are the Scandinavian MS Sweden, Denmark and Finland, which have formed the 'Nordic-plus' group together with the like-minded countries Luxembourg, the Netherlands and the UK. The observers or laggards are the Southern group including Spain (Alonso, 2005), Italy (Carbone, 2007, 2008), Portugal, Greece and France and arguably also the countries that joined the EU in 2004/2007 (Lightfoot and Szent-Iványi, 2014). All EU donors have been affected by the economic crisis, but the effect on the laggards has been considerable. Other MS such as Belgium, Austria and Ireland can be considered to be fence-sitters, although Ireland is sometimes also considered to form part of the Nordics. They generally care about development topics, and although they will not always support the Nordic plus, they sometimes take a leading role on specific issues.

Roughly speaking, four differences between the Nordic-plus and Southern groups can be distinguished (cf. Carbone, 2007; Hoebink and Stokke, 2005). First, the former tend to have relatively large aid budgets, historically often exceeding the 0.7 per cent target (e.g. Sweden, Denmark, Netherlands and Luxembourg). Their aid bureaucracies are also internationally recognized to be efficient and experienced. Second, the Nordic-plus countries have a more normative view on international development cooperation. They focus less on development *per se* and more on poverty reduction as well as social and environmental aspects of development. They have played a progressive role in debates on the international aid architecture and were instrumental in initiatives such as the 2000 Millennium Development Goals, the 2005 Paris Declaration and the 2015 Sustainable Development Goals. In contrast, the Southern group has a lower profile on development cooperation and is more inclined to linking aid policies with trade and foreign policy interests. Third, the Northern countries have been less enthusiastic about development policy integration at the EU level, giving preference to bilateral and multilateral aid policies. They have usually favoured the UN agencies whose views are considered to be closer to their own approaches to economic development (see McLean, 2012). Already in the 1970s, the Northern countries advocated, as part of a wider group of like-minded countries, a multilateral approach to global development issues. Within the group of Western donors, the like-minded group constituted the strongest proponent of a New International Economic Architecture. Their first concrete action was to support the 1976 UN Resolution on the Integrated Programme of Commodities (Hveem, 1980: 46, 82–3). Also after joining the EU, Nordic countries continued to be active within the link-minded group, which includes also non-EU countries such as Canada and Norway. Given their own track record in development issues, their preference for multilateral institutions and their close ties with like-minded countries outside the EU, it is not surprising that the Nordic-plus group tends to be critical of EU integration in development policy. Fourth, the Nordics put more emphasis on the quality of aid, which can be seen in the preference for certain aid modalities such as budget support. Southern donors tend to be more critical of budget support and rely more on project support.

This does not mean that the Nordics have been passive on the EU development front. They have lobbied for more progressive development policies within the international aid architecture, but at the same time, they have also attempted to influence the EU's development policies. Rather than favouring intra-EU foreign policy, the Nordic-plus group has engaged in inter-EU and intra-extra EU foreign policies. Inter-EU foreign policy, whereby EU MS cooperate outside the legal structures of the EU, may be an important yet often neglected dimension of EU development policy (see the Introduction of this volume). The Nordic-plus group has regularly coordinated on development issues, holding separate meetings on specific issues such as gender mainstreaming in development (Arts, 2004: 104; Elgström, 2000: 465). In this context, the Utstein group is also worth mentioning: in 1999, four female Development Ministers, namely Heidemarie Wieczorek-Zeul (Germany), Clare Short (UK), Hilde Johnson (Norway) and Eveline Herfkens (Netherlands) decided to meet regularly and show 'by example how common goals can be achieved by informal, practical cooperation' (GIZ, 2003). Some extent of intra-extra EU foreign policies also takes place, whereby MS use their presence in the EU framework as leverage to magnify their role in development debates. We see increasing examples of 'Nordicazation' of EU development policy, more so than Europeanisation (Elgström and Delputte, 2016). In the European Consensus, we see the Nordic-plus MS were relatively successful in guaranteeing that the European 'common vision' reflects the aid effectiveness agenda and the international commitments to poverty reduction and the MDGs, they were less happy with the greater coordination role granted to the European Commission (Bué, 2010: 206–10; Carbone, 2007).

Thus, what is interesting is that both groups hold different views not only on what aid should be (substantially) but also on the preferred forum for aid coordination (global versus EU). While the like-minded countries favour extra-EU and inter-EU foreign policies, the Southern MS have been more inclined towards intra-EU foreign policies. However, the Nordic-plus and the Southern European countries also have in common that they are members of the DAC. What is noticeable is that the European Commission has also been a member of the DAC since 1961 and that there has often been significant EU coordination (EU-15 and Commission) in the DAC context. This involves either the negotiation of a common EU position on important documents such as the high-level fora on aid effectiveness, or the more low-key meetings in Paris with a view to exchanging ideas and best practices (Verschaeve and Orbie, 2015). Therefore, the EU DAC members are also engaging in inter-EU foreign policy.

This leads to a second political cleavage within the EU, namely between DAC and non-DAC members. On the global level an important debate is going on about the new role of the emerging donors that are not part of the DAC, such as China, Brazil, South Africa and Turkey (see Dreher et al., 2013), but also inside the EU the arrival of new donors that are not a member of the DAC has been a noticeable evolution. The countries that became a member of the EU in 2004/07 are sometimes categorized under the Southern group of 'laggards' or 'observers' because development policy is not high on their agenda and because their low levels of aid. Aid budgets of the ten Central and Eastern European members are around 0.10 per cent of GNI while Cyprus and Malta's budgets are only slightly higher (see Table 12.3). It is clear that these countries are not following the EU's ODA commitment, repeated during the 2015 SDGs, lagging far behind the 0.33 per cent GNI benchmark that was envisaged for new MS. Similar to countries such as France and Spain they tend to prefer a European approach to development[6] issues which is not unlinked to broader foreign and security policy interests. However, these countries also differ from the 'traditional' donors in that until recently they did not have a development cooperation policy of their own. Most

Table 12.3 EU-12 aid figures

ODA EU-12	2011		2014	
	% GNI	*% to EU*	*% GNI*	*% to EU*
Czech Republic	0.13	57	0.11	60
Bulgaria	0.09	73	0.09	86
Cyprus	0.16	45	–	–
Estonia	0.12	63	0.14	43
Hungary	0.11	64	0.11	64
Lithuania	0.13	52	0.10	79
Poland	0.08	75	0.09	75
Romania	0.09	80	–	61
Slovak Republic	0.09	70	0.09	73
Slovenia	0.13	58	0.13	56
Latvia	0.07	87	0.08	79
Malta	0.25	–	0.20	31

Source: Own calculations based on OECD online database.

importantly, they do not have a colonial history in Africa and prefer a regional focus on the Eastern neighbourhood and the Western Balkans.[7]

Given the absence of a pre-accession development policy and the extensive enlargement process, one might expect significant Europeanisation to occur in the ten Central and Eastern European countries that became a member in the 2000s. This appears to be the case when looking at the channelling of the aid budgets. A remarkably high part of their ODA goes to the EU (compare Table 12.3 with Table 12.1). The bulk of the remaining budget is comprised of bilateral programmes whereas only a marginal part goes to non-EU multilateral institutions. However, it would be premature to conclude that, in terms of substance, a Europeanisation of these countries' aid policies has taken place (Lightfoot and Szent-Iványi, 2014). First, studies show that the impact of accession on development policy in non-DAC countries has in fact been limited. In the EU-12, we find that the commitment to development norms tends to be 'shallow' within the governments; there is little political 'demand' for increased development spending, the majority of aid goes to neighbouring states and within civil society and the development constituency remains under-developed (see Szent-Iványi and Lightfoot, 2015). Second, as far as their development policies and institutions have changed over the past decade, it remains uncertain to what extent this is the result of EU accession or rather of the wider donor community. For example the Busan agreement resulting from the Fourth High-Level Forum on Aid Effectiveness (2011) was signed by all the new members except Latvia and Lithuania.[8] The DAC has clear ambitions to include the non-DAC OECD members into the DAC as soon as possible, and this is also strongly supported by the Commission. The Czech Republic, Poland, Slovakia and Slovenia all joined the DAC in 2013, taking the DAC membership up to twenty-nine (of which nineteen are EU Member States). Four of the EU-13 states joining the DAC may weaken the cleavage, but much depends on the socialization within the DAC as within the EU structures. Again, it may be more accurate to speak of DAC-ization than Europeanisation, even if both processes seem closely intertwined.

Moreover, rather than fully embracing intra-EU foreign policies in development, these countries have used their access to EU policies and instruments to enhance their influence in the Eastern neighbourhood. In line with intra-extra foreign policy, the new MS have consistently attempted to ensure that the EU's Eastern neighbour countries would benefit from EU aid programmes. The Polish-Swedish initiative to establish the Eastern Partnership can be seen as an example of a new Member State trying to shape EU foreign policy. The focus on EU–Africa relations was seen to some new MS as needing to be balanced by a greater focus on the Eastern neighbours. As such the accession of the Central and Eastern European Member States has reinforced two closely related trends in EU development policies, namely a diversion of attention from former colonies in Africa towards Europe's neighbourhood and a growing engagement with the nexus between development aid on the one hand and foreign and security policy on the other hand. This link is explored in more detail in the next section.

Connecting development and foreign policy

Since 9/11, we have witnessed a shift from a poverty-reduction ethos to an explicit linkage between development and security objectives (Stern and Öjendal, 2010). The existence of a general correlation between poverty, instability and violent conflicts is undisputed. Also, within the EU, it has been recognized that there is a complex relationship between poverty and stability, which should be addressed in its external relations. By the mid-2000s, EU discourse had seen a change from mono-causal thinking whereby development determines security, to a more cyclical view on the complex relation between both concepts (Hadfield, 2007; Hout, 2010; Keukeleire and Raube, 2013). The Commission website states:

> Security and development are interdependent and mutually reinforcing. No sustainable development is possible in a country threatened by internal insecurity, crisis and conflicts. At the same time, there cannot be sustainable peace without development. Moreover, insecurity, crisis and conflicts can impede the efficient use of aid.[9]

However, critical observers have warned that EU discourse, aid disbursements and institutional reforms indicate a securitization of development aid. The involvement of the former DG Relex into EuropeAid decision-making, the abolition of the Development Council as a separate configuration, the European Security Strategy's statement that security is a precondition for development, the financing of the African Peace Facility from the EDF, the inclusion of clauses on anti-terrorism and weapons of mass destruction in aid programmes and the increased focus on geostrategically important countries in the neighbourhood may well indicate that development policy objectives are becoming subordinated to security objectives (e.g. Del Biondo et al., 2013; Manners, 2008). This debate has been further fuelled by the creation of the European External Action Service (Furness, 2010). DG DEVCO retains responsibility for implementation of development aid, but the geographical desks were moved into the EEAS. On the one hand, this could be seen as a positive move as it has the potential to 'reinforce the coherence of EU external relations with development cooperation' (Mackie, 2010). On the other hand, this removal of geographical desks could have been seen to have weakened the position of the Development Commissioner. Carbone argues the provision that proposals regarding developing countries must be jointly prepared by the EEAS and DG DEVCO 'strengthened the role of the Development Commissioner, who de facto had the final say on all development strategies, including for countries in Latin America and Asia' (Carbone, 2012). This is similar to the 'joint key' role envisaged by Gavas and Koeb (2010). Importantly, this joint key role exists for money. Carbone also argues that, although DG DEVCO lost some of its staff to the EEAS, the fact that it became responsible for EuropeAid could be seen as a victory for Development. Despite the Lisbon Treaty clearly stating 'in its contribution to the Union's external cooperation programmes, the EEAS should seek to ensure that the programmes fulfil the objectives for external action . . . and that they respect the objectives of the Union's development policy' (i.e. 'poverty eradication'), some observers fear that, given the relatively weak position of aid and development vis-à-vis diplomacy and security in the EEAS, aid money will be used to promote EU interests rather than focus on its core task (CONCORD, 2012; Van Seters and Klaver, 2011). Linked to that is the perceived lack of development expertise in the EEAS, which is being staffed mainly by diplomats. Will the European diplomatic service bring a more synergetic coherence between foreign policy and development aid, or will it facilitate the instrumental use of aid policies for security purposes (e.g. Del Biondo et al., 2013; Furness and Gänzle, 2013)?

At the EU MS level, we are also seeing an increased connection between security and development, with some degree of convergence in all MS. This can for example be seen in the growth of security-related aid. In March 2005, the DAC agreed that some expenditures related to security can be ODA-eligible,[10] which is in itself a reflection of the growing importance of the security-development nexus. What is clear is that security and development policies seem to have become increasingly intertwined both at the EU level and within the MS. Again, it is hard to disaggregate the driver behind these trends – do the MS follow an international trend or that of the EU? The former scenario seems most likely. The debate on the security-development nexus has re-emerged since the 1990s in various forms, for instance in the notion of 'human security' (associated with the UNDP and with Canadian foreign policy) and in the view that development aid should be employed in the fight against terrorism (associated with the US). Within the EU differences emerged between Germany which wanted to keep security separated from development policy and the UK which aimed to enhance the security-development nexus (Brzoska, 2008: 134). The Nordic countries have generally embraced the notion of human security. While the revised European Security Strategy in 2008 does mention 'human security' once, this concept has not been clearly operationalized at the EU level. The least one can say is that the EU has been struggling to define its views on the security-development nexus, something very evident during the negotiations for a European view on 'comprehensive security' (Del Biondo et al., 2013: 134–5).

This increased focus on security links to a broader politicization of the aid agenda, especially in relation to bilateral aid. Thus we see the DAC (2012) in their comparison of management systems for development cooperation, show that, in the vast majority of MS, the Ministry of Foreign Affairs is the key player, with the UK DFID model standing out alone. In newer donors, such as those states in Central and Eastern Europe, we find that development policy is a section or directorate within the Ministry of Foreign Affairs (MFA), with no cabinet presence, small personnel capacity (often diplomats rather than civil servants raise issues of institutional memory). There is also an issue of status, where development directorates are viewed as 'the least prestigious in the ministry' (Drążkiewicz-Grodzicka, 2013). The level of explicit politicization of aid is also high in these new donors, as is the link to security, although this trend is also evident in more established donors such as the UK under the current government (Heinrich et al., 2016).

The financial crisis, especially in the Eurozone, has contributed to this politicization. There have been two main impacts. The first is that the value for money angle has become visible in many MS. This promotes a sense of aid as an economic benefit to the donor state, with recent campaigns, such as the ONE campaign, highlighting the economic benefits to both the EU and donor states of providing aid. This can also be seen in the debate on budget support, which became more politicized. Even some of the Nordic plus (e.g. the Netherlands) are becoming more risk averse in relation to budget support. The other, rather obvious angle is that aid budgets in some MS have been cut. This issue became significant during the post 2015 development talks. As European Commissioner for International Cooperation and Development, Neven Mimica, put it, '[t]here have always been Member States that are very much below the average percentage of GNI directed to official development assistance (ODA) and countries that are above the 0.7% target. Unfortunately, there are more below than above the 0.7 line' (Barbiere and Jacobsen, 2015). Traditional 0.7 per cent donors such as Denmark, Finland and the Netherlands have all announced cuts to their ODA budgets, whilst states that have always found the target ambitious, such as Italy, Greece, Portugal and Spain, all allocate below 0.2% to ODA (Barbiere and Jacobsen, 2015).

Conclusion

Development is the oldest EC foreign policy, originating from the post-colonial settlement between MS and developing states. However, development aid still predominantly sits within national foreign policy structures. It did not become an EU competence until 1992 and even then only as a shared competence, divided between the EU and the Member States.[11] On the continuum that has been used in this edited volume, it would be situated in between 'shared parallel' and 'coordinated' competences. Despite the sheer size of the development budgets of the EU institutions, the influence of the EU on the MS' development policies has been qualified. Since the early 2000s, there have been several noticeable initiatives to streamline the aims, approaches and activities of EU donors. However, after one decade it remains hard to find tangible evidence anything more than a shallow form of Europeanisation. The familiar North-South division between the MS continues to exist. The enlargement with countries from Central and Eastern Europe has further diversified the donor landscape in Europe.

To be sure, there are indications of convergences between EU MS. First, there is a clear discursive commitment of all EU MS, including the recently acceded MS that aim to become a member of the DAC, to the international aid effectiveness agenda. There is also evidence that the changes at MS level development policy, since end of Cold War are trending towards support for poverty reduction over historical ties, even in Southern countries such as France. Both of these were visible during the 2015 development talks. Second, there is the increased focus on the development-security nexus at the EU and MS levels. Although a common EU vision on linking security and development has been difficult to achieve, the 2015–16 migration/refugee crisis has seen a coming together of the two areas, with aid budgets being diverted to support migrants within the EU (Elliott, 2016).

However, this may be more an internationalization, or specifically a DAC-ization, than an Europeanisation. This chapter has argued that, to the extent that MS' development policies have converged, this often reflects international trends that go beyond the EU. While it remains difficult to disentangle the differentiated impact of MS, EU and global trends, it seems unlikely that the EU institutions have been a driving force in the evolutions in MS aid policies over the past decade. These findings resonate with existing literature which qualifies the EU as a 'norm follower' rather than a 'norm setter' in development policy (Arts and Dickson, 2004; Farrell, 2008).

We argue that the evolution of MS development policy performance in terms of change and action is shaped more by domestic preferences and international commitments than EU-level norms, even if the European Commission has at times played a catalyzing role. It remains to be seen how the economic crisis, the refugee/migration crisis and the emergence of non-DAC donors will impact on both MS and EU development policies. It is already clear that new ways are being used to frame the debate on ODA (e.g. concepts such as 'ODA plus', 'high impact aid', private investment) and that development aid is becoming more instrumentalized (e.g. 'more for more', 'value for money', cash on delivery, Molenaers and Nijs, 2009). Changing geopolitical evolutions also seem to reinforce the trend whereby development policy becomes more closely linked to foreign and security policies, in line with preferences of the Southern MS and the CEE donors. We see this in the 2015–16 migration crisis and the fact that Turkey is now the largest beneficiary of EU aid, in part as a result of its significant role in the region.

That said, the Nordic-plus group might continue to play a distinctive role in within and without the EU. The extent to which these countries can play a progressive role in development debates, perhaps in alliance with the European Commission, remains to be seen, not only because these countries have not wholeheartedly supported an EU development policy but also because shifts towards more liberal-conservative governments have made some members of 0.7 per cent group less ambitious. This chapter has highlighted the specific role of the Nordics' inter-EU and intra-extra EU foreign policies, a subject that clearly deserves further research (cf. Olsen, 2013).

More broadly, it should be noticed that the Europeanisation of MS development policies has still an under-researched topic.[12] This chapter is mostly based on existing reports and on aid statistics. However, more detailed and qualitative research, including discourse analysis case study research, would be needed to thoroughly assess the impact of the EU on the policy, polity and politics of its MS in development. In doing so, we have highlighted that studies should not be limited to the interaction between the EU and its MS and also consider the impact of global institutions beyond the EU.

Notes

1   We are grateful to the editors, to Sarah Delputte and to Joren Verschaeve for useful feedback on previous versions of the chapter.
2   See the DAC Peer Review (DAC, 2012: 13–14); see also the Quality of ODA assessment (available online at http://international.cgdev.org/page/quality-oda-quoda).
3   The German case is an interesting one. Aid is fragmented across different line ministries, so we find that spending reflects political motivations more than an altruistic focus on poverty reduction in some departments and not others (see Nunnenkamp and Ohler, 2011).
4   See http://ec.europa.eu/europeaid/what/development-policies/financing_for_development/index_en.htm
5   It is worth noting that research suggests that, if Member States work together, they can influence Commission decisions in terms of the direction of EU ODA (see Schneider and Tobin, 2013).
6   An important reason why an important share of these countries' ODA goes through the EU is that there is not much additional budget on top of the compulsory contribution through the EU budget and the EDF.
7   For example, the Czech Republic's bilateral aid is concentrated in five countries: Afghanistan, Bosnia and Herzegovina, Ethiopia, Moldova and Mongolia. See http://www.oecd.org/dac/the-oecd-welcomes-the-czech-republic-to-the-development-assistance-committee.htm
8   See http://www.oecd.org/dac/effectiveness/busanadherents.htm
9   http://ec.europa.eu/europeaid/what/security-conflict/index_en.htm (accessed 13 July 2013).
10   The DAC guidelines allow for example the prevention and demobilization of child soldiers, the removal of landmines and security system management, while activities such as military capacity building or training military skills are excluded.
11   One important exception that has not been addressed in this chapter concerns the EU's trade relations with developing countries. Since 1999, the competence for trade relations with developing countries has shifted from DG DEVCO to DG Trade within the European Commission. In this

area, a stronger convergence can be seen around the preference for asymmetrical free trade areas, preferably on a regional basis and including a broad regulatory agenda. This has been witnessed in the negotiation of Economic Partnership Agreements with ACP countries and regions. Since the late 1990s, even Southern MS such as France have agreed to weaken the exclusivity of the ACP and to abandon the interventionist elements of the Lomé trade regime (Arts and Dickson, 2004). Compatibility with the rules of the World Trade Organization (WTO) became the leitmotiv of EU trade-development policies. Thus, here too, the question arises whether we witness Europeanisation of internationalization. Also, this chapter has not explicitly addressed the EU MS' different policies in relation to democratic conditionality and budget support (see e.g. Molenaers and Nijs, 2009).

12 See Orbie and Carbone, 2016, and Smith, 2016, although there are still many questions for further research.

Bibliography

Alesina, A. and Dollar, D. (2000) 'Who Gives Foreign Aid to Whom and Why?', *Journal of Economic Growth*, Vol. 5, No. 1, 33–63.

Alonso, J. A. (2005) 'Spanish Foreign Aid: Flaws of an Emerging Framework', in P. Hoebink and O. Stokke (eds.) *Perspectives on European Development Co-Operation*. London: Routledge, pp. 493–517.

Arts, K. (2004) 'Changing Interests in EU Development Cooperation', in K. Arts and A. Dickson (eds.) *EU Development Cooperation: From Model to Symbol*. Manchester: Manchester University Press, pp. 101–111.

Arts, K. and Dickson, A. (2004) 'EU Development Cooperation: From Model to Symbol?', in K. Arts and A. Dickson (eds.) *EU Development Cooperation: From Model to Symbol*, Manchester: Manchester University Press, pp. 1–16.

Barbiere, C. and Jacobsen, H. (2015) Commissioner Laments EU Development Aid Cuts [13.07.2015], Brussels: EurActiv.com. Available at: http://www.euractiv.com/sections/development-policy/commission-laments-eu-development-aid-cuts-316258, date accessed 14 November 2015.

Broberg, M. (2011) 'What Is the Direction for the EU's Development Cooperation after Lisbon? A Legal Examination', *European Foreign Affairs Review*, Vol. 16, No. 4, 539–557.

Brzoska, M. (2008), 'Extending ODA or Creating a New Reporting Instrument for Security-Related Expenditures for Development?', *Development Policy Review*, Vol. 26, 131–150.

Bué, C. (2010) *La politique de développement de l'Union Européenne. Construction et projection de l'Europe par le Sud* (PhD Thesis), Institut d'Etudes Politiques, Paris.

Carbone, M. (2007) *The European Union and International Development: The Politics of Foreign Aid*. London: Routledge.

Carbone, M. (2008) 'Mission Impossible: The European Union and Policy Coherence for Development', *Journal of European Integration*, Vol. 30, No. 3, 323–342.

Carbone, M. (2012) 'Development Policy in a Changing Europe: More Donors, New Challenges', in F. M. Bindi and I. Angelescu (eds.) *The Frontiers of Europe: A Transatlantic Problem?* Washington, DC: Brookings Institution Press, 151–164.

Carbone, M. (2013) 'International Development and the European Union's External Policies: Changing Contexts, Problematic Nexuses, Contested Partnerships', *Cambridge Review of International Affairs*, Vol. 26, No. 3, 483–496.

CONCORD (2012) 'EEAS One Year on: "Work in Progress" for Poverty Eradication'. Report. Concord: Brussels. Available at: https://www.bond.org.uk/data/files/EU_/EEAS-year-A4-lowdef.pdf, date accessed 16 October 2016.

DAC (2012) *OECD/DAC Peer Review European Commission*. Paris: OECD.

Del Biondo, K., Oltsch, S. and Orbie, J. (2013) 'Security and Development in EU External Relations: Converging, But in Which Direction?', in S. Biscop and R. Whitman (eds.) *The Routledge Handbook of European Security*. London and New York: Routledge, 126–143.

Delputte, S., Lannoo, S., Orbie, J. and Verschaeve, J. (2016) 'Europeanisation of Aid Budgets: Nothing Is as It Seems', *European Politics and Society*, Vol. 17, No. 1, 74–89.

Delputte, S. and Orbie, J. (2014) 'The EU and Donor Coordination on the Ground: Perspectives from Tanzania and Zambia', *European Journal of Development Research*, Vol. 26, No. 5, 676–691.

Drążkiewicz-Grodzicka, E. (2013) 'From Recipient to Donor: The Case of Polish Development Cooperation', *Human Organization*, Vol. 72, No. 1, 65–75.

Dreher, A., Fuchs, A. and Nunnenkamp, P. (2013) 'New Donors', *International Interactions: Empirical and Theoretical Research in International Relations*, Vol. 39, No. 3, 402–415.

Elgström, O. (2000) 'Norm Negotiations: The Construction of New Norms Regarding Gender and Development in EU Foreign Aid Policy', *Journal of European Public Policy*, Vol. 7, No. 3, 457–476.

Elgström, O. and Delputte, S. (2016) 'An End to Nordic Exceptionalism? Europeanisation and Nordic Development Policies', *European Politics and Society*, Vol. 17, No. 1, 28–41.

Elliott, L. (2016) 'The World's Poor Lose Out as Aid Is Diverted to the Refugee Crisis', *The Guardian*, 10 January. https://www.theguardian.com/business/2016/jan/10/poor-lose-out-as-aid-is-diverted-to-the-refugee-crisis-africa, date accessed 11/2/17

European Commission (2012) EU Accountability Report 2012 on Financing for Development: Review of progress of the EU and its Member States, Brussels, 09.07.2012, SWD (2012) 199.

European Commission/European External Action Service (2013) *Joint Communication to the European Parliament and the Council: The EU's Comprehensive Approach to External Conflict and Crises*, Brussels, 11.12.2013, JOIN (2013) 30 final.

Farrell, M. (2008) 'Internationalising EU Development Policy', *Perspectives on European Politics and Society*, Vol. 9, No. 2, 225–240.

Faust, J. and Messner, D. (2005) 'Europe's New Security Strategy: Challenges for Development Policy', *European Journal of Development Research*, Vol. 17, No. 3, 423–436.

Furness, M. (2010) 'The European External Action Service: A New Institutional Framework for EU Development Cooperation', *Discussion Paper*. Bonn: DIE-GDI.

Furness, M. and Gänzle, S. (2013) 'The European Union's Development Policy: A Balancing Act between "A More Comprehensive Approach" and Creeping Securitisation', draft unpublished paper.

Gänzle, S., Makhan, D. and Grimm, S. (eds.) (2012) *The European Union and Global Development: An 'Enlightened Superpower' in the Making?* Basingstoke: Palgrave Macmillan.

Gavas, M. and Koeb, E. (2010) 'Setting up the European External Action Service: Building a Comprehensive Approach to EU External Action', Overseas Development Institute (ODI) and European Centre for Development Policy Management (ECDPM), 16 March.

GIZ (2003) The Utstein Group. Available at: http://www3.giz.de/E+Z/content/archive-eng/03–2003/foc_art5.html, date accessed 1 December 2012.

Gunzburg, T. (2015) Time for EU to Lay Its Cards on the Table [24.06.2015]. DEVEX.com. Available at: https://www.devex.com/news/time-for-the-eu-to-lay-its-cards-on-the-table-86404, date accessed 14 November 2015.

Hadfield, A. (2007) 'Janus Advances? An Analysis of EC Development Policy and the 2005 Amended Cotonou Partnership Agreement', *European Foreign Affairs Review*, Vol. 12, No. 1, 39–66.

Heinrich, T., Kobayashib, Y. and Bryanta, K. (2016) 'Public Opinion and Foreign Aid Cuts in Economic Crises', *World Development*, Vol. 77, 66–79.

Hoebink, P. and Stokke, O. (2005) *Perspectives on European Development Cooperation*. Abingdon: Routledge.

Holland, M. and Doidge, M. (2012) *Development Policy of the European Union*. Basingstoke: Palgrave.

Hout, W. (2010) 'Between Development and Security: The European Union, Governance and Fragile States', *Third World Quarterly*, Vol. 31, No. 1, 141–157.

Hveem, H. (1980) 'Scandinavia, the Like-Minded Countries, and the NIEO', in E. Laszlo and J. Kurtzman (eds.) *Western Europe and the New International Economic Order: Representative Samples of European Perspectives*. New York: Pergamon Press, 45–98.

Keukeleire, S. and Raube, K. (2013) 'The Security: Development Nexus and Securitization in the EU's Policies Towards Developing Countries', *Cambridge Review of International Affairs*, Vol. 26, No. 3, 556–572.

Klingebiel, S., Negre, M. and Morazán, P. (2016) 'Costs, Benefits and the Political Economy of Aid Coordination: The Case of the European Union', *European Journal of Development Research*, 1–16. DOI: 10.1057/ejdr.2015.84

Larsen, H. (2009) 'A Distinct FPA for Europe? Towards a Comprehensive Framework for Analysing the Foreign Policy of EU Member States', *European Journal of International Relations*, Vol. 15, No. 3, 537–566.

Lightfoot, S. and Szent-Iványi, B. (2014) 'Reluctant Donors? The Europeanization of International Development Policies in the New Member States', *JCMS: Journal of Common Market Studies*, Vol. 52, 1257–1272.

Mackie, J. (2010) 'New Competition in Town', in E. Drieskens and L. van Schaik (eds.) *The European External Action Service: Preparing for Success*. The Hague: Clingendael, 27–32.

Manners, I. (2008) 'The Normative Power of the European Union in a Globalised World', in Z. Laïdi (ed.) *EU Foreign Policy in a Globalized World: Normative Power and Social Preferences*. London: Routledge, 23–37.

McLean, E. V. (2012) 'Donors' Preferences and Agent Choice: Delegation of European Development Aid', *International Studies Quarterly*, Vol. 56, No. 2, 381–395.

Michel, L. (2006) 'Commission Proposes Concrete Measures to Deliver EU Aid Better and Faster'. Press Release IP/06/256, Brussels, 2 March 2006. Available at: http://europa.eu/rapid/press-release_IP-06-256_en.htm?locale=en, date accessed 15 August 2016.

Molenaers, N. and Nijs, L. (2009) 'From the Theory of Aid Effectiveness to the Practice: The European Commission's Governance Incentive Tranche', *Development Policy Review*, Vol. 27, No. 5, 561–580.

Nunnenkamp, P. and Ohler, H. (2011) 'Aid Allocation Through Various Official and Private Channels: Need, Merit, and Self-Interest as Motives of German Donors', *World Development*, Vol. 39, No. 3, 308–323.

OECD (2015) *Multilateral Aid 2015 Better Partnerships for a Post-2015 World*. Available at: http://www.oecd.org/dac/multilateral-aid-2015-9789264235212-en.htm, date accessed 10 November 2016.

Olsen, G. R. (2013) 'The European Union's Africa Policy: The Result of Nordicization or Europeanization?', *Journal of European Integration*, Vol. 35, No. 4, 409–424.

Orbie, J. (2012) 'The EU's Role in Development: A Full-Fledged Development Actor or Eclipsed by Superpower Temptations?', in S. Grimm, D. Makhan and S. Gänzle (eds.) *The European Union and Global Development: An Enlightened Superpower in the Making?* Basingstoke: Palgrave, 17–36.

Orbie, J. and Carbone, M. (2016) 'The Europeanisation of Development Policy', *European Politics and Society*, Vol. 17, No. 1, 1–11.

Schneider, C. and Tobin, J. (2013) 'Interest Coalitions and Multilateral Aid Allocation in the European Union', *International Studies Quarterly*, Vol. 57, No. 1, 103–114.

Smith, M. (2013) 'Foreign Policy and Development in the Post-Lisbon European Union', *Cambridge Review of International Affairs*, Vol. 26, No. 3, 519–535.

Smith, M. (2016) 'Conclusions: Europeanisation, globalisation or (re)nationalisation? Revisiting development policy in the European Union', *European Politics and Society*, Vol. 17, No. 1, 136–141.

Stern, M. and Öjendal, J. (2010) 'Mapping the Security: Development Nexus: Conflict, Complexity, Cacophony, Convergence?', *Security Dialogue*, Vol. 41, No. 1, 5–30.

Szent-Iványi, B. (2012) 'Aid Allocation of the Emerging Central and Eastern European Donors', *Journal of International Relations and Development*, Vol. 15, No. 1, 65–89.

Szent-Iványi, B. and Lightfoot, S. (2015) *New Europe's New Development Aid*. Abingdon: Routledge.

Van Seters, J. and Klaver, H. (2011) 'EU Development Cooperation after the Lisbon Treaty. People, Institutions and Global Trends', *ECDPM Discussion Paper 123*. Brussels: ECDPM.

Verschaeve, J. and Orbie, J. (2015) 'Once a Member, Always a Member? Assessing the Importance of Time in the Relationship between the European Union and the Development Assistance Committee', *Cambridge Review of International Affairs*, Vol. 29, No. 2, pp. 512–527. DOI: 10.1080/09557571.2015.1015486

Younas, J. (2008) 'Motivation for Bilateral Aid Allocation: Altruism or Trade Benefits', *European Journal of Political Economy*, Vol. 24, No. 3, 661–674.

13 External facets of justice, freedom and security

Jocelyn Mawdsley

Introduction

In the last decade, the Area of Freedom, Security and Justice (AFSJ) has been the most dynamic field of European integration (Wolff, 2008). Encompassing the policy areas of police, customs and judicial cooperation, EU citizenship, border control, immigration, asylum, combatting discrimination and the fight against terrorism, organized crime, drug-trafficking and human-trafficking, the AFSJ has developed rapidly in terms of policy areas, institutional complexity and legislation. Its external dimension has also expanded quickly, because the EU's internal security objectives can only be achieved through cooperation with third states. Both the refugee crisis stemming from conflicts in the Middle East and terrorist attacks in Paris and Brussels meant that by 2016 the external aspects of the EU's AFSJ have become major challenges for the EU. However, rather than being a strongly Europeanised external policy, the reality is more nuanced and highly politicized. The chapter aims to answer two main questions:

- What is the dominant mode of Member State cooperation in this area, and is this changing?
- Is the external dimension of the AFSJ becoming more Europeanised or more nationalized over time?

This introductory section will briefly explain the division of competences in the AFSJ and outline the institutional complexity of its governance, before introducing some of the tensions that feature in its policy-making.

Until the Treaty of Amsterdam, cooperation in the field of justice and home affairs (JHA) was intergovernmental in what was known as the JHA pillar, with little involvement of the other EU institutions. The Treaty of Amsterdam moved the areas of asylum, immigration and judicial cooperation in civil matters into the Community pillar, but everything else remained in the intergovernmental JHA pillar. Policy-making was largely carried out through multiannual programmes, whose parameters were set by the European Council, and the Commission was tasked with proposing implementation measures. The Lisbon Treaty removed the JHA pillar, meaning the AFSJ is now subject to the ordinary legislative procedure, and should have heralded changes in policy-making dynamics. Indeed Kaunert (2010) has pointed to the importance the Commission granted to securing the changes in both the Convention on the Future of Europe, and the subsequent treaty negotiations, as evidence of Commission policy entrepreneurialism in this policy area.

However, there are some important limitations. The AFSJ remains an area of shared competence, meaning that Member States retain the right to exercise their legislative prerogative where full harmonization has yet to occur (i.e. in almost all AFSJ areas). States therefore can, and do, continue to conclude agreements on issues related to the external dimension of the AFSJ. Moreover, the Lisbon Treaty does not give any general competence for the EU to act in external AFSJ affairs (Monar, 2012). Since the Lisbon Treaty came into force, there is also evidence of the Member States in the Council trying to reassert their prerogative to set the contours of the policy against the will of the Commission (Carrera and Guild, 2012). However, the conflict between intergovernmentalism and supranationalism is not the only tension.

The policy area is not just legally but also institutionally complex. Within the EU institutions, the portfolio is divided between several Commission Directorates-General along with specialized agencies like Frontex and Europol. Each has its own institutional priorities, and these do not always match, meaning that a unified position can be challenging to find. These internal Commission tensions are mirrored by disagreement between the European Parliament and the Commission and Council, on the correct balance between security and freedom, with the Parliament sometimes (if inconsistently) taking a more liberal human rights-based approach.

Monar (2012) argues that the diversity of complex and politically sensitive areas covered by the AFSJ makes it unlikely to develop into a unified EU external policy.[1] It also means integration dynamics vary within AFSJ external policies. Broadly speaking, however, we can differentiate between the dynamics in **border and migration control** on the one hand and **counter-terrorism** on the other. While both policy areas have evolved largely in response to external events, they have done so in different ways. This offers an organizational logic for this chapter, so after offering a brief outline of the evolution of the external dimension of the AFSJ and an overview of Member States' positions, this chapter will examine the integration dynamics of external policies on border and migration control and on counter-terrorism.

Context: integration in the field of Justice and Home Affairs (JHA)

Until the ratification of the Single European Act, European integration was largely based on the concept of removing economic and legal barriers to the free movement of goods, capital, services and people. The removal of internal borders, however, meant that the security of EU citizens became dependent upon the control of the EU's external borders, while simultaneously ensuring that the removal of internal borders was not abused. Huysmans (2000) suggests that this linking of external and internal borders marked the transformation of the Single Market from a socio-economic project into an internal security project encompassing the wider Union. Certainly, the emphasis on protecting external borders means there has been an external dimension to JHA cooperation from the outset, and from the Hague Programme onwards (if not earlier), this can be reasonably described as having a security focus. The intensification of the refugee crisis from 2015 onwards, coupled with terrorist attacks in Paris in 2015 and Brussels in 2016, has further strengthened security fears, leading to some states unilaterally reintroducing national border controls within the Schengen area.

Evolution of the external dimension of the area of freedom, security and justice

Although for scholars like Balzacq (2009) there is earlier evidence of an external dimension to JHA cooperation,[2] according to Wessel, Marin and Matera (2011) three events have shaped the development of the external dimension of the AFSJ:

1   the 1999 Tampere summit,
2   the 9/11 terrorist attacks on the US, and
3   the 2004 Hague Programme.

The 1997 Amsterdam Treaty stated that the EU should work internationally on JHA concerns, and the changes in this treaty enabled the 1999 Tampere extraordinary European Council Summit conclusions, which for the first time clearly articulated the link between the EU's internal security policies and external relations and stated that all EU external relations instruments should be used to build the AFSJ (European Council, 1999). This marked the start of a policy-making mode whereby the AFSJ policy objectives were set out in multiannual programmes by the European Council. At the follow-up June 2000 Feira Summit, the European Council agreed to give priority to 'external migration policy, the fight against organized crime and terrorism, against specific forms of crime, drug-trafficking, and the development and consolidation of the rule of law in countries on the road to democracy' (Wessel, Marin and Matera, 2011: 281). This set the overall direction of the external dimension of the AFSJ.

The second key event was the 9/11 attacks, which focussed attention not just on counter-terrorism but on external cooperation with the United States. This cooperation has led to unprecedented agreements on data sharing for example but also more generally to the elaboration of cooperation with third states on counter-terrorism, an area where the tensions between freedom and security are at their strongest. It has meant that security concerns have played an even more prominent role in shaping the external dimension of the AFSJ than might have been the case.

Finally, the Hague Programme, agreed in 2004, saw the adoption by the European Council of a coherent strategy on the external dimension of JHA in 2005, which set the parameters for this field (Council of the EU, 2005). This strategy made it clear that the primary objective of EU engagement with third countries is the fulfilment of the needs of EU citizens, conceived primarily in terms of security.

Member States: the Stockholm programme and beyond

The Stockholm Programme was the most recent iteration of the full AFSJ programmes. Entitled 'An Open and Secure Europe Serving and Protecting the Citizens', the Stockholm Programme stated that external action should concentrate on five areas of action: migration and asylum, security, information exchange, justice and civil protection and disaster management (European Council, 2010). It was an ambitious document reflecting the 'depillarization' of the ASFJ in the Lisbon Treaty. However, it was also noticeable that the Stockholm Programme was substantially based on the 2008 Member State-dominated Future Group report, showing the continuation of intergovernmentalism prevailing at the policy framing stage of AFSJ. While certain states were very active in framing the Stockholm Programme – the Future Group included the first three trio presidencies of the programming period – Germany, Portugal and Slovenia; France, Czech Republic and Sweden; and Spain, Belgium and Hungary, along with the UK as a common law observer – this did not mean these states consistently supported Europeanisation in all of the agreed areas of action. In fact, the intensely politicized nature of the policy area means that Member States are inconsistent in their support or opposition and often develop their positions based on national politics or recent events. This also means that a Member State might be classified as a laggard in one area, while being a champion of further integration in others. Even formal treaty status is not helpful. For example, the UK is one of the more active Member States on the external dimension of the AFSJ but, like Denmark and Ireland, has a formal treaty opt-out from the AFSJ, although the UK and Ireland can choose to opt-in on a case-by-case basis.

The implementation of the ambitious Stockholm Programme was therefore not straightforward. As argued earlier in this chapter, positions in the Council fluctuated in response to recent events, but as Carrera and Guild (2012) point out, both the European Commission and the Parliament developed also specific alternative agendas, leading to a multiplicity of conflicting and overlapping strategies, agendas and legislative proposals. Although less ambitious framework guidelines were adopted in 2014 for the current programming period with the idea that 'less is more', they too have been overtaken by events, notably the refugee crisis and the terrorist attacks in Paris and Brussels.

Rather than a straightforward picture of Europeanisation envisaged by the Lisbon Treaty, the AFSJ currently represents a confused and conflicted policy agenda, with tensions over power and policy direction. It is therefore difficult to make an overall assessment of the policy-making dynamics and whether for the Member States the policy is becoming more Europeanised or nationalized. Moreover, within the policy area, the integration dynamics are differentiated between the policy areas subsumed under the external dimension of AFSJ. This chapter now will look at two key but differing policy areas – border and migration control and counter-terrorism and internal security – to assess whether any trends can be identified.

Border and migration control: policy change

While its inadequacies have been made clear by the worsening of the refugee crisis from 2015 onwards, the 2008 European Pact on Asylum and Migration still forms the centrepiece of EU cooperation on asylum and migration. It represents not just a highly successful uploading by the French EU presidency of French norms and concerns but also, as Kostakopoulou (2009) argues, the continuing power of the Member States to frame the issue of migration, and thus cooperation with third states, through their national concerns. Domestic political sensitivity about immigration is a key political issue in most Member States, and so there is a reluctance to cede sovereignty on migration including cooperation with third states. It is difficult to portray the area of border management and migration control as other than largely characterized by intergovernmental dynamics (both Mode II and Mode IV).

Since the entry into force of the Lisbon Treaty, the European Commission has tried to establish a series of narratives to enable the Europeanisation of the policy area; however, this has not been wholly successful. Kaunert (2009) for example suggests that the European Commission has acted as a norm entrepreneur on immigration, moving away from further securitization of asylum policy and instead focusing on adhering to international law. The more successful narrative has been around framing external border security as a technological problem, which has permitted the growth of supranational border surveillance. While the EU border management agency, Frontex, established in 2004, reflects an uneasy compromise between the European Commission's preference for an EU border guard and Member States' reluctance, the agreement on a European border surveillance system (EUROSUR), represents a supranational advance, underpinned by the Commission's growing role in the research and development of surveillance technologies. On the whole, though, this has been the exception rather than the rule.

Most recently, the dynamics of third-country cooperation have been dominated by the rhetoric of emergency, which has strengthened the intergovernmental logic and indeed meant a return to Mode IV activity. In responding to the developing refugee crisis in 2015–16, Member States have been more enthusiastic about cooperating through intergovernmental policies like the CSDP or non-EU bodies like NATO than they have on proposals that would deepen European integration. Here both Mode II and IV dynamics can be observed. Since May 2015, EUNAVFOR MED Operation SOPHIA has been working in the Southern Central Mediterranean to deter people traffickers, stem flows of illegal migration and prevent deaths at sea. Ardittis (2016) claims that the Council now hopes to deploy a civilian security mission to improve Libyan police, border forces and counter-terrorism operations in a further example of Mode II policy action. NATO also agreed to deploy its fleet in the Aegean Sea in February 2016 to deter people trafficking – this decision is thought to have come at the request of Germany and Turkey, following bilateral meetings (Zhukov, 2016), showing an example of Mode IV policy action. Similarly, the highly controversial 2016 EU–Turkey deal on the exchange of irregular migrants for refugees, was driven by German-Turkish bilateral negotiations (Kim, 2016). While it is tempting to see these dynamics as emergency responses, or perhaps a symptom of German hegemony in the EU, in fact, they conform well to general trends about EU states' behaviour as the next section will show.

Border and migration control policy performance: action and change

Although EU external border management policy is intended to be built on principles of burden-sharing and solidarity, in reality, it is characterized by individual Member States attempting to upload migration emergencies causing domestic political tension to the EU level (intergovernmental Europeanisation – Mode II), while non-affected Member States resist. However, this does not mean that states can be consistently identified as laggards or leaders as flows of migration, locations of most asylum claims and national responses (such as tightening of immigration legislation or closing of borders) vary over time. While this pattern has been at its most acute from 2015 onwards, it is not new. As Chou (2009) points out, Germany attempted to upload its domestic problems with refugees from the Balkans conflicts in the early 1990s but met with resistance and then turned into a laggard, blocking attempts to Europeanise asylum policy (Hellmann et al., 2005), but then in 2015, when its unilateral decision to suspend the Dublin regulation led to over one million asylum-seekers entering Germany, it favoured compulsory quotas for all Member States. Migration routes also vary meaning that the third countries that the EU and its Member States must negotiate with change. For example, in 2015, attention shifted from the central Mediterranean route (Libya to Italy/Malta) to the Eastern Mediterranean route (Turkey to Greece) as the numbers using the latter increased exponentially meaning that a previous focus on agreements with Libya shifted to Turkey, as shown in Figure 13.1.

Until the refugee crisis intensified in 2015 and more states were drawn in, either as transit states or final destinations, migration flows were concentrated on Southern European states bordering the Mediterranean, and the situation for some time had been encapsulated by a

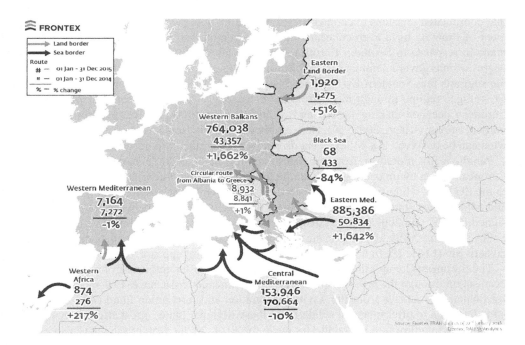

Figure 13.1 Major refugee routes to Europe

Source: © Frontex.

North-South divide (Wolff, 2008).[3] Bremberg and Britz (2009) suggest that more generally in internal security matters, there is a divide between Southern Member States, which are in favour of greater supranationalization (and thus in particular burden-sharing in the form of financial and technical assistance) and Northern Member States, which are opposed. For the Mediterranean states badly impacted by the financial crisis, their new internal security problems, especially those connected to immigration, are an additional expense that they are ill prepared to deal with, so some supranational proposals that would make all EU states share the burden are attractive; however, here too, there is resistance to ceding sovereignty. The 2015 intensification of the refugee crisis has also brought a new line of tension with many Central and Eastern European states stating outright opposition to any communitarization of individual states' migration problems and particularly rejecting national quotas for refugees (Hampshire, 2015).

While solidarity between EU states during migration emergencies remains low, there is some evidence that, in calmer times, states do have some success in uploading their national concerns to the EU level. The example of the French presidency shaping the 2008 European Pact on Asylum and Migration has already been given. Southern EU states for example have also enjoyed a degree of success in Europeanising their national concerns. The 2002 Spanish Presidency was able to upload its domestic concerns about combatting drug-trafficking and immigration from Morocco and to get agreement on the externalization of JHA policy in the Mediterranean. Since then, Wolff (2008) argues, Frontex activity has taken on a distinctly Mediterranean focus, due to continued intense pressure from EU Southern Member States. Spain, Portugal, Greece, Malta, Cyprus and Italy are periodically confronted by waves of migration from Africa, with which they are poorly equipped to cope. Wolff further points out that coordinated missions to counter illegal migration, both prior to and since the establishment of Frontex, have been concentrated on this region, and policy has accordingly been made in response to Southern European concerns (Wolff, 2008). Here, we can observe a degree of intergovernmentally fostered Europeanisation (Mode II). Klepp (2008) for example suggests that Southern EU Member States 'on different levels . . . are remodelling the EU-refugee regime through their "frontline perspective", pressuring for their positions in European decision-making forums and formalizing informal practices established in the border regions' (Klepp, 2008: 19). Here too though, despite some Mode II Europeanisation, what can be observed is a policy being driven by crises rather than forward planning.

Paradoxically, moreover, frontline states like Italy, Spain or Malta have been engaging in Europeanisation by uploading their immigration, asylum and border management concerns to the EU level, while simultaneously developing bilateral relationships with North African and Middle East states on migration control, like the agreements between Italy and Libya signed in 2003 and 2007 (Wolff, 2010). Here, we can observe the continuation of extra-EU policy relations (Mode IV) despite the presence of Europeanisation through intergovernmental activism (Mode II). In this sense too, the national interest appears to remain paramount.

The European Commission has been endeavouring to foster enthusiasm for greater Europeanisation through the provision of technical and financial assistance. EU states can apply for financial assistance from the Asylum, Migration and Integration Fund (AMIF), which aims inter alia to offer financial solidarity to those Member States, most affected by migration and asylum flows. In the budgetary cycle for 2014–20, the Commission has also established an Internal Security Fund: Borders and Visas with funding of €2.76 billion, to assist in these aspects of the implementation of the internal security strategy.[4] This would cover all aspects of border surveillance for Schengen states.

Moreover, the Commission has also attempted to frame border management as a collective technological challenge. Given that even the most resistant states accept that the external border is only as strong as the weakest EU state's controls, this has met with some success. Since 2003, the Commission has been financing the development of internal security technologies, particularly surveillance technologies, through first a preparatory programme, then the Seventh Framework Programme and now Horizon 2020. Edler and James (2012) regard this action as evidence that the Commission can act as a supranational policy entrepreneur in this field, as they had no initial buy-in from any of the other actors concerned. In 2011, Frontex was given the right to directly procure border surveillance equipment, which could create a more integrated, supranational dimension to external border control although its budget is small (European Union, 2011). A communiqué on the security industry also made it clear that the Commission intended the Internal Security Fund to fund testing and validation of such technologies (European Commission, 2012). The motivation for this focus on surveillance technologies is clearly linked to the new EUROSUR border surveillance system. In this sense, there is some evidence of the European Commission being able to leverage a more supranational dimension to border management through the use of existing communitarized policies such as research and development policy. It has also enabled it to present the highly political EUROSUR project as a primarily technical one.

The EUROSUR project has a substantial external element involving the externalization of EU external borders. The use of EU funding to provide border control technology to third states is not new. The Seahorse network involving Spain, Portugal, Morocco, Mauritania, Cape Verde, Senegal, Guinea-Bissau and the Gambia for example has been running since 2006, funded substantially by the Commission's framework for asylum and migration cooperation with third states. The initiative proposed and partially funded by Spain is based around a satellite-based communications network to share information on migrant movements. Here, we can observe a degree of Europeanisation, even if Spain and Portugal's leadership was driven by a desire to access EU funding to deal with a national problem. Similar networks exist in the Baltic and Black Seas with both EU and non-EU participants, and Spain has proposed a further one for the Mediterranean. EUROSUR, which would mark an increased supranation-alization of border control policy, would bring these networks together, thus bringing the EU more firmly into these regional arrangements. Frontex would be responsible for surveillance of the 'pre-frontier' area and third countries would be supplied with the necessary technolo-gies (backed up by the use of EU unmanned aerial vehicles) to attempt to ensure that potential migrants cannot reach EU territorial waters (European Commission, 2008). However, it is not clear that this is compatible with international law. Moreover, the sale or provision of sur-veillance technologies to governments with problematic human rights records raises difficult ethical questions (Wolff, 2008; Mawdsley, 2013). Finally, the credibility of this technological solution seems in question given the extent of the current refugee crisis.

To summarize this section, the external element of border management policy reveals a confusing set of integration dynamics. First, a general conclusion can be made that the policy area is predominantly marked by **intergovernmental decision-making** within the EU framework so Mode II (intra-EU cooperation) in the analytical structure of this book, although the refugee crisis has shown some evidence of wholly uncoordinated national activity. Second, however, the North-South divide means that Southern European states have been taking two rather contradictory steps. Their need for financial and technical assistance to secure their external borders has led them to support **supranational policies** and to apply for financial assistance from the available funds. However, even where there has been sub-stantial EU assistance to reform national practices, there is still a sense that **national inter-ests** prevail. Moreno Fuentes (2008), discussing the Spanish case for example, suggests that there is a marked dissonance between rhetoric and practice. This might suggest that even where **evidence of Europeanisation** can be found in terms of discourse and institutional adaptation; it does not necessarily translate into practice. This would also explain why the Southern EU states have also engaged in **bilateral activity** (Mode IV) in concluding agree-ments on migration control with third countries such as Spain and Portugal through the Seahorse network and the Italy–Libya agreements, which even if funded partially by the EU, resemble Mode IV four of foreign policy-making. The section also suggested that, despite a history of opposition to many of its proposals in this area, the Commission was carefully developing a successful framing tactic for more supranational integration through funding for the development and procurement of security technologies. The EUROSUR project would represent a considerable step forward in this respect but remains ethically problem-atic. Kaunert (2010) argued that the Commission had also attempted to reframe asylum issues through an international law framework. This stance has since been largely rejected by Member States, but the Commission's attempts to frame external border management as technical rather than political seemed more successful at least prior to the intensification of the refugee crisis in 2015.

Counter-terrorism and internal security: policy change

The interplay between the EU institutions and the Member States in terms of shaping the external dimension of counter-terrorism and internal security policy is complex. While countering political extremism was the original issue that prompted intergovernmental cooperation in JHA, formal counter-terrorist cooperation was not really pursued at the EU level until after 9/11. Since then, the external dimension of AFSJ counter-terrorism action has evolved quickly, sometimes through specific AFSJ policy instruments, sometimes through CFSP.

Once again, it is difficult to identify a constant grouping of states due to the high levels of politicization of the policy area and the domestic political imperative to need to be seen to respond to terrorist attacks. There are various cleavages along which Member States fall. The first cleavage divides states with higher or lower levels of concern about the balance between human rights and security. Most EU proposals have been focussed on security, and there has been reasonably constant reluctance from the Nordic states and the Netherlands about impairing civil liberties. More Atlanticist states like the UK and Poland have been keener to follow an agenda that has been largely set by a third state, the United States (Monar, 2012). Second, there is a divide between those states with high levels of competence and experience in counter-terrorism, and those that do not. The former, largely the UK and France, are more likely to try to upload their national priorities to the EU level but paradoxically can be quite resistant to any supranationalization of counter-terrorism because they fear the result would be less effective than their national processes and could damage intelligence-sharing with third states. With the less capable, the situation is reversed.

This section intends to make two main claims about the nature of the process since 2001. First, the European Commission has been able to act as a supranational policy entrepreneur on various issues and has been able to achieve agreement on previously intractable issues (Mode I). However, the Commission's agenda has been largely shaped by a non-EU state, the US. Second, large Member States have been reasonably successful at uploading geographical preferences for external EU counter-terrorist activity (Mode II). Britain and France have been notable in this respect. Active Member States, however, tend also to maintain bilateral activity in the form of extra-EU security and intelligence policy relations (Mode IV) with third states. Let us examine each of these claims in turn.

Counter-terrorism and internal security: policy performance

First, external cooperation on counter-terrorism has evolved rapidly as a policy field since 2001. In particular, the EU and its Member States, as close allies and trading partners of the US, had to respond to the demands of its post-9/11 security agenda not just in terms of counter-terrorism cooperation in third countries, but also to American efforts to secure its borders. Rees and Aldrich (2005) argue that strategic cultures related to terrorism are very different on both sides of the Atlantic. In contrast to the US, which declared a global war on terror, EU states have tended to view counter-terrorism as a matter of law enforcement and internal security rather than a military matter. This attitude seems to persist even after major attacks on Paris and Brussels in 2015–16. The more legalistic European approach meant that US policies like extraordinary rendition and Guantanamo Bay were controversial (Archick, 2011). Attitudes to citizens' rights on electronic surveillance and private data protection also differ between the US and EU (Rees and Aldrich, 2005). These differences have emerged particularly in European Parliament opposition to some Commission proposals.

However, some commentators suggest that EU–US stances on counter-terrorism have now converged. In part, some suggest this is due to the more multilateral approach of the second Bush administration and later the Obama administration, which reacted to EU civil rights concerns, particularly about the treatment of detainees (Archick, 2011). Others, however, stress the Commission's actions as a supranational policy entrepreneur. They point to the use that the Commission made of the shock of 9/11 to push for a rapid transfer of internal security powers to the EU level, something that Member States had traditionally been cautious about. The need for the EU to be seen to be doing something to assist the US on counter-terrorism, meant that measures which had earlier been proposed but not agreed were swiftly accepted.

This speed meant that the EU's emerging internal security policies were partially, if not primarily, constructed in response to the US' need for transatlantic cooperation (Lodge, 2004; Pawlak, 2009). Archick (2011) points particularly to the EU internal security strategy, which resembles the US homeland security concept, while Lodge (2004) considers the Commission's adoption of homeland security measures to be driven by subservience to the US rather than by internal imperatives. In this sense, we can observe the rapid emergence of a highly institutionalized, integrated policy area driven by a supranational actor but shaped or framed by a third party. However, it is questionable whether the Member States would have accepted this action had it not been for the external shocks of 9/11 and the Madrid and London bombings and the importance that most attach to their bilateral relationships with the US. Monar (2012) argues that the UK was active in pressing for greater EU–US counter-terrorism cooperation. Moreover, there are signs that the period of the EU acting as a fairly unified actor on counter-terrorism are over. The European Parliament is emerging as a more liberal (albeit very inconsistently) actor than the Commission and Council, and has made its concerns about internal security policy clear, particularly regarding data protection. The Parliament also raised concerns about and demanded revisions to EU–US agreements on the transfer of banking data (Swift Accord) and air passenger data (Passenger Name Record) (Archick, 2011). Brady (2010) suggests that in the post-Lisbon era the Parliament's new right of co-decision means that such clashes will occur more frequently.

The second contention is that some Member States have been successful in uploading their geographical preferences for external counter-terrorism action but simultaneously maintain bilateral extra-EU cooperation, suggesting that integration is rather limited. The states which have been able to upload preferences are usually large states, which have special interests in and thus more intense engagement with particular regions for historical reasons. Ironically, given its reluctance on AFSJ integration, one of the most successful uploaders has been the UK. Quite apart from its success in fostering intensive EU–US cooperation, Mackenzie (2012) points out that the UK has made consistent and eventually successful efforts to upload its own policy conviction that Afghanistan and Pakistan are important sources of terrorist insecurity to the EU level. It was also successful in shaping the 2012 draft Counter-Terrorism Action Plan for Yemen and the Horn of Africa, leading the House of Commons to question whether other Member States actually shared what appeared to be a UK-Danish vision (House of Commons, 2012). Similarly, France and Spain have been able to upload their particular concerns about the Maghreb.

However, this uploading can be secondary to national action. Although the UK has attempted successfully to upload its preference for counter-terrorism action in Pakistan, partly because it enables it to encourage action that is not enmeshed in ex-colonial tensions, it also maintains close bilateral relations (Mackenzie, 2012). This is not unusual. Despite France and Spain successfully uploading Morocco and Algeria as EU policy priorities, both North African countries prefer bilateral relations with EU states. Moreover, despite the intensity of EU–US cooperation, in 2008 Germany signed a bilateral agreement with the US on access to biometric data and the sharing of data on known and suspected terrorists (Monar, 2012).

To sum up this section, the pattern of integration in the external dimension of EU counter-terrorism policy is decidedly mixed. On the one hand, there has been a rapid expansion of integration sponsored by the European Commission, which could be viewed as evidence of **Mode I foreign policy-making**; that is external policy-making operating within the EU framework in an **institutionalized, integrated and supranational** fashion. However, this neglects the fact that there was an upload of **Member States'** preferences for close cooperation with the US, and the fact that the Commission largely responded subsequently to a US agenda. The opposition of the Parliament to some measures regarding data sharing shows the extent of the mismatch between EU and US cultures. This means that the Commission counter-terrorism agenda sits uneasily and may as a result be less effectively downloaded into national cultures. It is hard to describe this as authentic Europeanisation.

Moreover, in a counterbalancing trend there is evidence that bilateralism is thriving as individual Member States negotiate counter-terrorism agreements without reference to the EU, which fits well with the model of **Mode IV (extra-EU policy relations) foreign policy-making**. This is coupled with evidence of **Mode II (intergovernmentalism)**. In this sense, while Member States' abilities to upload their geographical preferences for counter-terrorism activities, reinforces Europeanisation, it simultaneously reinforces national policy-making dynamics.

Conclusion

The conclusion to this chapter will attempt to answer two questions:

* Is the external dimension of the AFSJ becoming more Europeanised or more nationalized over time?
* What is the dominant mode of Member State cooperation in this area, and is this changing?

From the outset of JHA cooperation, the external border has been portrayed as threatening and needing to be secured through cooperation with third states. While elements of the external dimension of AFSJ are closer to the general objectives of the CFSP, such as the global promotion of human rights, international judicial cooperation or efforts to improve data protection standards in third countries, much of the external dimension of the AFSJ is about securing the external borders and persuading third states to cooperate in this through the provision of financial and technical assistance. The complexity of the number of policy elements involved, and the mixed messages being conveyed by the EU institutions, have potentially limited the potential for downloading the field's policy objectives to the Member State level.

Attempts by the Commission to act as a supranational policy entrepreneur have seen various re-framings of AFSJ: adopting a US agenda in the early 2000s when the emphasis was on counter-terrorism, in the late 2000s through a framing of the external border in terms of human rights and international law (Kaunert, 2010) and most recently by framing external border security as a technical rather than a political issue. Despite the Commission's efforts to offer an overarching narrative, the external dimension of AFSJ remains predominantly reactive rather than proactive. While there has been a high level of activity in this field since the 1999 Tampere European Council summit, external events rather than internal imperatives have been the agents of change. The policy-making mode associated with the early JHA cooperation was intensive transgovernmentalism. While the particularities of the second pillar have been superseded by the Treaty of Lisbon, their legacy is still present.

This means that, in terms of this book, this foreign policy-making field can best be characterized as still more nationalized that Europeanised. Unpacking the external dimension of the AFSJ has shown that in the absence of real agreement on the correct strategies for the EU to take in terms of controlling illegal migration and counter-terrorism, action tends to come through reaction to emergencies such as the 9/11 terrorist attacks or the refugee crisis currently impacting Europe. This reactive tendency allowed a third state, the USA, to frame the emerging EU counter-terrorism strategy. Member States do upload their own preferences and are able to frame policies in their national policy-making style. Particular examples are the French EU Presidency in 2008 uploading its national preferences to the European Pact on Asylum and Migration, the 2002 Spanish EU Presidency achieving its national goal of externalizing JHA towards the Mediterranean. However, Member States, who are particularly concerned about a particular issue with a third state, remain prone to concluding bilateral agreements. In short, in terms of this book's analytical framework, the dominant modes of Member State cooperation are intergovernmentalism within the EU framework (Mode II) and extra-EU cooperation between EU and non-EU states (Mode IV).

The European Commission is striving to create a joined-up narrative for the external dimension of the AFSJ and has made several attempts to frame it in an acceptable manner for the Member States to accept supranationalism in this area. However, the high level of domestic sensitivity of the policy area and the lack of agreement on basic principles means the Member States tend to block. The EUROSUR integrated border management project represents a step forward but is controversial and raises both legal and ethical issues, which could undermine other areas of EU foreign policy.

It is not possible to consistently classify states as laggards or lead states on the external dimension of the AFSJ. One would expect Denmark, Ireland and the UK given their legal opt-outs, to be laggards. In fact though, the UK in particular has been quite activist in pushing for external action on counter-terrorism, and although as a non-Schengen member, it cannot be a member of Frontex, it attends meetings by invitation and has been a strong supporter of and participant in Frontex operations. Moreover, the North-South divide seen in border management policy does not apply to counter-terrorism. Support and dissent tend to be issue-specific and based on national interests. The issues that AFSJ tackles are too domestically sensitive across the EU for politicians to act otherwise. As the changes in policy-making adopted in the Treaty of Lisbon bed down, more established coalitions of supporters and laggards may emerge. As the issues at stake tend to be closely connected to fundamental rights, the coalitions may emerge though as party political rather than national. At present though, policy-making on the external dimension of the AFSJ remains predominantly intergovernmental, reactive rather than proactive and without clear guiding objectives other than internal security.

Notes

1 The Treaty of Lisbon, while extending the legal possibilities for ASFJ external action, also restricts them by emphasizing in Article 4(2) TEU that Member States have sole responsibility for maintaining law and order and national security. See Monar (2012) for a full account of this.
2 Such as the Edinburgh 1992 European Council, which established principles governing external aspects of migration policy, in particular the intention to establish readmission agreements with third countries and on coordinated action to address 'push' factors encouraging irregular migration into the EU.
3 There is also a long-standing North-South divide more generally in terms of immigration policy. In the 1990s, Northern states would put pressure on Southern states to adopt stricter immigration policies (King, Lazaridis and Tsardanidis, 2000).
4 EU Internal Security Strategy: http://www.consilium.europa.eu/uedocs/cms_data/docs/pressdata/en/jha/113055.pdf

Bibliography

Archick, K. (2011) 'US-EU Cooperation against Terrorism', *CRS Report for Congress RS22030*, Congressional Research Service, Washington.

Ardittis, S. (2016) 'From Turkey to Libya: The EU Refugee Crisis' Never-Ending Domino Effect', *Vocal Europe*, 22 March 2016, available at: http://www.vocaleurope.eu/2016/03/22/from-turkey-to-libya-the-eu-refugee-crisis-never-ending-domino-effect/

Balzacq, T. (2009) 'The Frontiers of Governance: Understanding the External Dimension of EU Justice and Home Affairs', in T. Balzacq (ed.) *The External Dimension of EU Justice and Home Affairs*. Basingstoke: Palgrave Macmillan, 1–34.

Brady, H. (2010) *EU JHA Co-Operation: After Lisbon, Reality Bites*, 24 June 2010, London: Centre for European Reform.

Bremberg, N. and Britz, M. (2009) 'Uncovering the Divergent Institutional Logics of EU Civil Protection', *Cooperation and Conflict*, Vol. 44, No. 3, 288–308.

Carrera, S. and Guild, E. (2012) *Does the Stockholm Programme Matter? The Struggles over Ownership of AFSJ Multiannual Programming*, CEPS Paper in Liberty and Security in Europe, Number 51 December 2012.

Chou, M.-H. (2009) 'The European Security Agenda and the "External Dimension" of EU Asylum and Migration Cooperation', *Perspectives on European Politics and Society*, Vol. 10, No. 4, 541–559.

Council of the EU (2005) *A Strategy for the External Dimension of JHA: Global Freedom, Security and Justice*, Document 14366/3/05, Brussels, 30 November 2005.

Edler, J. and James, A. (2012) 'Understanding the Emergence of STI policies in the EU: The Genesis of EU Security Research and the Role of the EU Commission as Policy Entrepreneur', *Manchester Business School Working Paper No. 630*, Manchester, June 2012.

European Commission (2008) *Examining the Creation of a European Border Surveillance System (EUROSUR)*. Brussels, 13.2.2008 COM(2008) 68 final, available at http://eur-lex.europa.eu/legal-content/EN/TXT/PDF/?uri=CELEX:52008DC0068&from=EN, date accessed 5 August 2016.

European Commission (2012) *Security Industrial Policy: Action Plan for an Innovative and Competitive Security Industry*, COM (2012) 417 final, Brussels, 26 July 2012.

European Council (2010) 'The Stockholm Programme: An Open and Secure Europe Serving and Protecting Citizens', Document 2010/C 115/01, *Official Journal of the European Union*, 4 May 2010, Brussels: European Union, C115/1–38.

European Council (1999) Presidency Conclusions, available at: http://www.europarl.europa.eu/summits/tam_en.htm, date accessed 12 July 2013.

European Union (2011) 'Regulation (EU) No 1168/2011 of the European Parliament and of the Council of 25 October 2011 amending Council Regulation (EC) No 2007/2004 Establishing a European Agency for the Management of Operational Cooperation at the External Borders of the Member States of the European Union', *Official Journal of the European Union*, 22 November 2011, Brussels: European Union, L304/1–17.

Hampshire, J. (2015) 'Europe's Migration Crisis', *Political Insight*, Vol. 6, No. 3, 8–11.

Hellmann, G., Baumann, R., Bösche, M. and Herborth, B. (2005) 'De-Europeanization by Default? Germany's EU Policy in Defense and Asylum', *Foreign Policy Analysis*, Vol. 1, No. 1, 143–164.

House of Commons European Scrutiny Committee (2012) *Thirteenth Report of Session 2012–13*, London: Houses of Parliament, http://www.publications.parliament.uk/pa/cm201213/cmselect/cmeuleg/86-xiii/8602.htm, date accessed 12 November 2012.

Huysmans, J. (2000) 'The European Union and the Securitization of Migration', *Journal of Common Market Studies*, Vol. 38, No. 5, 751–777.

Kaunert, C. (2010) 'The Area of Freedom, Security and Justice in the Lisbon Treaty: Commission Policy Entrepreneurship?', *European Security*, Vol. 19, No. 2, 169–189.

Kaunert, C. (2009) 'Liberty Versus Security? EU Asylum Policy and the European Commission', *Journal of Contemporary European Research*, Vol. 5, No. 2, 148–170.

Kim, L. (2016) 'Merkel's Dilemma', *Slate*, 10 March 2016, available at http://www.slate.com/articles/news_and_politics/foreigners/2016/03/angela_merkel_is_fighting_for_her_survival_as_the_leader_of_germany_and.html

King, R., Lazaridis, G. and Tsardanidis, C. (2000) *Eldorado or Fortress? Migration in Southern Europe*. London: MacMillan Press.

Klepp, S. (2008) 'Negotiating the Principle of Non-Refoulement in the Mediterranean Sea – Missions, Visions and Practices at the Southern Borders of the European Union', *Research Academy Leipzig, Working Papers Series* 1, 11/2008.

Kostakopoulou, D. (2009) 'The Area of Freedom, Security and Justice and the Political Morality of Migration and Integration', in H. Lindahl (ed.) *A Right to Inclusion and Exclusion? Normative Fault Lines of the EU's Area of Freedom, Security and Justice*. Oxford: Hart Publishing, 65–92.

Lodge, J. (2004) 'EU Homeland Security: Citizens or Suspects?', *Journal of European Integration*, Vol. 26, No. 3, 253–279.

Mackenzie, A. (2012) *The External Dimension of EU Counter-Terrorism*, PhD thesis, University of Salford, Manchester, UK, February 2012.

Mawdsley, J. (2013) *A European Agenda for Security Technology: From Innovation Policy to Export Controls*. Brussels: Flemish Peace Institute.

Monar, J. (2012) *The External Dimension of the EU's Area of Freedom, Security and Justice: Progress, Potential and Limitations after the Treaty of Lisbon*, Report Number 1, May 2012, Stockholm, Swedish Institute for European Policy Studies.

Moreno Fuentes, F. (2008) 'Dissonance between Discourse and Practice in EU Border Control Enforcement: The Spanish Case', in A. Chebel d'Appollonia and S. Reich (eds.) *Immigration, Integration, and Security: America and Europe in Comparative Perspective*. Pittsburgh: University of Pittsburgh Press, 254–299.

Pawlak, P. (2010) 'Network Politics in Transatlantic Homeland Security Cooperation', *Perspectives on European Politics and Society*, Vol. 10, No. 4, pp. 560–581.

Rees, W. and Aldrich, R. (2005) 'Contending Cultures of Counterterrorism: Transatlantic Divergence or Convergence?', *International Affairs*, Vol. 81, No. 5, 905–923.

Wessel, R., Marin, L. and Matera, C. (2011) 'The External Dimension of the EU's Area of Freedom, Security and Justice', in C. Eckes and T. Konstadinides (eds.) *Crime within the Area of Freedom, Security and Justice: A European Public Order*. Cambridge: Cambridge University Press, 272–300.

Wolff, S. (2010) 'EU Integrated Border Management Post Lisbon: Contrasting Policies and Practises', in R. Zapata-Barrero (ed.) *Shaping the Normative Contours of the European Union: A Migration-Border Framework*. Barcelona: CIDOB edicions, 23–36.

Wolff, S. (2008) 'Border Management in the Mediterranean: Internal, External and Ethical Challenges', *Cambridge Review of International Affairs*, Vol. 21, No. 2, 251–273.

Zhukov, Y. (2016) 'NATO's Mediterranean Mission: What the Alliance Is Doing in the Aegean Sea', *Foreign Affairs*, 21 February 2016, available at: https://www.foreignaffairs.com/articles/europe/2016–02–21/natos-mediterranean-mission

14 National aims and adaptation

Lessons from the market

Chad Damro and Alasdair R. Young

Introduction

Access to the European Union's market, the largest in the world, is a significant source of power for the EU as a global actor.[1] The size of its market gives the EU leverage in trade negotiations and means that its rules and regulations matter to foreign producers and service providers and that its competition policy decisions affect the operations of major corporations in other parts of the world. Trade, regulatory and competition policies are also vital components of EU foreign policy. The EU, for instance, promotes its regulatory and competition rules internationally while using its preferential trade agreements to promote development and enhanced access to its market as a carrot to encourage respect for human rights, including labour rights, and environmental protection. It has withdrawn trade preferences and imposed sanctions on third countries to enforce international norms. Trade, regulatory and competition policies are therefore critical interfaces between the Member States and the EU and the rest of the world.

These policies, however, are different from the other policies covered in this volume in several critical respects. Trade, regulatory and competition policies are, for instance, among the longest established and most highly integrated of all of the EU's policies. Critically, trade and competition policies are exclusive EU competences, that is Member States can no longer pursue individual policies, but must pursue common policies. The concentration of trade policy at the EU level has been a protracted and contentious process, but has largely been settled by the Treaty of Lisbon. Even though the EU must pursue a common trade policy, the Member States have different preferences regarding the substance of that policy, resulting in perennial tensions within the common policy. In competition policy, responsibility for approving large mergers and vetting state aids is concentrated in the hands of the European Commission. Thus, trade and competition policies fall within Mode I of the volume's spectrum on the relative degree of EU versus national content.

Regulatory cooperation is more varied. The Member States continue to adopt various national regulations that affect whether foreign goods or service providers can enter their territories, although many regulations are now adopted at the European level. In addition, EU representation in regulatory diplomacy is highly varied, with representatives ranging from the Member States' standard-setting bodies, to Member State governments collectively to the Commission. Thus, European regulatory action is sometimes supranational (Mode I) and sometimes intergovernmental (Mode II). These three policy areas, therefore, while they have more in common with each other than with the other policies in this volume, reflect different degrees of Europeanisation.

More specifically, while intra-EU integration is the dominant mode of policy-making in all three policy areas, there have been different degrees of further Europeanisation in the twenty-first century. In trade policy, there has been the most pronounced tightening of cooperation among the Member States, particularly with respect to foreign direct investment (FDI). There has also been Europeanisation in the external dimension of competition policy, despite some expectations that the recent 'modernisation' would lead to the renationalisation of competition policy powers. There has been no pronounced shift to closer coordination in regulatory policy since the 'completion' of the single European market in the early 1990s, although new common rules continue to be adopted. Thus, there are differences in the intensity of the process of Europeanisation.

Beyond these assessments, this chapter seeks to make two further points. First, because of exclusive competence in trade and competition policies and because of the dynamics of regulation within the single market, there is extensive, but contested, up-loading of national policy preferences. Second, despite extended and intense cooperation, distinct national preferences persist with respect to trade, regulatory and competition policies. This chapter, therefore, should serve as an important cautionary note about the limits to the approximation of policy preferences that can reasonably be expected in less intensely integrated domains of European foreign policy.

The body of this chapter considers each policy in turn. In each case, we provide some background on the development of the policy with an emphasis on the balance of authority between the European and national levels. Our focus, however, is on developments during the twenty-first century. In that regard, while our focus is on supranational policy-making (Mode I) and intergovernmental cooperation (Mode II), we also touch on Member States engaging independently with third parties (Mode IV). The discussion of each policy concludes with an assessment of the relative frequency and significance of these different instances and the direction of change. The chapter concludes by looking across the three policy areas to assess the balance of change in EU foreign economic policy.

Trade policy: the original external policy

Trade policy is one of the most established areas of cooperation in the EU and is more closely integrated than any other aspect of the EU's explicit external relations. It is an area where the EU exercises exclusive competence. Moreover, the EU's economic capacity, which trade policy seeks to harness, is central to depictions of the EU as a global actor. The EU has used trade policy to foster political relations with the former colonies of its Member States and the countries of its near abroad. It has offered enhanced access to its market to provide assistance to the world's poorest countries and to encourage others to implement multilateral environmental and labour rights conventions. The EU has withdrawn preferential access from countries – Belarus, Myanmar and Sri Lanka – that it considers to have violated international human rights norms. The January 2012 decision under the Common Foreign and Security Policy to impose sanctions on oil exports from Iran for its failure to comply with the Non-Proliferation Treaty[2] was implemented through the common commercial policy.[3] The EU has responded to Russia's aggression in Ukraine in part by restricting exports of goods and (financial) services.[4] In April 2014, the EU unilaterally granted Ukraine preferential access to the EU market until 31 December 2015 as part of supporting the Ukrainian regime.[5] Trade policy, therefore, is a potent and distinctive external EU policy instrument.

High and increasing integration

A central decision in the 1957 Treaty of Rome was to create a customs union and thus have a common trade policy with the rest of the world (Lindberg and Scheingold, 1970: Ch. 1; Moravcsik, 1998: 86). The core institutional arrangement chosen for this common policy – the common commercial policy (CCP) – gave the EU exclusive competence for issues falling within the CCP. That is, the EU and only the EU could act. Moreover, the Treaty of Rome delegated considerable responsibility to the Commission for implementing the common policy and foresaw decision-making in the Council of Ministers by qualified majority, giving the policy a strong supranational character from the outset (Lindberg and Scheingold, 1970: 14; Moravcsik, 1998: 153–6). Nonetheless, trade policy is conducted in close consultation with the Member States, which are represented at the official level in the Trade Policy Committee.

The product of a compromise among the founding Member States, which had different trade policy preferences, the scope of the common commercial policy was open ended. Although the Treaty explicitly included some trade policy instruments, it was silent on others, leaving open the question of precisely where the boundary between EU and Member State authority lay. At least in part, this was a reflection of the main preoccupations of the time – tariffs and quantitative restrictions – but meant that the policy did not include many elements that became the subject of multilateral negotiations beginning in the 1970s. With respect to these areas, which included trade in services and foreign direct investment, the Member States could and do pursue independent policies. In addition, until the creation of the single European market in 1992, some Member States maintained individual trade policy measures on products from particular third countries (Commission, 1997: 1; Hanson, 1998), and there have been persistent, although dwindling, differences in how Member States apply the EU's common customs code. Member States actively compete when it comes to export promotion. Thus, although the Member States' scope for autonomous action has dwindled over time, it has not yet entirely disappeared.

The imperfect overlap between the EU's exclusive competence and the more extensive international trade agenda from the 1970s into the 2000s presented a challenge to the EU's participation in international trade negotiations. The EU's Member States, however, found a variety of ways beyond the treaty-based common commercial policy to participate in international agreements. In the 1970 European Road Transport Agreement, the Member States participated by common action, excluding the Commission altogether (Young, 2002: 36–7). In the late 1990s, the EU's Member States participated both individually and collectively in the failed negotiation of a multilateral investment agreement under the auspices of the Organization for Economic Cooperation and Development (OECD) (Young, 2002: 94–104). In numerous other instances, the Commission and the Member States collectively participated. In the Uruguay Round of multilateral trade negotiations, which created the World Trade Organization in 1995, the Commission represented the EU and the Member States, but the Member States also participated, and the twenty-eight Member States, as well as the EU, are members of the WTO. Associated with these awkward cooperative arrangements, there were a series of tussles between the Member States and the Commission over competence before the European Court of Justice. As a result of the ensuing ECJ rulings, EU competence in trade policy gradually expanded until the 1990s, but was still far narrower than the rapidly expanding international trade agenda.

The Commission first sought to persuade the Member States to expand the scope of the common commercial policy as part of the Maastricht Treaty, but it was unsuccessful. The first substantive negotiated expansion of the common commercial policy occurred in the Treaty of Nice. Under Nice, most aspects of trade policy were brought within the EU's competence, but resistance from a number of Member States, particularly France, led to some services – audio-visual, education, healthcare and social services – being explicitly excluded and foreign direct investment in non-service sectors not being included. In addition, the Member States retained the authority to pursue and conclude agreements affecting service so long as they did not contravene EU law (Young, 2002: 46–7). Foreign direct investment in non-service sectors also remained outside the EU's competence. As of 2010, the EU's Member States had concluded nearly 1,200 bilateral investment treaties with non-EU countries (Commission, 2010: 4). The Treaty of Lisbon finally brought these excluded sectors within the common commercial policy, thereby making it 'comprehensive' (Woolcock, 2010: 383). Nonetheless, agreements affecting the sensitive service sectors must be ratified unanimously by the Council. In addition, in 2015, responding to pressure from some member states, the Commission asked the Court of Justice whether the EU's free trade agreement with Singapore could be concluded by the EU alone. In 2016, it bowed to political pressure and treated the Comprehensive Economic and Trade Agreement with Canada 'as if' it were a mixed agreement so as not to delay signature pending the Singapore ruling. Lisbon thus further integrated EU trade policy, but the Member States did not cede their prerogatives easily.

Member State action within an integrated policy

That trade policy falls within the exclusive competence of the EU means that, in most cases, Member States cannot pursue policies independently of the EU. The most notable exception is trade promotion activities, including diplomatic efforts to address trade barriers adversely affecting a Member State's firms.[6] The Member States are, however, extremely active in seeking to shape EU trade policies. This section discusses Member States' efforts to up-load their trade policy preferences.

Crucially, the Member States have significantly different trade policy preferences. On the basis of these fairly stable positions, the Member States are often grouped into liberal 'north' and protectionist 'south' (see Table 14.1). The Member State governments, however, often diverge from these general trade policy tendencies with respect to specific trade policies affecting particular industries (Baldwin, 2006: 931; Johnson, 1998; Woolcock, 2005: 390). Moreover, given the rough balance between the liberal and protectionist camps, the positions of 'swing states' are often the key to explaining policy decisions (Baldwin, 2006: 931). Conflict occurs when Member States seek to up-load competing trade policy preferences.

Clashes among different trade policy preferences were very evident in the run up to the 2005 Hong Kong Ministerial in the Doha Round of multilateral trade negotiations. Unhappy at the extent of the concessions the Commission had offered on agricultural market access, at a special meeting of the EU's foreign ministers on 18 October, France sought to force the Commission to withdraw its negotiating proposal (EurActiv, 19 October 2005). Although the French initiative was supported by the Greek, Irish, Portuguese, Polish and Spanish governments, it did not command sufficient support to be adopted. In particular, the British government, holding the EU's rotating presidency, and the Danish, Dutch, Finnish, German and Dutch governments opposed constraining the Commission (EurActiv, 19 October 2005). The Commission, however, undertook to strengthen the mechanisms by which it keeps the

Table 14.1 Member States' crude trade policy preferences (more engaged states only)

More liberal	*'Swing'*	*More protectionist*
Denmark	Austria	France
Estonia	Czech Republic	Greece
Netherlands	Finland	Italy
Sweden	Germany	Poland
UK	Spain	Portugal

Council informed about the negotiations. In addition, the Council (2005) confirmed that 'the [2003 common agricultural policy] reform is Europe's important contribution to the [Doha Development Agenda] and constitutes the limits for the Commission's negotiating brief in the WTO Round'. French President Chirac subsequently warned that France reserved its right to veto any agreement that went beyond the 2003 reform of the common agricultural policy (Parker *et al.*, 2005). This vignette illustrates both the persistent differences among the Member States and the capacity of the Commission, thanks to the common commercial policy's decision rules, to at least temporarily pursue a negotiating position not supported by all, or even a majority, of Member States.

Such episodes of conflict, while not infrequent, are not standard in EU trade policy. The prevailing norm in trade policy is for decisions to be taken by consensus. It is, however, a peculiar kind of consensus in which Member States do not object to others' trade policy preferences unless they have very strong reasons for doing so. EU trade-policy-making, therefore, is characterised by 'diffuse reciprocity' (Keohane, 1986: 21) or 'log rolling' (Ahnlid, 2005: 137; Kempton, 2001: 187; Winters, 2001: 21; Young, 2006). In trade negotiations, the emphasis on consensus can strengthen the hand of the Member States with more protectionist interests. For instance, several Member States, including Italy, opposed the EU-Korea Free Trade Agreement until they were reassured about the robustness of safeguard measures affecting car imports (Siles-Brügge, 2011). France and others secured the delayed liberalisation of sugar imports (among others) in the EU's landmark 2001 Everything But Arms initiative to assist the least developed countries (Carbone, 2007: 49; Faber and Orbie, 2009: 773). Diffuse reciprocity is also common with regard to foreign market access barriers, which means the weight of the EU is brought to bear on issues of particular concern to only one or two Member States (Young, 2006). There is thus significant scope for Member States to up-load their trade policy preferences.

Even closer integration

Trade policy has been highly supranational (Mode I) since the creation of the customs union in 1968. There have been episodes of intergovernmental cooperation in the past, but these have faded away as integration has progressed. A gradual and halting process of further integration occurred during the 1970s through the 1990s, but there has been a marked acceleration starting with the Treaty of Nice. As a consequence, the Member States primarily pursue individual trade policy objectives through a common policy, although there is dwindling scope for limited national policies (Mode IV).

Regulatory policy: varied modes of interaction[7]

By the beginning of the twenty-first century, the European Union had emerged as one of the two 'regulators of the world' (Sapir, 2007: 12) or 'great [regulatory] powers' (Drezner, 2007: 35–6). Although the EU adopts regulatory policies for internal reasons, they have three external dimensions. First, the EU's regulations affect whether foreign goods and service providers can enter the EU's market; they can be non-tariff barriers to trade. Second, in response to such adverse trade effects, foreign goods exporters may lobby successfully their home governments to align domestic rules with those of the EU, resulting in what David Vogel (1995) has termed 'trading up'. Third, the EU actively promotes its internal regulatory choices in international standards bodies or through bilateral regulatory cooperation; what might be termed 'regulatory diplomacy' (Chapter 7, this volume). The active and passive externalisation of the EU's regulatory choices is central to the characterisation of the EU as 'market power Europe' (Damro, 2012).

The single European market: internal focus, external impact

The single market programme, which was launched in the mid-1980s, sought to realise the objective of the free movement of goods, services, capital and people. It aimed to go beyond the customs union by addressing regulatory barriers to trade. The single market, therefore, focused on managing the differences among the Member States' rules.

Managing Member State differences

Regulatory barriers are challenging to deal with as they are not normally adopted for the purpose of affecting trade but in order to secure some other public policy objective, such as ensuring safety or protecting the environment. Regulatory barriers, therefore, cannot simply be removed. In some cases, rules might be similar in effect despite differences in their specifics. Products or service providers that comply with rules that are equivalent in effect can be accepted without compromising the underlying policy objective. In the EU context, this approach is manifest in the mutual recognition principle. In many instances, however, rules cannot be considered to be equivalent in effect. The EU has sought to address the adverse trade effects of such rules through harmonisation – the adoption of common, European rules.

In agreeing to common rules, the Member States that have more stringent rules have an advantage. The products (or service providers) of other states are excluded from their markets, while they have access to those Member States' markets. This gives them a strong incentive to hold out for rules close to their preferences and gives the others an incentive to compromise. Denmark, Germany, the Netherlands and Sweden have tended to be the 'leaders' among the Member States with respect to 'risk regulations', those addressing environmental pollution, public health and consumer safety. These Member States have tended to be supported in their efforts to adopt stringent European rules by the European Commission and the European Parliament. As a consequence, the EU has adopted some of the most stringent regulations in the world, most notably with respect to food safety, chemical safety, environmental protection, data privacy and financial services (Vogel, 2003; Young, 2007).

Regulatory power

The adoption of common European rules affects third-country firms' access to the EU's market. The EU's stringent regulations are now the most significant barriers to accessing the EU's market (ECORYS, 2009: xiii; Messerlin, 2001; USTR, 2010). The capacity to adopt, implement and enforce these stringent rules combined with the EU's large market have given the EU significant power in international regulation (Bach and Newman, 2007: 831).

The greater the importance of the EU's market relative to another country's domestic market and its other export markets, the more likely its firms are to adjust their practices to meet EU requirements (Keohane and Nye, 2001; Posner, 2009: 668; Vogel, 1995).[8] Having adjusted, they may seek to align domestic rules with EU rules in order to offset the costs of complying with competing foreign and domestic requirements and to gain an edge over domestically oriented competitors. If another country aligns its rule with the EU's rule, it is called 'trading up' (Vogel, 1995).

There are several prominent examples of EU rules propagating through 'trading up'. Several OECD countries, with the notable exception of the US, have adopted EU-style data privacy protection in order to avoid restrictions on data transfers from Europe to their countries (Newman, 2008: 2; with respect to Canada see Princen, 2004: 134). Several countries are reluctant to grow or even import genetically modified varieties that have not been approved in the EU for fear that exports of their entire crop to the EU would be blocked (Bernauer, 2003; Devereaux et al., 2006; Pollack and Shaffer, 2009). As the dynamics of trading up depend on the relative value of the EU's market to foreign exporters, it is more likely to occur in smaller markets. The Commission (2007: 4) concluded that the single market made Europe 'more influential in setting rules and standards worldwide'.

Regulatory diplomacy: varied participation and variable impact

Beginning with its 1996 market access strategy, the Commission has promoted actively EU regulatory approaches and solutions in international fora (Commission, 1996: 4). The EU seeks to export its regulatory solutions both multilaterally and bilaterally. These efforts are complicated somewhat by the varied nature of EU participation in different settings. The members of some of the critical international standards bodies – such as the International Standards Organization (ISO) and International Electrotechnical Commission (IEC) – are not governments, but national standard-setting bodies. Moreover, the European standard-setting bodies, which have wider membership than the EU, are not themselves members. European participation therefore rests on coordination among national standard-setting bodies. In some other standard-setting bodies – most notably the *Codex Alimentarius* Commission (CAC), which sets food safety standards – the EU is a member alongside its Member States.[9] In bilateral regulatory cooperation, the Commission leads on behalf of the EU as a whole. Thus, supranational policy-making and intergovernmental cooperation coexist in EU regulatory diplomacy alongside a private collective representation.

Strikingly, the EU is arguably most effective where its representation is most diffuse. The EU plays a particularly influential role in the ISO and IEC, with European standards often adopted as international standards (Büthe and Mattli, 2011: 186; Woolcock, 1991: 103). As discussed earlier, the EU's influence owes much to the importance of its market and its capacity to develop standards, which some authors attribute to the hierarchical structure of European standard-setting (Büthe and Mattli, 2011: 186). An additional source of influence is multiple European voices and votes supporting the same standard.

By contrast, the participation of all of the EU's Member State governments as well as the EU does not appear to have been as effective in the CAC. Although the EU has undoubtedly had successes, it has also lost on a number of high-profile decisions. In 1995, the EU was unable to block the adoption of maximum residue levels (MRLs) on five growth hormones in beef, which paved the way for successful complaints by the US and Canada before the World Trade Organization against the EU's ban on hormone-treated beef. In July 2012, it also failed to block the adoption of MRL's on another growth hormone, ractopamine. The EU has again indicated that it does not intend to change its policy (Council, 2012). These episodes illustrate that, despite the EU's significant power resources in multilateral regulatory diplomacy, its preferences do not always prevail. In addition, it is clear that, while the EU is eager to 'upload' its regulations to the international level, it balks at 'downloading' international standards that are not consistent with its policy objectives.

The EU is not alone in being reluctant to download regulatory solutions. Many of the world's largest markets, which are also the markets of greatest interest to the

EU's exporters, are too. Consequently, the EU has invested considerable and increasing effort in managing bilaterally the adverse trade effects of such regulatory differences. In these bilateral negotiations, the Commission represents the EU as a whole.

It is worth noting that, to date, bilateral regulatory cooperation has focused primarily on managing regulatory differences rather than overcoming them through the two parties adopting similar rules. For the most part, these efforts have entailed what is essentially specific negotiated mutual recognition, that is both sides will agree that specific rules that apply to specific products or services are equivalent in effect. This is the approach behind the veterinary equivalence agreements that the EU has concluded with a handful of countries, including the US. It also is the foundation of the mutual recognition of accounting standards with the US (Pollack and Shaffer, 2009: 99; Posner, 2009: 672). A particularly developed version of this type of agreement is the 2011 Civil Aviation Safety Agreement with the US. In these instances, the EU, while easing economic exchange, is not really exercising influence (Young, 2015a: 1236–9)

There have, however, been some instances in which the EU has gotten a partner to adjust its rules in such a way as to reduce the degree of difference. Many of these examples involve services, particularly financial services, and involve others, notably the US, changing in order to accommodate the EU, such as on the regulation of financial conglomerates and the implementation of Sarbanes-Oxley (Bach and Newman, 2007: 838–9; Posner, 2009: 673–4). There are, however, also many examples when there was no such accommodation, including the EU's ban on hormone-treated beef, moratorium on approvals of agricultural biotechnology and ban on the use of anti-microbial treatments to clean meat. Thus, transatlantic regulatory cooperation, which has been the most developed to date, has been most successful at managing differences when dealing with highly technical regulations where regulators have and are willing to exercise autonomy. More profound regulatory differences, which are often enshrined in legislation, have been more difficult to overcome.

Nonetheless, since the late 2000s, the Commission has intensified its efforts at bilateral regulatory cooperation, undertaking to 'negotiate trade agreements with a particular focus not only on market access, but also on regulatory convergence' (Commission, 2011: 22). The EU has subsequently concluded a number of these 'new generation' trade agreements, including with Canada, Singapore and South Korea. In 2013, it also launched such negotiations with Japan and the United States. The emphasis in these agreements, however, has been more on managing differences than securing alignment with EU rules (Young, 2015b: 1266–8). Regulatory cooperation, nonetheless, has taken a central place in the EU's bilateral trade negotiations.

The projection of European rules through any means available?

The single European market programme laid the foundations for the EU's emergence as a regulatory power at the beginning of the twenty-first century. It has led to the regulatory capacity and outputs that, coupled with the attractiveness of the EU's market, has made the EU a regulatory reference point. The agreement of common rules internally has facilitated the EU's representation externally whether it is by national standard-setting bodies, by Member State governments collectively or by the Commission. While there are sometimes profound differences among the Member States over regulatory policy, once a common policy is agreed on, those differences largely fade into the background. The resulting coherence of purpose and negotiating leverage, however, do not always translate into outcomes favourable to the EU, particularly when the other pivotal player is the US.

Competition policy: the dominance of supranational policy-making

Like regulatory policy, competition policy is not primarily an external policy. But it is different from many traditional regulatory policies in that it applies to all sectors in the single European market and is characterised by exclusive competence. Competition policy also increasingly exhibits an external dimension because the EU is called upon to review the business activity of foreign firms operating in the single market. EU decisions on such business activity – typically including cartels, monopolies and mergers – can have important external commercial and political repercussions.[10] The EU is therefore increasingly pursuing competition disciplines in bilateral and multilateral relations as an important component of its foreign economic policy.

Competition policy integration and the single European market

While EU competition law has only been formally recognised as an exclusive competence since the Lisbon Treaty, it developed over time into a supranational policy area in which the delegation of explicit executive competences equalled those found in trade policy (Pollack, 2003: 93). Cini and McGowan go further, arguing that 'in contrast to all other EU policy areas, competition policy is unique, for both the Council of Ministers and the European Parliament find themselves on the sidelines' (1999: 177). This uniqueness is not surprising when competition policy is understood as a fundamental tool for achieving an integrated regional market.

The Treaty of Rome gave the newly created Commission considerable authority for implementing the competition Articles 101 and 102. Since then, this policy area has exhibited consistent Europeanisation, with subsequent treaty articles, court decisions and regulations bolstering integration through the 1960s and 1970s. For example, Regulation 17 (1962) established the institutional structure for EU competition policy and 'created a competition law system in which the enforcement and policy-making prerogatives were centred in the Commission and the role of national legal systems was marginalized' (Gerber, 1998: 349). Within this system, the Competition Directorate General developed into a formidable competition agency whose decision-making authority was insulated from political interference by the Member States (Gerber, 1998: 351).

While the historical trend reveals a Commission-driven process of integration in competition policy, further significant Europeanisation took place in the context of the single market programme. This was particularly the case with merger review, which was seen as fundamental to market-making. The Merger Control Regulation of 1990 (revised 2004, 2009) firmly established merger review at the EU level and positioned the Commission as a 'one-stop shop' for firms seeking approval of mergers that met certain turnover thresholds. Given the level of these thresholds and an agreed referral system, most mergers that included foreign firms would be sizeable enough to require approval by the Commission. The 1997 Boeing-McDonnell Douglas and 2001 GE-Honeywell cases are oft-cited examples of the international tensions that can arise when the Commission opposes a merger between foreign firms that has been approved in a foreign jurisdiction (Boeder, 2000; Morgan and McGuire, 2004).

As international cross-border business activity has increased in the global economy, so too has the integration of competition policy gradually acquired an external dimension. Regardless of where a firm is headquartered, if it is active in the single European market, its business activity is subject to EU competition rules. Given its central role in the development and application of competition policy, these changes have ensured that the Commission's use of competition policy has become an important component of the EU's foreign economic policy.

Member State involvement within an increasingly integrated policy

While the Commission has played the central role in competition policy at the EU level, this is not to say that the Member States have been completely absent from this policy area. The Member States do have national competition rules, the development of which has varied in accordance with their own national experiences and preferences. At the time of the Treaty of Rome, Member States had 'a patchwork of different competition laws, some (e.g. Belgium) with none at all' (Damro, 2006: 34). But over time, EU Member States 'have enacted competition laws or modified existing laws in order to bring them closer to Community law' (Gerber, 1998: 428). As the Member States have adjusted their national competition laws, the Commission 'often enjoyed political support for its competition law initiatives because they have been perceived as necessary to break down economic barriers among states' in the pursuit of market integration (Gerber, 1998/2010: xiii).

The 2004 modernisation package enhanced the role of Member States in EU competition policy and provides some potential for increasing intergovernmental cooperation (Mode II). Among other measures, these reforms 'established the idea that Member States would be primarily responsible for the application of competition law and that the Commission would only take enforcement action under limited circumstances' (Gerber, 2010: 190). However, while elements of these reforms may have decentralised authority, the overall package has been seen as a successful effort by the Commission to reduce its workload and maintain its control over the development of competition policy (Riley, 2003; Wilks, 2005). According to Gerber (2010: 191), 'the Commission controlled the process. It drove the proposals forward, managing the meetings and controlling the agenda, and in the end it created a system in which it could more effectively control the development of competition law in Europe'.[11]

The reform package also established the European Competition Network (ECN), in which relations among Member State competition authorities would be conducted with the Commission as 'the dominant voice and the control organ' (Gerber, 2010: 190). The ECN is primarily designed to pool experience and identify best practices for the development and implementation of EU competition policy. While the ECN may appear to resemble a trend toward intergovernmental cooperation, it is a fairly informal network that is not intergovernmental in the traditional sense. In addition, the ECN still allows for 'control' by the Commission and requires the Member States to apply EU competition law.[12]

Given the central role of the Commission in the development of competition policy, there is scant evidence of nationalisation occurring in this policy area. First, interactions that would resemble traditional diplomacy among Member States do not tend to occur outside the EU's institutional structure. The national competition authorities that comprise the ECN carry out their functions 'inside' the EU as they apply EU competition rules. Also, because of the Commission's prominent role and 'control' of the network, there is little opportunity for individual national preferences to influence competition policy.

Second, traditional diplomacy with non-Member States also involves an active role for the Commission. The opportunities are therefore limited for the Member States to engage without the EU in external competition policy relations (Mode IV). For example, the Commission and EU Member States' national competition authorities are full members of the International Competition Network (ICN). Under this arrangement, the diplomacy that takes place in this international venue is still characterised by the full coordination of EU competition rules among the Commission and Member States. In the Organisation for Economic Co-operation and Development (OECD), a similar but slightly different arrangement exists. Since its origins, OECD members have agreed that the Commission should take part in the work of the organisation. While the Commission does not have the right to vote on decisions or recommendations dealing with competition issues, its participation goes beyond that of an observer: Commission 'representatives work alongside Members in the preparation of texts and participate in discussions on the OECD's work programme and strategies, and are involved in the work of the entire Organisation and its different bodies'.[13]

In the WTO's Doha Round, the EU initially pushed for including competition policy on the negotiating agenda as one of the Singapore Issues. This linkage to trade policy would have created potential opportunities for engaging independently with third parties within the WTO only if the Member States were able to negotiate the topic without EU involvement. Beyond this unlikely set of circumstances, following the 2003 Cancun Ministerial, the WTO's General Council decided that no work toward negotiations on competition policy would take place during the Doha Round.[14] As a result, the Commission remains intimately involved in all competition negotiations that take place in international venues.

The persistence of supranational policy-making

Due to its essential role in creating the EU's integrated market, competition policy has witnessed a long and sustained trend of Europeanisation via supranational policy-making (Mode I). While Member States have maintained their own national competition laws, these have been increasingly adjusted to conform with EU competition law. The 2004 modernisation package sustained the Commission's central role in the development and application of competition policy to EU and foreign firm activity in the single European market. The central role of the Commission in cases with external dimensions is therefore generally assured. Beyond the actual implementation of competition rules, the exclusive competence and extent of supranationalisation that has occurred in this policy area ensure that the Commission is also present in international venues that address the development of competition policy. Member States are full members of the ICN and OECD, but they are constrained in their international interactions by the need to apply EU competition law and negotiate alongside the Commission.

Conclusions

Trade, regulatory and competition policies are all highly supranational. All three policy areas began as core activities of the European project, and all three have experienced subsequent Europeanisation. Trade and competition policies, in particular, are among the EU's most closely integrated policies. Nonetheless, the scope for Member State action has not been entirely excluded.

There are, however, notable differences among the three policies in terms of the process of Europeanisation. In trade policy, integration took place through a combination of successive ECJ judgments and iterated treaty reform beginning with Nice. In competition policy, it occurred primarily through secondary legislation and court decisions, with the Lisbon Treaty, the first treaty change since Rome, confirming exclusive competence. In regulatory policy, the big integrative step was the single European market programme. Subsequent Europeanisation has been the product the incremental accumulation of new common rules.

Thus Europeanisation has taken different forms and occurred at different paces in the three policy areas.

There are also significant differences in the scope for individual Member State action. Competition policy decisions involving third-country firms are taken almost invariably by the Commission. The Treaty of Lisbon means that the Member States no longer have any meaningful independent authority in trade policy. They do, however, have a prominent collective role in monitoring negotiations and ratifying agreements. Member States can, subject to procedural disciplines, adopt national regulatory policies and participate individually in multilateral regulatory fora. Despite protracted close integration, the Member States maintain very different preferences in trade and regulatory policies. Attempts by Member States to up-load these preferences within and beyond the EU are contested. Formal and informal institutions enable the EU (sometimes) to overcome these differences.

We draw two critical lessons for the EU's foreign policy. First, intense and prolonged integration does not necessarily lead to the approximation of substantive policy preferences. Second, unity of purpose and acknowledged power resources do not always (in fact frequently do not) translate into desired outcomes. Europeanisation, therefore, is not a panacea for EU effectiveness in foreign economic policy or foreign policy more generally.

Notes

1 Although these common policies historically were associated with the European Economic Community and, subsequently, the European Community prior to the European Union, the EU is now the legally correct name. In order to avoid confusion, we follow convention and refer to the EU throughout.
2 Council Decision 2012/35/CFSP of 23 January 2012.
3 Council Regulation (EU) No 56/2012 of 23 January 2012.
4 "EU Sanctions against Russia over Ukraine crisis," Available at: http://europa.eu/newsroom/highlights/special-coverage/eu_sanctions/index_en.htm. Accessed 8 October 2015. Council Regulation 960/2014, 8 September 2014.
5 Directorate General for Trade, "Countries and Regions: Ukraine," Available at: http://ec.europa.eu/trade/policy/countries-and-regions/countries/ukraine/. Accessed 29 June 2015. In order to guarantee Ukraine's access to Russia's market under the Ukraine–Russia bilateral preferential regime and in conjunction with the Minsk Agreement, the EU in September 2014 postponed implementing the DCFTA until January 2016 while talks were conducted with Russia to address its concerns about the implementation of the DCFTA (Directorate General for Trade, "Outcome of the Trilateral Consultations on the Implementation of the EU-Ukraine AA/DCFTA Joint Operational Conclusions," 18 May 2015. Available at: http://trade.ec.europa.eu/doclib/press/index.cfm?id=1313. Accessed 29 June 2015.
6 In 2011, as part of its new emphasis on enforcement the Commission has sought to improve coordination among the Member States and with the Commission in addressing trade barriers (Commission, 2011: 10).
7 This section draws on Young and Peterson (2014).
8 Mitchener (2002) provides accounts from foreign firm that have had to change their practices in order to continue to do business in the EU.
9 The EU became a member of Codex in 2003.
10 For more on these different areas of competition policy, see Cini and McGowan (2009). On cartels, see McGowan (2010). EU competition policy also covers Member State activity in the form of state aid. For more on the external dimensions of state aid, see Damro (2013).
11 For an alternative interpretation of the modernisation package, see Kassim and Wright (2007).
12 Likewise, Joint Statement on ECN (http://ec.europa.eu/competition/ecn/joint_statement_en.pdf) clarifies central role of Commission:

> The Commission will be particularly well placed to deal with a case if more than three Member States are substantially affected by an agreement or practice, if it is closely linked to other

Community provisions which may be exclusively or more effectively applied by the Commission, if Community interest requires the adoption of a Commission decision to develop Community competition policy particularly when a new competition issue arises or to ensure effective enforcement.

(3–4)

13   OECD, Available at: http://www.oecd.org/document/25/0,3746,en_36734052_36761800_36999961_ 1_1_1_1,00.html. Accessed 29 May 2012.
14   World Trade Organization, "Doha Work Programme," Decision Adopted by the General Council on 1 August 2004, WT/L/579, Available at: http://www.wto.org/english/tratop_e/dda_e/draft_ text_gc_dg_31july04_e.htm#invest_comp_gpa. Accessed 29 May 2012.

Bibliography

Ahnlid, A. (2005) 'Setting the Global Trade Agenda: The European Union and the Launch of the Doha Round', in O. Elgström and C. Jönsson (eds.) *European Union Negotiations: Processes, Networks and Institutions*. Abingdon: Routledge, 130–47.
Bach, D. and Newman, A. L. (2007) 'The European Regulatory State and Global Public Policy: Micro-Institutions, Macro-Influence', *Journal of European Public Policy*, Vol. 14, No. 6, 827–46.
Baldwin, M. (2006) 'EU Trade Politics – Heaven or Hell?', *Journal of European Public Policy*, Vol. 13, No. 6, 926–42.
Bernauer, T. (2003) *Genes, Trade, and Regulation: The Seeds of Conflict in Food Biotechnology*. Princeton, NJ: Princeton University Press.
Boeder, T. L. (2000) 'The Boeing-McDonnell Douglas Merger', in S. J. Evenett, A. Lehmann and B. Steil (eds.) *Antitrust Goes Global: What Future for Transatlantic Cooperation?* Washington, DC: Brookings Institution Press, 139–44.
Büthe, T. and Mattli, W. (2011) *The New Global Rulers: The Privatization of Regulation in the World Economy*. Princeton: Princeton University Press.
Carbone, M. (2007) 'EBA, EU Trade Policy and the ACP: A Tale of Two North-South Divides', in G. Faber and J. Orbie (eds.) *European Union Trade Politics and Development: 'Everything but Arms' Unravelled*. Abingdon: Routledge, 43–59.
Cini, M. and McGowan, L. (1999) *Competition Policy in the European Union*. Basingstoke: Palgrave Macmillan.
Cini, M. and McGowan, L. (2009) *Competition Policy in the European Union*, 2nd edition. Basingstoke: Palgrave Macmillan.
Commission (1996) 'The Global Challenge of International Trade: A Market Access Strategy for the European Union', COM(96) 53, 14 February.
Commission (1997) *External Access to European Markets*, The Single Market Review, Subseries IV, Volume 4, Kogan Page.
Commission (2007) 'The European Interest: Succeeding in the Age of Globalisation Contribution of the Commission to the October Meeting of Heads of State and Government', COM (2007) 581, 3 October.
Commission (2010) 'Towards a Comprehensive European International Investment Policy', COM (2010) 343, final, 7 July.
Commission (2011) 'Single Market Act: Twelve Levers to Boost Growth and Strengthen Confidence: "Working Together to Create New Growth"', COM (2011) 206, 13 April.
Council (2005) 'Extraordinary Meeting of the General Affairs and External Relations Council', Luxembourg, 18 October, 13378/05 (Presse 267).
Council (2012) 'Follow Up to the Adoption of a Standard Setting Maximum Residue Levels (MRLs) on Ractopamine by the Codex Alimentarius Commission at Its 35th Session', 3193rd Agriculture and Fisheries Council Meeting, 22 and 23 October.
Damro, C. (2006) *Cooperating on Competition in Transatlantic Economic Relations*. Basingstoke: Palgrave.

Damro, C. (2012) 'Market Power Europe', *Journal of European Public Policy*, Vol. 19, No. 5, 682–99.

Damro, C. (2013) 'EU State Aid Policy and the Politics of External Trade Relations', *Journal of Industry, Competition and Trade*, Vol. 13, No. 1, 159–170.

Devereaux, C., Lawrence, R. Z. and Watkins, M. D. (2006) *Case Studies in US Trade Negotiation: Vol. 2: Resolving Disputes*. Washington, DC: Institute for International Economics.

Drezner, D. W. (2007) *All Politics Is Global: Explaining International Regulatory Regimes*. Princeton: Princeton University Press.

ECORYS (2009) 'Non-Tariff Measures in EU-US Trade and Investment – An Economic Analysis', *Official Journal of the European Union*, 2007/S 180–219493. Available at http://trade.ec.europa.eu/doclib/docs/2009/december/tradoc_145613.pdf (accessed 5 October 2011).

EurActiv (2005) 'Mandelson Free to Talk Farm Cuts in Hong Kong', EurActiv, Oct 19, 2005. Available at http://www.euractiv.com/section/trade-society/news/mandelson-free-to-talk-farm-cuts-in-hong-kong/ (accessed 27 August 2016).

Faber, G. and Orbie, J. (2009) 'Everything but Arms: Much More than Appears at First Sight', *Journal of Common Market Studies*, Vol. 47, No. 4, 767–87.

Gerber, D. J. (1998) *Law and Competition in Twentieth Century Europe*. Oxford: Oxford University Press.

Gerber, D. J. (2010) *Global Competition: Law, Markets and Globalization*. Oxford: Oxford University Press.

Hanson, B. T. (1998) 'What Happened to Fortress Europe? External Trade Policy Liberalization in the European Union', *International Organization*, Vol. 52, No. 1, 55–85.

Johnson, M. (1998) *European Community Trade Policy and the Article 113 Committee*. London: Royal Institute of International Affairs.

Kassim, H. and Wright, K. (2007) 'Revisiting Modernisation: The European Commission, Policy Change and the Reform of EC Competition Policy', Centre for Competition Policy, Working Paper 07–19, Norwich: University of East Anglia. Available at http://papers.ssrn.com/sol3/papers.cfm?abstract_id=1022283

Kempton, J. (2001) 'Decisions to Defend: Delegation, Rules and Discretion in European Community Anti-Dumping Policy', DPhil Thesis, University of Sussex.

Keohane, R. O. (1986) 'Reciprocity in International Relations', *International Organization*, Vol. 40, No. 1, 1–27.

Keohane, R. O. and Nye, J. S. (2001) *Power and Interdependence*, 3rd edition. New York, NY: Longman.

Lindberg, L. N. and Scheingold, S. A. (1970) *Europe's Would-Be Polity: Patterns of Change in the European Communities*. Englewood Cliffs, NJ: Prentice-Hall.

McGowan, L. (2010) *The Antitrust Revolution in Europe: Exploring the European Commission's Cartel Policy*. Cheltenham, UK: Edward Elgar.

Messerlin, P. A. (2001) *Measuring the Costs of Protection in Europe: European Commercial Policy in the 2000s*. Washington, DC: Institute for International Economics.

Mitchener, B. (2002) 'Increasingly, rules of global economy are set in Brussels', *The Wall Street Journal*, 23 April. Available at: https://www.wsj.com/articles/SB1019521240262845360 (accessed 13 February 2017).

Moravcsik, A. (1998) *The Choice for Europe: Social Purpose and State Power from Massina to Maastricht*. London: UCL Press.

Morgan, E. J. and McGuire, S. (2004) 'Transatlantic Divergence: GE-Honeywell and the EU's Merger Policy', *Journal of European Public Policy*, Vol. 11, No. 1, 39–56.

Newman, A. L. (2008) *Protectors of Privacy: Regulating Personal Data in the Global Economy*. Ithaca, NY: Cornell University Press.

Parker, G. *et al.* (2005) 'Chirac Fires Warning Shot on Trade Deal in Defense of Farm Subsidies', *Financial Times*, 28 October 28, 4.

Pollack, M. A. (2003) *The Engines of European Integration: Delegation, Agency, and Agenda Setting in the EU*. Oxford, NY: Oxford University Press.

Pollack, M. A. and Shaffer, G. (2009) *When Cooperation Fails: The International Law and Politics of Genetically Modified Foods*. Oxford: Oxford University Press.

Posner, E. (2009) 'Making Rules for Global Finance: Transatlantic Regulatory Cooperation at the Turn of the Millennium', *International Organization*, Vol. 63, No. 4, 665–99.

Princen, S. B. M. (2004) 'EC Compliance with WTO Law: The Interplay of Law and Politics', *European Journal of International Law*, Vol. 15, No. 3, 555–74.

Riley, A. (2003) 'EC Antitrust Modernisation: The Commission Does Very Nicely – Thank You! Part Two: Between the Idea and the Reality: Decentralisation under Regulation 1', *European Competition Law Review*, Vol. 11, 604–15.

Sapir, A. (2007) 'Europe and the Global Economy', in A. Sapir (ed.) *Fragmented Power: Europe and the Global Economy*, Brussels: Bruegel, 1–20.

Siles-Brügge, G. (2011) 'Resisting Protectionism after the Crisis: Strategic Economic Discourse and the EU – Korea Free Trade Agreement', *New Political Economy*, Vol. 16, No. 5, 627–53.

USTR (2010) *2010 National Trade Estimate Report on Foreign Trade Barriers*. Washington, DC: United States Trade Representative.

Vogel, D. (1995) *Trading Up: Consumer and Environmental Regulation in a Global Economy*. Boston: Harvard University Press.

Vogel, D. (2003) 'The Hare and the Tortoise Revisited: The New Politics of Consumer and Environmental Regulation in Europe', *British Journal of Political Science*, Vol. 33, 557–80.

Wilks, S. (2005) 'Agency Escape: Decentralisation or Domination of the European Commission in the Modernization of Competition Policy?', *Governance*, Vol. 18, No. 3, 431–52.

Winters, L. A. (2001). 'European Union Trade Policy: Actually or Just Nominally Liberal?' In: H. Wallace (ed.), *Interlocking Dimensions of European Integration*. New York: Palgrave, 25–44.

Woolcock, S. (1991) *Market Access Issues in EC-US Relations: Trading Partners or Trading Blows?* London: Pinter/Royal Institute of International Affairs.

Woolcock, S. (2005) 'Trade Policy: From Uruguay to Doha and Beyond', in H. Wallace and W. Wallace (eds.) *Policy-Making in the European Union*, 5th edition, Oxford: Oxford University Press, 377–99.

Woolcock, S. (2010) 'Trade Policy: A Further Shift Towards Brussels', in H. Wallace, M. A. Pollack and A. R. Young (eds.) *Policy-Making in the European Union*, 6th edition, Oxford: Oxford University Press, 381–99.

WTO (2011) 'Trade Policy Review: European Union: Report by the Secretariat', WT/TPR/S/248, 1 June.

Young, A. R. (2002) *Extending European Cooperation: The European Union and the 'New' International Trade Agenda*. Manchester: Manchester University Press.

Young, A. R. (2006) 'Punching Its Weight? The European Union's Use of WTO Dispute Resolution', in O. Elgström and M. Smith (eds.) *The European Union's Roles in International Politics: Concepts and Analysis*, Abingdon: Routledge, 189–207.

Young, A. R. (2007) 'The Politics of Regulation and the Internal Market', in K. E. Jørgensen, M. A. Pollack and B. Rosamond (eds.) *Handbook of European Union Politics*, London: Sage, 373–94.

Young, A. R. (2015a) 'Europe's Influence on Foreign Rules: Conditions, Context and Comparison', *Journal of European Public Policy*, Vol. 22, No. 9, 1233–52.

Young, A. R. (2015b) 'Liberalizing Trade, Not Exporting Rules: The Limits to Regulatory Coordination in the EU's "New Generation" Preferential Trade', *Journal of European Public Policy*, Vol. 22, No. 9, 1253–75.

Young, A. R. and Peterson, J. (2014) *Parochial Global Europe: 21st Century Trade Politics*. Oxford: Oxford University Press.

15 The EU in the world

From multilateralism to global governance

Robert Kissack

Introduction

The international system of 2016 is different from how it was twenty-five years ago when the Maastricht Treaty was negotiated, creating the tension between national foreign policies and a common European foreign policy upon which this book focuses. The year 1991 was the beginning of a decade of liberal internationalism, manifested in the globalisation of world economy, the creation of the World Trade Organization (WTO) – the only alteration to the architecture of the multilateral system designed after World War II (cf. Ikenberry, 2001) and the networking of transnational governance between states (Slaughter, 2004). It was also the decade of genocide in Rwanda and ethnic cleansing in the Balkans, shocking events that challenged the norm of non-intervention in the domestic affairs of states and led to the 1999 bombing of Kosovo in the name of humanitarian intervention. Europeans and Americans appeared to be re-writing the rules of Westphalian sovereignty, and the *sui generis* nature of the European Union and its foreign policy based on shaping international norms played a central role (Manners, 2002). For many Americans, this era ended on 11 September 2001; for the rest of the world, it ended on 15 September 2008, the day Lehman Brothers bank collapsed, and the US sub-prime mortgage crisis and subsequent recession spread globally. While the eurozone was mired in crisis, emerging economies led by China, India and Brazil remained virtually unscathed by the great recession and demanded political influence in multilateral institutions commensurate to their growing economic stature. Commentators see an international system undergoing 'partial repolarisation' (Crocker, 2015: 9), leading to a 'world adrift' characterised by the 'unregulated diffusion of authority, agency and responsibility' (Crocker, 2015: 15), caused by the 'rise of the rest' (Zakaria, 2008) and creating a post-hegemonic 'no one's world' (Kupchan, 2012).

This chapter focuses on the 'frozen configurations of privilege and bias' (Barnett and Duvall, 2005: 52) found in the International Monetary Fund (IMF), United Nations Security Council (UNSC) and the (reformed since 2005) UN Committee on Human Rights (CHR) that are increasingly called into question. EU Member States (particularly Western Europeans) are the primary beneficiaries of these frozen privileges as a legacy of their close cooperation with the US after World War II and their significance in the global economy during the Cold War. These are paradigmatic cases for this book because they represent the most significant and conspicuous platforms for EU Member States' national foreign policies, while simultaneously being core components of EU foreign policy goals and constitutive elements of the EU's international identity, namely (i) upholding international peace and security (which both the UNSC *and* IMF were originally tasked with, cf. Kennedy, 2006); (ii) the universal promotion of human rights; and (iii) contributing to effective multilateralism (European Council, 2003).

Large and small EU Member States use international organisations to pursue national foreign policy goals, working within (Modes II and III) and without (Mode IV) of European coordination structures. Yet in order to enhance the voice and influence of the EU, the answer is thought to lie in more Mode I and II actions. These cases demonstrate the tension between national ambitions for prominence on the international stage as sovereign states and aspirations for greater EU actorness through Europeanised foreign policy. The selection of cases represents variation in the degree of adjustment to partial repolarisation. In terms of human rights promotion, the numerical advantage of European states in the CHR was addressed in the sixtieth anniversary UN reforms in 2005 through the creation of the Human Rights Council and increased representation of African and Asia UN members. Changes to the voting shares and Executive Board composition to favour emerging economies and diminish European power were agreed by IMF members in December 2010 and were formally adopted in December 2015 after the US Senate passed legislation securing the necessary number of national parliament ratifications. Reform of the UNSC remains on the political agenda, albeit far off.

This chapter presents overviews of each case in turn, summarising context, Member State groups, policy changes and policy performance. It concludes that foreign policy Europeanisation is not achievable against the interests of the largest EU states in the organisations regarded as most salient for national projection – the UNSC and the IMF. When reforms have been made, the visible costs to Europeans have been compensated by benefits that are harder to discern, yet nonetheless significant. It argues that Mode IV action is an effective foreign policy instrument in a multilateral system increasingly comprised of important non-European players.

The Commission on Human Rights and the United Nations General Assembly

Context

EU Member States have been committed to the protection of human rights (HR) within and without their borders for decades. The Council of Europe's *Convention for the Protection of Human Rights and Fundamental Freedoms* was ratified by many West European countries during the 1950s and by Central and Eastern European countries in the 1990s, demonstrating the importance of HR in their national policies. For EU external relations, the importance of promoting human rights through frameworks of cooperation with third states has been of concern since the late 1970s. The two stand-out issues were Uganda's receipt of Lome I funds despite Idi Amin's regime of domestic brutality and the accession of recently democratised Greece (1981), Spain and Portugal (1986) to the EEC (Clapham, 1999: 632; Riedel and Will, 1999: 723). The first clause permitting the termination of assistance programmes for cases of HR violations was inserted into the 1989 Lome IV agreement with African, Caribbean and Pacific (ACP) states, and similar clauses now appear in all EU cooperation agreements. After the end of the Cold War, the prospect of EU membership for former communist states became a reality, and the June 1993 Copenhagen European Council agreed that respect for HR was essential for EU accession. Simultaneously in Vienna, the UN World Conference on Human Rights was taking place, aimed at reasserting human rights protection through the UN system freed of superpower stalemate. It was therefore an opportune moment for the EU to make promoting HR a constitutive value in its international identity and continues to this day: '[P]rotection and promotion of human rights is a silver thread running through all EU action both at home and abroad' (European Commission, 2011: 4).

Table 15.1 Distribution of seats by region, UNCHR and HRC

	Western European and Others Group (WEOG)	Eastern Europe	Latin America	Asia	Africa
UNCHR	10	5	11	12	15
HRC	7	6	8	13	13

Promoting HR in the UN system was a logical step for EU Member States. In the mid-1990s, there were three main UN bodies tasked with HR promotion: the Security Council (UNSC), the General Assembly (UNGA) and the Commission on Human Rights (UNCHR), a subsidiary body of the Economic and Social Council. The UNSC was reserved for the most serious violations and required the agreement of the veto-holding permanent members. The UNGA was dominated by states from the Non-Aligned Movement (NAM) and enthusiastically protected sovereignty over HR. In the UNCHR, EU Member States found it relatively easy to gain a majority of votes in support of resolutions thanks to UN membership expanding more quickly than revisions to the distribution of seats. There was a frozen bias in favour of representing the original members of the UN system at the expense of newly independent states in Africa and Asia. As will be elaborated later in this chapter, the reformed Human Rights Council 'unfroze' this bias, making it much harder for EU states to pass resolutions. Table 15.1 presents the two distributions of seats.

Since the purpose of Part II is to look at state actions, the abolition of the death penalty is used to illustrate the evolution of EU actions once numerical advantages were removed.

Policy change

In 1994, the Italian government presented a resolution to the Third Committee of the UN General Assembly calling for the abolition of the death penalty. Although it attracted forty-nine co-sponsoring states, the resolution failed to gain a majority, and some EU Member States regarded it as too premature an effort (neither the UK nor the Netherlands supported it). In 1997, the Italian government succeeded in passing a resolution on the same issue in the UN Commission on Human Rights (UNCHR), in large part due to WEOG, Eastern Europe and Latin American states occupying twenty-six of the fifty-three seats. In 1998, Italy steered another resolution through the Committee, and in 1999 the Finnish Presidency presented another in the name of EU Member States (Bantekas and Hodgkinson, 2000: 23; Smith, 2006: 160). EU resolutions on other issues were passed in subsequent years, with only women's reproductive rights and gay rights being beyond the scope of cooperation. Mode II action superseded Mode III action, in both cases coupled with wider Mode IV outreach.

In 2005, at the sixtieth session of the UN General Assembly, the decision was taken to replace the UNCHR with the Human Rights Council. A number of steps were taken to depoliticise the promotion of HR, including allocating more seats to Asian and African countries to more accurately reflect UN membership. EU Member States continued with Mode II actions, but despite higher levels of voting cohesion than were achieved in the UNCHR, they repeatedly found themselves in the minority because of the rebalancing of region constituencies (Gowan and Brantner, 2008; Kissack, 2010; Smith, 2010; Garský and Spolander, 2012; Macaj, 2012). Faced with difficulties in the HRC, EU Member States made a surprising strategic decision. Beginning in 2006, the EU campaigned for a moratorium on the use of the death penalty in the UNGA, a venue typically seen as the bastion of the Global South and the very antithesis of frozen privilege (Kissack, 2010, 2012). It was an unlikely place to promote such a divisive issue as ending the use of the death penalty. Nevertheless, Finland read a statement with eighty-seven co-signatory states to the General Assembly in support of such a step. It was the start of a campaign that continues to the present day, slowly but surely heading toward a tipping-point where the norm of restricting the use of the death penalty will be widely accepted (Finnemore and Sikkink, 1998).

Policy performance

In 2007, the Portuguese EU Presidency coordinated the drafting of a resolution on the death penalty to be presented to the General Assembly's Third Committee (Social, Humanitarian and Cultural Affairs). If passed there, it would be taken to the General Assembly. Italy had attempted the same thing in 1994, but failed to gain even the support of all twelve EU Member States, let alone the majority of UN members. The death penalty is a permitted punishment under international law and traditionally seen as a matter of domestic legal practice to be discussed in the General Assembly's Sixth Committee (Legal). Presenting the issue in the Third Committee framed the death penalty as a human rights issue and removed it from the sphere non-intervention in the domestic affairs of a sovereign state into a legitimate issue for UN-level scrutiny under the Charter. As the Ambassador of Singapore said during a Third Committee plenary session discussing the matter in 2008, the 'basic issue in question before us today is not capital punishment per se. That is not at all what this resolution is about. . . . It is about whether a country has the right to decide on this matter for itself' (UN, 2008). A resolution calling for a moratorium on the use of the death penalty and for the UN Secretary General to report on the use of the death penalty worldwide (A/RES/62/149) was passed in 2007. In 2008, a shorter resolution acknowledging the report presented by the Secretary General and calling for the issue to be revisited in two years was also passed. Since then, in 2010, 2012 and 2014, gradually more ambitious resolutions have been passed by greater margins, as shown in Table 15.2.

The EU should be acknowledged as a driving force behind the successful campaign to pass the resolutions, but it cannot take all the credit. There are a number of important factors to consider. First, the change in focus from abolition to moratorium nearly broke EU consensus on the resolution before it began. Hawkish HR states, led by Sweden, Finland and the Netherlands, were reluctant to dilute the ambition of the resolution from the 2006 statement. While they were around twenty states short of support, they preferred to wait than concede too early, while Italy advocated a result (in keeping with its long-term commitment to the issue). The issue was resolved *outside* of the EU27, as Portugal liaised with the nine states co-authoring the resolution, demanding collective control over drafting the resolution without the EU dictating from afar. Portugal used this to gain a high degree of agent autonomy

Table 15.2 Voting results in the UNGA for resolutions on a moratorium on the use of the death penalty

	2007	2008	2010	2012	2014
For	104	106	109	111	117
Against	54	46	41	41	37
Abstention	29	34	35	34	34

from its twenty-six Member States principals, playing a two-level game (Putnam, 1988) to force the EU into accepting text agreed by the ten co-authors using 'tied-hands' arguments.

This leads to the second point. The resolution was co-authored by ten states from the five regions of the UN system (Portugal, Albania, Angola, Brazil, Croatia, Gabon, Mexico, New Zealand, Philippines and Timor-Leste), making it genuinely trans-regional instead of explicitly European. The composition of states was influenced by the EU Presidency, which utilised relations with Lusophone states to identify co-authors. Other EU Member States were assigned third countries to lobby support for the resolution, tapping into linguistic and historical extra-European networks of influence. The passing of the resolution was a major foreign policy achievement for the EU, somewhat ironically given that the co-authors convinced the EU Member States that a *lower* EU profile was desirable, so as to discredit opposition grounded in claims of neo-imperialism. The 2008 French EU Presidency oversaw the coordination of co-authors for the following year's resolution, and in recent years (2012 and 2014) the responsibility of coordinating follow-up resolutions has been taken up by Chile.

This case shows how Mode III action between EU states in the UNCHR developed into Mode II action as the rotating Presidency assumed responsibility for coordination and representation of HR-promoting statements, coupled in both cases with Mode IV action to non-Europeans. However, when the WEOG, Eastern Europe and Latin American states required more than just a couple of Asian or African states to achieve a majority, as in the reconfigured HRC, the EU found it difficult to promote common positions despite increased coherence under Mode II. The EU took up the case of the death penalty by promoting a moratorium on its use in the UNGA, confronting head-on a more adversarial venue. The passing of the 2007 resolution can be attributed to increased Mode IV action, including a feedback loop into the Mode II EU common position negotiations to placate the doubts of hawkish states reluctant to do deals at any cost. Loosening frozen privileges was overcome by more communication with other states and accommodating the wider consensus of UN members within the EU common position.

The International Monetary Fund

Context

The purpose of the IMF was to maintain international financial order in the years after World War II, by helping 'maintain pegged but adjustable exchange rates, primarily between the industrialised countries of Western Europe and the United States' (Vreeland, 2007: 5). To do this, it performed 'two main tasks: (1) to monitor members' economies – especially their exchange rates and balance of payments, and (2) to act as an international lender' (Vreeland, 2007: 9). The funds available for lending are raised through members' deposits ('quota'), 'calculated on the basis of a set of formulae combining the ability to contribute, that is, national product, and the need for Fund resources, calculated on the basis of countries' vulnerability to external shocks linked, in particular, to openness to international trade' (Bini Smaghi, 2009: 64). Voting rights are allocated proportionally to quotas, meaning that the largest economies in the world are also the most powerful members of the IMF. Historically, since the creation of the IMF, Western European states have been among the richest in the world and seventy years after its creation still control around 30 per cent of votes.

The IMF has a twenty-four-member Executive Board, and each member – or Executive Director (ED) – represents a single state or group of states. Prior to the December 2015 adoption of the 14th General Review (IMF, 2015), the US, Japan, Germany, France and the

UK were the five largest contributors to the IMF and were automatically allocated seats. Some states, such as China, Russia and Saudi Arabia, also occupied single seats, while the remaining 180 members belong to constituencies represented by one member. Some, such as Belgium, the Netherlands and Italy were de facto permanent EDs, while others rotated the duties of ED among constituency members. Consequently, it was normal for six EU Member States to be present on the Executive Board, occasionally rising to eight or nine depending on the rotation within groups. Debate about the merits of this situation is divided between those advocating more coherent representation (McNamara and Meunier, 2002; Garnier et al., 2006; Wouters and Kerckhoven, 2013; EU, 2015); those advocating better coordination of (especially eurozone) EU states but not their elimination (Bini Smaghi, 2004, 2009; Pisani-Ferry, 2009); and those who question the feasibility of such changes within the structure of the IMF (Broome, 2013).

Member State groups

As of January 2016, EU Member States are represented by ten different EDs. As shown in Table 15.3, they are classified into five different types of representation: (i) national ED, (ii) de facto permanent ED by virtue of being largest member of a constituency, (iii) occasional ED as part of a rotation in a constituency, (iv) constituency member represented by another EU Member State and (v) constituency member represented by a non-EU Member State. Some groups are based on linguistic blocs, others on geography, others on rank within the IMF, such as the G-5 (US, Japan, Germany, France and the UK) that contain the majority of international banks within their financial systems (Breen, 2013). The reforms to the governance structure agreed in the 14th General Review meant that the Big-Three states will now have to be voted onto the Executive Board like other EDs, while countries used to being permanently represented on the Board will have to take a back seat as two Europeans are replaced by non-Europeans among the twenty-four EDs. For these states, their national prestige is clearly knocked, as the gap between them and Britain, France and Germany will widen.

EU Member States have historically been reluctant to give up national representation in the IMF. Although the creation of the euro meant that control over monetary issues relevant to IMF scrutiny of members' economies had been ceded to the European Central Bank (ECB), Germany and France were among the strongest voices rejecting calls for more coordinated representation (Broome, 2013). Pisani-Ferry compared the voting rules of the IMF with the

Table 15.3 Division of EU Member States in IMF Executive Board as of 1 January 2016 (largest member italicized)

Germany
France
United Kingdom
Belgium, Bulgaria, Croatia, Cyprus, Luxembourg, the *Netherlands*, Romania (plus 8 non-EU)
Greece, *Italy*, Malta, Portugal (plus 2 non-EU)
Denmark, Estonia, Finland, Latvia, Lithuania, *Sweden* (plus 2 non-EU)
Austria, Czech Republic, Hungary, Slovak Republic, Slovenia (plus 3 non-EU)
Spain (plus 7 non-EU)
Poland (plus 7 non-EU – largest Switzerland)
Ireland (plus 11 non-EU – largest Canada)

EU Council and argued that Member States with EDs enjoy greater voting power in the IMF than in the EU, explaining their preference for the status quo (Pisani-Ferry, 2009). One reason for this is that EDs vote with the aggregate total of their constituency, thus capturing the votes of members and magnifying power. The euro crisis and the establishment of much tighter EU oversight of national budgets (the 'Two pack' and the 'Six pack') elevated the question of EU representation in the IMF up the political agenda. In summer 2015, Juncker (2015) produced a report on 'Completing Europe's Economic and Monetary Union', to which the European Commission generated a number of policy proposals. Regarding the IMF, a three-step proposal for 'more consistent and effective external representation of the euro area' required '(i) strengthening coordination among Member States of the euro area; (ii) improved representation of the euro area within the IMF; and (iii) once the necessary adjustments to the IMF governance are made, a unified representation and single seat for the euro area' (EU, 2015). The Commission is advocating replacing Mode IV representation with Mode I, consistent with expectations that legal competencies shape foreign policy-making.

Policy change

Until the euro crisis, there was little discernible common EU policy in the IMF. The agenda of the Executive Board concerned lending to low- and middle-income states and reviewing adherence to conditionality. There is a considerable literature on the politics of these lending decisions, centring predominantly on degree of political influence exerted by the US (Dreher et al., 2009) and the degree of bureaucratic autonomy of IMF staff (Broome, 2013). Stone (2004) produces evidence showing Britain and France soften conditionality to former colonies, while Breen (2013) argues that Britain, France and Germany as G-5 members have strong interests in seeing the IMF bailout states on the verge of defaulting on sovereign debt to private banks. While there are weekly meetings between European EDs in Washington (Bini Smaghi, 2004), according to one former ED, they consist of informing each other of instructions received from national capitals and focus on avoiding conflicting positions, rather than establishing coherent common ones.

The decision to lend $2.1 billion to Iceland in October 2008 was the first IMF loan to a Western European country since 1976. While large, it was dwarfed by standby agreements (credit lines) provided to Hungary ($15 billion), Latvia ($2.4 billion), Romania ($17 billion) between winter 2008 and spring 2009, followed by even larger loans to Greece (€30 billion), Ireland (€22.5 billion) and Portugal (€22.5 billion) between 2009 and 2011. These loans were made possible after lending rules were changed in May 2010 to permit an 'Exceptional Access Policy' that in theory applies to all members but to date has only been used in these cases (Pisani-Ferry et al., 2013: 85). As a consequence of lending to EU Member States, the IMF has become increasingly intertwined with the European Commission and ECB. The Troika both designs structural reforms and monitors compliance with them, resulting in some non-EU IMF members expressing grave doubts about the reputational costs to the IMF (Pisani-Ferry et al., 2013: 86).

Without doubt, EU Member States have used the IMF during the euro crisis for a number of reasons to further various (and not necessarily complementary) goals, of which four are most clearly identifiable (Kissack 2016). The first is wealthy, Northern European eurozone members (Germany, Netherlands, Finland, Belgium, Luxembourg, France) seeking to transfer the adjustment costs of the eurozone to the IMF. By framing the crisis as a threat to systemic stability, the IMF can be legitimately called upon to help, providing around 30 per cent of the funds securing the monetary union. The second is closely related and concerns free-riding on the reputation and expertise of the IMF. The European Commission had no experience of handling financial crises, and financial market scepticism of its abilities risked increasing the cost of the bailout. For the same Member States wishing to transfer adjustment costs to the IMF, it also provided a greater guarantee of success. Hodson (2014) argues too that the Council delegated monitoring duties to the IMF in parallel to the Commission to prevent against agent slippage. The third reason is that G-5 members use the IMF to protect private banks in their national jurisdiction from sovereign debt default (Breen, 2013). The bailouts were in effect an enormous transfer of debt from private to public institutions, justified as the risks of banking collapse constituted a threat to an already fragile international financial system. Private banks in Germany, France and the UK were exposed to €250 billion of bad debt from Greece, and €600 billion factoring in the property market collapse in Ireland (Breen, 2013: 107–111). The final reason for turning to the IMF for help was that, for the states receiving the loans, it offered a counterweight to the terms offered by the EU (and driven by German rejection of underwriting the debts of other states). As early as November 2008, at the meeting of G-20 Heads of State in Washington, IMF Managing Director Dominic Strauss-Kahn presented a Keynesian inspired solutions to the global recession, and under Christine Lagarde, the IMF has maintained its softer stance of debt relief, clashing publicly with the EU (BBC, 2015).

Policy performance

The fiscally sound members of the eurozone that baulk at the thought to paying off the debts of other members have used the IMF to their advantage. The crisis has been averted, new rules are in place to consolidate oversight of national budgets and the European Stability Mechanism Treaty provides a framework to resolve future problems. The treaty formalises cooperation between the IMF and the EU in co-funding new loans (Article 13), pointing to agreement by all eurozone members (the treaty is an intergovernmental agreement) that IMF cooperation is desirable. Since its signing in 2012, positions on cooperation have changed, with Germany questioning the continued need for IMF participation, especially when its interventions go against the policy preferences of Berlin. To this end, locking in the IMF is a safeguard for states requiring loans because it provides a credible alternative to austerity-driven policies. However, whether the IMF will serve this role in future is uncertain because it is likely to limit its contribution to European bailouts to 10 per cent (Pisani-Ferry et al., 2013), thus allowing it to exit reforms programmes it does not agree with, while maintaining sufficient funds to lend to other IMF members. Frozen privileges remain significant determinants of EU Member State behaviour and mode of action. The IMF has been used to further the interests of its most powerful members, above all Germany and states supportive of its strict position on dealing with the crisis. France was for much of the crisis aligned with Germany, and had common interests in the protection of its banks, but saw the IMF as a way of locking in more left-lending economic policies. Mode IV will remain the dominant policy strategy for the foreseeable future.

United Nations Security Council

Context

The most conspicuous frozen privilege in the multilateral system is the allocation of five permanent seats with veto powers in the UNSC. Alongside the US, China and Russia are France and the UK, and although neither has used their veto since 1991 (Hill, 2006), their continual presence at the heart of the Security Council gives them a formidable platform for pursuing their foreign policy goals. EU Member States benefit from bias in the allocation of the ten rotating seats on the UNSC, with two allocated to the WEOG and one to Eastern Europe, permitting a maximum of five out of fifteen seats occupied by EU countries.[1] Participating in the UNSC elevates states to the role of executives charged with overseeing the most important of all UN activities, namely maintaining international peace and security. The purpose of the UNSC was to delegate decision-making power to a small group of UN members that could respond quickly to international crises, and during such times, the UNSC meets daily and the fifteen work around the clock to drafting resolutions and monitoring events. Of the EU28, only Estonia and Latvia have not served on the UNSC, showing how widely Member States see the significance of participation.

The current constitution of the UNSC is widely seen as deeply problematic. Its permanent members were identified during the drafting of the UN Charter in 1945 and omitting countries such as India, Japan, Germany and Brazil (G-4) is argued to reduce the legitimacy of the Security Council. Although this chapter is not about UNSC reform, mapping where various EU Member States stand on reform reveals their preferences for enhancing their national foreign policies.[2] Where states stand in terms of their own ambitions for future participation is informative when considering their voting on key resolutions. Britain and France, as existing permanent (P5) members, accept that other states have equal entitlement to the powers they enjoy and support limited reforms to increase the legitimacy of their continued privilege. As a member of the G-4, Germany regards itself as a prime candidate for enjoying an enhanced role in a reformed UNSC. There exists a group of states opposed to the G-4, led by neighbouring rivals (Italy, Mexico, Pakistan, South Korea and others) under the name of Uniting for Consensus. Italy is a founding member of the group, and Spain is another prominent European member and is using its UNSC membership for 2015–16 as a platform to raise awareness of the reform agenda during the seventieth anniversary of the UN.[3] Finally, there is the integrationalist position that the long-term goal of the Union should be an EU seat replacing the Member States (Mode I) and enjoying the privileges of veto. The EU is fundamentally divided on the question of UNSC reform because of its largest members' rival ambitions, demonstrating the importance of the UNSC for national foreign policies.

Policy change

The Lisbon Treaty states that, when the 'Union has defined a position on a subject which is on the United Nations Security Council agenda, those Member States which sit on the Security Council shall request that the High Representative be invited to present the Union's position' (Lisbon Treaty Art. 19 §b (iii)). The High Representative, as well as EU Special Rapporteurs, have addressed UNSC open sessions, which in turn are part of the push to make the Council more transparent by holding some meetings in public. Yet evidence from practitioners shows that open sessions push the 'real' discussions into behind closed doors where the fifteen members set the agenda and negotiate resolutions. Drieskens (2009) argues that, when EU Member States sit on the UNSC, they are rapidly socialised into Council routines, immersed in the ongoing agenda and required to take positions on all issues under consideration. While EU Member States may be more or less disposed to greater CFSP cooperation and willing to use their UNSC membership as a bridge to other Member States when they begin their two-year term, sooner or later the need for confidentiality to ensure the trust of other UNSC members wins over. This reality is also recognised in the Lisbon Treaty, in the *Declarations Concerning the Provisions of the Treaties*:

> [The] provisions covering the Common Foreign and Security Policy . . . will not affect the existing legal basis, responsibilities, and powers of each Member State in relation to the formulation and conduct of its foreign policy, . . . including a Member State's membership of the Security Council of the United Nations.
>
> (Declaration 14 Concerning the Provisions of the Treaties OJ 306/255 17.12.2007)

EU Member States have legally protected their obligations as sovereign states acting in the UNSC, prioritising Mode IV action.

The UNSC agenda covers a number of policy issues, ranging from norms setting (for example, women and security in the follow-up to UNSCR 1325 cf. Barbé 2016), peacekeeping and humanitarian actions (see Chapter 7), to the use of force to maintain international peace and security. This section focuses on the latter issue, as the decision to use military force is arguably the most important action a sovereign state can make. According to international law, the use of force is only permitted in self-defence or when sanctioned by the UNSC. As the EU has no military capacity of its own, the use of force is always a decision for national governments, but the European Security Strategy confirms the EU's commitment to the same norms by saying 'the fundamental framework of international relations in the United Nations Charter' (European Council, 2003: 9). We will consider two cases: the American-led intervention in Iraq in March 2003 and the decision to use force to protect 'civilians and civil populated areas' in Libya in March 2011. In both cases, some EU Member States deployed military forces, but in the former UNSC, authorisation was not forthcoming, while the latter secured approval. The following section focuses on the roles played by France and the UK as permanent members; Germany, Italy and Spain as aspiring enhanced members; the position of other EU states on the UNSC at the time; and decisions to support (or not) military action.

Policy performance

During the 1990s, the international community continued to monitor Iraq's capacity to produce chemical, biological and nuclear weapons under its post-Gulf War obligations to disarm. The inspection regime was reinforced when UNSCR 1284 (1999) established a subsidiary body of the Security Council, the United Nations Monitoring, Verification and Inspection Commission (UNMOVIC), to concentrate on the Iraqi situation. The United States, under the Presidency of George W. Bush and as part of the War on Terror following the attacks of 9-11, initially increased diplomatic pressure on Iraq to terminate its programmes. After a breakdown in the inspection regime in autumn 2002, the UNSC passed Resolution 1441, setting out the steps necessary for Iraq to comply with its disarmament obligations. The penultimate paragraph states that 'the Council has repeatedly warned Iraq that it will face serious consequences as a result of its continued violations of its obligations' (UN, 2002: §13). As Gordon and Shapiro (2004) detail in their excellent account of events, opinion was divided over whether a second resolution would be needed to use military force against Iraq, if it did not comply. German Chancellor Gerhard Schroeder, who had narrowly won the national election in September 2002, based his campaign on opposing any war with Iraq and would not support any intervention. Although France eventually opposed military action,

French military officials were in the US in early 2003 planning their participation in strikes against Iraq. Iraq made a number of concessions to the demands of UNSCR 1441 that drove a wedge between France and the UK and US; France indicated it would veto a draft resolution prepared on 7 March 2003 by Spain, the UK and US giving Iraq an unequivocal ten-day ultimatum (UN, 2003). While a veto by China and Russia could have been tolerated on the grounds of representing moral vindication, a veto by France would be more damaging to the legitimacy of action that no resolution at all. On 20 March, the US invaded Iraq with the assistance of many states, including the UK, Italy, Poland, the Netherlands, Spain, Denmark and Portugal, as well as smaller deployments from nine Eastern European countries.

The consequences of US Secretary of Defence Donald Rumsfeld's division between 'new' and 'old Europe are well known. Two letters demonstrate how widely supported US action was in Europe. The 'Letter of Eight' published on 30 January 2003 in a number of leading newspapers was signed by existing NATO members, the Czech Republic, Denmark, Hungary, Italy, Poland, Portugal, Spain (a UNSC member at the time) and the UK. A week later, a 'Letter of Ten' from Eastern European non-NATO members Albania, Bulgaria (a UNSC member at the time), Croatia, Estonia, Latvia, Lithuania, the Republic of Macedonia, Romania, Slovakia and Slovenia echoed their support for the US. Alongside France and Germany in opposition to action were Belgium, Luxembourg and Greece and the neutral states of Austria, Ireland and Sweden. This case was one of the most public and divisive splits between EU states on a foreign policy issue and led to a further questioning of the viability of a common foreign policy. The publication of the European Security Strategy in December 2003 went some way towards closure on the rift.

In February 2011, the Libyan government of Colonel Gaddafi began violently repressing peaceful protests and the situation quickly escalated into a civil war, with civilian areas targeted by government forces. The 17 February 'Day of Rage' drew international attention to the situation, and within a week, a UNSC resolution condemning the violence was passed, Libyan membership of the League of Arab States (LAS) was suspended, the African Union issued a statement of condemnation, and the UN Human Rights Council opened a committee of inquiry. As government violence increased, the Security Council referred the situation to the International Criminal Court. The 'LAS stopped short of calling explicitly for regime change but it made an unprecedented declaration on 12 March when it called for the UNSC "to bear its responsibilities towards the deteriorating situation in Libya"' (Williams and Popken, 2011: 254). Five days later, a French, Lebanese and British draft resolution was taken to the Security Council mandating the use of military action to enforce no-fly zones over Libya protecting civilians and civilian populated areas (Doyle, 2011). With the support of the US and members of the League of Arab States openly calling for military action, China, Russia, India, Brazil and Germany abstained from voting, and UNSCR 1973 was passed (UN, 2011), allowing France, the US and the UK to begin military strikes, initially in defence of the city of Benghazi. European Council President Van Rompuy and High Representative for Foreign Policy Ashton issued a joint statement declaring that the 'European Union is ready to implement this Resolution within its mandate and competences' (Van Rompuy and Ashton, 2011). This did not resonate with the divide in the Security Council between France, Britain and Portugal supporting the resolution and Germany, fearing forces participating in the mission 'could be drawn into a protracted military conflict . . . decided not to support the resolution and would not contribute its own forces to any military effort that arose from its implementation' (UN, 2011). Germany remained outside the NATO mission to enforce an arms embargo on Libya that began on 23 March 2011 and incorporated ships and aircraft from Belgium,

Denmark, Greece, Italy, Spain, the Netherlands and the UK, together with Canadian, Turkish and American forces (NATO, n.d.).

Germany's position was not without merit.

> The attack on Libya represents an unprecedented moment in the history of the UN Security Council and responsibility to protect. Specifically, resolution 1973 is the first time that the Security Council has explicitly authorised a military intervention against the will of a functioning government for humanitarian purposes.
>
> (Williams and Popken, 2011: 249)

Nor was it alone, as China, Russia, Brazil and India all abstained from voting, and South Africa announced soon afterwards it would have preferred to abstain that vote in favour. The conclusions of the European Council meeting of the 24 March 2011 papered over the cracks, stating that the Council 'expressed its satisfaction after the adoption of UN Security Council Resolution 1973' (European Council, 2011). But as NATO action protecting civilians shifted to air support for opposition forces, it overstepped its original mandate. On 2 November 2011, the 'Prosecutor of the ICC briefed the Security Council saying that the allegations of crimes committed by NATO . . . would be examined impartially and independently by the ICC's Office of Prosecution' (Ulfstein and Christiansen, 2013: 161). Once again, on the most significant issue before the UNSC, the EU was divided.

Comparing the non-UNSC mandated invasion of Iraq in 2003 and the mandated air strikes on Libya in 2011, we see an important difference and some degrees of similarity. The most important difference is their legality, with the latter initially complying with international law until NATO breached its mandate. By contrast, the legal basis for military action in 2003 in UNSCR 1441 is highly questionable. Variation in EU Member State support is partially explained by this. But the similarities that exist mean that other factors are at play too. First, the two permanent EU members of the UNSC are crucial actors in determining how events unfold, as expected due to their central position in the policy-making system. They operate in Mode IV action with the other members three permanent members and ten non-permanent members, of whom one, two or three are fellow EU Member States. Where do these other EU Member States stand? NATO membership is an important factor to consider both cases and is another example of Mode IV action. Support for US-led action against Iraq was gathered through NATO members (bridging EU and non-EU states) in the Letter of Eight and aspiring NATO members in the Letter of Ten. In 2011, NATO warplanes and warships carried out the air strikes under the UNSC mandate. Similarities exist too in the behaviour of states positioning themselves for greater participation in the UNSC after its (possible) reform. Italy and Spain supported both actions, presenting credentials as security providers capable of force project abroad. Although Germany also aspires to become a more influential UNSC member, it did not support either action in keeping with its great reluctance to send military forces abroad (Kosovo and ISAF being exceptions). In both cases, national foreign policy goals and cooperation with non-EU members were pursued at great expense to common EU foreign policy.

Conclusion

This chapter framed the most important issues for EU Member States' national foreign policies in the multilateral system in the context of frozen privileges in the UNCHR, IMF and UNSC. The three are at the nexus of EU Member States national prestige and the European pursuit of effective multilateralism, pinpointing the tension between national foreign policy and European common foreign policy. The changing distribution of power in the international system magnifies European bias and increases the pressure for reform. In the three cases, reform is at different stages of completion, allowing a comparison of EU Member State reactions. However, the varying degrees of salience between cases cannot be overlooked as it partially explains the willingness of privileged states to forgo their advantages. Nevertheless, a number of important conclusions are reached.

While Mode I action is a goal in the IMF and UNSC for integrationalists, at best, we see evidence of Mode II action (UNCHR and HRC). We see plenty of Mode III action, such as weekly coordination meetings between IMF EDs in Washington and some co-authoring of UNSC resolutions. By far, the most important action in all three cases is Mode IV, such as the P5 in the UNSC, the G-5 in the IMF and the use of regional co-authors in the UNGA. Mode IV action also takes place in the background, such as third state lobbying in support of the moratorium on the death penalty resolution and liaison with the League of Arab states via Lebanon drafting UNSCR 1973. In an international system comprised of increasingly important non-European players, Mode IV action is essential.

Privilege is a source of power, and in these cases, we see that the EU Member States with the greatest privileges used them to increase their power inside and outside the EU. In the case of UNSCR 1973, Britain and France *wanted* to bomb Libya and invested considerable political capital supporting the National Transition Council of Libya in various international conferences (UK Government, 2011). Germany, France and the UK used their influence in the IMF to protect their private banking sectors (Breen, 2013), while Germany, France and other Northern eurozone states successfully transferred a sizeable proportion of monetary union adjustment costs to the IMF. Crucial to this was the passing of the Exceptional Access Policy in May 2010, which was done prior to reforming voting shares, which lowered EU28 total voting power (Kissack, 2016). The role of power is discernible too in the case of the UNGA, although operating differently. In the General Assembly, where sovereign equality is highly prized, widespread wariness of the EU (as seen in the efforts to gain enhanced observer status in the sixty-fifth session) meant reducing the EU's profile and emphasising the ten co-authors. The powerful lead from behind to prevent the messenger becoming more important than the message. In conclusion, unsurprisingly in important multilateral organisations, *all* EU Member States want to maximise opportunities to promote their national foreign policy goals, not least the largest. The challenge for the EU is to stop seeing Mode IV action as being the antithesis of EU common foreign policy and to accept that it is increasingly essential in the twenty-first century.

Notes

1 Cyprus belongs to the Asia group and therefore makes the theoretical maximum number of EU members six, although it is yet to serve on the Council.
2 The key issues on reform that different groups argue over are (i) the number of additional seats (generally accepted at ten), (ii) the distribution of those seats, (iii) the method for allocating them (permanent or renewable terms) and (iv) use of the veto by new members and P5.
3 http://www.spainun.org/en/2015/03/the-reform-of-the-security-council-is-possible/

Bibliography

Bantekas, I. and P. Hodgkinson (2000) 'Capital Punishment at the United Nations: Recent Developments', *Criminal Law Forum*, Vol. 11, No. 1, pp. 23–34.

Barbé, E. (2016) 'Supporting Practices Inspired by Solidarist Ideas: The EU in the UNSC Open Debates on Women, Peace and Security', in E. Barbé, O. Costa and R. Kissack (eds.) *EU Policy Responses to a Shifting Multilateral System*, Basingstoke: Palgrave, 135–156.

Barnett, Michael and Raymond Duvall (2005) 'Power in International Politics', *International Organization*, Vol. 59, No. 1, pp. 39–75.

BBC (2015) 'Greece Debt Crisis: IMF Attacks EU Over Bailout Terms', 15 July 2015, available at http://www.bbc.com/news/business-33531845 (accessed 16 December 2015).

Bini Smaghi, L. (2004) 'A Single Seat in the IMF', *Journal of Common Market Studies*, Vol. 42, No. 2, pp. 229–248.

Bini Smaghi, L. (2009) 'A Single EU Seat in the International Monetary Fund?', in K.E. Jørgensen (ed.) *The European Union and International Organizations*, London: Routledge, 61–79.

Breen, M. (2013) *The Politics of IMF Lending*, Basingstoke: Palgrave.

Broome, A. (2013) 'The Politics of IMF-EU Co-Operation: Institutional Change from Maastricht Treaty to the Launch of the Euro', *Journal of European Public Policy*, Vol. 20, No. 4, pp. 589–605.

Clapham, A. (1999) 'Where Is the EU's Human Rights Common Foreign Policy, and How Is It Manifested in Multilateral Fora?', in P. Alston, M. Bustelo and J. Heenan (eds.) *The EU and Human Rights*, Oxford: Oxford University Press, 627–683.

Crocker, C.A. (2015) 'The Strategic Dilemma of a World Adrift', *Survival*, Vol. 57, No. 1, pp. 7–30.

Doyle, M. (2011) 'The Folly of Protection', *Foreign Affairs, Online Comment*, 20 March, available at: https://www.foreignaffairs.com/articles/africa/2011-03-20/folly-protection (accessed 25 February 2017).

Dreher, A., J.-E. Sturm and J.R. Vreeland (2009) 'Global Horse Trading: IMF Loans for Votes in the United Nations Security Council', *European Economics Review*, Vol. 53, No. 7, pp. 742–757.

Drieskens, E. (2009) 'Walking on Eggshells: Non-Permanent Members Searching for a EU Perspective at the UN Security Council', in J. Wouters (ed.) *Belgium in the UN Security Council: Reflections on the 2007–2008 Membership*, Antwerp: Oxford & Portland: Intersentia, 175–185.

EU (2015) 'Communication from the Commission to the European Parliament, the Council and the European Central Bank: A Roadmap for Moving towards a More Consistent External Representation of the Euro Area in International Fora, Brussels', 21.10.2015 COM(2015) 602 final.

European Commission (2011) 'Joint Communication to the European Parliament and the Council: Human Rights and Democracy at the Heart of EU External Action – Towards a More Effective Approach', Brussels, COM 886 final.

European Council (2003) 'European Security Strategy: A Secure Europe in a Better World', Brussels, 12 December, available at http://www.consilium.europa.eu/uedocs/cmsUpload/78367.pdf

European Council (2011) 'Extract from the European Council Conclusions', Brussels, 24 March.

Finnemore, M. and K. Sikkink (1998) 'International Norm Dynamics and Political Change', *International Organization*, Vol. 52, No. 4, pp. 887–917.

Garnier, C., D. Dado and F. di Mauro (2006) 'UN-EU Cooperation on Financial Issues: The Role of the European Union at the International Monetary Fund and the World Bank', in J. Wouters, F. Hoffmeister and T. Ruys (eds.) *The United Nations and the European Union: An Ever Closer Partnership*, The Hague: T.M.C. Asser Press, 115–134.

Garský, S. and C. Spolander (2012) 'When Values Fail? European Gains and Losses in Facing Competitive Forms of Multilateralism', Paper presented at the ISA Convention 2012, San Diego, USA.

Gordon, P. and J. Shapiro (2004) *Allies at War*, New York: McGraw-Hill.

Gowan, R. and F. Brantner (2008) *A Global Force for Human Rights? An Audit of European Power at the UN*, Brussels: European Council on Foreign Relations.

Hill, C. (2006) 'The European Powers in the Security Council: Differing Interests, Differing Arenas', in K.V. Laatikainen and K.E. Smith (eds.) *The European Union at the United Nations: Intersecting Multilateralisms*, Basingstoke: Palgrave, 49–69.

Hodson, D. (2014) 'The IMF as a de facto Institution of the EU: A Multiple Supervisor Approach', available at www.bbk.ac.uk/politics/IMFasdefactoinstitutionRIPE2014.pdf

Ikenberry, G.J. (2001) *After Victory: Institutions, Strategic Restraint, and the Rebuilding of Order after Major Wars*, Princeton, NJ: Princeton University Press.

IMF (2015) *'IMF Managing Director Christine Lagarde Welcomes U.S. Congressional Approval of the 2010 Quota and Governance Reforms' Press Release 15/573*, Washington, DC: International Monetary Fund.

Juncker, J.-C. (2015) 'Completing Europe's Economic and Monetary Union', available at https://ec.europa.eu/priorities/publications/five-presidents-report-completing-europes-economic-and-monetary-union_en (accessed 14 December 2015).

Kennedy, P. (2006) *The Parliament of Man*, London: Penguin.

Kissack, R. (2010) *Pursuing Effective Multilateralism: The European Union, International Organisations and the Politics of Decision Making*. London: Palgrave.

Kissack, R. (2012) 'The EU in the Negotiations of the United Nations General Assembly Resolution on a Moratorium on the Use of the Death Penalty', in J. Wouters, H. Bruyninckx, S. Basu and S. Schunz (eds.) *The European Union and Multilevel Governance: Assessing EU Participation in the United Nations Human Rights and Environmental for a*, Basingstoke: Palgrave, 103–121.

Kissack, R. (2016) 'The Global Financial Crisis and Emerging Economies: EU Accommodation and Entrenchment in the IMF', in E. Barbé, O. Costa and R. Kissack (eds.) *EU Policy Responses to a Shifting Multilateral System*, Basingstoke: Palgrave, 155–177.

Kupchan, C. (2012) *No One's World: The West, the Rising Rest, and the Coming Global Turn*, Oxford: Oxford University Press.

Macaj, G. (2012) 'Squaring the Circle? EU Outreach and Bloc Politics in the Human Rights Council', Paper presented at LISBOAN – ERASMUS ACADEMIC NETWORK: EU external representation and the reform of international contexts: Practices after Lisbon, Clingendael, The Hague, NL, 21–22 February 2012.

Manners, I. (2002) 'Normative Power Europe: A Contradiction in Terms?', *Journal of Common Market Studies*, Vol. 40, No. 2, pp. 235–258.

McNamara, K. and S. Meunier (2002) 'Between National Sovereignty and International Power: What External Voice for the Euro?', *International Affairs*, Vol. 78, No. 4, pp. 849–868.

NATO (n.d.) 'NATO Arms Embargo against Libya Operation UNIFIED PROTECTOR, Fact sheet', available at http://www.nato.int/nato_static/assets/pdf/pdf_2011_03/20110325 _110325-unified-protector-factsheet.pdf (accessed 22 January 2014).

Pisani-Ferry, J. (2009) 'The Accidental Player: The European Union and the Global Economy', in K.E. Jørgensen (ed.) *The European Union and International Organizations*, London: Routledge, 21–36.

Pisani-Ferry, J., A. Sapir and G. Wolff (2013) *EU-IMF Assistance to the Euro Area Countries: An Early Assessment*, Brussels: Bruegel.

Putnam, D. (1988) 'Diplomacy and Domestic Politics: The Logic of the Two-Level Game', *International Organization*, Vol. 42, No. 3, pp. 427–460.

Riedel, E. and M. Will (1999) 'Human Rights Clauses in External Agreements of the EC', in P. Alston, M. Bustelo and J. Heenan (eds.) *The EU and Human Rights*, Oxford: Oxford University Press, 723–754.

Slaughter, A.-M. (2004) *A New World Order*, Princeton, NJ: Princeton University Press.

Smith, K.E. (2006) 'Speaking with One Voice? European Union Coordination on Human Rights Issues at the United Nations', *Journal of Common Market Studies*, Vol. 44, No. 1, pp. 113–137.

Smith, K.E. (2010) 'The European Union at the Human Rights Council: Speaking with One Voice but Having Little Influence', *Journal of European Public Policy*, Vol. 17, No. 2, pp. 224–241.

Stone, R.W. (2004) 'Political Economy of IMF Lending in Africa', *American Political Science Review*, Vol. 98, No. 4, pp. 577–591.

UK Government (2011) 'Paris Conference on Libya, Foreign and Commonwealth Office: London', available at https://www.gov.uk/government/news/paris-conference-on-libya (accessed 29 December 2015).

Ulfstein, G. and H.F. Christiansen (2013) 'The Legality of the NATO Bombing of Libya', *International & Comparative Law Quarterly*, Vol. 62, No. 1, pp. 159–171.

UN (2002) *Security Council Resolution No. 1441, 8 November 2002*, available at: http://www.un.org/Docs/scres/2002/sc2002htm (accessed 1 August 2016).

UN (2003) 'Draft Resolution 7 March 2003', available at www.un.org/News/dh/iraq/res-iraq-07mar03-en-rev.pdf

UN (2008) Statement by Ambassador Vanu Gopala Menon, Permanent Representative of Singapore to the United Nations, to UNGA Third Committee (42nd meeting) 18 November 2008.

UN (2011) 'Security Council Approves "No-Fly Zone" over Libya, Authorizing "All Necessary Measures" to Protect Civilians, by Vote of 10 in Favour with 5 Abstentions', available at www.un.org/News/Press/docs/2011/sc10200.doc.htm (accessed 22 January 2014).

Van Rompuy, H. and C. Ashton (2011) 'Joint statement by President of the European Council Herman Van Rompuy, and EU High Representative Catherine Ashton on UN Security Council resolution on Libya', Brussels, 17 March 2011.

Vreeland, J.R. (2007) *The International Monetary Fund: Politics of Conditional Lending*, London: Routledge.

Williams, P.R. and C. Popken (2011) 'Security Council Resolution 1973 on Libya: A Moment of Legal & Moral Clarity', *Case Western Reserve Journal of International Law*, Vol. 44, No. 1, pp. 225–250.

Wouters, J. and S.V. Kerckhoven (2013) 'The International Monetary Fund', in K.E. Jørgensen and K.V. Laatikainen (eds.) *Routledge Handbook on the European Union and International Institutions*, London: Routledge, 221–233.

Zakaria, F. (2008) 'The Future of American Power', *Foreign Affairs*, Vol. 87, No. 3, pp. 18–43.

16 Conclusion

Amelia Hadfield, Ian Manners
and Richard G. Whitman

The stakes have never been higher for the European Union. Both the distinctive form of the EU, and the contents of its twenty-eight separate sovereign units, have as many issues dividing them as reasons to remain together. As illustrated in Parts I and II of this text, the challenge of constructing a foreign policy 'held in common' has simultaneously catalysed and impeded European collective action. Member States' own quarrelsome attitudes, as well as external perceptions of the EU as substantively diminished have together undermined the coherence and effectiveness of the EU's foreign policy for the better part of a decade. EU crises have radiated geopolitically and deepened in severity, neither containable within Europe as a 'domestic' issue nor tackled externally as an EU foreign policy challenge. Investigating both the Member State and EU-specific dynamics responsible for this uneasy state of affairs is challenging but necessary. Various studies point to the long-term ramifications of the EU's enfeebled internal governance and impoverished external policy-making, primarily in terms of weakened relationships with key partners (Chaban and Holland, 2014; Dinan, Nugent and Paterson, 2016). Equally, the EU's ability to move beyond this period of crisis will produce both opportunities to recalibrate its overall foreign policy actorness – whether larger or smaller in scope – and options for Member States to re-evaluate their own national preferences. These challenges should not be underestimated, particularly as regards the EU's relationship with its Strategic Partners. As recently argued by Merritt (2016), current American views suggest

> that bold, sweeping reforms are imperative to meet the challenges of the twenty-first century. Global warming, terrorism, globalised markets, mass migration, militarised geopolitics and the digital revolution all require supranational attention. On their own . . . the individual nation states of Europe, Britain included, are doomed to irrelevance.
>
> (Hockenos, 2016)

Nor are problems primarily political in nature. Galbraith argues that the EU may have wounded its Eurozone project fatally, having 'erred egregiously . . . in making draconian austerity policies the price of Greece's rescue while letting the continent's banks off scot free' (2016). The result has set centre-right governments against left-wing governments across the continent, deepening 'the wealth disparity between northern and southern Europe that will may undermine transatlantic trade and investment structures (Hockenos, 2016). External criticism highlighting inadequate EU policy responses, coupled with internal discontent from national and populist sources, together actively question the very *raison d'etre* of the EU, as well as the integrative limits of its policies. EU reform is clearly overdue. While there may be little post-Brexit appetite for enhanced political and economic integration, as Hockenos suggests, because 'Europe's political spectrum is fractured as never before, with national interests regularly trumping common cause, the lesser evil at the moment may be smaller, tactical interventions to complete the single market, invest in research, modernise infrastructure and strengthen foreign policy mechanisms' (2016). Member States have emerged once again as both the crucible of such changes and the harbinger of fragmentation. The question is whether between them they can summon the political will to construct a stronger series of working relations, shared policies and common perspectives.

As explored throughout Part II, referents pertaining to territory, neighbourhood, borders and boundaries and the crises that have arisen from them, operate as permanent scope conditions from which the national preferences of EU Member States originate and from which subsequent policy portfolios arise, divided between national imperatives and Europeanised policy reflexes.

How can studies of EU foreign policy contribute to this complex area? Clearer interdisciplinary connections between IR, FPA, EU integration studies need to be identified, and a sharper sense of the emergent body of work comprising EU foreign policy analysis (EU FPA) is required. Indeed, the fruitful but unwieldy area of foreign policy analysis must itself formulate methods that take the unique nature of the EU into account as an innovative foreign policy source. In this way, the overarching area of FPA itself will be better able to reflect the complexity of conceptualising the intrinsically sovereign instincts of EU Member States alongside EU-level policy-making structures. As explored in Parts I and II, the parts of the EU are as unique as the sum itself. As such, the EU's true *sui generis* attributes lie not merely in the institutional aggregate of the EEAS or the Council but – as observed in the first edition – in the ongoing 'distinctiveness of the foreign policies of European states who are members of the EU and the issues that this membership raises' (Manners and Whitman, 2000, p. 3).

As an emergent canon, EU Foreign Policy Analysis needs to be *reflective* about the chronological transitions of EU Member States (preferably via historical analysis), *reflexive* about the empirical stakes played by sovereign nations (preferably via comparative studies) and *analytical* about the discursive impact that policies have upon the ability of Member States to share greater types of power that itself is increasingly variable in form. A sharper sense of the strategic imperatives of membership is instructive in this respect. Membership has moved the original fifteen Member States through the first epoch of Union consolidation, from a post-Cold War era to market-driven complex interdependence to political integration. The period 2004–9 represented a second era in which the Union struggled to gain internal and external legitimacy as a collective. The most recent era has seen the Union strive to make strategic inroads as a foreign policy actor, by attempting to induce amongst its members a higher degree of institutional efficacy and actor effectiveness. In a post-Brexit climate, the entire method of joint decision-making and shared competences, as well as the philosophy of European integration will inevitably come under scrutiny, as well as the concept of membership itself.

The specific roles that key Member States have played in furthering or hindering the EU through these epochs tell us much about their judgement of the external gains and losses to be had by supporting or opposing the EU through these transitions. Member State foreign policies also explain their overall attitude to the differential integration that European foreign policy operates within (captured within Modes I–IV), and the variable forms of hard and soft power that the EU has established in its foreign policy toolbox. National role conceptions remain a vital part of the practice and scholarship of foreign affairs. Accordingly, EU FPA needs to move beyond the tepid trinity of explaining all state behaviour in terms of rational-actor realism, decision-making organisational/bureaucratic theory, and undigested 'cultural leftovers'. For instance, examining national role conceptions, foregrounded within EU actorness in a way that combines policy-based state-centrism and the structuration of institutional process would constitute an interesting contribution.

EU FPA must also engage with the complex challenges derived from governance and governance studies. Governance (qua Börzel, 2010) means exploring the specific forms of procedural interaction and substantive relations enacted between supranational, inter-governmental and transitional dynamics. Discerning the impact of EU membership upon the foreign policy inputs and outputs of specific Member States means a ready appreciation for the increasing modes of governance by which policies are made. Specifically, it means taking seriously the role of a spectrum whose policy responses range from being definitively Europeanised, to intergovernmental consensus, to defiantly national attitudes attempting to preserve sovereign latitude in the face of domestic grievance or external pressures. The result is two separate 'worlds of compliance' (Falkner and Treib, 2008), balancing policy convergence inspired by a common set of ideas, definitions and tools' put together at the EU level (crossing Modes I and II), and policy diversification arising from national political cultures (Rostan and Vaira, 2011, p. ix). In conceptual terms, what is required is the accommodation of 'convergence and diversity in a unitary theoretical framework' that situates these dynamics as not merely relational but symbiotic (Rostan and Vaira, 2011, p. ix). The concept of allomorphism (Vaira, 2004) could for example capture a range of top-down and bottom-up dynamics foregrounded in both structure and agency (i.e. as process-based inputs) and ensuing forms of convergence/divergence (i.e. as policy-based outputs).

IR theory-derived contributions could examine the constant fracturing between US and EU approaches which flag up the cyclical challenges of the state as role-maker, as institutional member, as leader or laggard, helping to expand the area of role studies. Equally, IR theory could widen its approaches to include the forms of hybridity springing from multilevel forms of governance. The European External Action Service (EEAS) for instance is an ideal case study for neoclassical realism, which focuses on the 'transmission belt' between inputs and outputs. Operating as a meso-actor between constructing and implementing, between creating and evaluation, the EEAS is an appreciably persuasive intervening variable, mediating Europe-anisation and nationalism. Equally, the EEAS can be studied on a policy-specific basis to gain a sense (as in this text) of the *type* of role being pursued *given* the policy and geopolitical value-set of the state, to reveal the impact of membership. This too helps deal with '**actorness**' more effectively. From our perspective, EU Member States will continue to operate within a distinc-tive foreign policy-making system in which there exists an abiding need to preserve national foreign policy value-sets and strategies, and which demonstrate change and action that interacts with Europeanisation directly, relationally or in opposition. EU-level foreign policy meanwhile remains a multilevel, and multiactor body of domestic inputs and regional and international outputs – simultaneously circumscribed by the national limits imposed on further integration and boosted by ambition, opportunity, and clout – the sources of both these being the Member States themselves. It is clear that robust and reflexive approaches to EU foreign policy will need to incorporate the foreign policies of EU Member States.

What contribution has the current text made?

First, this volume provides a restated central argument, namely that the foreign policies of each of the EU's individual Member States cannot be ignored in any wide-ranging analysis of EU foreign policy, because national actors inherently facilitate and constrain the con-struction of EU foreign policy. Second, its two-part structure provides a comprehensive understanding of the internal and external construction of EU foreign policy. Part I has dem-onstrated the importance of engaging with the distinct foreign policies of EU Member States, as they emerge from their respective geopolitical value-sets while Part II reveals complex balance of mode-based preferences in the construction of EU-level foreign policies.

Table 16.1 summarises the findings of Part I in mapping the distinctive characteristics of clusters of Member States foreign policies on the basis of geopolitical orientations. The chapters, empirically and comparatively, indicate the extent to which there is continuity or change in the foreign policy composition of key EU Member States, as found across the 'strong-weak competence spectrum', and on this basis explore the extent to which the resulting foreign policy **action** is similarly transformed, as found within the four key modes. The chapters in Part II provided a survey of the most well-established and also distinct areas of EU foreign policy. These chapters also provide insights upon three key questions: the **initial objectives** of a given EU-level policy (e.g. neighbourhood); the nature of key **Member State contributions** to a given EU-level policy relative to their own foreign policy objectives: operationalised as *changes to the input* of a given policy; and the **current composition** of EU-level policies, arising from the combination of EU-level and Member State foreign policy dynamics: operationalised in the *action of policy outputs*.

Table 16.2 demonstrates the mode of foreign policy actions that predominate across a four-mode spectrum that indicates the degree of EU versus national content and as outlined in the Introduction to this volume:

- **Mode I**: Member State foreign policy operating within established EU frameworks in a deeply institutionalised, integrated, potentially supranational fashion.
- **Mode II**: Member State foreign policy operating within the established EU frameworks, according to intergovernmental mechanisms.
- **Mode III**: Member State foreign policy conducted bilaterally or multilaterally between EU Member States, but outside established EU frameworks and/or the EU *acquis*.
- **Mode IV**: Member State foreign policy conducted between EU and non-EU Member States.

These four modes have provided an effective approach to mapping the different strands of the Member States' relationship to different strands of EU policy-making. Distinguishing between these modes has allowed for a more nuanced evaluation of the roles of Member States, most strikingly, that most policy domains present mixed-modes. Consequently, EU foreign policy-making is characterised as a complex decision-making eco-system with Member States remaining central to all strands of EU policy-making.

Overall, the analysis contained in Parts I and II of this volume demonstrates the existence of a hybrid system of foreign policy-making across different dimensions. It is noticeable that there is no convergence around a single mode of decision-making. Whether this is the settled future condition of European foreign policy-making rests on future developments in European integration. The post-Brexit climate may trigger the impetus to deepen arrangements in EU foreign policy-making; or it may hasten its fragmentation.

The volume demonstrates continuity with the earlier work on the role of EU Member States by highlighting that Member States operate within a distinctive foreign policy-making system in which the preservation of national foreign policy is uneasily blended with the conscious creation of an EU foreign policy. Further work remains in explaining the many forms of parallelism that arise between EU and Member State foreign policy, and the grounding of those investigations within a clearer canon of EU FPA scholarship.

Table 16.1 Geographic/geopolitical orientations by Member States

Accession–2000		2016 (2000–13 overview)	
Part I: Geographic orientations/geopolitics			
Geographical area	Short summary	Short summary	Change observed
Chapter 1: *Northern Europe*	**Denmark** Denmark had to expend some political capital in its efforts to limit the evolution of the EU's capacity in the area of foreign and security policies, formally opting out of CSDP provisions. Danish 'active internationalism', based upon rejuvenated Atlantic Alliance, contrasts with its traditional ambivalence towards a Euro-centric model. Accordingly, the Atlantic Alliance remains a founding part of Danish foreign policy. Similarly, Nordic cooperation has played a key role beyond that of the EU.	**Denmark & Sweden** Denmark and Sweden are countries with similar priorities, style and tactics. They both use a critical constructive and pragmatic approach in their foreign policies. **Neither are EU enthusiasts, but still demonstrate commitment to key foreign policy areas.** Thus, in both countries, both and support and laggard attitudes are present, depending on issue areas. For both countries, intra-EU cooperation on the intergovernmental level (rather than intra-EU integration) remains the dominant mode in their foreign policies, while elements of traditional national foreign policies and foreign policy elements outside an EU framework (most prominently, Nordic cooperation) are also present.	**Continuity and limited change**
	Sweden & Finland The Finnish and Swedish governments were quick to acknowledge that they would become active and full members of the CFSP. Both countries have been at the forefront of strengthening the CFSP's capabilities in crisis management and recognised that the CFSP is an 'opportunity' to further their general goals of 'internationalism', allowing Europe to play a collective interventionist role in human rights and peacekeeping questions. Despite this, however, both countries maintained substantial bilateral relationships and individual interests. Sweden has committed substantial financial and political resources in order to promote Swedish objectives in the Baltic Sea region. Finland's requirement for cordial relations with Russia remains an ever present concern, and may explain partly why they have resisted NATO membership. Taken together, the Union was viewed by the Swedes and Finns as a vehicle to provide additional collective weight to their governments' objectives. In effect, the two Nordic 'post-neutrals' were practicing selective 'semi-alignment' in which the only item that remains contentious is cooperating with EU and NATO counterparts in Article V-related collective security.	**Finland** **Finland has incorporated support of Germany alongside its role of northern balancer and on occasion, regional leader.** More recently, the role of a support state has seen less accent on support for Germany and more towards common EU foreign policies. Finland has also been one of the most vocal supporters of the EEAS, and the HRVP role. The financial crisis however, revealed a different Finland, more assertive of its interests. Traditional Finnish support for supranational intra-EU integration has been balanced by preferences for a more intergovernmental intra-EU cooperation mode.	**Sweden** **Continuity and limited change** **Finland** **Shift from supranationalism to intra-EU intergovernmentalism**

Table 16.1 (Continued)

Accession–2000	2016 (2000–13 overview)	Change observed

Part 1: Geographic orientations/geopolitics

Geographical area	Short summary	Short summary	Change observed

New Northern Europe: the Baltic

Estonia, Latvia & Lithuania

The Baltic countries possess similar foreign policy priorities due to their shared history and geography. All three countries operate as support states in EU foreign policy Lithuania has been more outspoken and self-assured, whereas Estonia and Latvia have adopted a more pragmatic approach and a tendency to avoid confrontations, sometimes acting as 'laggards'. With regards to Russia, the Baltic states have adopted a degree of Finnish pragmatism, while also appreciating Sweden's and Denmark's more outspoken and critical approach. Estonia and Latvia have made a conscious effort to shrug off the image of 'agenda-spoilers' in EU–Russia relations by supporting shared positions. Lithuania, by contrast, has aimed to be among the lead states on Russia, pushing for a more critical EU approach, and promoting stronger EU support for the Eastern Partnership. In case of future multispeed developments in the field of EU foreign policy, all three would likely opt for the 'avant-garde' because of their security concerns, but they are unlikely to promote differentiated integration.

Chapter 2:
Western Europe

There is little evidence to suggest that membership of the EU has led to the widespread transformation of British national objectives. Decades of European foreign policy collaboration do not appear to have led to a new and wholly different European identity for British foreign policy. Policy-makers have simply used the EU as a new arena for the pursuit of national objectives. With the important exception of trade competences, membership of the EU appears to have left the majority of British objectives remarkably unchanged.

Britain

Brexit will force a comprehensive re-evaluation of the UK's role in the world. Despite pioneering key facets of CSDP, its tacit support of CFSP, including support for enlargement, neighbourhood, development and humanitarian assistance, Britain's historic inability to explain its role within the EU project to its own national constituency has now resulted in the most serious geopolitical challenge to the EU since its founding. Whether it remains integrated, aligned or autonomous from key EU foreign policy structures remains to be seen.

Very limited change

For Irish foreign policy, the impact of EU membership has been to challenge preferred national security and defence policies. The government was confronted with policy choices they would not otherwise have had to face and raised significant domestic opposition. Ireland was also conscious of the possibility of its foreign and security policy being marginalized as a consequence of NATO's relative success in peacekeeping. This fear brought about a determined effort to bring Ireland closer to the European security mainstream.	**Ireland** In the case of Ireland, the only area within the EU foreign policy in which integration it advances are visible is in intra-EU cooperation, where the Irish participation in the CSDP has been notable and accelerating. There is, however, evidence of a significant shift towards a renationalisation of inter-EU foreign policy. This in turn is connected to intra-EU policy debates surrounding the collapse of the Irish economy and the role of the Troika. There is also evidence of a renewed focus on the bilateralisation of Irish foreign policy, most especially vis-à-vis the United States and China.	**Significant shift towards renationalisation and bilateralisation of Irish foreign policy**
Both the Netherlands and Belgium can be categorised as states with extensive networks of external relations beyond the EU. At the same time, however, they represent the type of Member States that historically act in concert with the EU. Both countries consider CFSP as their main point of reference. The Benelux group considers itself to be the catalyst of European integration.	**Benelux** In several respects, Belgium and Luxembourg are exemplars of Europeanisation. While the Netherlands displays benign satisfaction at the development of the EEAS, there are no signs of markedly pioneering Europeanisation of foreign policies already; most are already well settled within existing policy structures. Belgium for example is content to 'remove' their national policy, for instance on China, to the EU level.	**Very limited change**
Chapter 3: *Eastern and* *Central Europe* In terms of foreign policy, Austria's adaptation to EU membership has progressed smoothly. With the Cold War coming to an end and new security threats emerging in Central and Eastern Europe, Austria found itself in a position where neutrality could no longer be relied upon as a guarantee for the country's security. Hence, Austria's willingness to participate in the CFSP and its wish to establish an active role for the EU in conflict prevention and involvement in the Balkans while supporting Eastern enlargement.	**Austria** Austria has the self-image of a state in a 'balancing mediatory position', particularly active in conflict resolution processes. It has also pursued a multilateral approach in its foreign policy. Current Austrian status is no longer that of a neutral state but rather 'an alliance-free' one and an active supporter of a common security policy of the EU. Austria has been very active in promoting the European perspective for the Western Balkan states, which was one of key priorities for its presidency in 2006. Recent national emphasis has however been seen; most notably in the migration crisis. **Slovenia** Slovenia's foreign policy towards Eastern Europe and the rest of the world has been almost entirely conducted through the European Union. However, Slovenia's contribution to CFSP has been limited due to scarcity of the resources. It has tried to	**Very limited change**

(Continued)

Table 16.1 (Continued)

Accession–2000	2016 (2000–13 overview)	
Part 1: Geographic orientations/geopolitics		
Geographical area	Short summary	Change observed
	Short summary	

present itself as a committed European and 'a normative power contributor' that can fulfil the role of a 'bridge between the EU and the Western Balkans'. During Slovenia's presidency in the Council of the EU, its top priority was to assist the Western Balkans on their road to the EU membership and specifically to conclude the Stabilization and Association Agreements.

Romania & Bulgaria

Romania and Bulgaria have been engaged in promoting initiatives in a Black Sea area. Romania has been particularly active in attempts to raise its profile. The Romanian government made attempts to mend relations with Russia, which unfortunately produced the opposite effect of worsening the strained relationship. The Bulgarian position has been less active than the Romanian one. Given its dependence on Russian gas, The Bulgaria pursued bilateral relations with Azerbaijan and Central Asia, outside the EU framework. Both countries have been primarily engaged within their own region and in issues that directly affect them rather than demonstrating a distinct commitment to specific EU foreign affairs.

Slovakia, Czech Republic and Poland

The majority of the foreign policies of three of the Visegrad Four are conducted through or with the EU. Since accession, Poland has considered itself as a large Member State, with responsibilities to express positions on all aspects of CFSP and take the lead on the EU's relations with Eastern neighbours. It has aspired to be a 'bridge' between the 'Big Three' and the smaller Member States in the region, after failing to become a new 'bridge' between the United States and the EU. The Czech Republic and Slovakia generally see themselves as vulnerable, small countries that need alliances in order to be protected from the big players in the region. Still, they have also expressed ambitions to be among the 'shapers'

Visegrad Four

of some policies, concerning human rights or enlargement. However, there is an understanding that while the Czech Republic and Slovakia are able to offer ideas, they have few resources to back them up. Increasingly, Poland has emerged as a leader of EU policy towards Russia, adopting a more radical approach. Both Czech and Slovak policies on Russia are less confrontational, not least due to the energy dependence. Slovak policies on migration throughout 2015–16 were distinctly nationalist in tone, running counter to Europeanising efforts on asylum.

Hungary

A strong element of Hungarian foreign policy is what is defined as a 'responsibility for minorities living abroad'. This stands in stark contrast to robustly nationalist attitudes to the 2015–16 migration crisis. Hungary, much like Austria, is engaged in the EU's policy towards Western Balkans, as the key area of their interest within the CFSP. Energy security also plays a central role in Hungary's foreign policy with 'uploading' efforts promoting the North-South gas route, ensuring diversification of its own gas supplies. Hungary's policy towards Russia is more restrained than that of its Visegrad partners, especially Poland.

France

The mid-2000s witnessed a weakening of France's political position in Europe, an 'Atlanticist shift' in French foreign and security policy, initiated by a rapprochement to the US, culminating in France's return to NATO's military structure in 2009 and the Lancaster House military agreements with the UK in 2010. As a result of changes in German foreign policy, France seeks to reinvigorate its 'Western' and 'Atlantic' persona, and look 'South' to make up for its progressive loss of centrality in European affairs from meta-regional support in the Union for the Mediterranean to security and defence ops in Mali and Libya.

A noticeable shift towards extra-regional foreign policy

Chapter 4:
Central European states

French governments have promoted the EU's international activity as a vehicle for those initiatives which France alone cannot accomplish, and which are intended to supplement French efforts at national level. The European presence is useful in areas where French influence is weak, American hegemony is strong and where economic aid and investment is beyond its bilateral capabilities. French governments have sought to keep their *domain privé* in those areas where France had historic national influence, and which are vital if it is to continue to lay claim to the status of a world power.

(Continued)

Table 16.1 (Continued)

Accession–2000

Part 1: Geographic orientations/geopolitics

Geographical area	Short summary	2016 (2000–13 overview) Short summary	Change observed
	German foreign policy displays remarkable continuity despite fundamental changes in its environment. Germany's approach was characterised by both idealism and pragmatism. It pushed for foreign policy integration in order to harmonise and accommodate its own geographical position and power and to restrain any potential 'renationalisation' of foreign policy among the Member States. Germany wanted to see a more cohesive EU actor in foreign and security policy situated within the Atlantic context, while maintaining its status of a 'civilian power'. Core beliefs in German foreign policy generally reproduce the CFSP ethos itself: human rights, moderateness of approach, willingness to seek compromises etc. Despite this continuity, there were also visible changes, particularly on the view of using military force outside territorial defence to address instabilities and threats, such as the conflict in the Balkans.	**Germany** The 1992–2005 period represented the peak of Franco-German togetherness, and the 'centrality' of the Franco-German engine in European politics. Eastern enlargement, however, strengthened Germany's strategic position in Europe. Germany has become increasingly more 'central' to the European integration process with increasing influence and leadership in the EU. Berlin has turned out to be the main political sponsor of 'civilian CSDP' strengthening it institutionally and placing the notion of 'civ-mil' integration at the centre of CSDP doctrine. Tensions still exist between its balancing role with Russia (e.g. on energy security) and its responsibilities to Eastern Member States. This has produced more assertive attitudes in Germany, but which also take the form of a Europeanised response on the issue of sanctions over Russian intervention in Crimea, or a collective response to the 2015–16 migration crisis.	**Some continuity and increasing leadership position within; influence on and centrality to EU politics**
Chapter 5: *Southern Europe*	European integration had a decisive influence on Spanish foreign and security policy orientations, providing the Spanish government with the ideal template with which to provide Spain with a coherent national foreign and security policy more in line with that of the EU as a whole. Spain embraced the NATO Alliance, integrated itself into other chief instruments of European defence and effectively subordinated the two traditional regions of Spanish policy concern – the Mediterranean and Latin America. Its foreign policy since 1996 has been notably more low-key, with regards to Spain's position on the world stage, and more pragmatic to present its position in terms of Spanish national interests.	**Spain** Spain was one of the frontrunners in joint efforts to build common institutions for the CSDP and to establish a common European defence industry. Spanish foreign policy displayed strong Atlanticist traits in early 2003 when it openly supported the US-led invasion of Iraq. However, Spain refused to recognise Kosovo and its declaration of independence from Serbia issued in February 2008. In terms of uploading Spanish foreign policy, there is emphasis on the 'bridge' role that Spain (together with Portugal) has played in the EU's policies towards Latin America, just prior to and immediately after, and since membership as well as attempts at regional leadership in Mediterranean projects. Such uploading, however, often only amounts to 'transferring' a number of national problematic issues 'up' to the EU level, not in order to try and find a European solution to them, but instead in order to try and 'score points' at the domestic level.	**Incremental Europeanisation with signs of renationalisation**

In the late twentieth century, Portugal had to remake much of its internal political culture and its external post-empire identity; its main focus in this transitions that of accession to the EU. Since 1992, there has been a narrowing of the gap between EU and Portuguese foreign policy with Portuguese special relationships no longer conducted without the EU. On the contrary, the initiatives of the Portuguese foreign policy complement the CFSP. After twenty-five years of democracy and thirteen years of EU membership, Portuguese influence in the world had increased substantially. But this influence is that of a small country which subscribes to the principles of the UN and the EU.	**Portugal** Portugal, like Spain, was also keen to participate in joint efforts to build common institutions for the CSDP and to establish a common European defence industry. At present, it is participating in all current CSDP missions. Portugal, has also displayed strong Atlanticist traits, opposing any Franco-German-inspired Europeanisation efforts of the invasion of Iraq. The further involvement of Portugal in efforts to redevelop and secure the Mediterranean remain a foreign policy potential.	**Incremental Europeanisation with signs of renationalisation**
Italy has consistently maintained its 'triple' role of founding member, poor relative and laggard. Compared to the pre-Maastricht era, Italy's European policy has not fundamentally changed its goals, but it has significantly changed its means. 'Staying in Europe', specifically within the integrationist core and with a higher profile, has become a particularly challenging task for the Italian political and administrative system. The Foreign Ministry was no longer the sole nor the main policy-making body for EU affairs. The intra-governmental division of labour in relation to EU affairs was also in a state of flux.	**Italy** Until 2010, Italy had the highest number of nationals (16) representing the EU abroad as heads of delegations. Further, Italy successfully achieved the appointment of Federica Mogherini to the post of High Representative of the European Union in the Juncker Commission since November 2014. As for CSDP and conflict resolution, Italy participates in all EU CSDP missions and operations, regardless of whether these are of a civilian or military nature. For example, during the invasion of Iraq, Italy was trying to portray itself as a bridge-builder between 'Old Europe' and 'New Europe'. In terms of migration, Italy and other southern countries have become highly pro-active and influential on the EU level since 2008. However, Italy's attempts at forcing '"European solidarity" through the back door' can be interpreted as subverting the principle of sincere and loyal cooperation.	**Incremental Europeanisation with signs of renationalisation**
EU membership has had a significant impact on Greek foreign policy. Despite setbacks, Europeanisation and modernisation have progressed in many areas of domestic political life and there are signs of their extensions in others. Participation in CFSP has contributed to the raised international status of	**Greece** The Greek government strongly rejected any military action in Iraq that was not backed by a UNSC resolution, thus joining the anti-war camp within the EU. Greece refused to recognise Kosovo and its declaration of independence. Beyond its historic support for stability in the Balkans, Greece has struggled to	**Incremental Europeanisation with signs of renationalisation**

(Continued)

Table 16.1 (Continued)

Accession–2000	2016 (2000–13 overview)	

Part 1: Geographic orientations/geopolitics

Geographical area	Short summary	Short summary	Change observed
	Greece and the socialisation of policy-makers and diplomats has facilitated the increasing number of common positions and gradual convergence of Greek foreign policies to these.	identify a wider leadership role in the Mediterranean. The economic convulsions of Grexit as well as the challenges of dealing with the migration crisis have inevitably spurred nationalist responses to key external challenges.	
		As far as the Cyprus conflict is concerned, Greece was successful in uploading the issue to the EU level, thereby ensuring that the island's division was not an impediment to its EU accession, and it even succeeded in shifting the position of other Member States.	
New Southern Europe		**Malta**	
		Due to Article 1 (3) of its constitution, stipulating Malta's neutrality, the country's Europeanisation efforts were comparatively more limited, although it is now clear that it is no longer a formal obstacle to participating in the CSDP. The Maltese government strongly rejected any military action in Iraq that was not backed by a UNSC resolution, thus joining the anti-war camp within the EU.	
		Cyprus	
		Cyprus as a consequence of accession to the EU gave up membership in the Non-Aligned Movement in May 2004. Its attempts to join NATO remain blocked by Turkey thus limiting any real impact on EU–NATO security and defence collaboration. During the financial crisis, sought support from Russia in 2011 and 2012, asking for loans totalling EUR 7.5 billion amid the country's lock-out of international debt markets and concerns over its domestic banks. This was complemented by talks over financial assistance with Beijing and a recent decision to cooperate closely with Israel on gas exploration in the Mediterranean. These develpments in Cypriot foreign policy regarded in Brussels with scepticism and potentially run counter to a further Europeanisation of EU foreign policy. Cyprus, together with Spain and Greece, refused to recognise Kosovo.	

Table 16.2 Foreign policy dimensions by mode

Part II: Foreign policy dimensions

Policy area	Short summary	Mode*
Chapter 6: *Diplomacy*	The Lisbon Treaty produces two possible scenarios: A) The first is that greater involvement of national diplomats in the EEAS will have a socialising effect and will lead to further Europeanisation of Member State foreign policy. B) The second scenario sees little socialisation and minimum Europeanisation. Under this scenario the inter-EU policy relations would reassert themselves, especially among the largest EU members. It is also possible that the expansion of national diplomatic exposure to the EU institutions will trigger a dual effect: on the one hand it may further Europeanise national foreign policy and diplomatic practice while, at the EU level, make the institutions far more sensitive to national preoccupations and concerns.	**Mode II and Mode IV**
Chapter 7: *Security and defence*	The dominant mode of cooperation in this field is increasingly that of intra-EU cooperation; that is, an intergovernmental mode of cooperation within the CSDP framework facilitated by processes of Brusselisation and socialisation. There are no signs, however, that Member States are going to move towards intra-EU integration in the near future. Furthermore, while cooperation at the EU level is more intense than ever before, it coexists with significant bilateral cooperation with other Member States outside the CSDP context (inter-EU policy relations) and with other security actors outside the EU, mainly the US and NATO (extra-EU policy relations).	**Dominant mode is II, co-existing with Modes III and IV**
Chapter 8: *Military operations*	There has been a significant move towards further intra-EU cooperation in the foreign, security and defence realm in the period observed (2000–13). The European Security Strategy and the follow-on report on its implementation explicitly stated the MS's shared ambition to further align – although not fully integrate – in this policy area. This illustrates a mode of change focused on intra-EU cooperation although MS still can and arguably will continue to cooperate outside the EU framework and with non-EU actors in security and defence matters as well. The questions of enhanced use of CSDP and of building a European security union however have emerged from recent geopolitical and migration volatilities.	**Dominant mode is II, coexisting with Modes III and IV**
Chapter 9: *Enlargement policy*	The dominant mode of operation in enlargement up until 2007 seems to be a combination of the EU-level and MS foreign policy dynamics. The enlargement policy, as a result, has become Europeanised. However, increasingly after 2008, the EU enlargement policy became subject to individual Member States' vetoes, and it is possible to see the EU members uploading their own preferences to the EU level.	**After 2008, Mode I**

(Continued)

Table 16.2 (Continued)

Part II: Foreign policy dimensions

Policy area	Short summary	Mode*
Chapter 10: *Energy security*	Energy security remains within the realm of national policies. MS responses beyond the specific purchase of energy supplies are hard to categorise, particularly between forms of intra-EU cooperation and inter-EU policy relations. Some EU legislation (e.g. Third Energy Package) impel intra-EU cooperation, but projects are often undertaken by national energy actors and justified as national solutions inherent to inter-EU policy relations.	**Predominantly Modes III & IV with some signs of Mode II**
Chapter 11: *Neighbourhood and migration policy*	With a few exceptions, Member States have remained largely ambivalent to the ENP. The ENP has provided key opportunities for regional patronage with the Union for the Mediterranean, and the Eastern Partnership. Within the ENP, Member States demands are an overlap of intergovernmental cooperation of an EU-design (Mode II), fostering Member States extra-EU cooperation (Mode III), while prioritising their own foreign policy preferences with non-EU others (Mode IV).	**ENP:Dominant modes are II, III & IV Migration:modes I, II, III & IV**
	An anchor of neighbourhood policy, and leader in the migration crisis, Germany has strengthened its authority across Europe through a skilled blend of Modes I and II regarding the ENP, a combined Modes I, II and III response to migration, and Mode IV relative to Russia.	
	Within the southern dimension of the ENP, **Greek** participation reflects the intergovernmental agreements found in Mode II. Migration responses have fostered Mode III interactions with Member States beyond established ENP policies, and migration and asylum legislation, and fostered Mode IV interfaces with Balkan states, Turkey and MENA partners.	
	Despite supporting key EU goals, contemporary **Slovak** preferences operate within the regional-specific process of 'Visegrad-isation', preferring intergovernmental coalition-building of Mode II, and Mode III extra-EU regional diplomacy via the Central European Initiative (CEI), the Danube Cooperation Process, the Adriatic-Ionian Initiative, to the intrinsically Europeanised dynamics of Modes I or even II.	
Chapter 12: *Development policy*	Development aid rests predominantly within national foreign policy structures. On the continuum that has been used in this edited volume, it would be situated in between 'shared parallel' and 'coordinated' competences. Since the early 2000s, there have been several noticeable initiatives to streamline the aims, approaches and activities of EU donors.	**Between Modes I, II & IV**
	Indications of convergences between EU MS include a clear discursive commitment of all EU MS to the international aid effectiveness agenda. Second, there is the increased focus on the development-security nexus at the EU and MS levels. However, this may be more the result of an internationalisation, or specifically a DAC-isation (*OECD Development Assistance Committee*), than a Europeanisation.	

Table 16.2 (Continued)

Part II: Foreign policy dimensions

Policy area	Short summary	Mode*
Chapter 13: *External facets of justice, freedom and security*	This foreign policy-making field remains more nationalised than Europeanised. The dominant modes of Member State cooperation are intergovernmentalism within the EU framework and extra-EU cooperation between EU and non-EU states.	**Dominant modes are II & IV. Southern Europe: Modes I, II and IV**
	Border and migration control: The external element of border management policy reveals a confusing set of integration dynamics. A general conclusion can be made that the policy area is predominantly marked by intra-EU cooperation.	
	However, the North-South divide means that Southern European states have taken two rather contradictory steps. They supported policies stemming from intra-EU integration, but where substantial EU assistance led to reform of national practices, there is still a sense that national interests prevail.	
	Counter-terrorism policy: The pattern of integration in the external dimension of EU counter-terrorism policy is decidedly mixed. On the one hand, there has been a rapid expansion of integration sponsored by the European Commission. On the other hand, there is evidence that bilateralism is thriving as individual Member States negotiate counter-terrorism agreements without reference to the EU.	
Chapter 14: Trade, regulations and competition	While intra-EU integration is the dominant mode of policy-making in all three policy areas, there have been different degrees of further Europeanisation in the twenty-first century. In trade policy, there has been the most pronounced tightening of cooperation among the Member States. There has also been Europeanisation in the external dimension of competition policy, despite some expectations that the recent 'modernisation' would lead to the renationalisation of competition policy powers. There has been no pronounced shift to closer coordination in regulatory policy since the 'completion' of the single European market in the early 1990s, although new common rules continue to be adopted. Thus, there are differences in the intensity of the process of Europeanisation.	**Dominant mode is I**
Chapter 15: *Multilateralism and global governance*	**Human rights:** Intra-EU cooperation with signs of increasing extra-EU policy relation.	**Modes I, II, III & IV, depending on the institutional setting**
	International criminal justice: Action falling under intra-EU integration umbrella on ICC matters are well established and accepted.	
	Multilateral military operation: The EU MS support Responsibility to Protect through intra-EU cooperation.	
	In the case of Libya, there is a sizable gap between the EU statements (falling in the intra-EU integration category) and the actions undertaken by Member States under extra-EU policy, of NATO members cooperating with non-EU NATO members.	

(Continued)

Table 16.2 (Continued)

Part II: Foreign policy dimensions		
Policy area	Short summary	Mode*
	Multilateral economic management: Extra-EU policy relations are preferred, when actions stemming from inter-EU integration or cooperation would increase the voting power of the EU while conceding some of its voting share to emerging economies.	
	EU commitment to supporting these issues is stated by the Council President and the EU High Representative (intra-EU integration), documents are prepared by the Council (intra-EU cooperation), but in practice, the implementation of these policies is through intra-EU cooperation or inter-/extra-EU policy relations.	
	Inter-EU and extra-EU policy relation actions do not always imply nationalisation as a movement away from Europeanisation; it can be the reducing EU profile in situations where it engenders more hostility than support or because the formal institutional rules of membership limit EU participation.	

* The modes identified in this table represent only the general and most common pattern of behaviour identified across the majority of EU Member States in a particular area of foreign policy. This does not mean, however, that all Member States follow the same model at all times within any given policy area.

Bibliography

Börzel, T., (2010), 'European Governance: Negotiation and Competition in the Shadow of Hierarchy', *JCMS: Journal of Common Market Studies*, Vol. 48, Issue 2, pp. 191–219.

Bretherton, C. and Vogler, J., (2013), 'A Global Actor Past Its Peak?', *International Relations*, Vol. 27, Issue 3, pp. 375–390.

Chaban, N. and Holland, M., (eds.) (2014), *Communicating Europe in Times of Crisis*, Basingstoke: Palgrave Macmillan.

Dinan, D., Nugent, N. and Paterson, W., (eds.) (2016), *The European Union in Crisis*, Basingstoke: Palgrave Macmillan.

Falkner, G. and Treib, O., (2008), 'Three Worlds of Compliance or Four? The EU-15 Compared to New Member States', *Journal of Common Market Studies*, Vol. 46, Issue 2, pp. 293–313.

Galbraith, J. K., (2016), *Welcome to the Poisoned Chalice: The Destruction of Greece and the Future of Europe*, London: Yale University Press.

Hockenos, P., (2016), 'The E.U. Is in Crisis: Two Economists Disagree on Why', *The New York Times*. Available at: http://www.nytimes.com/2016/08/21/books/review/slippery-slope-giles-merritt-welcome-to-the-poisoned-chalice-james-k-galbraith.html?smprod=nytcore-ipad&smid=nytcore-ipad-share&_r=0 (Accessed August 22, 2016).

Manners, I. and Whitman, R., (eds.) (2000), *The Foreign Policies of the European Union Member States*, Manchester: Manchester University Press.

Merritt, G., (2016), *Slippery Slope: Europe's Troubled Future*, Oxford: Oxford University Press.

Rostan, M. and Vaira, M., (2011), Questioning Excellence in Higher Education: An Introduction', in Rostan, M. and Vaira, M. (eds.) *Questioning Excellence in Higher Education*. Rotterdam: Sense Publishers, pp. vii–xvii.

Vaira, M., (2004), 'Globalization and Higher Education Organisational Change: A Framework for Analysis', *Higher Education*, Vol. 48, Issue 4, pp. 483–510.

Index

Note: Figures and tables are denoted with italicized page numbers; end note information is denoted with an n and note number following the page number.